Writing in Multicultural Settings

Modern Language Association of America

Research and Scholarship in Composition

Lil Brannon, Anne Ruggles Gere, Geneva Smitherman-Donaldson, John Trimbur, Art Young, Series Editors

Writing in Multicultural Settings

Edited by
Carol Severino,
Juan C. Guerra, and
Johnnella E. Butler

The Modern Language Association of America
New York   1997

For information about obtaining permission to reprint
material from MLA book publications, send your request by
mail (see address below), e-mail (permissions@mla.org),
or fax (212 533-0680).

The essay "Contrastive Rhetoric: Implications for Teachers of
Writing in Multicultural Classrooms" is adapted from chapters 1
to 3 in Ulla Connor, *Contrastive Rhetoric: Cross-Cultural Aspects of
Second Language Writing*, New York: Cambridge UP, 1996.
Reprinted by permission of the publisher.

Library of Congress Cataloging-in-Publication Data

Writing in multicultural settings / edited by Carol Severino, Juan C.
  Guerra, and Johnnella E. Butler.
      p.   cm — (Research and scholarship in composition ; 5)
    Includes bibliographical references (p.) and index.
    ISBN 0-87352-583-3 (cloth). — ISBN 0-87352-584-1 (paper)
      1. English language—Rhetoric—Study and teaching—
  United States.   2. Intercultural communication—United States.
  3. Multicultural education—United States.   4. Language
  and culture—United States.   5. Pluralism (Social sciences)
  I. Severino, Carol, 1949–   . II. Guerra, Juan C., 1949–
  III. Butler, Johnnella E.   IV. Series.
  PE1405.U6W75   1997
  808'.042'07—dc21   96-49853

ISSN 1079-2554

Published by The Modern Language Association of America
10 Astor Place, New York, New York 10003-6981

Contents

Preface to the Series

The Research and Scholarship in Composition series, developed with the support of the Modern Language Association's Publications Committee, responds to the recent growth of interest in composition and to the remarkable number of publications now devoted to it. We intend the series to provide a carefully coordinated overview of the varied theoretical schools, educational philosophies, institutional groupings, classroom situations, and pedagogical practices that collectively constitute the major areas of inquiry in the field of composition studies.

Each volume combines theory, research, and practice in order to clarify issues, synthesize research and scholarship, and improve the quality of writing instruction. Further, each volume reviews the most significant issues in a particular area of composition research and instruction; reflects on ways research and teaching inform each other; views composition studies in the larger context of literary, literacy, and cultural studies; and draws conclusions from various scholarly perspectives about what has been done and what yet needs to be done in the field.

We hope this series will serve a wide audience of teachers, scholars, and students who are interested in the teaching of writing, research in composition, and the connections among composition, literature, and other areas of study. These volumes should act as a lively orientation to the field for students and nonspecialists and provide experienced teachers and scholars with useful overviews of research on important questions, with insightful reflections about teaching, and with thoughtful analyses about future developments in composition studies. Each book is a spirited conversation in which you are cordially invited to join.

Series Editors

Acknowledgments

We would like to thank all the thoughtful, dedicated, and supportive people at the Universities of Iowa and Washington who helped with the preparation of this book, especially Cindy Stretch, Becky Soglin, Andy Bartlett, Elaine Wood, Ann Franzenburg, and Wendy Swyt. Our thanks and appreciation also go to Geneva Smitherman of the series board for helping shape and expedite this project.

Acknowledgments

Introduction

Over the past three decades, dramatic social and cultural changes have transformed the student populations that United States colleges serve. Three developments—the establishment of equal opportunity programs in the wake of the civil rights era, the implementation of affirmative action, and an increase in immigration from non-European nations—have changed the college and university population and the needs of college and university students. Today's institutions of higher education enroll students very different from the once predominantly white male student pool. As a consequence, constituencies on and off campus—students, faculty members, administrators, and parents—have been forced to confront an idea that many find confusing and some consider threatening: multiculturalism.

We define multiculturalism as the effort in the latter half of the twentieth century to encourage citizens in the United States to embrace the racial, ethnic, class, gender, religious, age, and physical-ability differences in our population; multiculturalism is an approach to living that respects, incorporates, and mediates the differences and similarities of our population. It suggests a reckoning with the erasure of cultural identities inherent in the melting-pot ideal and with the possible essentialist interpretations of the salad-bowl or jambalaya metaphors, which serve better the more desirable goal of a cooperative, relational pluralism.

The problem of defining and implementing multiculturalism in higher education has challenged most disciplines and interdisciplinary units within colleges and universities. Departments and academic affairs and student affairs units wrestle with determining how multiculturalism should apply not only to curriculum and campus climate but also to policies that affect the college, the university, and the larger society. One of the settings deeply affected by this concern is the writing classroom, because writing as artifact is a form of both personal and cultural expression. Traditional curricula and approaches to writing must be reexamined, not only to address heterogeneous classes (in which twenty-five students may be writing from just

1

as many different racial, ethnic, and cultural backgrounds) but also to teach relatively homogeneous classes of mainstream students who must learn to interact and communicate with an ever-growing variety of people on and off campus. Before we can fruitfully critique any curriculum or approach to writing, we need at least a rudimentary history of the discipline and an understanding of the principal factors behind the tensions informing our teaching.

Tensions in Composition Teaching

For the first sixty years of this century, the teaching of writing was governed by a set of tacit assumptions that scholars in composition studies have come to refer to as the "current traditional paradigm." The primary goal of this approach was to assimilate students into the conventions and expectations of the academy. Richard Young has identified five overt features of the paradigm:

1. the emphasis on the composed product rather than the composing process;
2. the analysis of discourse into words, sentences, and paragraphs;
3. the classification of discourse into description, narration, exposition, and argument;
4. the strong concern with usage (syntax, spelling, punctuation) and with style (economy, clarity, emphasis); and
5. the preoccupation with the informal essay and the research paper.   (31)

John Clifford has further described the paradigm's discipline-centered approach to teaching:

1. Only finished products are considered; assignments are turned in, evaluated, and returned for optional revision.
2. Students sit in rows.
3. Commercial texts are used for examples, drills, and reference.
4. The instructor is the sole teacher, audience, authority, and evaluator.
5. Instructors set up guidelines for organizing, developing, and editing compositions.
6. Revision occurs after the paper is submitted.

7. Instructors make corrections and suggestions, write a brief overall summary, and assign a letter grade to each piece of work. These are averaged for a final grade. ("Composing" 44)

When writing teachers began to interrogate the paradigm's assumptions in the highly charged political atmosphere of the 1960s, their critiques led to a series of oppositional theoretical approaches, which in turn have led to the development of composition studies as a legitimate academic field. No matter how any one of these different approaches has been framed or manifests itself, they all attempt to answer the question that writing teachers have long asked themselves: Is the purpose of writing instruction to help students find their voices and cultivate expressions from alternative social and cultural locations, or is the purpose to initiate students into the academy and the society it serves?

Supporters of the expressivist approach, the first to emerge as a consequence of a growing interest in writing as a process, heralded a revolutionary approach to teaching writing. Because many expressivists conceived of writing "as an unteachable act, a kind of behavior that can be learned but not taught," a teacher's primary responsibility was, as James Berlin argues, to "provide a classroom environment in which the student learns to write . . . through dialectic." Expressivist teachers invited the student to write from the heart and in a voice that expressed his or her individuality. Students were encouraged to sit in circles and to share their writing, not so that they could critique one another and search for ways to meet some external set of expectations or respond to the needs of some outside audience, but "to get rid of what is untrue to the private vision of the writer, what is, in a word, inauthentic" ("Contemporary Composition" 16). Above all, expressivist teachers wanted student writing to be honest, fresh, and personal (Macrorie).

In the 1970s some theorists and researchers grew concerned about the lack of shared objective standards among the expressivists and became influenced by the work in cognitive-developmental psychology (Britton et al.), especially in artificial intelligence (Flower and Hayes). These scholars focused on a search for the "cognitivist" strategies that all good writers share. In addition to invoking the importance of audience and arguing that students could not be effective writers if they wrote only for themselves, cognitivists used the methodology of protocol analysis, whereby students were urged to report aloud what they were doing as they wrote. Cognitivists wanted to understand the process writers went through in "real writing situations." They also developed research projects that compared professional or expert writers with beginning or poor writers to produce a description of the composing process and explain the differences. Inevitably, some cognitivists developed complex diagrams and flowcharts to illustrate their interpretation of a universal writing process (e.g., Flower and Hayes). These cognitivists' implicit goal became to make poor writers self-conscious about their writing processes so that they would mimic those of good writers and so that the writing experience would become an act of discovery.

The social constructivist approach emerged in the early 1980s as a response to the cognitivist approach. Social constructivists were disturbed by the idea of a universal model of the composing process and argued that it was impossible to define expertise "outside of a specific community of writers" (Faigley, "Competing Theories" 47). For these reasons and as a consequence of the experiences many social constructivists had teaching students from diverse cultural backgrounds, they began to posit the idea that the practice of writing was socially situated, not individually realized. In their view, students brought to the classroom multiple composing processes and voices, which writing teachers had to honor at the same time that they looked for ways to initiate the students into what social constructivists called the academic discourse community (Bizzell, *Academic Discourse*). Because this was the first serious encounter between composition and multiculturalism, social constructivists tried to respond directly to many of the conflicts and questions facing teachers in writing classrooms that reflected a new demographic reality.

While social constructivists have widespread support in the field, critics have expressed concerns about the often rigid definition of the academic discourse community. Some, like Joseph Harris, have warned about the often unproblematized concept of community within an academic context. Kurt Spellmeyer, John Trimbur ("Consensus"), and Greg Myers have criticized the social constructivists for, above all, failing to recognize "a dimension of dissent in the ongoing formation of knowledge itself and also in a social life of any kind" (Spellmeyer, *Common Ground* 162). Adherents of what some call the postprocess approach have also questioned the dichotomous view that suggests that the purpose of writing instruction is either to accommodate students by encouraging them to find and use their authentic voices or to acculturate them by initiating them into the academy and the society it serves. For them, the goal of "a post-process, post-cognitivist theory and pedagogy" is to "represent literacy as an ideological arena and composing as a cultural activity by which writers position

and reposition themselves in relation to their own and others' subjectivities, discourses, practices, and institutions" (Trimbur, "Taking" 109). Unfortunately, while the important notion of repositioning has been widely described in theoretical terms, there are still few examples of how it manifests itself in the writing classroom.

Questions Raised by This Book

While *Writing in Multicultural Settings* offers theoretical and practical explanations and insights from the wealth of our contributors' teaching and research experiences, it offers no easy answers, no quick fixes; it raises as many questions as it answers. Its purpose is to articulate the issues and describe how cultural conflicts play out in interactions among students, teachers, and texts in the writing classroom.

Because the twenty-six writers of these twenty essays and four crosstalks are immersed in the multicultural settings of their classrooms, writing centers, institutions, cities, and towns, they speak from a lived experience that is rich and deep. These contributors are intimately involved in their students' writing and speaking; they read and respond to their students' writing and form relationships with them through spoken and written texts. This rendering of immersion in the students' "discourses," lives, and cultures makes reading sections of this book somewhat like reading ethnographic narratives. But the "thick" descriptions of classroom events are balanced by careful and critical reflection. Daily in their classrooms and offices and nightly in their homes, teachers struggle with the fundamental challenge of multiculturalism, which is played out in different styles with different dynamics throughout this book: the conflict between ideas of difference and the similarities present in apparent difference, all of which we should consider seriously in our theory and practice.

The contributors to this volume continually ask themselves, their students, and their readers a variety of critical questions: How different from or similar to one another are we? How fluid or fixed are such differences (Hesford; Jamieson; Evans; Troutman)? How different are our students from one another and from us (Soliday; Mangelsdorf; Rodríguez Milanés)? How much do we as teachers want to emphasize difference or similarity in our teaching (Evans; Miller; Severino; Gilyard; Jamieson; Okawa)? How do underrepresented students feel in mainstream classes that stress difference (Miller; Jamieson)? How do mainstream students feel in classrooms that stress difference (Chappell)?

How different are the students' discourses from academic discourses (Guerra; Gleason; Hamp-Lyons; De and Gregory)? How do expectations about student writing abilities at elite institutions compare with those at schools with broader admissions policies? How do those expectations frame pedagogies, practices, and students' responses (Hesford; De and Gregory)? What rights and opportunities should students have to maintain and express their own different discourses (Troutman; Campbell) or native-language discourse patterns (Connor; Blalock; Leki)? How different is first-language writing and teaching from second-language writing and teaching (Harris; Silva)? What opportunities do students have to write stories and analyses of their own different histories and traditions (Evans; Lisle and Mano; Grijalva; Hesford; Mangelsdorf)?

How the Book Was Developed

In the long process of developing this book, we have ourselves attempted to put theory into practice. Our methodology and motivation for selecting and revising articles therefore can be characterized as generative—that is, there are correspondences among the writers, the essays produced, and the processes of creating the book. As in four-year institutions, scholars and teachers of color have been underrepresented in mainstream publications. When we selected essay proposals from the eighty we received, we strove for diversity and balance, first of all, among the contributors, over half of whom are Asian American, Native American, African American, and Latino or Latina. A multiethnic, multiracial editorial team ourselves (a Chicano, an Italian American, and an African American), we intend the book to feature the new voices not always heard and read in the profession. Just as we sought representativeness in the contributors' voices, we looked for essays that featured the writing and perspectives of students whose voices are seldom heard, especially students of color and students who are speakers of other languages and dialects. The articles in this book resound with student voices—excerpts from their essays and from their spoken discourse in and about the classroom.

We also wanted to bring to the profession scholarship representing the diverse institutional settings in United States higher education. We were interested in essays on working with specific populations (Evans; Campbell; Troutman; Mangelsdorf; Grijalva; Chappell), on working with heterogeneous populations (Guerra; Soliday; Gleason; Lisle and Mano; De and Gregory; Hesford), on working in predominantly mainstream settings (Jamieson; Chappell; Miller), on writing

centers (Harris; Blalock), and on testing situations (Gleason; De and Gregory; Hamp-Lyons). We also sought institutional and geographic diversity. The contributors are from private and public institutions of different degrees of selectivity all over the country (including Alaska)—the East and West Coasts, the Midwest, the Southwest, and the South. For instructional purposes, we included several perspectives from institutions and sites with a long history and experience of diversity, especially New York City and Los Angeles. Lastly, we sought both theoretical diversity (including a range of postmodern and expressivist pedagogies) and disciplinary diversity (integrating perspectives from composition, linguistics, and literature).

Like the first four volumes in the MLA series Research and Scholarship in Composition, this one is weighted in favor of composition as a bridge between literature and lingusitics. In particular, our search for correspondences and connections between first-language (L1) and second-language (L2) pedagogy led us to include part 3, on ESL issues. A number of the contributors focus on a mix of native speakers, bilinguals, and ESL speakers (Soliday; Gleason; Severino; De and Gregory; Hesford; Lisle and Mano; Hamp-Lyons; Blalock), which we believe is a positive trend. Studies of first-language, second-language, and bilingual writers have been compartmentalized for too long. Moreover, the very purpose of this book—to examine writing in multicultural settings—demands attention to all the elements that shape the teaching of writing: ESL and basic writing, the use of multicultural material in classes with both students of color and European American students, and the politics of writing instruction.

The book begins and ends with views of the tensions and conflicts in the multicultural classroom as a microcosm of the larger society: part 1, "Cultural and Linguistic Diversity," and part 4, "Sociocultural and Pedagogical Tensions." In between are two sections with a more specific focus: part 2, "Teachers and Texts," and part 3, "ESL Issues." Each section contains three to six essays and a "cross-talk" response that synthesizes and critiques the essays with a reviewer's eye for what is missing or controversial.

Writing in Multicultural Settings, therefore, is theoretically wide-ranging, regionally and racially representative, and multidisciplinary; it is also coherent and focused in its goals to integrate theory and practice and to articulate questions about similarity and difference in teaching writing in diverse multicultural settings. For these reasons, we see it not as a collection but as a generative work, encouraging interaction between theory and practice, reflection and action, and inviting further research and writing.

CS, JCG, and JEB

PART I

Cultural and Linguistic Diversity

Introduction

The essays in this section focus on the students in multicultural classrooms, both native and nonnative speakers, and on their diverse backgrounds, needs, attitudes, and discourses. Celebrating the diversity of student texts, Bonnie Lisle and Sandra Mano describe how composition students engage in fieldwork to investigate the discourse practices of their home cultures. Denise Troutman looks closely at issues of African American dialect features and writing.

Michelle Grijalva writes about using storytelling to help Native American students overcome the sense of shame they may have from living in a society that has been bent on destroying their native cultures. Addressing the inevitable assessment of students' writing for placement purposes, Liz Hamp-Lyons shows how a small sample from the multicultural classroom interprets typical standardized essay-exam prompts. Kermit Campbell, like Troutman, argues for African American students' rights to their own languages and voices as keys to their identity and literacy. Through three case studies, Susan Blalock examines cross-cultural conflicts in the writing center that have implications for relationships in one-to-one writing conferences and in writing classrooms. In her cross-talk, Gail Okawa demonstrates the danger of terms like *multiculturalism* becoming part of "the academic wallpaper," arguing that teachers should "bifocally" examine their own cultures—how they see themselves and how others see them.

Embracing a Multicultural Rhetoric

Bonnie Lisle and Sandra Mano

Diversity is a hot topic in composition: conferences and journals are alive with talk about new canons, multiple discourse communities, social construction, intertextuality, multivocality, and heteroglossia; publishers advertise a new "multicultural" text in every issue of *College English*. Working as we do with an extremely diverse, multiethnic mix of students, we are delighted to see so much attention focused on issues that we encounter daily in our classrooms. But we detect a gap between professional talk and professional practice. A glance at current textbooks, which offer a rough measure of what goes on in most composition classrooms, suggests that, while the profession celebrates heteroglossia and difference, most rhetoric instruction remains monologic and ethnocentric. Publishers' rush to get on the multicultural bandwagon has produced a welter of texts purporting to be multiethnic, but few show evidence of having thought through the implications of teaching writing to students from diverse linguistic and rhetorical traditions. We begin by reviewing some of the cultural limitations of current rhetoric instruction and continue by outlining our alternative vision of a genuinely multicultural rhetoric.

Invisibility and Tokenism in Current Rhetoric Texts

Most rhetoric texts remain ethnocentric, ignoring the particular needs and interests—and sometimes even the existence—of culturally diverse students (see Jamieson, this volume). Some make unwarranted assumptions about students' linguistic and cultural backgrounds. These words, from the introduction to one rhetoric, are clearly intended to reassure the novice writer:

> Like all writers, you're already a sophisticated user of your native language. When you speak, you don't consciously think about words; you think about meaning, and the words tend to come

12

out correctly. Unless you are scared, subjects and verbs usually agree, sentence structures work, vocabulary is appropriate. In addition to that, you also react almost intuitively to your social situation. . . .   (Elbow and Belanoff 6)

By suggesting that "you" are expected to have a native's fluency and knowledge of social customs, such advice assumes a reader who is middle-class and fully assimilated into the dominant culture; it consigns other readers to invisibility. Far from being reassured, our students—most immigrant or bilingual, many working class—would read these words as irrelevant or alienating.

Perhaps the authors assumed that nonfluent speakers would all be placed in separate ESL courses. But as Guadalupe Valdés points out, the distinctions we typically make among bilingual students, speakers of nonstandard English, and basic writers are crude and inadequate; for instance, some monolingual students born in this country will nevertheless speak "a contact variety of English" containing many nonnative features because they have learned the language from their bilingual families and communities (103). Whatever courses we teach, we can't afford to make assumptions about our students' "intuitive" grasp of language and rhetorical effectiveness. The advice that rhetorics often give to listen for what sounds right or to rely on a felt sense of what works will backfire for many students, reinforcing the fear some have that there's something wrong with them or leading them to suspect that the teacher who makes such suggestions doesn't care about or understand them.

Some rhetorics contain nods to cultural diversity in the form of readings by writers of color or sample essays by students with Asian or Latino surnames. But the additive approach is merely a quick fix: multivocality demands much more than token representation. A few rhetorics now claim to offer a "cross-cultural" or "multicultural" approach to writing, but while they include more multiethnic reading materials, they uncritically endorse familiar Euro-American rhetorical conventions. Although they demonstrate a desire for fresh approaches, they seem trapped by tradition, failing to address the serious challenges that ethnic diversity poses to our assumptions about language and rhetoric.

Cultural Constructions of Identity

While it is easy to assume that our values and rhetorical practices are natural or self-evident, studies of writing in other cultures indicate that both content and form are based on principles that vary widely from country to country. An international study found that student essays written on the same topic differed considerably in focus and patterns of coherence, as well as the use of concrete detail, figurative language, and personal references. For example, students from Australia, Italy, and Thailand produced highly metaphoric, ornamented prose, while students from Finland, Nigeria, and Japan, like those from the United States, wrote in a much plainer style (Purves, "Rhetorical Communities" 42).

A far more basic difference among rhetorics concerns the construction of the writer's identity within the larger culture. Many United States rhetoric texts emphasize personal voice or begin with personal writing on the assumption that students find it easy and engaging to write about themselves. But assuming that expressive and personal writing is natural reflects a peculiarly American emphasis on individualism as the basis of identity—an idea not shared by all cultures. Fan Shen, a Chinese writer who attended college in the United States, recalls that his instructors' repeated directions to "be yourself" and "write what you think" were more confusing than helpful, for

> the image or meaning that I attached to the word "I" or "myself" was, as I found out, different from that of my English teacher. In China, "I" is always subordinated to "We"—be it the working class, the Party, the country, or some other collective body. Both political pressure and literary tradition require that "I" be somewhat hidden or buried in writings and speeches; presenting the "self" too obviously would give people the impression of being disrespectful. . . . (460)

Although changes in China's political climate have eased such rigid prohibitions of individual expression, Carolyn Matalene, an American teacher living in China, found that, for many of her students, keeping journals of personal reflections was difficult and foreign, not the liberating activity that many textbooks assume it is (791). Some of our American students echo the discomfort with personal writing described by Shen and Matalene. Even writing a personal-opinion essay can run counter to some students' cultural training. One Vietnamese immigrant student, writing about the cultural clashes he experienced in the United States, described his difficulty reconciling his teachers' demands that he speak up and express his ideas with his family's insistence that "children" (even eighteen-year-olds) remain silent—that only adults may express opinions.

For some students, personal writing is difficult not because individualistic constructions of self are foreign but because such writing is fraught with risk. In a society that overtly or tacitly condones bigotry, students from nonprivileged groups may resist sharing their experiences as a matter of pride or self-preservation. In a collection of autobiographical essays, bell hooks explains that initially it was hard for her to write about herself because

> so many black folks have been raised to believe that there is just so much that you should not talk about. . . . One of the jokes we used to have about the "got everything" white people is how they just tell all their business, just put their stuff right out there. One point of blackness then became—like how you keep your stuff to yourself, how private you could be about your business.
>
> (*Talking Back* 2)

Reticence may serve as a necessary shield: an African American student in one of our classes fabricated an entire family history to avoid sharing his painful past. Likewise, lesbian, gay, and bisexual students often feel constrained about expressing themselves, given the homophobia and heterosexism that pervade the larger culture and, too often, the classroom itself. (Virginia Uribe and Karen M. Harbeck document the personal and institutional bigotry that such students encounter in school.) One gay student who was just coming out wrote eloquently about the joy of daring to speak in an uncensored voice after years of hiding behind a "safe" but colorless classroom persona.

While the imbalance of power in the classroom can make it risky for any student to open up, the potential danger is compounded when students see the teacher as representing an unjust or hostile social order. To shun self-revelation within an oppressive dominant culture is a reasonable response to what Molefi Asante calls the rhetorical condition—"the structure and power pattern, assumed or imposed, during a rhetorical situation by society" (*Afrocentric Idea* 22). Although the rhetorical condition powerfully shapes a writer's self-definition as well as her or his public reception, textbooks ignore or greatly oversimplify the social and political complexities inherent in the writer's task.

We don't mean to suggest that all, or even most, students from a particular cultural background or social group will resist personal writing. In fact, personal writing plays a central role in our own rhetorical approach. However, we do not assume that such writing will come easily or spontaneously to all students, we explicitly acknowledge

cultural differences in rhetorical style, we encourage students to analyze the rhetorical condition in which they write, and we try to offer
options to accommodate those who feel uncomfortable or awkward
with personal disclosure.

Challenging Ethnocentric Models of Persuasion

Because textbooks do not acknowledge or teach cultural variation in
rhetorical strategies, they tend to represent persuasive writing as necessarily thesis-driven and linear. This approach, holding up the propo-
sitional model as the only appropriate form for academic writing,
excludes the wide range of styles and rhetorical strategies many students bring with them. Moreover, a survey of persuasive strategies in
other cultures suggests that as a measure of rhetorical effectiveness
the logocentrism of Western tradition is the exception rather than the
rule; both oral and literate traditions of non-European cultures challenge the straight-edged geometry of Western rhetoric. While few of
our students may be familiar with the formal rhetorical traditions of
any particular culture, Shirley Brice Heath's *Ways with Words* reminds
us that students' families and communities may teach them to express
their ideas in ways that make our academic conventions seem alien. If
we as teachers fail to acknowledge such ways of writing, we effectively
silence such students. It's vital, then, to counter our ethnocentric biases
by learning about as wide a range of rhetorical models as possible.

Matalene and Shen identify one traditional form of academic essay
in China as *ba gu*, or the "eight-legged essay," whose hallmarks are indirection, repetition, and associative rather than hierarchical development. In direct contrast to the front-loaded organization Western
academics prefer, the logic and structure of *ba gu* resembles an onion
that must be peeled layer by layer "until the reader finally arrives at
the central point, the core" (Shen 463). Although *ba gu* has been dis-
missed by other scholars as "a minor and poorly regarded form" not
taught in modern Chinese schools (Mohan and Lo 519), at least one
of its features persists—the onion-like organization. Indeed, immigrant Chinese students in our classes have told us that they were
taught to devote the opening paragraph of an essay to statements of
universal truth; only after that was it appropriate to broach the topic
of the paper.

Other Asian rhetorical traditions value what we would dismiss as
digressions in the body of an essay. John Hinds reports that a highly
regarded form in Japan, *ki-shoo-ten-ketsu*, mandates that the third sec-

tion of the essay (*ten*) consist of at least one tangentially related sub-topic "brought up with few overt transition markers" ("Reader" 150). Another study suggests that "a Korean preferred rhetorical structure, *ki-sung-chon-kyul*, appears to follow the same pattern" (Eggington 156). Since both studies focus on essays written in the native language, we cannot assume that such features would carry over in the work of Japanese or Korean speakers writing in English. Nevertheless, the widespread use of such forms reminds us that our own conceptions of effective organization and coherence are culture-specific.

The rhetoric of American Indian storytelling provides another alternative to linear, thesis-centered writing. Leslie Marmon Silko, describing Pueblo tradition, explains that "the structure of Pueblo expression resembles something like a spider's web—with many little threads radiating from a center, criss-crossing each other" (54). In constrast to the Western analytic model, which emphasizes distinction and division, Pueblo discourse emphasizes connections and inclusiveness: one story leads to another, and even individual words within a narrative may have their own stories that also must be told. Thus "one story is only the beginning of many stories" (56), and what would appear irrelevant or digressive to Euro-American eyes is meaningful and integral to the Pueblo sensibility.

In Arabic rhetoric, the Koran serves as the ultimate rhetorical guide; thus "the power of words [lies] not in their ability to reflect human experience, but in their ability to transcend it, to reach toward . . . the divine" (Janice Anderson 98). Verbal artistry and emotional impact are the primary measures of persuasive power: rhythm, sound, repetition, and emphatic assertion carry more weight than factual evidence, and organization may depend more on metaphor and association than on linear logic. Indeed, among educated Arabs, poetry "frequently functions in a political context to motivate action, and, as such, it is accorded as much weight as a scholarly dissertation" (97). We know a student who began her first paper in graduate school with a poem to enhance and strengthen her argument; she was crushed when her professor refused to accept the paper until she changed the opening. Studies of Arabic-speaking students writing in English suggest that, while these students' rhetorical strategies do not always differ this dramatically from those of native English speakers, their texts do show demonstrable differences in content, discourse style, sentence structure, and narrative pattern (Ostler; Soter).

African rhetorical traditions like *Nommo* (the power of the word) and *Kuntu* (the unity of sound and sense, of word and action) also value sound and rhythm as highly as logical analysis (Asante, *Afro-centric Idea* 49–51). Although the languages and cultures of Africa are tremendously diverse, many scholars argue that African communication styles share certain deep-structure similarities—characteristics that sharply contrast with the conventions of European rhetoric (see, e.g., Smitherman, *Talkin* 74–75; Asante, *Afrocentric Idea* 59–63). Moreover, certain African rhetorical patterns have been preserved and adapted through black American oral traditions like call and response and signifying. According to Geneva Smitherman, "Indirection and circumlocutory rhetoric are also a part of African discourse strategy, and Afro-Americans have simply transformed this art to accommodate the English language" (*Talkin* 99). Indirection thus became a persuasive device in some African American speech communities: "By 'stalking' the issues, the speaker demonstrates skill and arouses hearers' interest. The person who goes directly to the issues is said to have little imagination and even less flair for rhetorical style" (Asante, *Afrocentric Idea* 51). The persistence of this tradition is at least tentatively reaffirmed by a recent study in which African American high school students, when asked to choose among different organizational strategies, consistently chose nonlinear forms like circumlocution, narrative interspersion, and recursion in preference to conventional "academic-based patterns" (Ball 519). While younger African American respondents in Ball's study did not show this marked preference for nonlinear organization and while we certainly cannot assume that every African American student will be conversant with the oral traditions described by Smitherman and Asante, the existence of alternative rhetorical styles, even among American-born students, compels us to revise ethnocentric conceptions of organization, logic, and persuasion.

Redefining the Writer's Role

Like linear organization, the classic rhetorical triangle is an inadequate representation of discourse in most cultures. Isolating speaker, message, and audience makes little sense to people from cultures in which the oral tradition remains strong. Asante points out that because public expression in African tribal cultures is often communal and participatory, "traditional African philosophy cannot make the distinction of 'speaker' and 'audience' to the same degree found in rhetorical traditions of Euro-American society. . . . *Nommo* must be a collective activity" (*Afrocentric Idea* 66). Pueblo tradition collapses the triangle even further, seeing words as inseparable from the speaker and blurring the boundary between message and audience: "a great deal of the story is believed to be inside the listener, and the storyteller's role is to draw the story out of the listeners" (Silko 57).

Even where literate culture is well established, writers often bear an entirely different relation to their audiences and subject matter than we typically assume. Hinds distinguishes between rhetorical traditions like ours that stress the writer's responsibility to make meaning clear and other traditions, like Japan's, that place the burden of understanding primarily on the reader. The assumption of reader responsibility in Japan means that writers may seldom revise, may use fewer and more subtle transition markers than Western writers use, and may favor ambiguous or imprecise language in literary and some expository prose: "Japanese authors do not like to give clarifications or full explanations of their views. They like to give dark hints and to leave them behind nuances. . . . It is exactly this type of prose which gets the highest praise from readers" (Hinds, "Reader" 145).

While Americans see rhetoric as "an avenue for the individual to achieve control by saying something new in a new way," in China "the primary function of rhetoric is to preserve the general harmony and to promote social cohesion; and therefore, its appeal is always to history and to tradition" (C. Matalene 795). The use of set phrases—primarily from classical literature—is a central element of effective Chinese rhetoric: "the Chinese writer or speaker who can use them frequently is not only ensuring that his message will be understood, he is also revealing his own superior education, his own knowledge of the literary tradition" (792). The common (to us) textbook admonitions to develop "original ideas," to use "fresh language" and shun clichés directly contradict this rhetorical wisdom. Shen remembers resorting to what he calls "reversed plagiarism" in writing papers for his classes in China; when he couldn't find a respectable authority to quote, he attributed some of his own ideas to other sources to make his argument more powerful (460). Conversely, some of Matalene's students imitated models so assiduously (a virtue according to their prior training) that she initially accused them of plagiarism.

The assumption underlying Western academic views of plagiarism—that ideas are the property of individuals—is foreign to many cultural groups. Some American colleges experienced conflict during the 1970s when a large influx of students from Iran brought with them accepted practices of working together on exams as well as on assignments. Likewise, scholars editing the papers of Martin Luther King, Jr., generated tremendous public controversy several years ago when they announced their discovery that King had "plagiarized" extensively in his sermons and writings. But in a recent study of King's rhetoric Keith D. Miller argues that King was in fact practicing "voice merging"—an established tradition in black folk preaching. In this rhetorical tradition, ministers

> borrow partly because their culture fails to define the word as a commodity and instead assumes that everyone creates language and no one owns it. . . . Borrowing also enhances a preacher's status with an audience that demands authority, not originality; appropriateness, not personal expression, the gospel of Jesus Christ, not the views of an individual speaker.   (26)

The Western academic tradition's insistence on individual achievement and originality thus runs afoul of established practices within United States culture as well as abroad.

We're not suggesting that college writing courses suddenly begin teaching students the intricacies of *ki-shoo-ten-ketsu* or encouraging them to borrow freely without citing their sources. Nor do we mean to imply that students' cultural backgrounds automatically determine their linguistic habits and rhetorical patterns. Many other variables also shape student writing: the length of time in the United States, the degree of assimilation, prior schooling, home and community culture, and personality. Given the complexity of such influences, it would be foolhardy to make hasty assumptions about any student's rhetorical knowledge. We do argue, though, that diverse rhetorical practices demand that teachers develop new sensitivities and skills: (1) we as teachers need to acknowledge the many rhetorical styles students may be familiar with; (2) we need to help students understand academic habits of mind and language in relation to their own cultural and rhetorical knowledge, whether that knowledge has been shaped by Pueblo storytelling, MTV, or both; (3) we need to provide opportunities for students to wrestle with the cultural conflicts that are raised by their immersion in academic culture—the changes it demands of them, the ways it may threaten to silence or censor them, and the ways it may separate them from their home communities and families—as well as the new voices and communities it may open to them; (4) we need to make clear to students that the rhetorical practices we're teaching them are culturally constructed and subject to change, not fixed and absolute; (5) we need to examine the rhetorical condition in which writers write—to help students recognize patterns of exclusion and power within dominant discourses and resist or challenge those patterns when they are disabling.

Envisioning a Multicultural Rhetoric

To implement these goals in our own courses, we have been developing an approach that highlights the languages and cultural knowledge students bring with them to the university. As Gloria Anzaldúa poignantly writes, "Ethnic identity is twin skin to linguistic identity—I am my language. Until I can take pride in my language, I cannot take pride in myself" (*Borderlands* 59). Many of our students have echoed these feelings. School experience has taught some that their home language is somehow deficient or incorrect; these students often worry that gaining proficiency in academic English constitutes a betrayal of family and community. Others are eager to learn the "language of power" but fear that they will lose (or are already losing) their native tongue. For these students, as well as for many who belong to the language majority, linguistic issues can interfere with success at the university. We have found that openly discussing these topics and exploring students' many cultural and language communities enhances learning.

We begin with storytelling. Stories, because they occur among all groups, cut across cultural boundaries, yet since types of stories and storytelling patterns can vary radically, they also clearly illustrate cultural differences. First, we read a range of narratives by writers from various ethnic groups; then we ask students to tell their own stories. Those who are comfortable with personal narrative may write about a moment of crisis or change in their lives. Those whose cultural or personal bent is to shy away from self-revelation can recount traditional stories from their cultures or describe important customs and ceremonies in their families and communities. Because stories are appealing and familiar to students, they can help bridge home and academic cultures. As Terry Dean points out, "Most often, it is not the home culture that causes problems, but a fear on the part of students that elements of that culture will not be accepted in the university environment" (36). Our experience, like Dean's, suggests that giving students the opportunity to talk and write about their cultural heritages, identities, and conflicts can diminish that fear and help ease their transition. We move on to investigating the influence of culture on the development of texts. We read essays, like Silko's "Language and

Literature from a Pueblo Indian Perspective," that place storytelling styles in their cultural contexts. Then, as students continue to work on their own stories, we encourage them to begin thinking analytically about the personal and cultural values their narratives reflect. Greg Sarris has observed that in his own classes such assignments were particularly useful for students outside the dominant culture, "bridging the chasm between life experience and classroom activity and personal anecdote and critical thinking" (182).

By using storytelling to examine the cultural basis of values and assumptions, students can also learn to understand more fully the sources of their differences. Unlike those traditionalists who warn that multiculturalism will doom us to balkanization, we believe that exploring the roots of our differences through stories opens communication rather than reinforces barriers. Reading the stories of marginalized groups can, as Henry Giroux explains, "help privileged groups listen seriously to the multiple narratives that constitute the complexity of Others historically defined through reifications and stereotypes" ("Postmodernism" 244). Indeed, storytelling can help combat stereotypical thinking among all groups. Sarris recounts that when a class discussion of sexism led to a shouting match between a feminist Jewish American student and a conservative Arab student, the class asked the disputants to tell stories about what had shaped their attitudes toward women. He concludes:

> While these stories did not solve the differences between these two students, they allowed them, and the rest of us in the classroom, the opportunity to explore mutual prejudices in a broader historical and political framework. After class, the Jewish woman approached the Arab and said, "I do not agree with you, but I understand you better." (183)

Explorations of difference thus become a central part of our classes. One assignment, for example, asks students to interview someone whose background is significantly different from their own and to write a profile of that person, discussing how the subject's experiences or opinions challenge, complicate, or confirm the writer's own views. When our students share their stories in class through peer response groups, reading aloud, and class publications, they are brought together "despite great distances between cultures" (Silko 69).

Next, students extend the range of their writing to examine the intellectual habits and formal conventions of the discourse communities they are entering. Lisa Delpit argues that this process is particularly essential for students of color, for if we neglect to teach them the codes of the "culture of power," at best we reinforce their marginalization within the academy and at worst we ensure their failure. But she does not advocate unquestioning assimilation: "even while students are assisted in learning the culture of power, they must also be helped to learn about the arbitrariness of those codes and about the power relationships they represent" (296). We invite our students to explore how their membership in different language communities and cultural groups influences their interpretation of the world and as a result their development as writers. Students read selections that discuss the many ways in which cultural influences—whether from home, school, or the larger society—can censor and nurture the writer. Writing assignments include descriptions and comparisons of two language communities or social groups the students belong to, discussions of the ways the students must alter language and behavior as they move between these groups, and analyses of how the values of each community reinforce or conflict with each other and contribute to the students' identities. An alternative assignment asks students to write two versions of a brief editorial, one appealing to the general campus community, the other to a different speech community or cultural group to which they belong. This assignment allows students to become conscious of certain expectations of college writing without devaluing the patterns of literacy they bring with them.

Although students learn conventional forms, we also encourage them to be flexible—to multiply their rhetorical options. We provide many examples of writing that draw on different rhetorical traditions and violate the boundaries of what is considered appropriate according to Western conventions. Works like Anzaldúa's *Borderlands / La Frontera*—which blends autobiography and scholarship, English and Spanish, prose and poetry—challenge conventional rhetorical wisdom and open spaces for new kinds of academic writing. We compare these experimental forms with more conventional ones and ask students to weigh the purposes, powers, and risks that reside in the authors' rhetorical choices. In this approach, we follow Min-Zhan Lu's suggestion that

> we might intentionally complicate the classroom scene by bringing into it discourses that stand at varying distances from the one we teach. We might encourage students to explore ways of practicing the conventions of the discourse they are learning

> by negotiating through these conflicting voices. We could also
> encourage them to see themselves as responsible for forming
> or transforming as well as preserving the discourse they are
> learning.   ("Silence" 447)

We provide frequent opportunities for language play and for experimentation with forms of expression beyond the thesis-driven essay:
students may "translate" an essay into a poem, represent a subject
such as their literacy history in a drawing, or develop an idea apposi-
tionally rather than propositionally. We believe that fostering innova-
tion helps students not only to appreciate the strengths and limitations
of academic thinking but also to challenge its boundaries.

The examination of differences among diverse language groups
and rhetorical styles enables students to understand that correctness
is contextual, not absolute. We ask students to examine the university
as a collection of social groups, each with its own cultural values, customs, and language conventions. We read analyses and critiques of
academic culture so that students begin to see scholarship as a form
of inquiry that functions within specific cultural contexts. Writing
assignments involve fieldwork in the university—observing, inter-
viewing, gathering data. One assignment has students interview a professor in a field that interests them and report on the types of research
and writing, the use of evidence, the important theoretical perspectives, and the major current debates within the field. Examining the
values and expectations of academic culture prompts discussion and
debate about issues of assimilation: what one gains and loses—social
mobility, power, identity, connection to family and friends—and
whether or how to negotiate the often contradictory demands of
home and school. As Lu argues, we shouldn't try to avoid the cultural
conflicts students encounter in the academy; rather we should work
toward "helping students reach a self-conscious choice on their position towards conflicting cultural values and forces" ("Conflict" 906).
This approach stresses the dialectic relation between personal experience and academic analysis—the ability of each form of knowledge to
deepen and enrich the other. Kurt Spellmeyer argues that it is only
through negotiating the tension between one culture or discourse and
another that we can learn to become active shapers of knowledge: "we
cannot understand either without the other, without, that is, an inside
and an outside. . . . The very word 'discourse,' in its root sense a 'running back and forth,' implies the need for such a doubleness" ("Foucault" 722).

As students come to realize that academic writing is, like all language, culturally based, we begin working more intensively with interpretation. Since all texts and events are open to multiple constructions, academic writing becomes a specialized form of storytelling. Scholars have begun to identify the stories or "master narratives" embedded in the discourses of many academic disciplines (see, e.g., Gergen and Gergen; Journet; Papke). Presenting academic analysis as an extension of narrative—a mode of thinking already familiar to students—helps demystify it. We read conflicting accounts of current events or scholarly essays that offer competing interpretations of the same material, and we talk about ways of evaluating these alternative narratives. Students then produce their own competing texts: a freewriting exercise asks students to recall an argument they've had recently and to describe it first from their perspective and then from the other person's, writing both accounts in the first person. Other activities include retelling a story from the perspective of a character other than the narrator, writing alternative endings to stories, or writing imaginary dialogues between the authors or narrators of different texts. In lengthier essays, students synthesize divergent points of view or propose several possible interpretations of an event or a text and then discuss which interpretation works best. The emphasis on multiple perspectives pushes students to think through issues in more complex terms. David Perkins's studies of everyday reasoning suggest that the most consistent problem students encounter in constructing an argument is not fallacious logic but failure to consider alternative lines of analysis before coming to a conclusion. A writing course based on cultural difference and multivocality can thus help students develop the intellectual complexity most valued by the academy.

Perhaps more important, such an approach enables students to consider how their personal and academic histories have been socially constructed, sometimes by others. We discuss the rhetorical condition in which writers write, investigating how power relations shape discourse and its reception. June Jordan's essay "Nobody Mean More to Me Than You . . ." is a powerful case in point that raises complex questions about whether or how marginalized writers can make themselves heard in the dominant culture without compromising their integrity. We also read the work of writers who have consciously resisted, disrupted, and reshaped the rhetorical condition itself—writers who, like Anzaldúa, "write to record what others erase when I speak, to rewrite the stories others have miswritten about me, about you" ("Speaking" 169). As students learn how language and stories have been used to oppress as well as to resist oppression, they are sit-uated "to engage critically the strengths and limitations of the cultural and social codes that define their own histories and narratives" (Giroux, "Postmodernism" 248). When students gain the confidence to challenge dominant cultural narratives, they can begin to construct more inclusive narratives of their own and thereby "undertake the knowledge-transforming violence that distinguishes the empowered from the powerless" (Spellmeyer, "Foucault" 719).

We believe a rhetoric such as the one we describe will foster an awareness of varied audiences, purposes, and social contexts for writ-ing through an examination of students' linguistic and cultural com-munities. When students can make connections between home and academy and look critically at each culture through the lens of the other, their experiences at the university will be enriched. As they ex-plore the complexities of multiple perspectives and struggle with the challenges of communicating across differences, they can develop the dialogic thinking essential to critical analysis. By learning that lan-guage conventions are fluid, contested, and enmeshed in relations of power, students can make better-informed choices as they negotiate the complexities of communicating in a tremendously diverse—and tremendously inequitable—world.

Because multiculturalism is fast becoming a reality of our daily lives, not just a fashionable bit of professional jargon, instructors as well as students must engage in a learning process. Rethinking long-held as-sumptions about rhetoric is a difficult task, one requiring us to ques-tion reflexive beliefs about language, teaching, and our own position in the world. Delpit acknowledges the difficulty of genuinely under-standing students' cultural differences, suggesting that "we must learn to be vulnerable enough to allow our world to turn upside down in order to allow the realities of others to edge themselves into our con-sciousness" (297). The rhetoric we are proposing demands more than constructing a new curriculum—it also requires self-transformation. Committing ourselves to the long process of learning and relearning that this effort entails must be our first step toward embracing a truly multicultural rhetoric.

Whose Voice Is It Anyway? Marked Features in the Writing of Black English Speakers

Denise Troutman

In sociolinguistics, linguistic features that are not usual or normal are called "marked." "Unmarked" features are those that are accepted as the norm. The usage of the dominant group in a society is generally established as "normal." We can more fully understand the concept of markedness by considering the conventional definition of the term *marked*. A marked object or person stands out prominently, the proverbial sore thumb, different from all others. Marked features in writing are the unaccepted kids on the block.

The following proscriptions warn against marked features in written English. Students are encouraged to make sure these nonstandard forms do not carry over from their speech into their writing.

> *a, an*. Use *an* before a vowel (an eye for an eye); use *a* before a consonant (a desk).
>
> Double negative. Double negatives say no twice. In standard English, a double negative is a no-no.
>
> *he don't, she don't. Don't* instead of *doesn't* is nonstandard for one single person or thing. Wrong: She don't live here.
>
> *knowed, blowed, had went*. Irregular verbs signal the past by a change in the root word. Know the standard forms.
>
> *and* and *but* at the beginning of a sentence. Many composition teachers still observe the rule banning *and* and *but* at the beginning of a sentence.
>
> *you* with indefinite reference. Never use this device in formal writing.
>
> Shifts in tone. Be sure to maintain a consistent tone.

Proscriptions like these appear in standard usage handbooks and are typically taught in English classrooms. What happens, though, when

27

the marked forms occur with regularity in students' essays? What happens when the marked forms serve an unmarked function for a particular cultural and racial group? Do English teachers and other evaluators proscribe away the authentic voice that students bring to their writing?

Language and Culture

As a college English teacher of developing writers, I focus this essay on African American students who are speakers of Black English (BE)—a linguistic variety of English that is socially stigmatized and is spoken by many, though certainly not all, African Americans—and suggest a method to improve assessment of their writing. Specifically, I address "cultural leftovers," which are marked, in the writing of African American students. *Cultural leftovers* is a phrase of my devising that parallels Melville Herskovits's "cultural carry-overs" (8). Herskovits focused on the carryover of African traditions and traits, in areas such as language and food, throughout the African diaspora. Cultural leftovers are distinctive spoken features used by African Americans that are left intact in written discourse. This phrase can have a positive connotation since flavors are often enhanced in leftovers. I discuss the issue of voice in relation to the marked cultural features and offer suggestions for improving the "at-writing-risk" status of this group of writers.

The marked features listed above are common BE features. BE is an oral language not used in print except experimentally. It survives in the minds and hearts of its speakers primarily as a spoken language, and its speakers pass on its oral forms from one generation to the next.

Among African descendants in the New World, "reverence for" and "preservation of" the oral tradition have survived "the move to a different continent, . . . a geographical Diaspora, centuries of slavery, and another century of racial discrimination" (Kochman). As in African society, verbal artistry is highly significant among speakers of BE, who exhibit great verbal skill. For example, in the dozens, a verbal game in which players try to cap each other or generate the most apposite, cogent, and spontaneous retort, usually about the opponent's mother, speakers must speak persuasively, getting and holding the audience's attention and approval. This verbal game involves establishing close engagement between speaker and audience. Getting the audience involved is also evident in the evangelical preaching style of African American ministers. Using and sharpening the speaker's verbal skills as well as engaging the audience, pulling it into the linguistic event, are distinctive characteristics of the BE speech community.

Since language reflects a speech community's way of thinking and worldview, I hypothesized that preference for the oral tradition would show up in the writing of college-level BE speakers, specifically, that their writing would reflect the oral attributes of the speech community, even though these students have become aware of the social stigma attached to BE.

The primary impetus for this analysis stems from my observations of numerous comments on and low evaluations of student papers by BE speakers. For example, the following sample essay, taken from Geneva Smitherman's research on National Assessment of Educational Progress–generated essays ("NAEP Writing"), received a low rater score of 2:

> I am a sad bird. Nobody wants me because I am so weird-looking. But some day just like the Negro they will realize that I am something. Maybe I do have a long beck. They shouldn't juge me that way. I might look dumb to them but I have some sense. They just won't give me change to show it. They just left me out here all by myself. They don't relize. that I'm blood and skin. I'm just as good as any other bird.

Perhaps the evaluator(s) of the essay did not seriously consider the consistent tone, the effective emotional appeal to readers, the concrete imagery and sustained metaphor, the consistent parallel between the bird and the "Negro," and the personal quality that establishes an authentic voice and a lively evangelical style. The BE speech community, in fact, values these features highly.

College Writers

I examined the writing of first-year college speakers of BE in developmental writing classes at a large midwestern university. I was able to assess students as speakers of BE by working with them closely in classes that met four days a week for two-hour sessions. These BE speakers used the following distinctive features:

> Completive aspect ("Like we done come from apes")
> Remote aspect ("We been done did our work")
> Habitual *be* ("The world be trying to clog up our minds")

Zero copula ("Like he adult")
Multiple negatives ("I don't know nothing about nobody no way")

Throughout the ten-week term, I collected final drafts of these students' essays, which had gone through in-class peer revision sessions. I did not give the BE speakers (or the non-BE speakers) written comments during the drafting of the essays, although during individual conferences we talked about paper objectives, content, organization, grading criteria, and other questions raised by the students.

Out of a total of forty collected essays, more than half the BE speakers used language reflective of the BE speech community. In fact, the proscribed marked features listed above are among the very ones that appear in these papers. I found that oral strategies, although devalued in Western societies, persistently carried over into these students' writing.

In their narrative essays, the students used conversational devices heavily, as if speaking directly to a visible audience:

Sample A

I had no reason not to trust him, I mean he talked as though he were honest, he even looked trustable if thats possible, and I was always a kind person, still am. So when he asked to borrow three of my dollars for lunch the word no never entered my mind. Maybe thats were I went wrong. He ate his free meal as if he were extremely grateful. He didn't smack or slurp, but you could tell it was of his nature and a struggle for him not to do so. This was on a Friday by the way, and we agreed Monday he would pay me back, which kindly did. I was extremely pleased that I had made a new friend, not that I had trouble doing so, but it was usually hard when money was involved. Our friendship grew stronger each day, we weren't best friends or anything like that, I mean we just never felt the need to be that close. And how we had met, or more importantly how I had at one time loaned him money, never came back into play until about two months later. I was raised you see, as the type of person never to borrow money, or beg for food.

Sample B

The officer on the passenger side opened the door and said, "Put your hands on the car. "What did we do?" "Don't worry about that, just do it!" he shouted. We stood there with our hands on the car and the cop staring at us. He went and mumbled something at the officer and started smiling. In a harsh voice he said, "Now get off the car before you get it dirty" and laughed. We were all angry and embaressed, you could see the water in our eyes.

. . . The cop said with his hands on his side, "Don't you worry about them, you're the one with the problem." The cop that was driving yelled though the window and said, Yall don't have no business out here." I thought who is he our father.

Sample C

In my adolescence, I've been in many embarrassing situations. Some of the situations took place the same day because of the same thing. Situations with my car, the noise making smoke machine, seems to be the most embarrassing. One day in my senior year of high school stands out. Well, a few days stand out but I'm only going to talk about one. . . .

The interpersonal function seems primary in the students' narratives. The writer in sample A uses an oral discourse style in a number of ways. First, there is little reliance on punctuation. To set apart ideas orally, speakers use intonation, rate of speech, and other prosodic cues. The commas, then, differ from standard usage; in the student essays, they indicate vocal pauses for breath. For example, "Our friendship grew stronger each day, we weren't best friends or anything like that, I mean we just never felt the need to be that close." (The writer in sample B uses commas similarly: "We were all angry and embaressed, you could see the water in our eyes.")

Second, the writer in sample A uses the oral discourse forms "by the way," "I mean," and "you see." Here the writer seems to pull readers directly into the text, creating close involvement, as if carrying on a conversation. For groups stemming from a "primary literate culture" (cf. Walter Ong's "primary oral culture"; 31), written language often has a detached, impersonal quality, unlike the language in this sample. Third, the writer in sample A stitches ideas together with *and*, *but*, and *so*, conjunctions used heavily in conversation: ". . . and I was always a kind person, still am. So when he asked to borrow three of my dollars. . . ." Fourth, the writer in sample A and the writer in sample B attempt to establish close engagement with readers through the use of *you*: "I was raised you see . . ." (sample A); "We were all angry and embaressed, you could see the water in our eyes" (sample B). As used here, *you* is a means of addressing the audience directly, involving it in the linguistic event, and establishing a personal tone. Thus the audience does not remain detached from the context but becomes part of it.

Sample B contains two additional oral features characteristic of BE. First, the sentence form exemplified by "He went and mumbled something at the officer" occurs in BE as a means of reporting action carried out by an interlocutor. The syntactic structure—noun or pronoun—plus *went* plus *and* plus verb plus -*ed* plus complement—intensifies meaning in that an agent executes not one action ("went") but two ("mumbled"). The appropriate use of this form dictates that the utterer conveys displeasure and dissatisfaction with the interlocutor's action.

Second, the writer of sample B uses a standard rhetorical mode of BE, called signifying. According to Smitherman, to signify is to make a humorous, indirect comment that puts down or makes fun of the receiver of the message. Signifying is most often openly "directed at [a] person or persons usually present in a situational context (siggers do not talk behind yo back)" (*Talkin* 121). The student in sample B, however, does not signify on the officer openly because of the possible repercussions; instead, she does so by thinking that he does not have the right or obligation to tell her or her friends what they should be doing or where they should be ("I thought who is he our father"). It is highly significant here, then, that the student writer incorporates central BE features used commonly in face-to-face interactions.

In sample C the writer uses an oral style in two ways. First, he uses the term *well*, which commonly functions in speaking to introduce a main point. Second, he explicitly acknowledges a speech act in writing ("I'm only going to *talk* about one"); thus an oral form surfaces in a literate one.

The BE speakers used oral strategies not only in their narrative essays but also in their expository essays:

Sample D

Racism. The first thought that comes to my mind is the Deep South with its old signs of 'Whites Only' and 'Colored Only'. In a sense of violence it brings to mind the thoughts of the Ku Klux Klan. Even though the signs of 'Whites Only' and 'Colored Only' have vanished within today's modern society, racism is something that just cannot be rid of.

> I have never personally encountered racism. I mean, I may have but it never came across my mind that it was intended as racial. I have always grown-up in promidently white neighborhoods and I cannot recall once when any of my white playmates parents did not allow them to play with me or spend the night because I was black. If anything, they were nothing but nice to my family and me. Maybe that is why I might of never noticed it. Living in my 'white' world, I could see no difference except the little girls had long, straight, blond hair when I did not. And besides our color of skin I always considered ourselves basically the same. Oh, yes, I knew of racial stuff but to me it just did not evolve around my world. . . . Who did the white people think they were? They are no better than anybody else. OK, in some cases they have better hair but that is about it.

The writer in sample D began her essay with a speech-making strategy especially popular among African American ministers—the intentional use of fragments for emphasis. These fragments allow pauses for reflection by the audience. The period after the opening fragment, "Racism," signals a pause for breath similar to that in sample A. If someone familiar with oral traditional style read the essay aloud, she or he would pause for effect after uttering "Racism," a word that would call up various intended images in the listeners' minds.

Just as the writer in sample A does, this writer uses oral forms as if she were carrying on a conversation. The forms "I mean," "Oh, yes," and "OK" reverberate with a conversational intimacy. Rarely, if ever, would writers from "primary literate traditions" use these features in writing. This writer addresses her readers directly through these forms. "Might of" is an orthographic form, deriving from speech sounds, not written words. Last, this writer uses another rhetorical mode of the BE speech community—sounding. In this mode a speaker expresses extreme displeasure with, indeed anger at, a particular outcome deemed undeserved, unjust, or demeaning by talking loudly, "sounding off" on the receiver. Sounding allows the speaker to avoid internalizing anger, to embarrass the receiver by telling others within hearing range about the injustice, to attain compensation from the receiver (if in fact a disservice occurred), and, for stage lovers, to gain a platform to pontificate on the mistreatment. The writer in sample D becomes indignant as she begins discussing whites' presumption of superiority. The perturbed attitude and pontification can be heard in the last three sentences of the sample: "Who did the white people think they were? They are no better than anybody else. OK, in some cases they have better hair but that is about it." Given additional time and space, the writer probably would have taken the platform longer.

The next student writer also employs an oral rhetorical strategy very common to BE. For centuries, African Americans have used repetition in speech as a valuable and desirable manner of presenting ideas. Even though the literate tradition teaches against repetition, especially within a short space, African American oral style relishes it, particularly for the rhythmic pattern it creates and the emphasis it provides:

Sample E

Racism was something I thought existed in the days of Dr. Martin Luther King, Jr. I thought racism was over. I thought we could all live together as one. . . . During those days I thought we were created equal. I thought wrong. Before entering college I remember racism at the University of Michigan being plastered across television and newspapers. I remember the incidents of racial violence, I remember the racial slurs and I remember the hurt and anguish across many faces who thought as I did. . . . Our ancestors fought out of slavery to be free, they fought to be able to vote, they fought for equality not only for their equality but for their descendants equality. . . .

There is no prescribed number of times that speakers or writers should repeat a particular word, phrase, or idea; the amount depends on the mood of the speakers or writers, their adeptness in creating meaning with the repeated forms, and the emotion they want to invoke. In this sample the repetition of words is systematic. The writer repeats "I thought" five times. The last "I thought" not only creates a rhythmic and emphatic pattern but serves as a common oral signifying retort in BE: a speaker making an erroneous statement beginning with "I thought" would be sharply told, "You thought wrong." The writer uses a variation of this retort to correct herself deservedly. Next, "I remember" occurs four times, followed by a final recurrence of "thought." Then "fought" appears in several phases, with a particle, with an infinitive, and with a prepositional phrase. Finally the writer repeats "equality" twice.

This type of repetition of words, phrases, clauses, and ideas occurs, for example, in Jesse Jackson's oratory: "Africa would if Africa could. America could if America would. But Africa cain't and America ain't"

(Smitherman, *Talkin* 3). This community of speakers uses repetition powerfully and effectively. Interestingly, the student writer of sample E constructed her introduction as if she were delivering a speech (reminiscent of sample D), which poignantly highlights the culture and language connection discussed throughout this paper.

Other examples of features in BE speakers' writing abounded in their expository writing, for example, storytelling devices, elements from rap, cultural expressions ("acting a fool," "picked with him"), and BE syntactic forms ("I be taking this all in"). The following excerpt from a college-level BE speaker's essay helps lead into my final point:

Sample F

Well, this is how I'll evaluate my academic performance, not the way I expect my grades to be. I was having trouble with my [writing course] because I was lacking how to write a essay paper, and that was where my biggest fault was. I tried to write the way I heard my teacher spoke, but I couldn't it wasn't me. She would make comments on my paper telling me this wording isn't right, this doesn't make any-sense. I knew this wasn't high school anymore, that it was the real world. I hop when I pass in my paper that it will lift my grade up a little higher than it is now. . . . I used to think my [writing] teacher was a threat to my friend & myself. It seem that we were the only two black girls, that she would put down our papers, and give us low grades. This white girl wrote her paper on Santa Claus, a legend that little kids believe in. It was no better than mine she get an good grade, I get a low grade so I ask the teacher why she tells me, that I don't get to the point, I talk in circles. How do she expects me to talk when I'm doing a paper on abortion, you have to when they're young teenagers getting aborting.

This sample contains some of the oral features discussed above. The writer constructs a conversational style through the absence of some punctuation and the use of "well" and other marked oral features: "a essay," "I talks," and "how do she." More important, the student explicitly identifies a central point: she could not imitate her instructor's voice because it was not her own authentic voice. This poignant statement and the one about the numerous teacher comments scribbled on each page immediately raise the question Whose voice do writing instructors want students to use? Walk a mile with me in my cultural and racial moccasins as in the standard BE style, I switch tones in the next section, preaching, teaching, advocating a new direction in the assessment of BE speakers' writing to help students improve their skills.

Whose Voice Is It Anyway?

Shouldn't students be given the right to discover and warm up their authentic voices before they add on other voices? Isn't that precisely the philosophy we prescribe but do not practice? Do we aim to create humanoids who write in simulated voices, not possessing individualized senses of self? Or do we attempt to see the worth in the written creations before us? Yes, the superficialities of language and punctuation may need work to enhance communication with some audiences, but we should look at the imagery, the ideas!

If we follow the proscriptions against marked BE features, we deny BE speakers affirmation of their linguistic heritage and teach them "linguistic self-hatred" (Sledd 1309). These proscriptions work against intrinsic features of the oral traditional style that many African American students use to project their voices.

Yet isn't it our job as teachers of English to lead students away from "cultural leftovers"? As Keith Gilyard attests and I reaffirm, getting rid of such features is not requisite to acquiring literacy (160). As in speech, people can retain their native linguistic codes or styles and add on others. Discovering, grasping control of, and retaining authentic voices, with which writers develop and reinforce who they are, allow students to become confident as writers and as members of a distinct speech community.

Nancy Sommers intertwines an article with a discussion of voice and authority, highlighting that one of the most empowering experiences of students' lives is learning to write from the authority of their own voices. She writes about the absence of her voice in her own work. In reviewing a talk she presented at a 1987 conference, Sommers found that she used

> a distant, imponderable, impersonal voice—inaccessible, humorless, and disguised. . . . I speak in an inherited academic voice; it isn't mine. I simply wasn't there for my own talk. . . . I, like so many of my students, was reproducing acceptable truths, imitating the gestures and rituals of the academy, not having confidence enough in my own ideas, nor trusting the native language I had learned. . . . Against all the voices I embody—the

voices heard, read, whispered to me from off-stage—I must bring a voice of my own. I must enter the dialogue on my own authority, knowing that other voices have enabled mine, but no longer can I subordinate mine to theirs. The voices I embody encourage me to show up as a writer and to bring the courage of my own authority into my classroom. I have also learned about the dangers of submission from observing the struggles of my own students. When they write about their lives, they write with confidence. As soon as they begin to turn their attention toward outside sources, they too lose confidence, defer to the voice of the academy, and write in the voice of Everystudent. . . . They disguise themselves in the weighty, imponderable voice of acquired authority. . . .   (27–29)

Two articles published in the same journal as Sommers's essay each contain two different voices (Zawacki; Clark and Wiedenhaupt). At the end of the collaborative essay by Beverly Clark and Sonja Wiedenhaupt, a teacher and a student, the latter ends the essay, thanking her professor for nudging her to complete the honors thesis that had given her writer's block for over a year: "I don't think it is an easy task to make a student trust their own voice" (71). These articles argue for encouraging students to discover, explore, and develop their authentic voices, because of the confidence and strength that result. Indeed, the writers seem focused on changing the academy, not the student.

Overall, the findings in this analysis show that in the first year of college most BE speakers used linguistic features prominent in their oral culture in their writing. Obviously, the BE speakers did not all use the same features, although some overlap inevitably occurred. My findings are corroborated in Arnetha Ball's research. Ball found that in organizing written expository discourse urban African American high school students "indicated a strong preference for using vernacular-based organizational patterns [narrative interspersion and circumlocution] for academic written as well as conversational tasks" (524). That BE-speaking student populations used oral traditional strategies in their formal writing tasks suggests that the thinking, the oral traditional worldview, of African Americans is reflected in language, even written language.

With these findings as a resource, scholars may be able to make recommendations addressing the issues of "excellence" or literacy and of educational equality. One possible step in solving literacy problems for speakers of BE is to accept their cultural voice. But to do so requires a new type of instruction. As Gilyard admonishes, "there must be an

insistence that educators understand and indicate by their actions the importance of cultural and linguistic pluralism in educational settings" (163). We must learn to accept difference in writing styles and stop evaluating it as deficient. In fact, the former editor of *College Composition and Communication*, Richard Gebhardt, remarks on that journal's acceptance of different writing styles: "It seems clear to me . . . that *CCC* is open to strongly-voiced submissions, to personally-grounded articles, and to articles that take risks with structure or style" (9). It would appear timely for those entrusted with the training of students to adopt such openness. Educators must recognize the students' need to develop skills in a wide variety of literacies, not just a written literacy (Applebee, Langer, and Mullis). We must allow these students to use their cultural forms in writing, since the oral forms promote a sense of self and help develop confidence. "The challenge of the next decades is to reinstall written language with the vitality of oral language. . . . Within *any forms* of a living language lie a multitude of concrete worlds . . . and an open challenge to promote creative and critical thought" (Heath, "Where"; emphasis added). Since cultural differences are communicated by writing, educators, especially teachers of writing, must help African American students affirm who they are through the use of BE. John Oliver Killens, in the foreword to *The Cotillion*, unequivocally communicates the point about cultural voice and cultural preference:

To Whom It May Concern
(and to all you all who ought to be)

I'm a writer, understand. And I just finished the novel that I'm forwarding to you, dear readers. I used to write my novels as I lived them from Rio all the way to Zanzibar. In the oral tradition of my African ancestors.

This book is kind of halfly autobiographical and halfly fiction, all based on facts as I have gathered them. I got my log together, baby, from the natural source, the horse's mouth and his hinder parts. Also from the lips of the sweetest girl on this terrible wonderful earth. Dig it, and like I went to one of them downtown white workshops for a couple of months and got all screwed up with angles of narration, points of view, objectivity, universality, composition, author-intrusion, sentence structure, syntax, first person, second person. I got so screwed up I couldn't unwind myself for days. I said, to hell with all that! I'm the first, second and third person my own damn self. And I will intrude, protrude, ob-

trude or exclude my point of view any time it suits my disposition. Dig that. I read all the books on writing. Egri, John Howard Lawson, Percy Lubbeck, McHugh, Reynolds. You name it. I know all about the dialectical approach, character development, cause-and-effect and orchestration, the obligatory scene, crisis, climax, denouement, and resolution. I was uptight with the craft [stuff]. Can you dig it?

    I decided to write my book in AfroAmericanese. Black rhythm, baby. Yeah, we got rhythm, brothers, sisters. Black idiom, Black nuances, Black style.   (1–3)

Like Killens, the African American students in the present study and in earlier research appear not to want to give up culturally learned modes of discourse; they seem to prefer the cultural style (Troutman; Ball). Beginning where these students are—at the cultural level—may lead to successful writing experiences.

Teaching American Indian Students: Interpreting the Rhetorics of Silence

Michelle Grijalva

> *I can remember reading that the robins were heading south for winter, but I knew that all winter the robins were around Laguna. It took me a long time to figure out what was going on. I worried for quite a while about the robins because they didn't leave in the winter, not realizing that the textbooks were written in Boston.*
>
> —Leslie Silko

Leslie Silko's anecdote about Laguna Pueblo in New Mexico highlights a perceptual problem facing many Indian children on reservations in the Southwest as they struggle to master English and literature from textbooks that ignore cultural and geographic difference. I was acutely aware of this problem of perspective when I began teaching comparative literature and writing to precollege Hopi and Navajo students at the University of Arizona. The summer of 1993 was the sixth and last summer teaching sophomores, juniors, and seniors from Tuba City High School, because our grant from the Josiah Macy Foundation ended.

Tuba City is about 350 miles north of Tucson on the Navajo Reservation, which encircles the Hopi Reservation in northeastern Arizona: "The 25,000 square mile Navajo Reservation, about the size of West Virginia, extends into Utah and New Mexico, though the majority of its land is in Arizona. There, the Navajo and Hopi share land for hunting, gathering, sheep grazing, and religious purposes. And there, most Hopi make their homes on the three stone fingers called First, Second, and Third Mesas" (Hillerman 59). The Hopi refer to their homeland as Tuwanasavit, "The Center of the Universe." Hopi and Navajo rites, language, and traditions are extremely different. Navajo is an Athabascan language; Hopi is Uto-Aztecan. Ranching is very important for the Navajo, who build their homes far apart; Hopi homes, built of red stone, are clustered around a central plaza. Both tribes believe their home-lands to be sacred ground, however, and both have complex cultural foundations and rich oral traditions that begin in time immemorial.

Tuba City is not your typical city at all. Rather, it is a ragtag mix-ture of trailers and mobile homes, a hospital, a police station, a trading post, a high school, a junior high school, an elementary school, a couple of hotels, prefabricated houses, old stone buildings left over from government projects, a Mexican restaurant, and a few fast-food places—all scattered about in no apparent pattern. The wind blows ceaselessly in the afternoons, raising a fine dust that knits the town together.

My first visit to Tuba City was in July 1988. I had been asked to de-sign and teach an advanced English course for students who would be attending second-session summer school at the University of Arizona. The course was an experiment initiated by Bio-Prep, the high school honors program, which prepared students for advanced courses in math and science. These courses were going well, but the students were uninterested and performing poorly in their English classes. Manny Begay, director of the Bio-Prep program, believed that students would benefit from a rigorous English class at a major university. Not only would the students be able to concentrate on one course, but they would also see what it was like to live in a dormitory, visit a large city, and attend a university.

Because I had never taught high school students before, I was ap-prehensive about the choice of books, but I knew I wanted to empha-size American Indian literature. I visited the reservations so I could get a feel for the land, and I believe the visit helped me better understand my students. Specific mountains and landscapes play vital parts in the oral traditions of the Hopi and Navajo. The San Francisco Peaks near Flagstaff are considered holy by both tribes. Called Dook 'o'oosliid by the Navajo, these mountains mark the western boundary of their homeland. For the Hopi, the sacred mountain is Nuvatekiaqui, gate-way to the home of the kachinas, spirit beings that link the Hopi to their creator. "The *kachinas* create the clouds and bring rain, fertility, and all blessings. They live among the Hopi during the half-year be-tween planting and harvesting, then return to the spirit world through the mountain" (Hillerman 60). These mountains and the long expanse of a Navajo sheep camp invested the Native literature I had studied with a vitality that is often missing from the dusty pages of ethno-graphic research reports. To see the Hopi mesas was to understand finally why the Hopi language sounds angular and hard-cut; it mirrors a way of life cast in gray stone and red rock.

I decided to visit the acting superintendent of curriculum while I was there. Even though I was not expected, I was graciously received. I showed him two books I was thinking of using for the course: *Earth Fire: A Hopi Legend of the Sunset Crater Eruption* and *Between Sacred Mountains: Navajo Stories and Lessons from the Land*. A Navajo man, the superintendent was kind and patient, but he was concerned about my choice of texts. He said candidly, "I'm sorry, but the students will not read these books. Maybe they'll peek at them around midnight in their dorms, but they won't read them. They're ashamed of their cultures." I was alarmed by his comment. American Indian literature was not being taught in the high school, even though in 1988 ninety-seven percent of Tuba High's 1400 students from Arizona, Colorado, New Mexico, and Utah were Native American, giving it the largest Native American student body of any high school in the country. I emphasized that this sense of shame had to be explored, and a starting point could be using American Indian literature in the classroom. He agreed but wondered if it would work. So did I.

Underlying this sense of shame is a long and complex history. To understand the psychological, political, legal, and cultural dilemmas faced by many American Indians, one must understand the historical and contemporary consequences of conquest, subjugation, and colonialism, especially from an indigenous perspective—clearly a daunting task but a mandatory one.

We might begin by examining the history of Indians and boarding schools. In 1879, the Carlisle School for Indians, the prototype of the Indian boarding school, was established, the brainchild of Richard Pratt, whose pedagogical strategy was to "kill the Indian and save the man." Pratt solicited hundreds of Indian children for the school. By the late 1880s, well-intentioned yet misguided American educators were compelled to "civilize" Indian children by removing them from their homes, enrolling them in boarding schools (many of which were designed on the Carlisle model) hundreds of miles away from their families, prohibiting them from speaking any language but English, denying them visits home for five years, demeaning their tribal traditions, cutting their hair, discarding their traditional clothes, and teaching them that to be civilized was to deny their cultural heritage and language. The fine documentary *In the White Man's Image* details the suffering, oppression, and dehumanization of those who survived the "noble experiment." However, killing the Indian and saving the man was an unprecedented failure, producing countless individuals who felt trapped between cultures—liminal men and women shunned by the dominant society and isolated from tribal traditions. Finally, in the 1930s, the experiment was abandoned, but the insidious portrayal of the Indian as backward and inarticulate still flows in the undercurrents of our educational systems.

At Tuba City High School in 1988, literature was indeed being taught, but the curriculum clearly denied that Indian traditions, cultures, or languages had any literary or artistic merit. The emphasis was on the classics. Roger Dunsmore, the scholar in residence for the Arizona Humanities Council at Tuba High for 1988–89, explains that "the students were fed a steady diet of Anglo standards—*Beowulf*, Shakespeare, Wordsworth—and most had little sense of their own literature or history" (36). Dismayed at the lack of Indian literature at the high school, he met with the English department to discuss including Native American works in the curriculum. He encountered staunch resistance:

> There were teachers who said openly that to bring in the Native literature was an attempt to take us all back to the cave. "We all started in caves!" was the exact comment. And when asked about the environmental wisdom contained in that literature, we were told by this teacher: "We don't need it. When we ruin this planet, we'll get into our spaceships and go to another, and when we ruin that one, we'll go to another, and when we ruin that one, we'll go to another, and another, and another. That's what technology is for." (38)

Clearly, the atmosphere at Tuba High was not conducive to teaching American Indian literature.

Because my class was taught at the University of Arizona as English 195, I had the freedom to choose the texts and films. Entitled Places of People in the Landscape, the course emphasized the connection between identity and place. I used a variety of books to place Hopi and Navajo literature into a world canon. Besides *Earth Fire* (Malotki) and *Between Sacred Mountains* (Bingham and Bingham), we read Rudolfo Anaya's *Bless Me, Ultima*, Yukio Mishima's *The Sound of Waves*, and N. Scott Momaday's *The Way to Rainy Mountain* and viewed a series of videos: *Iisaw: Hopi Coyote Stories* (Evers), with Helen Sekaquaptewa; *Running on the Edge of the Rainbow: Laguna Stories and Poems* (Evers), featuring Leslie Silko; *In This Song I Walk: Navajo Stories and Songs* (Evers); *Natwaniwa: A Hopi Philosophical Statement* (Evers); and *Itam Hakim, Hopiit: We the Hopi* (Masayesva).

In the first class, I had thirteen seniors accompanied by Percy Piestewa, their friend, guardian, and counselor. Percy grew up in Tuba City, works at the junior high there, and often travels with students as their chaperone. It was her job to live with them in the dormitory and help them adjust to life in the big city. Several of them had never been away from home. All the students could understand their native language, Hopi or Navajo, but most could not speak it. A few, however, were fluent speakers of their native language as well as English. For all, writing English was harder than speaking it. Some students clipped the ends off English words when they spoke. They explained that this pronunciation is considered a "reservation accent" and is mocked by Anglo teachers at the high school.

I was not sure how to begin the course. The students were incredibly reticent, enveloped in a silence that seemed impenetrable. They did not want to open up and certainly did not want to talk about their cultural traditions. In my research, I had found no truly useful guides or texts that would help me teach American Indian literature to American Indian students, so I decided to tell them about my own cultural experience. I asked, "Do you know what a *curandera* is?" They shook their heads, but at least I had their attention. A tall, lanky Hopi boy asked quietly, "What language is that?"

"Spanish," I replied. "A *curandera* is a healer, a medicine woman. In Yaqui, she is called an *hitebi*. My father's godmother was a healer, a *curandera*, and she lived out at Old Pascua." I pointed northwest, explaining that Old Pascua was the village where we celebrated our sacred Easter ceremonies. "When I was a child, I was an *angelita*, a little angel, and on Holy Saturday morning, all the *angelitas*, the deer dancer and singers, and the *matachin* dancers gathered on the steps of the church to defend it against the evil *chapayekas*. I had to dress all in white—all the kids dressed in white—and my mother braided white roses into my hair. We stood in front of the church and threw sacred flowers, *sewam*, at the evil *chapayekas*, ending their reign of terror. They had taken over the village after Lent and tormented every living creature. Each *chapayeka* dancer made his own mask, and each mask was the incarnation of evil, although only the best and most virtuous men were dressed as *chapayekas*."

"What did they make the masks out of?" asked the same boy. "Different hides," I answered. "It depended on the man, but there was a sacred way of hunting for the animal." The students murmured softly, while the student and another Hopi boy took turns explaining, "You have to pray to the animal you are hunting, thanking it for its life, and you have to have a clear mind and good heart when hunting."

"That's true in our tradition, too," I replied. "My grandfather always said that you have to hunt with *tu'i hiapsimak*, a good heart. Now that I think about it, my grandmother used to say the same thing—that you have to cook with a good heart, *tu'i hiapsimak*." This made the girls giggle, and one Navajo girl commented, "Our traditions sound similar. My grandfather's a singer, and during a sing—" She was cut off by a Hopi girl who asked quietly, "Is that when they cure someone who's sick?" The Navajo girl nodded her head and continued, "You have to have really good thoughts and a good heart or you can mess up the cure." Then she asked if we had singers like that in my tradition. "Well, that takes me back to the *curandera*, who is a powerful healer. If the healer is a man, then he is a *curandero*. My grandmother used to tell me this story about a Yaqui *curandero*." I proceeded to tell the story, and they slowly began telling theirs.

"You know," I encouraged them after they told a few of their stories, "there's a lot of wisdom hidden in stories like these. They are a lot of fun, but they also teach us a great deal, don't you think?" One boy, who spoke Navajo fluently and English carefully, explained, "My grandfather's always telling us stories. My uncle is really good at *yana* stories." Puzzled, I asked, "What's a yaha story?" The class laughed. He clarified, "No, no, *yana* story y-a-n-a. *Yana*." When I couldn't get the pronunciation, he said, "Like banana, you know, *yana* like banana."

"Oh, OK, I got it. So, what are they?" Again, laughter. "Stories about witches, skin walkers, spooky stuff like that." "Well," I said, "Sounds like you guys know a lot of stories. Why don't you write some up for your first assignment?" The students were excited but startled. "Really?" "Yes. I'd like to read them. In fact, I'd love to hear them too. Maybe by the end of the semester, each of you can tell the class one of your favorite stories." The students agreed, but clearly they were surprised that I would not only tell stories from my tradition but also encourage them to tell stories from theirs.

But inexplicably on the following Monday morning the class was beyond quiet or even hesitant; they were encased in a silence that bordered on collective solitude. It was as if they were engaged in a conspiracy of silence that held them together or would somehow protect them. Protect them from what? from me? What was happening here? The students refused to talk. I was stumped. Class ended and we had got nowhere. Finally, Percy confided in me.

Over the weekend, a drunk Navajo boy, a student from another program and another dormitory, somehow turned up on our students' floor. He behaved obnoxiously and attached himself to the group, though they didn't know him or want him around. The boy couldn't hold his liquor, and he was sick all over the floor and in the main study hall. Since it happened on Saturday night, no one could be found to clean up the mess on Sunday. In the July heat and simmering humidity, the stench became unbearable. But far worse than the smell was the shamefulness of the boy's actions. The Tuba City students couldn't believe what he had done, and they certainly didn't condone his drunkenness. But what bothered them the most was that other people in the dormitory acted as if our students were to blame for this stranger's outrageous acts. Because the Tuba City students were Indian, they were all scorned and made to feel guilty; it didn't matter whether they were Hopi or Navajo. Cutting remarks were made, and it was the first time that many of the students felt the sting of racism. In the eyes of the other dormitory residents, they were all "drunken savages." The treatment was irrational and cruel. Percy was furious. Our students wanted to go home.

It was interesting and ironic how quickly and categorically Indians were stereotyped by the dormitory community. Our students were victims of an interpretation. They were told who and what they were, and their sense of internal integrity and autonomy was negated. The other dormitory residents were, albeit unknowingly, participating on a small scale in a long tradition of domination and dehumanization in which non-Indians have spoken for indigenous peoples.

As I surveyed our situation in the dorm, I felt that if our students returned home, then my students and I would also be participating in this history of subjugation. Following James Clifford's lead, we chose to assert our own ethnographic authority, that is, we refused to accept either the dormitory residents' invectives or Pratt's misguided dictum of killing the Indian and saving the man. In his essay "Man Made of Words" Momaday addresses the question "What is an American Indian?" His answer is an appraisal of the relation between language and experience:

> It seems to me that in a certain sense we are all made of words; that our most essential being consists in language. It is the element in which we think and dream and act, in which we live our daily lives. There is no way in which we can exist apart from the morality of a verbal dimension . . . An Indian is an idea which a given man has of himself. And it is a moral idea for it accounts for the way in which he reacts to other men and to the world in general. And that idea, in order to be realized completely, has to be expressed.   (162)

Momaday's essay is a difficult one; arranged by juxtaposition, it reads like a spiderweb, with many different threads radiating from a central core, so the narrative is nonlinear, and the essential points can converge in many different ways as the pattern falls into place. Momaday weaves together pieces of stories, strands of memories, and evocations of landscapes into a powerful analysis of the imagination.

We talked about his essay in class the next day and came to understand that identity, like a story, can be considered a rhetorical construction—it is, among other things, a performance that constantly changes, playing itself out in "our daily lives." Consequently, identity for us became "conjunctural, not essential" (James Clifford 11), and we learned that you must "tell your story in pieces, as it is" (Edward Said, qtd. in James Clifford 11). The way to tell our stories in pieces, we learned from good storytellers like Momaday, is to use multiple voices, personas, and genres. Learning this lesson necessitated an intimate knowledge of writing and speaking; that is, we had to learn to imagine ourselves. As Momaday emphasizes, "We are what we imagine. Our very existence consists in our imagination of ourselves. Our best destiny is to imagine, at least, completely, who and what, and *that* we are. The greatest tragedy that can befall us is to go unimagined" (162).

By the second year of the program, the class size had doubled. I team taught with Patrick Baliani, and we continued to focus on the image of the storyteller, and I invited the Navajo poet Luci Tapahonso to visit our class and discuss writing from a Native perspective. Luci emphasized that no sacred stories may be told during the summer; it was against Navajo custom. I explained to her that the students in the first year had asked me why we couldn't talk about these sacred narratives, and I had to confess that I didn't know. I knew that when the snakes are awake in the summer, no sacred tales could be told or we would risk snakebite, but I didn't have a rational explanation. Luci seized on my point and emphasized that in American Indian traditions, it wasn't necessary to know. In fact, she didn't know why certain traditions existed either. She echoed Julian Hayden's point that "there are, as any desert [dweller] knows, many things in the desert that can't be explained logically or on the basis of existing knowledge. These things are to be accepted and not worried about" (227). This concept of knowledge is central to an understanding of Native American literature. American Indian oral traditions are paradigms of mystery, incorporating beauty, humor, and fear into moving constructions of language.

Using Luci Tapahonso's and Julian Hayden's comments as a point of departure, I encouraged our class to understand silence as an effective rhetorical tool that gives shape to sound and meaning—not to confuse it with the inarticulate and illiterate or with the inchoate place of nonbeing, a void that lends itself to shame and insecurity. Rather, the silence of storytellers can remind us that there is such a thing as the unspeakable, something we might call the silence of the sacred, or it can simply signal an inappropriate time to speak. Storytellers teach us that silence is the beat and pulse, the rhythm keeper of the oral tradition. Storytellers who are not afraid of silence can hold their audience; they are survivors.

In the last six years, I have shared my own stories, interweaving dozens of Yaqui tales into my classes, creating our own text. Along with those tales, which in their silences resonate with the sacred, I have told stories about the policy of deportation and extermination that the Mexican government, under Porfirio Díaz, implemented against the Yaquis. I talked about how my grandparents had to flee Mexico to survive and how the Yaquis were not recognized as American Indians until 1978. We discussed the burdens that these hardships placed on the Yaquis, their traditions, and their language. The students responded to these stories and to the Native works we read by writing powerful, evocative essays, stories, and poems that came out of their own struggles with cultural identity and survival. A Navajo girl wrote about her grandparents:

> My grandparents know very little English; I know very little of my native language. Since I was young my mother had always told me I spoke good Navajo. And she could never understand why I stopped speaking it. Maybe I was more involved in modern society, listening to Michael Jackson. Or maybe I thought that knowing about my native tradition wasn't important to me. And for sure, I was definitely wrong about that, because these days everyone is trying to learn about their culture. And those who don't will soon learn the consequences about that which will be lost.

This student's paper captures the struggle of most Indian students on reservations to negotiate between traditional values and the customs of American teenagers in the late twentieth century. Cable television, rock music, fashion fads—orange hair, shaved heads, pierced noses, shredded jeans—contemporary movies, rivalries over sports stars, junk food, and the rest exist on the students' reservations with kiva dances, fry bread, traditional songs, and seasonal ceremonies, as well as Native languages and hogans and centuries-old stone houses. It is not an easy existence or a friendly collaboration. The student ends her paper with her grandfather worried about his grandchildren, hoping that they understand and carry on their traditional ways:

> Grandfather sat on his rough chair in the cool shadow of the afternoon, resting. The clouds then filled the sky of the heavens. Yet, there is no rain. Just the breeze of cool air rushing upon his brown wrinkled face. What surrounded him was a small sandstorm coming from the ground where once my ancestors lived and told their stories of how the *Dine* [the people] came. Through his eyes, I could see the reflections of my ancestors coming closer to me. . . . "My grandchildren," [he said], "look into my eyes and see the darkness brought upon your people. Your grandmother and I are so old. We see the selfishness of the people losing their tradition. Is this the way we all should live? You are the leaders of tomorrow, and you should do something about it, now. We are old and you are young. This is the beginning, where you should be an adult and teach yourself and others to know who you are, a Native Indian. You are the shadows of your ancestors and do what they say."

It is clear that the students we worked with resist efforts to eradicate Indian traditions and culture, yet their struggle to hold on to their Native languages is not easy. A Hopi student explains:

> Early in my childhood I learned how to speak and write in the English language, but at the same time I was learning the Hopi language from my parents. It was hard for me to learn both because most of my friends spoke English, but when I got home I had to flip over to the Hopi side. I can say, I know how to speak and write in the English form, but I don't know it fluently. Then there is the Hopi language, where I can understand it fluently but not speak it fluently, which is kind of odd. . . . I could say I'm caught on a bridge, where one end has the Hopi language and the other end has the English language; I have never been able to reach one side where I am completely aware of what I am speaking or listening to.

He says that if a lecture in English is given too quickly, he gets a bit lost; whereas the difficulty in speaking Hopi is that there are "different dialects of Hopi being spoken between each village. In some villages the language is spoken with a lot of emotion; whereas in other villages the language would be spoken [in a] monotone which makes it really boring." His piece shows that he has a keen ear for languages, even if he is struggling to master both. He ends his essay with an excellent linguistic analysis:

> A perfect example of the different dialects is between the villages of Shungopavi and Moencopi. Take the sentence: *Hep owi idam by bep gadudani*, meaning: Yes, we will sit there. That is the way it would be said in [a] Moencopi dialect, where the endings of "hep" and "bep" would end with the "p" sound. Whereas in Shungopavi dialect, the endings would be changed from "p" to the "f" sound. It would read: *Hef owi idam by bef gadudani*. Therefore, in the Hopi language you would be expected to know the different dialects.

Hopi is not a written language, so this student was creating one as he tried to transcribe and capture Hopi on paper. His dedication and determination were shared by all the students. In those six years, I never encountered students who were not interested in their cultural backgrounds or languages once they overcame the initial awkwardness or shame of making that interest public.

Luckily, the students were true collaborators, and the program evolved into something much greater than the sum of its parts. The students struggled with difficult cultural problems but continually found themselves "going home"; that is, they became cultural translators, explaining to themselves and their teachers the trials and tribulations of being an American teenager as well as a Hopi, Navajo, or mixed breed. Consistently, their writing involved collective voices of family and tribe, and it was concerned with understanding their histories. As Momaday explains,

> When the imagination is superimposed upon the historical event, it becomes story. The whole piece becomes more deeply invested with meaning. No defeat, no humiliation, no suffering was beyond the power to endure, for none of it was meaningless.
>
> ("Man" 169)

Exploring Bias in Essay Tests

Liz Hamp-Lyons

Educators regularly raise the concern that minority students are disadvantaged in testing situations. This kind of disadvantage is known as test bias. In its psychometric sense, test bias refers to situations in which groups identifiable by race, class, gender, language background, or any other variable besides the ability being tested receive systematically lower scores on a test. When systematic test bias is observed, it becomes necessary to discover whether the test instrument is itself biased or whether factors in the educational or broader social contexts of specific groups might explain their disappointing performance. Roscoe Brown, Jr., demonstrates a consciousness of this distinction:

> [We must] persist in our evaluations of the test instruments, insist on the coupling of tests with other criteria whenever appropriate, and accelerate the recent trends toward the creative use of testing as a facilitator and not as a roadblock. Moreover we should strive to improve the quality of education experienced by blacks and other minorities so they will have a better chance to perform well on tests. (98)

While Brown is concerned about specific issues such as bias in test content, the predictive accuracy of test scores for minority students, and the uses of test results, he is also concerned about general social equity. He points out that variables in the testing context itself—speededness, the test taker's experience of tests and their outcomes, the test taker's level of anxiety—can affect students from minority groups more than others. This effect becomes test bias when the test does not measure the same aspects of achievement for different groups.

While the bias in standardized, multiple-choice tests (because of culture-specific or culturally offensive content or test takers' unfamiliarity with testing practices) is well recognized, concerns about bias in

51

direct essay testing have surfaced only more recently. The *Code of Fair Testing Practices in Education*, developed by the American Educational Research Association, the American Psychological Association, and the National Council on Measurement in Education, tells us that test developers should "indicate the nature of the evidence obtained concerning the appropriateness of each test for groups of different racial, ethnic, or linguistic background tested" (2). Yet because of citizens' legal rights not to declare their ethnicity or have it revealed, many writing assessment programs find it difficult to obtain and use background data on race and ethnicity and thus to investigate test bias. In fact, few studies examine performance on writing tests by ethnic origin. In one such study, Edward M. White and Leon Thomas look at the scores of over ten thousand California State University students on the TSWE (Test of Standard Written English, a multiple-choice grammar test that is part of the College Board's Scholastic Aptitude Test) and on the EPT (English Placement Test, administered by the Educational Testing Service for California State University), which includes an essay test. White and Thomas used self-reported ethnicity information and compared students' TSWE scores with their EPT essay-component scores; on the basis of the comparison, they concluded that the TSWE is biased against African American, Mexican American, and Asian American students. They argue for expanded essay testing of minority students and reduction of multiple-choice testing. But while educators often assume that collecting writing samples is a fairer means of testing students in racial, cultural, and linguistic minorities, a study by Miriam Chaplin shows that merely changing from standardized to essay testing does not eliminate test bias against minority students.

Both Chaplin and Brown suggest that minority students are often inexperienced with the formal, conventional genres that they are expected to use on writing tests. This concern applies not only to African American students but also to Hispanic students and immigrant groups from non-English speaking backgrounds, among whom the most common are Chinese, Koreans, and Vietnamese. We might also expect that visiting international students, who are penalized in the United States academy by having to write outside their dominant languages, would be even more severely handicapped on tests, especially essay tests, that demand the use of written language skills under stressful circumstances. While some college literacy events may be unfamiliar or inimical to students outside the mainstream, essay tests are especially threatening. Not only are they conducted under depersonalized conditions and time pressure, they are also high-stakes assessments; grades, permission to enter a major or special program, and the obligation to take (and pay for) remedial courses all hang on the outcome. Given the serious consequences of essay tests and given that these tests have been claimed with little empirical evidence to be far less biased against culturally or linguistically diverse student groups, it is important that we explore further the possibility of bias in them.

To understand these issues better I talked with a number of student writers, focusing only on the aspects of topic and task embodied in the set of essay-test instructions that writing-assessment specialists call the prompt. Below I report on my conversations with four of these writers (two bilingual, one ESL, and one standard English as a second dialect) about how they interpreted and responded to an essay-test task. I asked them to talk to me either while they read and interpreted a prompt from a university essay test and planned strategies for responding to it, or while they reread a prompt they had already written on and recalled how they had approached and responded to it in a timed essay. I did not intend to investigate all aspects of this test instrument, which, as I describe elsewhere, is a much larger task (Hamp-Lyons, "Second Language Writing"); I sought only to understand better how culturally and linguistically diverse students make sense of topic and task in this narrow academic context.

I knew none of the students personally; I dealt with them as an administrator when they came to me to request late placement or a change of placement. Although I audiotaped each student's think-aloud or recall of his or her interpretation of the prompt and plan for response, the recordings were not experimental protocols. Thus I interacted with the students and sometimes asked them questions to elicit increasingly detailed responses. While I tried to maintain an observer's stance, for example, by not making suggestions, I was concerned to establish a role as friendly advocate; I felt that to add a formal protocol context to the already intimidating situation of an essay test or a placement appeal would be educationally unacceptable.

What Students "Know" about Essay Tests

Arvind (all students' names are pseudonyms) is a bilingual (actually trilingual) international student who came from India as a junior. He had, he said, plenty of experience taking tests in writing (ellipses in the transcript extracts indicate a pause):

> The way I did the test was the same way I would have written it in India . . . They like to have a little bit of history, you know . . . and then try and get something in the present . . . They like much

more points than just a few points . . . building up . . . they like a much wider area to be covered . . . and that's what I tried . . . I think that what you're looking for here is very different from what they are looking for there . . . I think now I have a slight idea of what you people want, and I daresay I might be able to write it according to the way it should be here.

As Arvind read the brief background paragraph that had been his prompt (see app. 1), he responded that "it's a little too specific" and "I don't know too much about that." He spoke mostly about the gulf he felt between his experience at Delhi University and what he had seen so far at his new university. When I eventually directed his attention to the last paragraph, which states the essay readers' expectations, his response was "I really don't pay too much attention to that . . . just try to do your best." In India once a paper is given to a professor, Arvind said, whatever the course or the context, "you never ever see it in your life again . . . You can't do a thing about it."

Listening to Arvind talk about the prompt, learning his lack of analysis of the prompt's meaning, I was tempted to think he lacked the language skills to pick up on its messages. But Arvind was educated wholly in English, and as he spoke it was clear that, orally at least, he is a native speaker, although of a different dialect. The evidence suggests he did not lack language skill. Did Arvind's experience leave him unprepared to respond to this prompt, which after all was developed for mostly native speakers of United States English? As I probed for Arvind's views on education, I had to rule out this possibility. Let us hear him further:

I would say that a wide education would be a good thing to do . . . one of the reasons why I have come here is because here is not just book learning as it is in India. In India you just go to college and if you have a few courses . . . if you do economics you just do economics and nothing else . . . but out here you get a much wider variety . . . I especially agree with what's written with this thing because I was in a school till my tenth grade where everything was just book knowledge, you know, you went home and studied everything by heart . . . and then I was shifted to a boarding school, and there you had to take part in all sorts of activities . . . and I did feel that it helped me out in life . . . I'll write basically of my experience there . . . I can't really write very much on the topic I was given, but basically . . . I'll just write about my experiences . . .

From what Arvind said as the result of direct prompting, it became clear that he did have specific ideas and responses to bring to bear; more important, he had direct comparative experience, evidence of the kind that studies show is much valued by essay readers and that few entering students have. In content, we may say, Arvind should actually have been at an advantage. But, despite being educated in English, Arvind did not have the American college student's view of the prompt as an important artifact. He saw it vaguely and imprecisely and assigned little value to its elements. College-level ESL courses tend to include lessons in study-skills in which students are generally taught how to analyze a prompt and get at the heart of what readers are looking for—to "psych out the test," as American students often say. Arvind did not take such a course because of his high level of oral English and grammatical control; perhaps he missed an opportunity to pick up a kind of pragmatic knowledge not necessarily related to oral or written grammatical proficiency.

In fact, Arvind did not write about his personal experience at all. Rather, he wrote a long and abstract theoretical discussion that does not engage the powerful realities that he is ideally equipped to deal with, inhabiting as he has two cultures in his home country and, now, two countries. Arvind relied on his knowledge of expectations in his own culture, using the formula that is successful there. The Indian linguist Yamuna Kachru has described the Indic discourse tradition as cyclic and nonsequential, as valuing poetics and drama over coherence and cohesion; within this context, Arvind's approach would have been appropriate. But in the United States context we might say that Arvind's case is one of pragmatic failure, that is, failure to respond according to the practical expectations and needs of the situation.

Joe is an African American athlete from Detroit who by his own account loves to write. When Joe and I discussed how he would go about writing the in-class test essay, in his case a practice essay written early in the course (see app. 2), he began:

> Well . . . I never had much to do with computers. They must be a good thing . . . I wish I knew about them . . . it's why I like this class, I never had a chance to learn to use them before . . . I sent in a[n e-mail] message, I hope he got it. If you don't know computers you can't get much of a job. But it's not that hard to learn once you get the chance . . .

Joe continued in this way for several minutes, expressing general approval of the computer revolution but anxiety about his ability to participate in it. I asked him about access to computers at his high school; he answered that he was not sure if there were any but that he never got near one. When I pressed him for specifics on how computers and the need for computer knowledge had affected his own life, he talked about the automated teller machine. I realized that Joe had little notion of computers' functions in daily life. I asked him about the prompt's reference to the dangers of decreased human contact and devaluation of individual differences. He responded, "Yeah, but . . . you know . . . it's different . . . your friends, your family, that's nothing to do with computers . . ." There was a lengthy pause. Joe could not form a connection. I moved on, asking him how he thought he might start the essay. He said, "Well, I'll try to describe the benefits and problems, like it says . . . I'll give my opinion . . . and . . . I'll give some other ones . . ." Another lengthy pause. Joe understood that in an argumentative essay (which he had been told was the genre here) he was expected to do a "pros and cons kind of thing," and he was willing to apply the formula. But I could see that he had little to say about the prompt, that it did not touch his world much at all.

The essay Joe wrote after our conversation shows some follow-through on his plan to talk about benefits and problems, but mostly it shows his unfamiliarity with the topic. Once he had written about the twenty-four-hour money machine, its convenience, and the problems that result when the cards are damaged, he ran out of text, ideas, and experience. Joe's case, then, demonstrates another kind of pragmatic failure: Arvind had experience he did not use; Joe had no experience to use. Given this problem and Joe's uncertain command of organizational patterns of discourse and sentence grammar, readers saw little to commend in his essay.

Kon is a Korean American who moved to the United States as a preschool child with his family. He considers himself equally proficient in English and Korean. Kon's spoken English is fluent and idiomatic but contains many systematic errors. Kon said he felt that he got off to a wrong start in his essay, that it was "off the topic" but that he didn't think he could do anything about it, even though he had finished well before his time was up.

When Kon talked with me about his prompt (see app. 3), he began by describing his strategies:

> If I were going to write about this topic—which I am going to [laughs, realizing that he already has written about it]—I will think about it for quite a while before deciding on which side I

should take . . . I'll write the pro and con and list them and the one with . . . the most issues will be the one I'll write about.

Kon said he normally uses mind mapping as his prewriting strategy, but this time anxiety got the better of him, so he did not. He described his mind maps as an outline, and his references to pro and con sides suggest a training that emphasized the duality of issues facing societies today. We might say that Kon has learned to think in good-guy-bad-guy terms. Asked whether he would say anything about the other side of the issue on this prompt, Kon said, "I might, but I doubt it, because . . . that would make me look a little bit indecisive and . . . I might . . . er . . . just a couple of lines . . . but not much." Asked how he might arrange his answer, Kon said:

> I would first talk about how the animals came into the use of this experiment. . . . I would say things like . . . "human beings have learned to use animals blah blah blah" and then . . . in my . . . at the end of my introductory paragraph . . . I would take my position and say like . . . whether it is good or bad. And from then on I would just like . . . write the topic sentence . . . um . . . from the strongest to worst . . . um, and then just write the body and then the conclusion.

The prompt cues the writer to look at the issue from more than one point of view (long-term and short-term, for a start). But when I asked Kon if he planned to do so, he responded that, no, he would choose a side and stick to it. His greater concern was to "come up with an original idea, an idea that the reader would never think about" in order to show his perceptiveness. But he also said that the approach sometimes caused him to waste time in fruitless searching.

Kon's essay is unimpressive—desperately short, vague, and unfocused. Containing neither an original idea nor the structure Kon had described, it reads as though he had nothing to say. For almost the entire session Kon talked about how he would write the essay, not what its content would be or how its pieces would form a whole picture. Kon's essay structure, it seems, is an empty shell, containing no substance. Readers gave his essay almost the lowest possible score on a scale whose extreme ends are rarely used, and Kon knew that. Yet he continued to believe that he had strategies for approaching the task and for putting together a satisfactory response. He described himself as "a pretty good writer." Kon completed his K–12 education in American schools where he learned a specific and, in that context, adequate way of coping with writing tasks. He planned to keep using his approach even though it had already let him down in the more rarefied atmosphere of college. This is another kind of pragmatic failure: although Kon knew his essay was unsuccessful, he had no plan to change his approach.

Kris came from Norway specifically to get a degree in the United States, and was exempted from an ESL writing course by his performance on an ESL writing test. At our interview I gave him his very first essay prompt in the United States, for a late placement (see app. 4), and asked him to plan aloud how he would write it. Faced with a prompt about teenage employment, Kris's first thoughts were that he would

> be defending a point . . . you know . . . I think you shouldn't work while you're in school . . . I didn't work myself . . . well, I did sometimes, but I always found that those periods were the periods where I found that I had the worst results . . . when you do a job, unless it's extremely interesting, it just draws all the energy from you, wears you out.

Kris's initial response, then, was to take a particular point of view and to bring in his own experience immediately. But having said that, Kris went back to the prompt and reread it. He spoke in broken phrases— "Yes, you could do that . . . Well, but what about summer jobs?"—and then in longer segments, showing his awareness of my presence:

> Most people live at home anyway, and you don't get all that much feel for what money's worth, not having to pay the rent, or the utilities bill, or . . . whatever . . . it takes a long time before you experience all that . . . with the bills and everything . . . so . . . if you think you can be without it, I'd say, "Don't do it in high school."

After this long oral response to something in the prompt that had acted as a trigger, Kris fell silent, rereading the prompt to himself. He started in:

> Oh well, that's [he did not explain what "that" was] one thing . . .
> yeh, I'd tend to go in that direction, but . . . yeh, you know . . .
> I see, I see, some of the points they have too . . . of course it is

valuable to be responsible for your own money and . . . er . . . and also I think it's bit different in the States 'cos . . . you tend to want to . . . also save money for college . . . in Norway you don't have to do that, 'cos you get everything financed.

Kris spoke for over ten minutes, drawing on the prompt again and again, each time seeing a new point he or his "opponent" could make. At last he began to think about how to start writing. "I think I should make a little outline," he said, and he began to do so, commenting, "I'll try to write the general stuff, and as I go along I'll hope to find the details. If I have to find all my points before I start, I'm not going to be done." His outline in fact follows his scheme, with three or four main points on each side but no specifics. Asked if there is anything he would keep in mind while writing, he said:

Ah, yeh, that I'm consistent. If I'm not careful I might start off meaning one thing and end up meaning something else . . . if I do find more arguments later for the other point of view, at least I will round it up saying something really contradictory to what I started out saying [laughs] . . . don't want that.

Kris commented that the paragraph describing the readers and their expectations was both helpful and a problem. It's surprising, he said, to find such a paragraph, but he saw it as threatening. When you read it carefully, he said, it's really just a paragraph about how to write essays, nothing unusual, but it seems at first as though "they" want something special. He picked up on the request to develop ideas with evidence or examples, saying that normally he might have just put down his ideas as general statements but not supported them much ("paragraph—statement; new paragraph—statement"). Now that he had seen this, he would take care to supply evidence, to think about what sort of statements he could support.

Kris began to think, really think about the prompt from the beginning and spent a good deal of time doing so. He examined it from several points of view, seeming to hold a dialogue or an argument with himself as he read, reread, and found new points. In talking about structure, Kris was concerned with meaning ("[don't want to] start off meaning one thing and end meaning something else"). Kris read and commented on the paragraph that referred to the readers and the criteria. Having noticed it, he spoke of how he would adjust his strategy accordingly. First, he took what he had been told as the truth; second, he apparently accepted the information and expectations as reasonable. Kris seemed to have strategies to take new expectations into account. This kind of response is only possible, I suggest, for a writer already familiar with the general conventions that underlie the new expectations. Kris was not accustomed to this overt statement about the readers of the text, but he was clearly familiar with the concept that writing is for a reader and that the reader is an intelligent, responsive shaper and sharer of ideas. In this respect he was far removed from Arvind, who saw "them," the judges, as a barrier to cross. Kris spent his energies engaging the ideas, not trying to second-guess the ideas the readers might want him to have or the structure the readers might want him to use. Kris's response fits with the definition of excellence implicit in the current view of the writing process and the goals of writing.

Discussion

Three of the four students seemed to rely on formulaic approaches, and two of those seemed to be hampered by lack of experience or knowledge to inform their writing. Only Arvind seemed to have conflicting cultural expectations about what types of ideas, material, arguments, and text structures might be acceptable in the United States academic context. The other international student, Kris, appeared to share many of American students' expectations about what is legitimate in formal college writing. Both Arvind and Kris are middle-class in their own countries, but Kris comes from a European, hence "Western," academic tradition, while Arvind, despite the British influence on the Indian upper and middle classes, comes from an Eastern tradition that values text making of quite different kinds. Robert Kaplan and others have long argued for the notion of contrastive rhetoric, and there seems to be an element of rhetorical conflict here ("Contrastive Rhetoric"); Arvind edited his experience out before it ever reached the page. He seemed unaware, or unable to believe, that his readers would value the kind of experience he has to offer, so he suppressed it.

On the basis of these four interviews, I cannot draw conclusions about whether essay tests disadvantage culturally and linguistically diverse college students. Not only is this sample far too small, I have not provided comparative interviews with so-called mainstream students. Mike Rose's *Lives on the Boundary* and work by others, such as Joy Ritchie ("Beginning Writers") and Tom Fox ("Basic Writing"), suggest that problems like Arvind's, Joe's, and Kon's are not unique to linguistically and culturally diverse students. But I did expect to find indications that ESL writers would be more disadvantaged than bilingual writers, who would in turn be more disadvantaged than African American writers. But on the contrary Kris is the only one of my four students who attained a standard definition of excellence in both written product and writing process.

I must pause here to reflect on this "standard definition of excellence." As Marcia Farr has shown, an individual's "ways of speaking" (32), by which she means verbal performances, whether oral or written, may be seen as inappropriate for what she calls "essayist literacy," using John Goodlad's term. David Bartholomae has argued that college students are often expected to "invent the university" for themselves, and the gatekeeping essay test is clearly a genre in which essayist literacy is expected ("Inventing" [1985]). Students are expected to perform to the norms of this kind of literacy, even when they have not yet learned them well enough to integrate the new genres into their existing literate practices. While of the four students I interviewed Joe may have been the closest to the mainstream of society, he turned out to be the farthest from the mainstream of the academy. In his thinking aloud, Joe could talk only of lack of knowledge, lack of opportunity, and lack of experience. No one had yet taught him that he could turn the story of his lack into a compelling story—an argument—about technology and social injustice: He could not see this experience of life outside the computer revolution as evidence powerfully relevant to the prompt. Arvind, with his very different educational and cultural experiences, was in other ways equally distant from the conventional essayist literacy of the Western academy. As he talked to me, Arvind revealed the personal experience at the center of his thinking, contrasting and linking two kinds of experience in his culture to his experience across two cultures, building a range and depth of personal evidence. But he was culturally constrained from sharing his experience with his readers. Arvind and Joe each had an important story to tell, but for different reasons neither of them told it.

Kon learned (or thought he learned) his essay-test strategies in school; at least, he left school equating the shape of a legitimate genre with its substance. While Farr argues for explicit instruction in the kinds of literacy that gatekeepers (in this case, essay-test readers) value, Kon's interview reminds us that explicit instruction can be superficial. Our understanding of the contrasting verbal styles of writers from other cultures must go deeper than our ability to observe their deviation from the norms of the placement-essay genre or the five-paragraph theme. Perhaps Kon learned the lessons of school too well, accepting the easy surface strategies, unaware that underlying them must be ideas, raw material to be strategically shaped. In the interview, Kon never seemed to consider what he felt, what he knew, or what he had experienced; he went straight to the level of strategy and stayed there. His essay cannot show strategic skill because he had no evidence, personal or otherwise, to bring to it; strategies, after all, work only on material, not in place of it. Kon's empty shell is, perhaps, the husk of superficial instruction.

In contrast, Kris was a product of a Western European culture that shares many values with the United States and other countries of the so-called First World. Although English is his second language, Kris was in every way at home in the elite academic culture. He encountered some unfamiliar expectations in the United States, but he had the confidence in his skills and the flexibility to attend to and adjust to those unfamiliarities. As Kris considered the prompt, his thoughts ranged from his personal experience to wider issues and back. He re-created his feelings and reactions to his experiences over and over, looking at his own responses from different viewpoints. He argued with himself, and in that process he set up a model for structuring an argument. He used the sophisticated academic writing strategy of building evidence from story, a strategy that many so-called mainstream American undergraduate and even graduate students have not acquired. He incorporated his story in his essay, interpreting it in a wider context for readers.

Is it merely coincidence that Kris, the European, possesses skills and strategies that the essay readers, and most well-read composition instructors these days, value and reward? What would I have discovered if the sole ESL writer I interviewed had Kris's facility with language but was from, for instance, Saudi Arabia, whose cultural values and schooling practices differ significantly from those of Europe and the United States? Of course, I do not know. But is Kris most like us, the majority of composition teachers—middle-class and of European ancestry—and thus most familiar to us, and are we thus most familiar to him? Is he most like us in his control of essayist literacy? Do we reward him for excellence or for sameness? Have teachers' attempts to initiate Kon into the demands of the academy taken something from him and made him appear weaker, or is he an inherently poor writer made marginally better by the addition of some rudimentary strategies? Would Arvind and Joe be better helped by some work with text structure and genre or by the liberation of the stories within them?

Four interviews cannot answer our concerns about bias in essay tests. But four interviews were enough to convince me that we must seriously consider that essay tests may contain as much test bias as standardized tests. Furthermore, rater judgments, which I do not explore here, are likely to embody biases of several kinds (Hamp-Lyons, "Raters Respond"). While essay tests may reduce some kinds of bias found in standardized tests, it is simplistic to think that bias exists only within the design and conduct of test instruments and not also within the larger context the student inhabits. When we administer one-item tests such as essay tests, we make assumptions about the shared experiences of young people living in the United States, yet we hardly need research studies to tell us that some of those assumptions are unjustified. We make assumptions about what students know about genre conventions, for example, and we find Arvind, who believes that the conventions of academic writing exclude personal experience and narrative. We find Joe, who has not been taught that he may challenge the assumptions in the tasks set by white middle-class university teachers, and we find Kon, who thinks that genre is a shell and who is not concerned with what is inside that shell. We make assumptions about topics, and we find Joe, who has no experience with computers; Kon, who sees content only as an "original" idea; and Kris, who already knows that ideas and knowledge can be generated from inside the self. Bias can only be countered when we begin to pay serious attention to essay tests, and it is past time for us to do so. The least well understood elements of a writing test are the students themselves and their reactions to the test; this essay attempts to begin a discourse of discovery of linguistically and culturally diverse students' encounters with essay tests.

Appendix 1: Arvind's Prompt

Read the following paragraph, then write an essay as you are asked in the paragraph in boldface:

James Duderstadt, the President of the University of Michigan, believes that "We must not view undergraduate education at Michigan as simply aimed at extracting knowledge from our vast information characterizing our society. Instead . . . our students must learn how to extract wisdom from knowledge and through that wisdom learn the art of life itself." While many people share his point of view, trends such as the dramatic increase in undergraduates choosing business majors emphasize the view of college education as the development of skills which can be used for work or career. In the modern world, finding a balance between conflicting goals and needs is difficult.

Write an essay explaining your view of the purpose of a college education. Make your reasons for holding that view clear, but also consider the arguments of other people who hold different views.

Remember that your essay will be read by college writing instructors. These readers expect to find that you have thought seriously about the complexities of the subject. They look for development of ideas and supporting evidence or examples. They also expect you to have organized and presented your essay clearly.

Appendix 2: Joe's Prompt

Read the following paragraph, then write an essay as you are asked in the paragraph in boldface:

The computer revolution has had a tremendous impact on the lives of people throughout the world, but expecially on those in technologically advanced countries such as the USA. We all recognize that computers are changing the ways in which we acquire and shape knowledge. Those who welcome the computer revolution point to how computers increase access to information needed by professionals, businesses and government agencies, and to how they are capable of performing a variety of tasks with great efficiency and accuracy. Others, however, are concerned that because computers decrease direct contact between people, the world will become a less humane place, where individual differences are less likely to be understood and valued.

Write an essay in which you explore the benefits and problems of the computer revolution. Establish and explain your own perspective and your reasons for holding that perspective. As you develop your essay, keep in mind that others may hold a different perspective, and consider how society will in future be able to take account of differing views of computers.

Remember that your essay will be read and judged by college writing instructors who expect to find that you have thought critically about the complexities of the subject, have developed your ideas and supported them with evidence or examples, and have organized and presented your essay clearly.

Appendix 3: Kon's Prompt

Read the following paragraph, then write an essay as you are asked in the paragraph in boldface:

Life-saving advances in medicine, for example, cancer, heart disease, and muscular dystrophy have been achieved through the use of live animals in medical research experimentation. There have, however, been concerns about the pain and suffering experienced by animals at experimental labs and animal abuse in the homes where animals are kept. Researchers appointed to investigate this issue have recommended that alternatives to the use of animals in research and testing be found whenever possible, but they have also stated that the likelihood of the complete replacement of animals in medical research is zero for the foreseeable future.

Write an essay in which you address the issues involved in the use of animals in medical research. Establish and explain your own point of view, and take into consideration the reasons why others might not agree with your perspective.

Remember that your essay will be read and judged by college writing instructors. These readers expect to find that, as far as possible in the time available to you, you have thought seriously about the complexities of the subject. They look for development of ideas and supporting evidence or examples. They also expect you to have organized and presented your essay clearly.

Appendix 4: Kris's Prompt

Read the following paragraph, then write an essay as you are asked in the paragraph in boldface:

In the USA, many people believe that an after-school job is a good experience for teenagers: However, many other countries do not share that view. In fact, even US researchers have found that while young people who work during high school gain a better understanding of money and feel more responsible and self-reliant, they are also likely to spend less time with their families and less time on their schoolwork, and are more likely to become involved in drug use.

Write an essay in which you address the issues involved in the question of whether young people should be encouraged to work while attending high school. Establish and explain your own point of view, and take into consideration the reasons others might not agree with your perspective.

Remember that your essay will be read and judged by college writing instructors. These readers expect to find that, as far as possible in the time available to you, you have thought seriously about the complexities of the subject. They look for development of ideas and supporting evidence or examples. They also expect you to have organized and presented your essay clearly.

"Real Niggaz's Don't Die": African American Students Speaking Themselves into Their Writing

Kermit E. Campbell

> Tryin' to make a Nigga extinct
> because they fear me
> but never want to hear me.
> —NWA, *Niggaz4life*

> *The language of blackness encodes and names its sense of independence through a rhetorical process that we might think of as the Signifyin(g) black difference.*
> —Henry Louis Gates, Jr., *The Signifying Monkey*

This essay bears the title of a paper I received from Ronnie (all students' names are fictitious), a college basic writer. I was intrigued by his spelling of the word "Niggaz's" and what he meant by the title. As I've discovered since then, the phrase derives verbatim (excepting the 's) from the title of a song by the now-defunct rap group NWA (Niggaz With Attitude). Leaving aside the issue of plagiarism, I'm struck by Ronnie's appropriation of this perplexing title. What are real niggaz? And why don't they die? Of course, in its own way, the content of the paper bears out the meaning conveyed rather obliquely by the title.

I read the title and much of the paper as an example of a form of vernacular discourse called signification, or what Henry Louis Gates has conveniently labeled "Signifyin(g)" to suggest the distinctively black usage of the term. Though there's no singularly precise definition, according to Geneva Smitherman, the term generally refers to "the verbal art of insult in which a speaker humorously puts down, talks about, needles—that is, signifies on—the listener" (*Talkin* 118). Since the time of slavery signifying has existed in many forms, both direct and indirect, playful and serious (see H. Gates, *Signifying*). A few of these appear below:

> "You so ugly look like you been hit by a ugly stick."
>
> "Yo natural [hairdo] look like this broad on the wall." (pointing to a picture of Medusa)
>
> Reverend Jesse Jackson, merging sacred and secular siggin in a Breadbasket Saturday morning sermon: "Pimp, punk, prostitute, preacher, Ph.D.—all the P's—you still in slavery!"
>
> (Smitherman, *Talkin* 120)

Ronnie's title signifies in two ways. First, to borrow Gates's interpretation, *niggaz* is a repetition of the standard English pejorative label *niggers*, applied to those who, particularly in the minds of racists, are the worst sort of black people. Yet it is a repetition with a (black) difference (see Gates, *Signifying* 45–46); the standard English suffix *-ers* is supplanted by the black vernacular *-az* to affirm absolutely and positively hard-core blackness with the corresponding denial of anyone or anything that poses a threat to blackness. In traditional rhetoric, this kind of sound and letter change is a form of *agnominatio*—"two words of different meaning but similar sound brought together" (Lanham 3).

Interestingly, this affirmation of blackness (of selfhood) is reminiscent of the inverted, signifying way in which militant African American prose writers of the 1960s used *nigger* in the titles of their works. Dick Gregory's *Nigger: An Autobiography*, H. Rap Brown's autobiography *Die Nigger Die!*, and Cecil Brown's *The Life and Loves of Mr. Jiveass Nigger* are but a few examples. H. Rap Brown expresses the complex and varied uses of the term most powerfully in the introduction to his autobiography. The passage below, I believe, expresses what NWA and Ronnie mean by *real niggaz*.

> To be Black in this country is to be a nigger. To be a nigger is to resist both white and negro death. It is to be free in spirit, if not body. It is the spirit of resistance which has prepared Blacks for the ultimate struggle. This word, "nigger," which is taboo in negro and white america, becomes meaningful in the Black community. Among Blacks it is not uncommon to hear the words, "my nigger," (addressed to a brother as an expression of kinship and brotherhood and respect for having resisted), or "He's a bad nigger!," meaning, He'll stand up for himself. He won't let you down. He'll go down with you. When Blacks call negroes

"niggers," however, it takes on the negativeness of white and negro usage.

 Negroes and whites have wished death to all Blacks, to all niggers. Their sentiment is "Die Nigger Die!"—either by becoming a
negro or by institutionalized or active genocide. Blacks know,
however, that no matter how much or how hard negroes and
whites may try, ultimately it will be the negro and his allies who
will "D[i]e, die, die!"   (ii – iii)

A second way in which Ronnie's title signifies is that it reverses or re-
buts the assumption that oppression categorically yields death or de-
feat, for the "real niggaz" are those who "don't die." Rather, according
to NWA, they "multiply."

Vernacular Voice, the Self, and Writing

In this essay, I explore how a group of African American college students speak themselves into their writing, which I mean to suggest
that through their use of vernacular forms of discourse like signifying,
African American student writers present their most authoritative
voices, their most affirmed sense of self in written academic work.
Helping nonmainstream students position these voices in their academic prose, I argue, may be the most important task for writing
teachers, for it legitimates and affirms the students' social and cultural
identities, which, though by no means monolithic, are nonetheless
questioned, if not categorically denied. Nonmainstream students need
this legitimation and affirmation if they are to acquire and use academic literacy.

 Far from making the writer's voice the be-all and end-all of writing
instruction, however, I envision, as Houston Baker does in *Blues, Ideology, and Afro-American Literature*, "language (the code) 'speaking' the
subject," that is, at least as I read it, language, the vernacular, constructing (and affirming) the cultural identity of the writer (1). Cecil
Brown, in fact, sees black speech as "reality construction at its best"
(xxxiii). To put it another way, the various African American vernacular English forms that appear occasionally in the autobiographical
writings of African American college students and of published writers effect a kind of stance or posturing of black cultural identity in
the face of white or mainstream cultural-linguistic dominance. Referring to the various African American vernacular expressive forms,
Baker similarly comments, "Blues, work songs and hollers, and such

verbal forms as folktales, boasts, toasts, and dozens are functions of the black masses' relationship of 'identity' vis-à-vis mainstream culture" (68).

To demonstrate how the same holds true at times for students' language, I refer to several written examples from African American male college students enrolled in an at-risk program at a large, predominantly white university in the Midwest. I focus on African American male students in particular to demonstrate the linguistic versatility of this often feared and yet woefully misunderstood group.

I begin with examples from two students—Ronnie and Gerald—who wrote explicitly about street language and culture. About a third of the way into his paper, Ronnie expresses his heartfelt sentiment toward his cronies, "the real niggaz." What's impressive about this expression is not the sentiment alone but its relation to Ronnie's opposite feelings about society.

> Rob's crib was known as the honey comb hideout. His moms and all the rest of the niggaz would make [me] feel as though that I was home. Ai-ski, my ace would usually be the first to say what's up "the horse is in the howz." . . . I will never forget the feeling just walking through the hideout and seeing the rest of the niggaz. I knew that I could say Fuck you! to society and its shitty rules because I was in a society of my own a very special one and everyone in this room loved me.

The last sentence of this passage expresses a categorical rejection, if not displacement, of mainstream culture ("society") and its mandates ("its shitty rules"). Without interview data, one can only speculate about the cause of the rejection. But I don't think it would be far-fetched to say that racism is a factor. In any case, what's truly interesting about the rejection is Ronnie's posturing of a black group identity—one constructed through vernacular naming practices (e.g., "crib," "honey comb hideout," and "horse")—vis-à-vis mainstream language and culture.

Such rhetorical posturing even manifests itself in attitudes toward dress:

> It was funny because I see people going to parties dressed up but we use to purposely look down (dress careless) everyone had on there Carhart pants and jacket and black hoodee topped [off] with black forums (adidas). I mean from appearance you would

think we were straight criminals. I think our dress t[y]p[i]fied who we really were we wanted to be the outcast because we were the outcast.

Obviously, one's appearance as a criminal makes one a virtual "outcast," but perhaps, Ronnie's tautology suggests, no more so than young black men are by definition. Ronnie's final paragraph sums up nicely the positive effect that "the real niggaz" had on him.

Being a part of the real niggaz made me realize that there was more to life than just women, money, and power. There was friendship, trust, unity and a sense of self awareness the real niggaz were not together because they just loved each other from the beginning we were together because society had put us all in the same situation where [there was] the need to have someone in your corner because you had to fight daily to stay afloat. So there lay six brothers united by something thicker than blood but by an understanding of each others lives and a self awareness of who they were. So Like to give sho[u]ts out to my family "The Real Niggaz" D-nice, Ant-dog, Ai-ski, XL, and Rob Gee thanx for giving me a sense of belong[ing].

In the light of Ronnie's earlier rejection of mainstream society and affirmation of his own, it comes as somewhat of a surprise that "the real niggaz" formed not out of love but out of an apparently desperate need to survive. Again, one can only speculate about what harm society might have inflicted on these young men, but I believe one thing is certain: society has defined or constructed a black male identity largely through negative images and exclusion.

In the academy, this negative imaging and exclusivity is nowhere more evident than in the stance toward nonstandard language varieties. There has not been widespread acceptance let alone use of non-mainstream language varieties in university writing classes, in spite of concerted efforts to the contrary (e.g., the CCCC 1974 resolution "Students' Right to their Own Language" [Committee]). Marcia Farr and Harvey Daniels have proposed that in teaching writing to non-mainstream writing students we utilize and build on the linguistic resources they bring with them to the classroom (42). But their idea elicits little credibility or favor from the followers of E. D. Hirsch, who propose a model of academic excellence that privileges a narrowly de-fined "literate language" (Hirsch 3). These academics, no doubt, find little praiseworthy about the "nonliterate" language Gerald describes in the passage below:

> Nutrition was the best time of the day; it was when all the heavy lingo broke out. Everyone in the Mob [a close-knit group of football players] always meets at the same table so that we can chill together. Besides, our table was where all the highnas (girls) went. We had a distinct language that not many people could decipher. We used it sorta like the mescans [Mexicans] used Spanish. My boy, Gee-o, stepped to me and said, "Damn, Bone, that chili over there is really on your nuts. What up? Are you going to step to it and get a fever or what?" I just told him that if my chocolate was not sweet to me, my mouth just might end up on fire. He just laughed and said, "Don't get burnt."

Although much of the language Gerald displays here amounts to little more than popular street slang (e.g., "chill," "highnas"), its metaphoric and improvisational qualities would doubtless make useful resources for writing instruction, especially since the metaphors the two interlocutors play on are not improvised arbitrarily but based on concrete objects natural to the setting. Their dialogue contradicts the common charge that basic writers cannot move easily from the concrete to the abstract and vice versa (see Farrell).

Admittedly, the clever repartee Gerald depicts also possesses a phallocentric bias, not unlike the bias of many of today's rap lyrics. While I do not endorse such language, neither do I censor what may, in part, constitute the very identity construction I seek to explore. Besides, such language use is deeply embedded within black street culture and must therefore be judged with respect to the values and worldview of that culture.

Let's consider, for a moment, some of the qualities of Gerald's language use. Gerald's friend Gee-o uses the word "chili" to inform him that some girl has the "hots" for him, or, more accurately, would be hot *to* him since from this chili he could catch a "fever." Picking up on the food-heat metaphor, Gerald hints that he might taste the chili (i.e., at the least, pursue the girl; at the most, well . . .) and his "mouth might just end up on fire." Gee-o, adding another layer to an already dense metaphor, cautions him, "Don't get burnt."

Juxtaposed with the hot-dish metaphor is another metaphor that appears in Gerald's conditional response to Gee-o's question. He says that his mouth might catch fire "if my chocolate is not sweet to me." Gerald's "chocolate" is his girlfriend, who, as such, should be sweet to him. The play on the intrinsic qualities of chocolate and chili—sweetness and sauciness—clearly indicates the richness of our students' language. The sense of belonging, or affirmation engendered by such verbal exchange is evident in Gerald's comments:

> It was nice to just sit at the table and see all the fellas just chill. I knew by seeing them all together that we could not ever be stopped or broken up. We were in full stride and could not be taken out by anybody.

The Signifying Voice in Prose

Signifying affirms African American cultural identity in writing by signaling a voice that in a way resists the very prose of which it is a part (see K. Campbell, *Signifying*). The personal narrative of another basic-writing student, Patrick, provides an example of this function. Patrick was required to write about a time in his adolescence when he had changed. He begins his narrative as follows (I have fictionalized the proper names in this excerpt):

> I grew in the city of East Manville. the percentage of blacks are 98%. there is only one high school called Wash High, which enrolls 3,000–4,000 students. It was a so-called ghetto. There was ways that you could show that you were mature and a man in the eyes of this society One was to join a gang. Even though it was wrong it was a way of having clout and money b[y] ways of threat and robbery.

Although this passage exhibits no particular vernacular discourse forms, it suggests, like the examples from Ronnie's essay, a society (and thus a corresponding social identity) at odds with the mainstream. Gang activity of the kind Patrick describes, the folklorist Roger Abrahams reasons, allows the member to demonstrate his manliness by "striking out against an almost impersonal foe" with little damage to himself, even if he loses. More important, gang membership and activity give inner-city boys "a sense of place and a constant set of friends upon whom they can rely" (34).

One is tempted to extend this textual analysis by applying Baker's economic approach, for the affirmation of self (manhood) partially depends on the ability to acquire through subversive action mainstream entitlements such as money and power. But, such an approach would be beyond the scope of this essay. Having been steered by his parents to choose college over gang membership, Patrick thus sums up the socially accepted view of maturation and manhood:

> Growing up in the inner city you have to make many decisions. Ones I had were to be a true man in the eyes of my culture by not joining a gang and to go to college.

True manhood, Patrick was persuaded, comes not through delinquent activity but through mainstream education. Still, Patrick did not immediately and totally denounce street life, for it furnished the very things that school deprived him of:

> Growing up in the hood and going to private school was interesting, because I had the best of both worlds. I could chill out with the fellas on the street and still have a good enough chance of being something with the name and the education that my parents would make me receive. I never liked school I liked the streets, I liked the freedom of the streets, I liked the brothership of the fellas in the neighborhood and I liked the excitement and danger of the streets that was caused by us and others. Seeing the older gangsta niggaes mess up, I learned what and what not to do. I felt that these lessons were more important than any school books.

In spite of the apparently favorable attitude Patrick developed toward school, I don't want to dismiss cavalierly the function of his discourse to affirm the value of street life over schooling. Patrick rhythmically repeats the phrase "I liked" in a series of sentences; the signifying voice here and in the last two sentences, though mild by street standards, essentially hinges on the idea that the streets are where real education takes place. Thus the student signifies on teachers and the type of learning privileged in school. Or, to put it another way, the student reaffirms the value of mother wit (i.e., wisdom or street knowledge) over book learning (Smitherman, *Talkin* 76).

H. Rap Brown similarly affirms the value of street knowledge over schooling:

> THE STREET is where young bloods get their education. I learned how to talk in the street, not from reading about Dick and Jane going to the zoo and all that simple shit. The teacher would test our vocabulary each week, but we knew the vocabulary we needed. They'd give us arithmetic to exercise our minds. Hell, we exercised our minds by playing the Dozens.   (25)

Another student, Gary, was required to write a short autobiography focusing on significant events in his adolescence. Notice how his use of the word "shit" resembles that in Brown's mockery of "Dick and Jane." (In general, Gary's essay lacks much-needed revision, but his voice comes through clearly enough.)

> for that school year the girls started to bloom, I started to get hair up under my arms "dam" this time when I started to do the girls I got this funny feeling I thought I had to use the bathroom but it was white I didn't know what the hell it was but it felt good coming, when I was about ten that is when I had my first sexual intercourse I did not feel anything at the point in long ago time, but when I reached twelve I could not be stop until I asked my mother what is the white stuff, and she told me without hesitation; see my mother is the type of mother who would tell me things straight up she did not play that birds and the bees shit, and when she told me what the white stuff was she also told me to wear rubbers; at first I thought she was talking about rubber boots when she took me [to] revco she told me that I should always wear these rubbers, because they would keep me from having babies, and from the hospital.

"Shit," I believe, accentuates Gary's signifying voice. Signaled also by vernacular expressions like "straight up" and "did not play that," this voice pits a parent who discusses sexual matters straightforwardly with her children against parents (presumably white mainstream) who relate such matters euphemistically, as suggested by "the birds and the bees." Obviously, for Gary, sex is not a taboo subject but a subject to be celebrated, even boasted about—virility being another demonstration of manhood. Here again we see the writer's construction of self (of cultural identity) resisting construction or definition by a dominant mainstream.

Brown echoes this sentiment:

> Sometimes I wonder why I even bothered to go to school. Practically everything I know I learned on the corner. Today they're talking about teaching sex in school. But that's white folks for you. They got to intellectualize everything. Now how you gon' intellectualize screwing? At the age when little white kids were finding out that there was something down there to play with, we knew where it went and what to do with it after it got there. You weren't a man if you hadn't gotten yourself a little piece by the time you were seven. (30)

Brown's verbal onslaughts, especially the final two statements, verge more on the comic than Gary's do. Both in verbal dexterity and in sexual know-how, Brown ranks black street culture as superior to mainstream culture. This is not, however, to claim the unquestionable veracity of such pronouncements, for the art of signifying depends least of all on absolute truth (e.g., that white kids are, or were in the 1950s, completely naive about sex) and most of all on the imaginative potency of the signifier.

Positioning Vernacular and Academic Voices

These explorations into the written texts of male African American students demonstrate the resourcefulness of black vernacular discourse in writing instruction. The inclusion of vernacular discourse in our writing pedagogies would affirm the social and cultural identities of many African American students. It would empower them to add their own voices to the dominant academic voices and resist the "silencing potential" of these voices (Cook 24).

One way of achieving this goal is to allow students, as Ronnie and Gerald's teacher did, to explore their uses of language in nonacademic contexts. Although teachers shouldn't necessarily expect or require students to write about street talk, they should encourage them to write about whatever language variety or language group is most meaningful to them, since one can never really speak of language without considering a community or group. Along these lines, Michael Linn recommends that African American students be assigned a persuasive theme based on shucking (a way of speaking used to deal with a person who symbolizes white oppressive authority), such as "How to Talk Your Way out of Something" (153).

What I have in mind, though, is having students write, as ethnographers do, narratives describing their participation in particular language groups. These narratives could take the form of a research paper or, more likely, an essay that is part narration and part exposition. Students could, on the one hand, display some of the verbal and social dynamics of the group (as in Gerald's and Ronnie's examples) and yet, on the other hand, closely examine the stylistic qualities of the language used in that group. If it is true, as Grace Holt argued, that "whites 'progress' from literal language to metaphorical language" but "Blacks 'progress' from metaphorical statement to literal statement" (94), then it would be stimulating for black inner-city students to see this difference between their language and the academy's. Exploring through writing their membership in uninstitutionalized discourse communities will allow them to put in perspective their occasionally disconcerting attitudes toward academic language and literacy.

Another approach (albeit more a complement than an alternative to the first) is to expose black students to African American autobiographies that use vernacular forms of discourse. In addition to Cecil Brown's, H. Rap Brown's, and Gregory's works, I would include *The Autobiography of Malcolm X*, Zora Neale Hurston's *Dust Tracks on a Road* and her semiautobiographical folklore study *Mules and Men*, and Claude Brown's *Manchild in the Promised Land*. Students' careful reading of these texts should introduce them to black writing and literacy as a form of resistance to dominant mainstream discursive practices. Gates points out that

> Through autobiography, [black] writers could, at once, shape a public "self" in language, and protest the degradation of their ethnic group by the multiple forms of American racism. The ultimate form of protest, certainly, was to register in print the existence of a "black self" that had transcended the limitations and restrictions that racism had placed on the personal development of the black individual.   (*Bearing* 3)

Teachers could offer at least two types of writing assignments based on critical reading and discussion of these texts. First, students could keep reading journals commenting on the use of language in an autobiographical text, the function of vernacular forms vis-à-vis standard English forms, and the effect of these forms on particular audiences.

Second, students could compose their own autobiographies—that is, records of their experiences with oral and written language. But teachers needn't ask students to model their compositions after those they have read; rather, published autobiographies should serve as examples of the uses of vernacular forms of discourse in published writing. Or, as Thomas Fox puts it:

> These texts function more than as prose models for students to copy; they work to provide historical and political contexts within which African American student writers can position themselves. African American literature, presented in the context of these cultural issues, argues forcefully against the separation of school literacy from the traditions of African American writing, against the notion that learning to write is learning to be white.   ("Repositioning" 300)

Positioning students' vernacular voices in relation to academic voices enables students to participate readily, as David Bartholomae and Anthony Petrosky would have it, "as speakers with place, privilege or authority." Teaching nonmainstream African American students "the conventions of the highly conventional language of the university classroom" isn't sufficient to meet these ends (4). Isolated and alienated as they often are in predominantly white universities, these students need to feel that, apart from their facility with the conventions of academic discourse, they do belong and already are speakers with place, privilege, or authority.

By positioning students' voices—that is, by allowing students personal "spaces" in which to write (Cook)—we can help them reclaim their authority as speakers. We should never be content that African American students (or any students for that matter) merely appropriate existing spaces (the dominant discourse). Rather, we should advise our students as the elegant Mrs. Flowers did the bookish but reticent Maya Angelou, "Words mean more than what is set down on paper. It takes the human voice to infuse them with the shades of deeper meaning" (82).

Negotiating Authority through One-to-One Collaboration in the Multicultural Writing Center

Susan Blalock

Writing center tutoring, even more than one-to-one conferencing between teacher and student, offers tutors and students opportunities to discover cultural connections and to explore differences. Tutors can negotiate; teachers often legislate. Despite twenty years of attempts to shift to an awareness of process and student-directed learning in the classroom, a hierarchy that places the teacher as grader and rule maker over student performance defeats collaborative learning. Lisa Ede and Andrea Lunsford articulate the problem:

> Most day-to-day writing instruction in American colleges and universities still reflects traditional assumptions about the nature of the self (autonomous), the concept of authorship (as ownership of singly held property rights), and the classroom environment (hierarchical, teacher-centered). (112)

Because the tutor is free from the formal classroom and from the responsibilities of designing the assignment and grading it, the tutor and the student can approach the writing project through the student's skills and expectations rather than through the teacher's.

As director of a writing center staffed primarily by English department teaching assistants and peer tutors interested in teaching, I think tutoring provides the best training ground for prospective classroom teachers to experience the student's point of view and participate in student-directed learning. The tutor discovers the student's perspective and learns to negotiate with the student's cultural expectations and assumptions. The students, in becoming aware of their own expectations, are empowered to choose among competing authoritative claims. They take responsibility for their text as a response to a conversation between peers or at least between mutually respectful people whose fields of authority overlap.

Such conversations resemble Kenneth Bruffee's dialogues among peer learners; they provide a "social context" in which learning is a "two way street" and is, therefore, "collaborative" ("Peer Tutoring" 4). But, as John Trimbur reminds us, we must also recognize the institutionally validated position of the tutor, particularly the TA-tutor working with undergraduates. In order "to resocialize [themselves] as collaborative learners within student culture," these tutors also must often "unlearn" the traditional values they have assimilated in becoming successful individual learners ("Peer Tutoring" 27). A multicultural setting intensifies this attention to the individual student's cultural expectations and tolerances.

Unlike the students in many case studies involving tutoring, including Anne DiPardo's brilliant study of "ethnically underrepresented and academically underprepared students" in *A Kind of Passport*, the three students in this study—like most students using the writing center at the University of Alaska, Fairbanks (UAF)—are academically successful (4). They are maintaining B averages or better. Their very success in adapting to the traditional hierarchical academic setting complicates the renegotiation of authority and the tutoring process in fascinating ways. The tutors' experiences with these three students show how, in the collaborative dialogue between the tutor and the student, authority varies not so much by degree as by the manner of its exercise. All these students accord the tutor authority; the problem is usually to give students the power to take chances and make choices among cultural alternatives that require managing conflicting claims to authority.

I have named each student in this paper after a person of the student's choice, as DiPardo did in the case of Fannie's grandmother, or I have chosen the first name of a friend of similar ethnic background. The first student, Wanda, a graduate student from China, wanted editing help. Although she actually needed help with content, her reverence for institutional authority and for grammar and rhetorical models required that tutoring begin at the level of form and build toward content. Sophie, a Yupik student from a Koyukon village in rural Alaska, succeeded after several attempts to reconcile her culture's regard for indirection with the composition teacher's insistence on an assertive thesis statement. Her tutors learned to subordinate their authority as composition teachers (or successful English students in the case of peer tutors) to Sophie's greater need to use juxtaposed narratives rather than linear argument to structure a research paper. She negotiated an organization that combined her talent for narrative as an Alaska Native storyteller with the research component her instructor required. Finally, Dan, a white Vietnam veteran, discovered how to impose stylistic order on emotional chaos. As his tutor, I restrained my teacherly fear of emotionally charged topics, accepted his right to choose which risks to take, and became the sympathetic audience he sought.

No single strategy or prescriptive group of strategies guarantees true collaboration. The tutor-teacher learns as much as possible about the students' cultural values and expectations and devises strategies that give the students the most authority over the project. Although learning about particular cultures is important, only the experience of otherness will make an instructor sufficiently attentive to the way students respond to their assignments and tutors.

New TAs at UAF confront that otherness immediately. The ways of life in Alaska mirror the extremes in climate. Dealing with temperatures that vary from sixty degrees below zero Fahrenheit in winter to ninety degrees in summer requires considerable adaptation. Many students, regardless of ethnic background or gender, live in cabins without running water, but most have electricity to hook up their computers and compact-disc players. Cross-country ski trails and dog-mushing and snowmobile trails provide access from home to school for those who choose not to drive.

The director of composition and I orient new TA-tutors and peer tutors to basic teaching and assessment techniques, tutoring practice, and services for rural students. The writing center operates two on-campus centers: the main center, in the same building as the English department, and The Connection, in the on-campus Rural Student Services complex. Alaska Natives represent about ten percent of the approximately nine thousand students. Together, members of other American minority groups and international students compose about forty percent. The rest are "white" and "other." The main center conducts approximately 2,500 sessions a year, which are augmented by sessions in Rural Student Services. Tutors now also serve students at rural sites by telephone and fax. This combination of a center, a satellite, and distance delivery has succeeded in creating a clientele whose ethnic mix and class standing reflects the makeup of the university as a whole.

But most writing center TA-tutors are white. All TAs in the English department work in the center. Only two of twenty TAs have ESL experience, and none speaks any of the numerous Alaska Native languages. One of our main tasks, then, is to sensitize our predominantly white staff to our students' cultural backgrounds and writing problems.

Learning about and participating in our students' cultures must be an ongoing process, but we always start with a pleasant introduction to Alaska Native cultures. During the first week of training, the counselors and students from Rural Student Services invite the new TA-tutors to their center. During a slide show on villages that are home to Alaska Native students, the students explain a little about their subsistence lifestyles and their schooling in one-room buildings with living quarters for the single teacher or the couple who share in teaching the twelve grades.

In addition, the Rural Student Center usually treats tutors to such delicacies as seal oil or Eskimo ice cream, made from Crisco, sugar, and berries. While this introduction to Alaska Native life appears exotic to the new TAs and alerts them to important differences between Native students' home culture and the academic environment, they also experience commonalities. The Alaska Native students involved in these presentations are succeeding in a university setting. The new tutors' first experience with Native students at this university is one of learning from them rather than teaching them.

"You're the Boss, Right?" Rechanneling Misplaced Authority

As I was handling the front desk one mid-October afternoon a half-hour before closing, Wanda breezed up to the desk, looked at the appointment book, and smiled at me. "I only need a little help with grammar," she said. I replied, "Well, yes, that's fine, but . . ." I explained that all the tutors were busy and that I was answering phones and couldn't tutor her. She looked at me and said, "You're the boss here, right?" I knew that to accede would immediately skew the balance of authority, but a moment's hesitation gave me away. She quickly assured me that she didn't mind telephone interruptions and that whatever we did in thirty minutes would be fine. I acquiesced.

Two motives led me to agree. First, our attempts to attract international students to the writing center were only beginning to succeed after six years of canvassing their professors and labs. We had progressed from one such session or two each semester to approximately forty. Second, I felt that the short session time would not allow Wanda to trap me into word-by-word editing. But we were about to repeat a pattern characteristic of most of our tutoring experiences with international students.

Wanda had first come to the writing center the preceding spring term, when she wanted help with a paper for a technical writing class for international students taught by an experienced ESL instructor from the English department. She soon began coming for help with her graduate anthropology short reports and papers. She came five times the first semester and saw two tutors. She returned the next term for seventeen visits and saw eleven tutors. Wanda's repeated visits indicate she must have felt she was being helped, but she had built no ongoing, trusting relationship with any of her tutors, as students who return to the same tutor or tutors do. When a tutor and a student have established a background of skills and approaches, their conversation can turn quickly to higher-order concerns. But Wanda never requested a specific tutor until she found "the boss."

Once she discovered that I was available to the intrepid seeker, Wanda would sometimes come by my office or catch me in the hall and make an appointment. She wanted me to bring my authority to bear on mechanical correctness. In our first session she interrupted an explanation of a point of grammar by commenting, "You are an expert, good." My institutional status was validated by a demonstration of grammatical expertise. While the use of grammatical terms can sometimes intimidate and distract United States students (Meyer and Smith 162–63), Carolyn Matalene documents her Chinese students' great respect for demonstrated expertise at every level of textual production, from the single character to grammatical and organizational models. She concludes, "The usual Chinese response to a literary text is to repeat it, not to paraphrase, analyze or interpret it" (791).

In his illuminating piece "Walter Mitty in China," H. W. Matalene relates this reverence for the authority of the text to the authority given to the teacher. He suggests that despite Marxist influences mainland Chinese students grow up in a Confucian culture in which they learn to defer to authority and to expect kind, paternal wisdom in return (133). Carolyn Matalene adds, "Certainly, [Chinese students] are not in the habit of questioning their teachers" (792). Despite Wanda's respect for her tutors—perhaps because her tutors felt this respect as a legitimate need—she usually manipulated them into sentence-level correction by appealing to their authority as language experts.

Most of Wanda's tutors succumbed to her desire for correctness. Their comments are remarkably similar. "Wanda had a good sense of organization. . . . She was mostly concerned with usage and technical errors, so we worked on those," wrote one TA-tutor. The next report sheet in the file reads, "We went over Writing Conventions (grammar, punctuation, and spelling), that's all." In only one session in two semesters did someone mention working on "developing the analysis of an article." The tutor adds, "We also addressed spelling/grammar issues as they arose" in the thirty-minute session.

While Wanda's organization appeared clear in the first paper I saw, that clarity resulted from surface technique, not the structure of the content. She brought in a paper she said was the basis of an oral report to be given in a graduate anthropology seminar. It had no working title; instead, it was divided by headings: "Introduction," "Economic Importance of Walrus Hunting," and "Symbolic Importance of Bowhead Whaling." I was concerned because the paper's point eluded me. My questions about the paper's purpose and focus elicited replies related to the assignment rather than to the content: "Oh, I'm just giving a fifteen-minute report" instead of "I'm trying to explain the relations between Eskimo subsistence hunting and community ritual." Since we now had little more than twenty minutes left, I had her read the paper aloud. I hoped for the sort of explanations that often accompany oral readings, but we spent most of the time correcting verb-tense problems. At the end of the session I was still feeling uneasy. I asked her to bring me a copy of the finished version she handed in.

My misgivings were confirmed by the first line of the final copy. The title, "Economic versus Symbolic Hunting among the Bering Strait Eskimos," implied a contrast I did not recall. Instead, the paper described the topography of the villages of Gambell and Savoonga and the accessibility of whales and walrus. It briefly described proper behavior toward each mammal but did not mention a "symbolic hunt." One short paragraph warned against bad behavior by a walrus hunter: "If somebody speaks badly of walrus or brags about killing them, the walrus will be aware of it from a distance and can take revenge by punching holes in boats with their tusks and show other aggressive behavior towards hunters."

Wanda devoted more space and detail in the bowhead whale section to proper behavior by the *umialiq*, the whaling boat captain, his wife, and the village as a whole. The *umialiq*s are the most revered men in the village. They have ultimate authority over the hunt, choose their crews, and oversee the division of meat among the community. But Wanda did not show any opposition between the hunt's communal economic motive of feeding the village and the behavior of the *umialiq*.

The whaling section ended with a quotation from an interview with the captain and Wanda's evaluation of it: "'What's the point of catching a whale if I don't just give away as much as I can?'" says the captain. Wanda commented, "Although it is a statement by a senior Point Hope *umialiq*, it does represent the attitude of Eskimo people toward whaling." Wanda is right; the statement is representative. Patricia Kwatchka and Charlotte Basham designate "qualification," or "circumspection with regard to direct assertion," as "the most pervasive" characteristic of Eskimo discourse (417). The *umialiq's* closing rhetorical question and his use of a qualifier or deintensifier, such as "just," are common techniques for avoiding direct assertion. The more powerful the captain, the less need he has of overt assertion.

I was also surprised to find a new ending on Wanda's final version. Her conclusion, like the *umialiq's* rhetorical question, avoids assertion:

> The question is why there is no adequate report on symbolic large marine mammal hunting among Bering Strait Eskimos since quite a few anthropologists did many research works on this area. . . . As a matter of fact, Gambell people held whale ceremony every year, while Savoonga had walrus ceremony annually. I hope the answer to this question will provide more deep understanding of the traditional cultures and the social lives of Bering Strait Eskimos.

While the captain's question is based on personal experience and communal values, Wanda's statement of the question of symbolic hunting reveals her reticence to evaluate without textual authority. Carolyn Matalene reports a similar finding: "To be indirect in both spoken and written discourse, to expect the audience to infer meanings rather than to have them spelled out is a defining characteristic of Chinese rhetoric . . ." (801). Too many of the essential elements in the cultural context we were operating in did not connect. Wanda had invested my status as "boss" with her reverence for correctness, and I had not perceived the cause of her paper's indirection. Bruffee's "kind of conversation peer tutors engage in" was stifled by a deference that none of my questions could penetrate ("Peer Tutoring" 7).

Collaboration requires that both participants in a one-to-one relationship have authority. At first Wanda listened to me only when I addressed matters about which she granted me authority. She could not understand why I should concern myself with her area of expertise, the subject. In subsequent tutoring sessions I used Wanda's respect for my expertise in grammatical structures to move gradually toward a dialogue about higher-order concerns.

This strategy of moving from lower-order concerns to higher ones reverses the writing process, but I get to those higher-order concerns through the student's cultural expectations. My goal remains process-oriented. As Wanda and I established a background of work on these anthropology projects and she educated me in the subject, she began to answer my questions about content as though I were a peer instead of a teacher. She responded with information or questions of her own instead of answering by talking about the assignment. Wanda gained power even if the change was not so dramatic as Harvey Kail and John Trimbur's "crisis of authority," in which the hierarchical structure of transmission and generation is leveled and "the authority of knowledge" is defined as a "relationship among people" (12).

Peter Elbow (*Writing*), Muriel Harris (*Teaching*), Emily Meyer and Louise Smith, and Thomas Reigstad and Donald McAndrew correctly advocate that collaborative learning begin at the level of subject matter of the student's piece. It is often difficult to remember, under the pressure of the student's dependence on the tutor's authority or the desire for a good grade, that our concern must remain the student's progress, not the perfection of a paper. Stephen North states the issue succinctly: "Our job is to produce better writers, not better writing" (438). Even with ESL students, as Phyllis Brooks points out, content matters first: "The fact that a student is working on acquiring a second language should not obscure the fact that he or she is learning to compose" (51). But I advocate finding the most culturally satisfying way to get to that process (see Muriel Harris's essay in this volume).

"I Can Tell a Story, but I Just Can't Write!" Combining One Kind of Authority with Another

Sophie, a Yupik woman in her thirties, was one of the first Alaska Native students to come to the writing center regularly. In the relative safety of Rural Student Services a Native student would have been surrounded by other Alaska Natives, while in the main writing center such a student might have been the only Native. In 1992 the Alaska Native student population was 1,222, but we had only 52 tutoring sessions with Native students. That semester we held 31 sessions with Yupik speakers; Sophie represented 17 of those. We opened the Rural Student Services writing-center site in spring 1993, and we now average 100 sessions between the two sites.

Yupik speakers are proud of their language and still cultivate its use among their children despite the intrusion of television and of English in the schools. Other Eskimo languages, such as Inupiat, and the various Athabascan languages are not widely learned by young people of those language groups. The Yupik people's love of language also extends to storytelling, and Sophie, we discovered, is famous in her village as a fine storyteller. Now in her second semester of college, she confronted freshman composition and a teacher much younger than she.

Seemingly undaunted by classroom protocol, Sophie was openly enthusiastic about speaking out in class. Her problems with sentence structure, verb forms, and mechanics were similar to those of many rural Alaska Natives, both Eskimo and Athabascan. Sophie's diligent but frustrated attempts to impose an organizational scheme onto her research material was initially so distressing to her that her tutors fell into the trap of offering overly directive organizational strategies. Sophie's tutors were aware of the dangers, voiced by Stephen North and Peter Carino, of reducing the center to a fix-it shop. We gradually learned that she, not we, must find models by choosing among options available from her oral culture combined with those from the written one.

Sophie's frequent visits and hard work inspired experienced tutors to comment, "As always, working with Sophie is a joy" or "Sophie's paper is flying along—she's writing rapidly and has hit the groove concerning *what* to include." Only one of the nine tutors she saw that semester expressed skepticism. He wrote, "Sophie agrees with criticism quickly—as well as all suggestions. Please make sure she *really* understands and accepts them before moving on." Although Sophie's tutors read the previous tutor reports and established continuity between sessions, their caution was counteracted by her cheerful participation in brainstorming details and her apparent acceptance of proposed models of organization. So why was Sophie unable to settle on an organizational structure? The story of her ultimately successful experience illustrates how her tutors abandoned abstract models of organization and how she worked through her own cultural values to gain authority over her research project.

Sophie spent four sessions with various tutors on a paper about alcohol-related suicide in rural Alaska. While we encourage students to return to the writing center to polish their work, Sophie was testing out different tutors without making progress. Each tutor tried to help her reorganize the same material. Clarice, her first tutor, felt that the paper was in the prewriting stage and reported, "I helped Sophie organize her ideas into a chronological outline." Sophie returned two days later. A new tutor wrote, "We discussed getting started on a preliminary draft (i.e., coming up with an organization scheme)." A few weeks passed, and Sophie returned to another tutor, who wrote, "We looked at ways to reorganize the paper." Finally, a week later, Sophie returned to Clarice, and again they worked on organization: "Exciting session! Got out scissors and tape. She hacked up paragraphs and regrouped them into sensible clusters." Two important processes occurred: Sophie took physical possession of the project, and she organized it into "sensible clusters."

Only after reviewing Sophie's file and talking with her tutors did we finally realize that generating models was not effective for her. As Ron Scollon and Suzanne Scollon point out, rural village life in this extreme environment requires communal cooperation combined with respect for personal accomplishment. Valid information is provided by personal experience or direct observation of the experiences of others known intimately for a lifetime, not from written texts or abstract paradigms (*Interethnic Communication* 18). When the tutors transposed an abstract organizational system, even a chronological one, onto the separate narratives of suicide cases taken from printed sources and personal experience, they erected an insurmountable cultural barrier. Like Carolyn Matalene's Chinese students, Sophie was too polite to reject her tutors' advice outright, but she did not use any of it. Sophie's significant and intensely painful personal experiences with suicide and alcoholism in her village were not being integrated into the thesis-oriented freshman research paper meaningfully.

Clarice chose a new tactic when she saw Sophie the second and final time. An experienced ex–high school teacher and TA-tutor, Clarice exercised restraint, watching Sophie cut and paste for an hour. An occasional encouraging prompt was the only "tutoring," but Sophie made real progress. Sophie's polite acquiescence might make her appear less independent and sure of herself than her more assertive urban counterparts, but in returning to the writing center until she found a satisfactory form for her content, she took on far more personal responsibility than they often do.

In seeing our own cultural penchant for verbal assertiveness reflected in Sophie's gregariousness and extroverted behavior, we assumed she had internalized our predilection for thesis statements and linear argument. In fact, her verbal facility may have resulted from her skill as a storyteller rather than from acculturation. In any case, she, like the whaling captain from Gambell, retains the deeply ingrained cultural value of indirection. By organizing her essay as a progression of narratives about individual suicides, Sophie made the stories become parables of personal and cultural failure from which readers can draw their own message and connections.

Although every tutor recognized the advisability of dealing with organization before grammar or mechanics, we could have used the clues in Sophie's characteristic use of the conditional verbs had we known their cultural significance. Patricia Kwatchka links verb use to Native values:

> If we consider that "can/will" assert and "could/would" hypothesize, it is clear that the second conforms more with Athabaskan beliefs about the way people should relate to their environment. The Koyukon regard this relationship as delicate and subject to upset from many potential sources, some within and some beyond the individual's control. A statement about the likelihood of future events ("I will . . .") appears not only fatuous but possibly offensive to some components of the balance, endangering relationships with the environment. . . .   (32)

Among rural Alaska Natives, both Athabascan and Yupik, qualifying statements, like qualifying verb forms, indicate a proper social attitude. As Kwatchka explains, Koyukon social discourse prohibits any form of bragging: "Thus unqualified assertions of personal ability and/or intent offend socially, and are considered egocentric and inept to the point of rudeness" (32). The value the composition teacher and the tutor place on direct assertion in the thesis statement erects a serious cultural barrier to the rural Native student.

A strong opening thesis statement, one of the major goals of the freshman research paper, dooms the project from the outset since in Yupik culture it is unwise to predict. In addition, without sufficient personal experience, any outright assertion amounts to bragging. Simply directing the student to eliminate qualifying strategies as we had done with the verb forms is not productive. The tutor must negotiate with the student how much acculturation he or she wants to achieve in the assigned piece.

Sophie wanted an appropriate organizing structure; Clarice understood that negotiating form by talking about it was not the key. Instead, she allowed Sophie to act under encouraging guidance and reinforced Sophie's desire for "sensible clusters," discrete narratives rather than linear development. Tutor and student began with a false sense of similitude, each trying to satisfy the other's idea of "organization." They ended by communicating across difference, each responding to the other's encouragement. Sophie did not return again before handing in the paper. She did, however, usually make an initial visit in which she discussed other assignments with a tutor before beginning to write. She was, in a sense, sizing up the cultural boundaries and thinking about negotiating strategies. Her mechanical problems persisted, but her tutors commented that she often recognized how to correct them once they were pointed out.

Not only did working with Sophie help her negotiate cultures, but the process also helped the tutors negotiate among alternative structures. The exuberance expressed in Clarice's note on the successful session represents one of those emotionally charged moments when real collaboration takes place. In fact, Clarice discovered a personal affinity with Alaska Native culture, as her statement summarizing her semester's experience tutoring at Rural Student Services attests:

> Working with Alaska Natives is enjoyable because, like many of them, I tend to be soft-spoken and laid back. I don't think this would be the place for a high-energy dynamo tutor or for someone who prefers scheduled time and rules to enforce. Rather, it's a good place to absorb some of another culture, where nontutoring time can be spent observing and interacting with people from a variety of backgrounds and languages.

"I Was Making Sure There Wasn't an Ambush": Looking for Some Recognition of Authority

He walked into the center much as most students who have been required to come do. "This is a waste of my time" was written on his face. His more than two-hundred-pound frame was covered in blue jeans, a T-shirt and a black leather jacket with "The Outpost: Farthest North Harley Davidson" embossed on the back. A POW cap covered his thick but graying shoulder-length hair. Dan, like Mike Rose's veterans, was determined to be "let into the academic club" but he wasn't sure if I was the bouncer or the valet, a potential obstacle or a facilitator (*Lives* 141).

His assignment for his freshman composition class, due the next day, was a comparison-contrast essay. In it he compared his visit to the Vietnam War Memorial to his experience of combat in Indochina twenty years earlier. As a teacher, I have cringed at the prospect of a student's writing on such a topic since grading the assignment verges on judging the quality of the student's life rather than his writing. Yet here I was with a paper full of sentence fragments, a comparison I couldn't quite get, and one of the most intense and tense individuals I had sat down with since I began teaching in urban junior colleges in the early 1970's, when the Vietnam vets first came back to school on the GI bill. Dan's return to school was funded by a special program for veterans suffering from posttraumatic stress disorder.

Although I was not at all sure what the focus of the paper was meant to be, I resisted the impulse to ask about it. Instead, I asked him to read the paper aloud. After reading the first two paragraphs, he began to explain what he "meant to say." Since I had not visited the monument, I told him how I had long wanted to do so and asked him about the addition of the statue of the three unknown soldiers. He answered that he was so struck by this statue that he had hidden in some nearby bushes to cry. It took him hours to get himself under enough control to—in his words—"crawl toward the wall." By this point in the session, we both were leaning on our elbows over the table, facing each other almost nose to nose. I leaned back and commented, "Your approach to the wall sounds a lot like an approach in combat."

His breath exploded. He could hardly contain himself. How could he have missed it? Yes, of course, it was just like battle. I was nearly as excited: Yes, yes, this would make the comparison work. I was agreeing, but my role as authority had vanished. The discovery was mutual and almost simultaneous. I didn't tell him how to make the comparison clear or how to generate an outline; he was too excited to remember such instructions. I pointed to a couple of fragments that seemed to punch up the tempo and intensity and then asked him what the other ones were doing. He hadn't realized these phrases were fragments, so I suggested he not worry about them yet since he was rewriting the comparison anyway. We set up another appointment for two days later. Even though he was turning in a draft the next day, his TA encouraged students to revise their papers until they were satisfied. Dan planned to spend more time on this one.

Dan returned for his appointment with a rewrite. He had found a way of incorporating his combat experience directly into the language of his description of the approach to the wall. After a twenty-minute discussion of this scene's power and of what other information in the paper contributed to that power, we returned to the sentence fragments for the last five minutes or so. In the calmer atmosphere of this session, we considered which of the fragments might work and why others did not.

When Dan brought me his final version of the paper, the battle imagery was even stronger. He had decided to eliminate all the fragments—even the ones I liked—because he wanted the sentences to appear more controlled. The two focal paragraphs follow a short description of his arriving at Union Station "wearing a cami-jacket with Vietnam memorabilia and carrying an 80 pound pack." He had walked up Constitution Avenue and sat down to rest on a bench:

> While still sitting on the bench I began to feel as if I were delaying the inevitable. I was fighting to not do what I knew I had to do. I felt like I was on a twenty mile forced march.
>
> I stood up and continued down Constitution Avenue. I sensed that the Memorial was nearby. Then I saw a brown sign with yellow lettering which read, "Vietnam Memorial." I had arrived. Trembling I entered the area from the east side and behind it, almost like I was making sure there wasn't an ambush. As it came into full view I completely broke down. I stepped over a small wire fence, tripped, then crawled about 50 feet to a small grove of trees above the "Wall," and looked down at it. I sobbed silently as I stared at it.

Dan had negotiated his stance in this essay to his satisfaction. He asked me to help him with his final persuasive paper, but he did not return to the center that semester when I suggested another tutor who would be good with that subject. He did, however, find a wider audience than a Vietnam-era reader. He submitted a longer essay to a college-wide essay contest at the end of that term and won honorable mention. He also returned after a semester break from English classes and saw both TA-tutors and me.

The intensity of this man's experience produced a creative moment for me as well. I could share in the pride of his accomplishment in writing an essay that gained him some emotional control over both the experience and the process of writing about it. As a tutor I had the courage or vulnerability to accept the force of emotion that generated the topic, but I could not initially control it. Relieved of the responsibility of giving that assignment, which resulted in such an outburst, and relieved of the pressure of grading it, I didn't need to set up barriers parallel to his. As a young female teacher in the 1970s, I would have been prompted by Dan's apparent hostility to erect a wall of artificial authority equal to the imagined strength of his initial resistance.

The TA-tutors in the writing center at UAF seem to develop confidence in themselves and their students sooner than the TAs I went to graduate school with who did not tutor. TA-tutors repeatedly comment that tutoring other teachers' students has led them to see their own stu-

dition, they say they feel more relaxed in one-to-one conferencing. One TA-tutor discovered the secret of listening and waiting, a skill that can take years to develop: "I'm better at waiting for what a student really wants from me," she wrote.

Tutoring expertise and confidence also transfer to the classroom. One TA-tutor claims that "thinking on the hoof" in tutoring has made her much less defensive about classroom discussion. Jay Jacoby and Stan Patten declare that "service in a writing center is the best possible method of professional development in writing instruction" (158). I believe that one-to-one collaboration without the institutional force of the grade is the best environment for Bruffee's "conversation," in which similarity and difference create a balance of authority. A multi-cultural negotiation of authority can certainly teach the teacher how pervasive her or his own ties to traditional authority often are, despite the best efforts toward student-directed learning. Only by recognizing and articulating these assumptions can we move toward real collaboration.

Cross-Talk: Talking Cross-Difference

Gail Y. Okawa

In the postmodern academic world, there are some who drone on: *Diversity. Multicultural. Multiculturalism.* Such terms, when their speakers see them only as terms, become momentarily fashionable, sometimes co-opted to the point of meaninglessness and thereby ignorable. They fade into the academic wallpaper of words, which obscures the reality that we are all, in fact, culturally and linguistically different and that we are here in academia—students and teachers alike—trying to find ways of seeing and being seen, hearing and being heard.

The writers of this section suggest revision: they push us against the wall beyond, challenging us to resee language—the speakers and writers of different cultural backgrounds and varieties of language, the environments in which we talk about it, its inextricable connection to identity—and testing what we mean by the words. I like what they do, although I have some reservations, mainly the uneasy feeling that some of this might be a little too neat.

Reading the opening essay, I appreciate the way Bonnie Lisle and Sandra Mano provide a broad critical and pedagogical framework for viewing issues of cultural and linguistic multiplicity in literacy education, allowing us entry into this complex subject. They offer a critique of current traditional ethnocentrism in texts and teaching. They explore the demands of true multivocality as opposed to the token representation resulting from additive approaches to curricular change. They discuss with particular insight how they acknowledge their students' varied cultural orientations and rhetorical styles; the relations between students' rhetorical traditions and their cultural identities; and the need for new teacher sensibilities, attitudes, and knowledge to embrace the diversity of students in our classrooms. Through closely knit theory and practice, the authors have fostered student literacy and identity in the academy; their essay is helpful not only in providing a more inclusive approach to students' cultural and rhetorical orientations but also in bringing to light deep-seated assumptions of the dominant United States culture. It goes to the core of the issues of multicultural revision and transformation of students, curricula, and instructors.

The authors of the essays that follow Lisle and Mano's narrate and theorize more specifically their experience with and studies of students from wide-ranging linguistic and cultural backgrounds, in the classroom as well as in the writing center and in testing situations. It is the particularity in these essays that reaches me, that inspires me to explore and implement the authors' theories and methods. The intimacy of Michelle Grijalva's narrative on teaching precollege Navajo and Hopi students carries me furthest into the realm of experience. With compelling detail, Grijalva relates what happens to her as a Yaqui teacher facing the cultural eradication of her Navajo and Hopi students, their voicelessness. By telling the stories of her own language and family history, by drawing out and drawing on the stories of her students, and by introducing them to writers like N. Scott Momaday and Luci Tapahonso, Grijalva works with them so that they learn new ways of seeing their own cultures and cultural selves—becoming "cultural translators" with their sense of cultural identity and pride restored through their writing. In her narrative, she takes me with her, draws me into her classroom, lets me hear her students speaking—a layering of narratives. As Grijalva's experience illustrates and as I believe, this self-revelation by the teacher is critical in cross-cultural teaching and learning.

In the next essays Kermit Campbell and Denise Troutman provide us with ways of reading African American students' discourse as assertions of cultural and personal identity. Campbell shows how we writing teachers may hear and read the vernacular voices of male African American students. By analyzing how identity is constructed through specific rhetorical forms, he demonstrates that cultivating an environment for students to develop "authoritative voices" is the path to affirming student identities and a means to students' successful acquiring of "academic literacy." In the writing of Ronnie, Gerald, and Patrick, we see how integral the relations among each student's discourse, identity, and voice are. Like Grijalva and Lisle and Mano, Campbell argues that students should become ethnographers of their own languages and discourses.

Troutman similarly affirms the need to create opportunities for African American students to situate their voices in the university. Through a close sociolinguistic analysis of African American students' discourse, she upholds the need to revise the academy's perceptions of what discourse is. Troutman and Campbell's views of Black English Vernacular (BEV) discourse as a generative factor in African American student literacy is clearly supported by Geneva Smitherman's recent study of student writers:

> . . . What our analysis of essays by several hundred African American student writers indicates is this: given a paper with both BEV grammar and BEV discourse, the greater the degree of Black discourse, irrespective of the degree/amount of BEV grammar, the higher will be the rating . . . for fluency/accomplishment of the rhetorical task.   ("'Blacker the Berry'" 94)

Seeing literacy and language in terms of cultural practices, teachers may follow the lead of Geneva Smitherman-Donaldson, Joshua Fishman, Roseann Gonzalez, Harvey Daniels, and others in seeing the speakers of language varieties in this country as resources rather than as liabilities. Further, we may foster a broad scale of language development (see, e.g., the CCCC *National Language Policy* [Conference]) rather than undermine it.

Moving from the classroom, Susan Blalock foregrounds the writing center as a prime site for teacher training and for tutors and writers of differing cultural and linguistic backgrounds to negotiate authority issues through a recognition of otherness and different rhetorical orientations. Shifting from exposition into narrative, she presents the case of Wanda, Sophie, and Dan at the University of Alaska, Fairbanks, where the student body is fifty percent nonwhite and TA-tutors are predominantly white. She helps us see the new relations that tutors and student writers may establish when tutors are sensitized to their students' cultural backgrounds, rhetorical expectations, and "writing problems." Through the particularity of her case studies, we witness how the tutors' discovering and acknowledging the writers' cultural perspectives lead to the fuller development of the students' voices and hence their literacy. I heartily agree with Blalock that confronting authority issues in the writing center is critical to student writers' maintaining their cultural identities through their writing. But I am uncertain what she means when she says the TA-tutors experience otherness because she describes only their confronting new living conditions and the extremes of Alaska's climate. I am also somewhat troubled by the "pleasant introduction" to Alaska Native students' cultures that seems to foster exoticism and its attendant hazards. And as I have discussed elsewhere, I wonder if the ethnic composition of the TA-tutor cohort shouldn't be a focal issue when writing is taught in settings like Alaska, where there is a history of social and academic colonialism. Perhaps authority issues would take on different dimensions if students like Sophie were themselves to become tutors.

Liz Hamp-Lyons raises provocative questions about another setting encountered by students from diverse cultural and linguistic backgrounds: the test. By examining student writing under testing conditions, she explores the interactions between student assumptions and teachers' and institutions' biases to see how student essay-test writing may be assessed well before testing. Her interviews with Arvind, Joe, Kon, and Kris—again, rich with the particularity of narrative—illustrate the need for educators to probe the damage done to students by testing instead of probing the deficit of student performance.

The most powerful theme among these essays concerns a refocusing of vision: the authors establish the integral relations among the cultures, rhetorics, identities, voices, and literacies of diverse student writers. Beginning with an explicit or implicit critique of the academy's Eurocentric rhetoric and worldview, each contributor elaborates on this critical connection, which is at the heart of an inclusive multicultural rhetoric. Campbell and Troutman explicitly call for the tightly formalized conventions of academic discourse to expand and to include the oral and literate forms exemplified in their discussions of Black English Vernacular. When teachers recognize that students' cultures and culturally constructed rhetorics are intimately tied to students' identities, they must also recognize their responsibility to promote varied forms of discourse so that student voices and literacy may be realized.

Having learned the value of narrative in my current research, I am also happily struck by the use of story in all these pieces. Narrative, after all, is "both phenomenon and method" (Connelly and Clandinin 2). Lisle and Mano employ narrative to tap into their students' knowledge, cross cultural boundaries, and bring differences to light, and then to form a basis for analytical thought. Campbell, likewise, suggests using narrative with African American student writers. Grijalva herself tells stories within stories. From writers' narratives, we can learn how they understand the meaning in their lives through what Maxine Greene refers to as "the inclusion of those of us who read" (x). The overall effect is that we hear multiple voices and varieties of language and discourse—from the Yupik, the Pueblo, the Navajo, the Hopi, the African American, the Chinese, the Korean, the East Indian, and others. When the writers give me new ways of seeing students and discourse and myself, I feel enlightened and grateful.

Now, I think, we need to push ourselves harder against the wall—beyond the smooth, neat surface of academic wallpaper—to look at the cracks and fissures, to feel the rough surface scraping our faces, to touch the uncertain, loose plaster that we wish we could not see. As we come to know through these essays and our own experience, learning and teaching and writing in settings where people come from different cultural and linguistic backgrounds is a messy business: lots of talking cross-difference, dissonance, unpredictability.

Academic culture doesn't usually appreciate such untidiness, especially among newcomers, as Patricia Bizzell ("What Happens"), David Bartholomae ("Inventing" [1985]), Mike Rose (*Lives*), and others have discussed and as Grijalva and Hamp-Lyons illustrate; the structure of academic culture is as dictated by tradition and convention as its discourse is. So narrow is its definition of the acceptable, this culture paradoxically elevates the individual in the name of individualism while it individually isolates and denigrates personal and other-cultural voices and subjectivities. In *Bootstraps: From an American Academic of Color*, Victor Villanueva, Jr., reveals this contradiction in the experience of those who traditionally have stood outside the university:

> The liberal ideology of individualism allows for the unchecked continuance of the bootstrap sensibility. It allows for things like English Only legislation. . . . It allows for the confusion between immigrant and minority, an ahistorical perspective which doesn't make for seeing how long some groups have been without boots. Even when some within those groups manage to put on boots, the boots are not of the same quality as others' boots, the legacy of internal colonialism. Individualism alone . . . allows those who are of color, like the students in the traditional freshman composition class of my first research study—like me—to attempt to deny or to downplay our races or cultures or class affiliations in the name of individual achievement.   (121)

When student writers bring with them different languages, discourses, cultures, and worldviews, the culture of the academy would leech out their cultural uniqueness, absorb them, assimilate them, graduate them uniform in their uniforms. Admittance requires conformity and the attendant cultural loss. Ronnie, Gerald, Patrick, Sophie, Wanda, Kon, Arvind: as language can be the great equalizer, so can it be the great nullifier.

But demographics and retention rates in secondary schools and colleges reflect that students from nonwhite minority backgrounds often refuse that absorption, overtly or covertly (Gonzalez). Some, following H. Rap Brown's lead, "get their education" in the street, as Campbell illustrates; in school, they resist, they don't participate, they drop out, they fail (Erickson).

That is, they do unless they see the possibility of cultural coexistence; Patrick in Campbell's essay writes about having "the best of both worlds"—the hood and school—in that order. An equity of power among those who embody different cultures is essential for cultural coexistence: a sharing of knowledge and authority, a revising of relationships, and, most critical, a recognizing of one's own difference.

Such equity has little chance of developing unless individuals make the underpinnings of their subjective cultures explicit, especially to themselves, as the cross-cultural theorist Felipe Korzenny writes:

> Culture is like water for the fish: We are in it and a part of it but we do not see it. . . . Implicit or subjective culture is invisible, but it is the dimension of culture that is most likely to affect human interaction. The values, beliefs, attitudes, behavioral patterns, and role relationships that different cultures hold dear are difficult to detect by members of each culture as well as by those who are alien. Making culture explicit will therefore help us understand ourselves in contrast to others. (57)

In an academic setting, this critical self-reflection must begin with the one who would have authority, the teacher, as Lisle and Mano assert in their conclusion. What they do not discuss, however, is how each of us as teachers must practice a bifocality of difference—seeing one's difference, one's cultural self up close as well as from a distance, as others may see it. This process is quite natural for those of us from subordinated groups who must constantly define and redefine our selves vis-à-vis the dominant culture. The European American teacher and student, privileged by race or class, must begin to understand the personal and societal value of reconsidering their location—their dominance, their otherness—and the limitations and restrictions of these perspectives. They need to engage an unrealized bifocality themselves to comprehend or interact equally with those who have been traditionally subordinated.

Then, too, as many have written, we teachers must recognize how we are traditional upholders of classroom authority, how to varying degrees we are culpable and complicitous in this undemocratic venture (e.g., Bullock, Trimbur, and Schuster; Fox, *Social Uses*; Villanueva, "Considerations"). And how we are ignorant. Especially in multicultural settings, after all, we do not know others beneath their surfaces. Vinh The Do writes, "If we realize that we are all culture bound and culturally modified, we will accept the fact that, being unlike, we do not really know what someone else 'is'" (qtd. in Barna 345). When we move in cross-cultural spaces, then, our real authority, if based on superficial knowledge, becomes empty, void of substance. Grijalva sees this with her Navajo and Hopi students: Facing their initial silence, she is at a loss; through sharing her own experience and encouraging them to tell their stories, she affirms and learns from their vast cultural knowledge.

This sharing of authority should be not only a personal act but also a programmatic and political one. I learned this through experience. In the mid-1980s, I assumed the responsibility of training the peer tutors in the university writing center where I worked. Though supervising was new to me, as a longtime classroom teacher I found that assuming habitual authority was not. But our writing center served students in the university's Educational Opportunity Program (EOP), a group incredibly diverse in experience, ethnicity, culture, age, and socioeconomic-class and linguistic backgrounds. On-the-job training made me painfully aware that I did not and could not know everything in this cross-cultural setting. I came to realize that tutors of different ethnicities, ages, and social, cultural, and linguistic experiences might be able to work with students differently and thus provide one another and me with insights that would make us all more effective tutors. Equally important, a diverse group of tutors would provide role models for EOP students—physical evidence that language rights could be shared. It became more and more essential for me, practically and ideologically, to recruit tutors from American Indian, Latino-Latina, African American, and Asian American as well as European American backgrounds. We ended up creating our training program together. In contrast to the individualism of the academy, the collective, the community of tutors became an essential component of the program. In their writing about their experiences with tutoring, tutors have referred repeatedly to the importance of their peers as a source of cultural growth and identity (see Okawa; Okawa, Fox, Chang, Windsor, Chavez, and Hayes).

The changes that I experienced as a teacher were contingent first on my recognizing my cross-cultural ignorance as a bicultural Asian American woman. Like Grijalva, I had to reveal my life stories to the tutors I worked with to become a part of the collective. Reading Paulo Freire's *Pedagogy of the Oppressed* during this period, I felt affirmed in my beliefs that learning and teaching can and must be egalitarian, that teaching is not banking, that mine was not some idealistic pipe dream.

I also came to understand that we convey a social and political message to students when the racial and ethnic composition of the tutoring staff—and of the English teaching force as a whole—perpetuates historical power relations. But awareness was not enough; not until I made programmatic changes in tutor recruitment, hiring, and training did theory become praxis in Freire's sense. No matter how well-meaning teachers or tutors of the dominant culture may be, in multicultural language settings the internal colonialism among the colonized and the colonizers that Villanueva discusses in *Bootstraps* continues to exist in our visual imagery until our images are revised.

Those in positions of dominance—racial, cultural, linguistic, academic—need to acknowledge what they have and what they will lose and gain when they accept their difference in relation to others. Those who are subordinated must, as Frantz Fanon asserts in "Racism and Culture," rediscover and delineate their cultural traditions (42–43). This is true of students, teachers, and writers alike in multicultural, heterogeneous societies like the United States where some cultural groups like African Americans, Latinos and Latinas, Asian Americans, and American Indians have historically been colonized and misrepresented by those in power. In such cases, the subordinated must not only consciously construct their unique realities and identities but also maintain them lest they be subsumed into and by the dominant society and its stereotypes. Through their own writings or those who would write for them within their groups, the people of minority cultures must create a body of knowledge about their individual selves, and their collective self, their history, and their culture—in relation to themselves and to the dominant society. Grijalva's experience illustrates this imperative. Like Grijalva and her students, the writers of these cultures are charged or charge themselves with etching out the forms of their group's common experience against the backdrop of the dominant community.

Abdul JanMohamed and David Lloyd call this rhetorical perspective "collective subjectivity," a culturally affirming and transforming concept and strategy. In this view, the culture of a community is "not a mere superstructure"; rather, "the recognition of its culture as viable" is essential to the group's physical survival (9). Such cultural viability is preserved and conveyed through the group's discourse, as Grijalva, Campbell, Lisle and Mano, and Troutman illustrate. What is central to this discussion is that the writers of minority discourse, including students, write not in a vacuum but in response to a long tradition of dominance by the majority culture, a culture in which their histories and identities have been written according to and determined by dominant-culture stereotypes and assumptions.

These writers must assume this critical rhetorical posture for the sake of cultural survival. As JanMohamed and Lloyd assert, "The collective nature of all minority discourse . . . derives from the fact that minority individuals are always treated and forced to experience themselves generically. Coerced into a negative, generic subject position, the oppressed individual responds by transforming that position into a positive, collective one" (10). The individual fuses with the collective. It is the "carving of the face" that Gloria Anzaldúa writes about (*Borderlands* 73). As Ramón Saldívar points out in *Chicano Narrative*, however, this discourse is not simply counterhegemonic and reactive. I believe it is generative and creative and communal. We carve out our own faces.

We must be wary of wallpaper neatness. Acquiring knowledge about the cultures and rhetorics of others, as Blalock and Lisle and Mano suggest, can be an important step toward sharing knowledge and developing respect for those from cultures outside one's own. But there is always the danger of developing no more than highly sophisticated stereotypes. To reiterate Do's comment: "being unlike, we do not really know what someone else 'is.'" Instead, we—teachers and students learning to communicate in multicultural settings—must be prepared to confront our own difference and our own ignorance, be prepared to hear and see the exciting, the unexpected, the unsettling, because nothing is predictable. Discovering ourselves and our voices through our writing can be discomforting for both the writer and the reader. If we do reenvision our personal difference, it will be messy. Then we must do our share, as the writers in this volume do, in examining and challenging what the academy values and why, in changing what discourse is viable and acceptable, in allowing students to provide us with more options for their self-expression. Perhaps it is a matter of letting ourselves go in order to participate in our own and others' multiple rhetorics and discourses. Mitsuye Yamada writes of layers of masks:

> My mask is control
> concealment
> endurance . . .
> Over my mask
> is your mask
> of me . . .   (114)

When the masks come off, like the wallpaper, there is much to be reckoned with.

PART II

The Roles of Teachers and Texts

Introduction

The authors here examine different multicultural reading and writing curricula in largely heterogeneous classrooms and in largely homogeneous ones, focusing on the reading and writing of specific texts and on roles assumed by the teacher. Carol Severino's essay uses excerpts from taped classroom conversations to show how students interacted around culturally based narratives in two settings that differ in the type of text and in the role of the teacher. Esha Niyogi De and Donna Uthus Gregory problematize the roles of teacher and Western academic discourse as "colonizers" of the multicultural classroom. Examining the changing social construction of texts and identities, Wendy S. Hesford develops a theoretical framework for a pedagogy of autobiography. The next two authors focus on reading experiences: Sandra Jamieson on the way many currently used multicultural anthologies negatively affect the identities of minority students and the thinking of minority and mainstream students, and Virginia A. Chappell on the way a class of mainstream students initially resisted a narrative of Japanese internment. Cecilia Rodríguez Milanés points out the problems these essays raise that need to be addressed more fully, especially the effects of the teacher's race on how teachers, texts, and students interact.

Two Approaches to "Cultural Text": Toward Multicultural Literacy

Carol Severino

Although all composition teachers are concerned about which curricula and teaching strategies best bring about engaged discussion and writing, the choices are especially critical to teachers of students from diverse ethnic backgrounds. As teachers and researchers in multicultural classes often observe, classroom practices that work well with students from some ethnic backgrounds cause difficulty for students from others. Fan Shen points out that some Asian students struggle in writing first-person essays that require thesis statements and topic sentences, because these features can go against their cultural traditions (see also Lisle and Mano in this volume). And according to Susan Phillips's research, some Native American students find the small-group activities common in today's writing classes threatening because of the potential for losing face among peers. Terry Dean recommends "cultural topics" for discussion and writing because many students are in the throes of negotiating between the values, practices, and "ways with words" of their native cultures and those of mainstream groups in the United States. Paulo Freire has advocated using cultural conflicts (and resolutions) from students' daily lives to ground literacy curricula, and in *Critical Teaching and Everyday Life* Ira Shor has adapted the approach for the United States college English setting. Dean, Freire, and Shor emphasize how raising cultural themes in speaking and writing not only helps students individually but also builds community as students gradually learn from one another's experiences. Such cultural discourse, in effect, becomes the class text and works to build multicultural literacy—the knowledge of the beliefs, practices, and roots of the cultures in one's environment and the ability to communicate such knowledge in oral and written discourse.

Two other teacher-researchers and I developed two pedagogical approaches to cultural text, tested them against each other, and fine-tuned them over several years. Teaching and doing research on composition classes in an academic opportunity program at a large, urban, public commuter university, we were interested in experimenting with uses of text and types of teacher authority in the classroom. I examine here the dynamics in two multicultural classes taught by the same instructor. The classes differed in the ways in which the cultural text was used and in the kind of authority the teacher exercised. In both classes, however, the curricula and teaching strategies employed texts related to the students' diverse backgrounds as topics for discussion and writing. Both cases demonstrate that students' ethnic texts can be invaluable resources for building multicultural literacy.

The Students in the Classes: A United Nations Microcosm

The forty-five students in the two classes came from twenty cultural backgrounds, reflecting the ethnic composition of the midwestern city in which the university is located. Over one-third of the students in the classes were African American; a little less than a third were Caucasian; approximately one-sixth were Latino or Latina; and another sixth were Asian. Graduates of local public and Catholic high schools, the students had all been admitted to the university through the opportunity program because their standardized test scores or high school ranks were too low for admission through regular channels. Thus many of the students were considered high-risk by the opportunity program and the university and basic writers by the composition program.

But to label students by their race or rank is to oversimplify and stereotype. This multicultural student sample, like many freshman writing classes at the university, was a United Nations microcosm. Of the Asian students, three students had parents born in China; three, the Philippines; and one, Burma. Of the Latino and Latina students, the parents or grandparents of six were born in Mexico, and the parents of one in Puerto Rico; another student had just arrived from Colombia. Of the white students, one was from the Soviet Union, one from Lebanon, one from Poland, and one from Yugoslavia. The parents of three were from Greece, and the parents of one had escaped from Lithuania during World War II. Other white students were of German, Czech, Polish, or mixed European ancestry. Of the African American students, one was from Jamaica, and most had parents or grandparents from the South.

Contrasting Curricula: Two Uses of Cultural Text

Contrasting the curricula in the classrooms meant using text in two different ways. The first class focused on student-produced text, excluding commercially published readings because these readings can intimidate basic writers and interfere with their invention processes. The second class focused on published texts—stories and essays representative of some of the ethnic groups in the class. Instead of using traditional anthologies, which often exclusively collect white male authors such as E. B. White or Jonathan Swift, students read Alice Walker, James Baldwin, Martin Luther King, Jr., Maxine Hong Kingston, Harry Mark Petrakis, Tillie Olsen, Luis Valdez, Samuel Betances, and others who have recently begun to appear in multicultural readers (see Jamieson and Lisle and Mano in this volume). Thus both classes used ethnic texts: student-written texts in the first class, published texts in the second. As for the writing assignments, the first class wrote more directly about their own experiences, and the second wrote more directly about their class readings.

What is often perceived as a conflict between writing about experience and writing about reading is represented in the ongoing dialogue between Peter Elbow and David Bartholomae at the Conference on College Composition and Communication and in publications of the National Council of Teachers of English. Elbow defends students' rights to describe and reflect on their experiences, unencumbered by outside readings, although he says readings related to students' topics may be brought in later. Bartholomae advocates that students relate their experiences to published texts. Thus comparing and contrasting the two approaches to cultural text plays out the differences between what Lester Faigley ("Competing Theories") has identified as the more expressivist pedagogies, which emphasize writing about experience, and the more social pedagogies, which emphasize writing about reading.

Contrasting Teaching Strategies: Two Teaching Roles

Both the use of text and the mode of teacher-student interaction differed in the two classes. In the first class, teacher and students interacted in teacher-facilitated peer-response groups. Students sat in circles and took turns responding to read-aloud student work, an approach that two composition teachers in the opportunity program adapted from Marie Ponsot and Rosemary Deen. Because students spent most of their class time listening to and commenting on one another's work, I call this class, for the sake of easier identification, the listening class. In it, learning is inductive or discovery-oriented. The teacher doesn't lecture on rhetorical or literary matters until the students raise them. Hence turn taking is not the only pattern of classroom talk; students are encouraged to interrupt the round-robin discussion with comments or questions. If the instructor and fellow students respond to and expand on a student's point, it is what Ann Berthoff calls an "emergent occasion." From these occasions emerge rhetorical and literary lessons.

The second class interacted more traditionally with the teacher, who stood in front of the room leading the discussions based on the ethnic readings, which he often had to help students interpret. Because the students spent most of their time discussing the ethnic readings and related issues, I call this class the reading class. Both classes were taught by the same instructor, Carlos Gonzalez (a fictitious name), a bilingual, bicultural Chicano with particular empathy for students who were dealing with cultural issues and conflicts in their personal and academic lives. As the researcher, I visited the classes once a week, audio- and videotaped sessions, and collected data on students' attitudes toward reading and writing and on their literacy backgrounds. The students' names have also been changed.

Contrasting Classroom Dynamics

To illustrate the contrasting classroom dynamics, I present typical scenes from both classrooms. Focusing on the narrative (student-produced narrative in the listening class, published narrative in the reading class), the scenes illustrate an important goal of multicultural literacy—to discover unity and cultural universals while discussing diversity and cultural differences.

The Listening Class: Writing Ethnic Literature

One of the listening class's assignments was to write a family story commonly told at gatherings of relatives and passed down from one generation to the other. Like ethnographers or folklorists, the students wrote down the oral tradition of their culture. Many of the stories produced were ethnically based. Jose, a second-generation Mexican student, for example, told his uncle's version of the Mexican folktale "La Llorona" ("The Weeping Woman"), about a woman who killed her children and who walks in the woods at night searching for their bodies. Reading the story, excerpted and transcribed below exactly as Jose read it to the class, simulates the experience of hearing it as did Jose's classmates, who did not have copies of the story:

> The story I'm about to tell goes back many years, and has been narrated by numerous people in different ways. But the way I'm going to tell it, is the way my uncle told me a few years back. She was known as La Llorona or "The Crying Lady." No one knew her real name or where she was born. She was of average height, and lived near a small creek adjacent to Guanajuato, Mexico, where my uncle also lived. . . .
>
> So every night at the midnight hour La Llorona would come out of hiding and cry for her children. "Mis, mis hijos," meaning, meaning "my children" down the streets of the town and scared the daylights out of some innocent people. One of those people happened to be my uncle. He once owned a bar on the outskirts of town. One late night on his, ah, on his way back from work, he noticed a glowing, a glowing [pause]. One late night on his way back from work, he noticed a glowing object in the distance. He stopped and just kept staring. The object kept coming closer and closer. He remembered the tales of La Llorona and realized it was her. His heart began to beat faster and faster, and he finally thought it was time to run, and, boy, did he run. I think, um, I think my uncle might have had a few too many that night, and the night he told me the story. But the tales of La Llorona goes on and on.

As usual, Jose's reading was followed by round-robin comment from each student in the circle on features of the piece. The participants in the segment of comment excerpted below were Carlos, the instructor; Alfredo, a first-generation Mexican; Shana, a second-generation Jamaican; and Frank, of German descent. Because this session occurred toward the beginning of the course and thus the procedure was new to students, Carlos had to help them make their observations more specific and detailed. All speech in these excerpts, including hesitations, repetition, and dialect features, is faithfully transcribed.

> CARLOS: OK. Who would like to begin reading their observations? OK. Go ahead.
> ALFREDO: OK. It needs more smoothness in the connection of the ideas. Otherwise, it is acceptable.

CARLOS: OK. We'll go to your left.

SHANA: Uh-huh, I say the story was very clear, as he said, and he expressed his way as the way his uncle saw it.

CARLOS: OK. What was the last statement?

SHANA: That he expressed himself the way, very well, like his uncle would have said it or seen it.

CARLOS: Instead of through his eyes, it's through his uncle's eyes, the person who experienced it.

SHANA: Yeah.

CARLOS: OK. Frank?

FRANK: He gave good information about Llorona, where she came from, how she killed her kids, how she . . .

CARLOS: OK. Do you remember any specifics about that, give us an example of what kinds of things you remember him saying?

FRANK: That she was jilted by the townspeople or by herself, and she went mad because she took it personally.

CARLOS: OK. [Observations continue]

"Observations" do not have to be critical comments; instead, as Ponsot and Deen recommend, they can be features that the listener noticed or observed (57–64). If many listeners observe the same feature, for example, a shifting point of view, the writer realizes he or she must attend to it in revising. Later in this class session, listeners voiced confusion about the story's point of view: Who was telling the story, Jose or his uncle?

In this pattern of interaction, every student must comment on the essay to aid the writer in revising. The listening class calls for universal participation; unlike the reading class (or the Fifth Amendment), it does not allow any class member to remain silent. Thus it helps prevent the more vocal or perceptive students from monopolizing the discussion. But interruptions are encouraged to keep the observer-instructor-observer pattern from becoming monotonous.

The following segment of dialogue represents an emergent occasion interrupting the pattern of turn taking: it involves Camelia, a Colombian student; Sam, an African American student; Stephanie, a second-generation Greek student; as well as the rest of the class. Students and teacher discover that what seemed to be only a belief of Latinos and Latinas is a belief of other cultures too.

CAMELIA: But that story doesn't belong to Mexico only.

CARLOS: That's true.

CAMELIA: They have it throughout all Latin America, the story.

CARLOS: Where do you think it comes from, Camelia? Do you have any idea since you just came from South America?

CAMELIA: No, I don't have any idea, but my father—he has a farm, and the, the *campesinos*, the people who work on the land—

CARLOS [translating *campesinos* for the students]: The peasants.

CAMELIA: —believe in those kinds of stories of La Llorona and everything, that she's in the woods and at night you can hear her crying, and I know many people who have heard that before.

CARLOS: And, I mean, other cultures have things like La Llorona. Do any of your cultures have something, something ghostly that you remember? In black culture, there are no—spooky little— women running around? [Class laughs.] No one else has—In the Soviet Union [to Svetlana, who is from Russia] you don't have that, strange stories about—I mean, other cultures like you know, uh, some countries have Dracula, vampires; other countries have the story of Frankenstein and other stories, you know, some of them were made up, by writers, and they're not part of the myth of the culture. Yeah, Sam.

SAM: I remember a story where we was told that if we looked in the mirror in the middle of the night and you say "Mary Jane," you'll see, you say "Mary Jane had a little baby" ten times, you'll see a picture of this lady in the mirror.

MANY STUDENTS TOGETHER: I thought it was Mary Worth.

STEPHANIE: Mary Worth, you're supposed to say "Mary Worth" a hundred times and hold a candle in front of your face in front of a mirror, and she's supposed to come out and scratch your eyes out. [Class laughs.]

Thus Carlos, responding to Camelia's initiation, has gradually opened up the discussion of the Mexican story to include students from other cultures.

The Reading Class: Reading and Writing about Published Ethnic Literature

In the reading class, Carlos introduced the notion of cultural univer- sals, unity in the midst of diversity, by pairing ethnic short stories for study. In the example presented here, students comment on a story by a working-class Jewish author, Tillie Olsen's "Here I Stand Ironing," and the African American writer Alice Walker's "Everyday Use," which Carlos paired because, as students came to discover, the family situa- tions in the stories are remarkably similar. The following excerpt is from a discussion in which Carlos asked students to compare and contrast the stories. As in the scene from the listening class, in which a Latino student was the first to discuss a Latino text, the initial discussion here, about Alice Walker's story, is between the instructor and the African American students—Arlene, Lisa, and Theo—whose text is being discussed, but again the instructor gradually opens up the discussion. Carlos suggests common cultural patterns and problems and the other students join in, especially as the discussion touches on family and economic issues related to Walker's story about a southern, rural African American family. The other participants include Greg, a Greek American; Snejina, who had recently immigrated from Poland; Leticia, an African American; and Kevin, of Czech descent.

CARLOS: OK, are there any other similarities either about the story, or about how it's done, or whatever? Yeah.

ARLENE: They both, you know, maybe, talk about two daughters and . . .

CARLOS: OK, good. There's two mothers and each one has two daughters. OK. Yeah?

LISA: They both have favorites.

CARLOS: OK. The mother has favorites. In the first story, there's a favorite, and who's the favorite in the first story?

STUDENTS: Susan.

CARLOS: Susan is the favorite, and the girl out of favor, is . . . Emily. Right? In this one, who is the favorite daughter? What is different about the two stories insofar as the relationship between the mothers and daughters? . . . In relation to what she just said?

THEO: Well, in this story, the mother—she favors the one that's withdrawn—

CARLOS: Yeah.

THEO: —over the one who has everything.

CARLOS: Exactly, so in this story, the mother is siding with the *poor* child, the one who has had all the problems, and the other one, she sided with the girl who had everything. OK? What other similarities do you notice? Hm?

GREG: Well, in a way, it's not like both families are rich.

CARLOS: OK. Good.

GREG: They both have problems. They grew up with problems.

CARLOS: Apparently, they all had trouble.

GREG: Right.

CARLOS: What else? Just keep . . . off the top of your head.

SNEJINA: Poor families.

CARLOS: They're both poor families. Anything else? I mean, there's bunches of similarities. Yeah?

ARLENE: I think Emily and Maggie, uh, personalities are the same.

CARLOS: OK, in what way are they the same?

LETICIA: They're both shy and to themselves, except at the end Maggie started to open up a little, but they're withdrawn.

CARLOS: Does, does Maggie ever change? Would you say Maggie ever changes? You don't think she changes? OK, we'll discuss that later.

ARLENE: Um, Emily is not as afraid of Dee, not Emily, but Maggie's not as afraid of Dee anymore. At first, she used to be afraid of her, but now she . . .

CARLOS: OK. So, there's a slight change, but it's real subtle. OK. That's good. Some more changes. I mean, there's so many and they're all important. Kevin, do you have any changes?

KEVIN: No . . . similarities because . . .

CARLOS: Excuse me.

KEVIN: Uh, we never hear from their fathers. The mothers are raising up all the children.

CARLOS: OK, so they're almost examples of single-parent families. The fathers are never around generally. It's just the mother and the two daughters. OK? What about the way in which the story is written? . . . The tone, the tense, any of those kinds of, uh, technical features.

GREG: Similar plots.

CARLOS: OK. The plot is similar.

LETICIA: Both of the stories reflect on the past and bring it to the present.

CARLOS: OK. Good. They both reflect on the past and bring it to the present. Any others? OK. Remember the tense? of the first story?

GREG: First person.

CARLOS: OK, they're both first person, and they're both in the present. OK, so that again the writer by using the present tense is trying to create a sense of immediacy, OK, by writing the first, the present tense, you feel as though you're there because every thought, every movement is reflected immediately so that it's almost as though you were part of the scene, as opposed to, you know, being separated from it by time. OK? There's a lot of similarities, and when we start discussing what happens in the story,

I think we'll touch on some of the differences. OK. So what is the setting of this particular story?

SEVERAL STUDENTS [replying at once]: A house. The South. The country.

CARLOS: OK. It's a house, in the South, it's a country setting. Anything else that you remember? How does that compare with the first story?

STUDENTS: The city.

GREG: An apartment.

CARLOS: Yeah, the other one was in the city in an apartment, so there's a difference there because we have two completely different environments. The other one was in an apartment with people downstairs and in the back, and it's crowded, and it's urban, and here we have a country setting where the nearest neighbor is God knows how far away. So there's a sense of isolation; in addition to the personal isolation, there's physical isolation. And then, we discussed point of view already in passing. They're both told from the first person, in the present tense. The mother is the "I"; it is not a third-person story. . . .

Hence Carlos emphasizes how unity exists in the midst of diversity—the stories have disparate settings (rural vs. urban) and ethnicities (African American vs. Jewish) yet similar family and economic situations and similar first-person, female points of view. The connections Carlos helped students find emphasized that attempting to treat one's own different children fairly while struggling against poverty is not necessarily race- or culture-bound. For one of the essay assignments, the students compared their family situations and their status as children or siblings with those of the children in the two stories. Their experiences resembled those of either Susan and Dee, the favored children, or Emily and Maggie, the less favored children.

But emphasizing commonalities does not mean erasing or minimizing differences, conflicts, and tensions based on race, culture, class, gender, and sexual preference. Carlos presented "Everyday Use" as an African American story by an African American author and "Here I Stand Ironing" as representative of the white working-class experience. He led a discussion of the civil rights and black power movements so that the class could understand Dee and her newly discovered black nationalism in relation to Maggie, for whom preserving her heritage is an integral part of life rather than a political statement. The discussions in both classes dealt with matters of gender, race, and class—factors that have become fighting words in the culture wars of the university and the nation—but Carlos did not browbeat, dictate, or proselytize in approaching the cultural texts and conducting the discussions.

Building Multicultural Literacy

Using differing kinds of texts and teaching modes, the listening and reading approaches help students recognize cultural differences and similarities; students get to know one another and one another's cultural backgrounds. This knowledge provides an antidote to the racial and ethnic strife that afflicts many communities and much of the world. Neither approach encourages divisiveness or a sense of victimization or entitlement, exacerbates racial tensions, or promotes "particularisms on parade" (Gates, "Weaning" 83). Neither approach fits Chester Finn's exaggerated depiction of multicultural education, in which "people fundamentally identify with their subgroup, are steeped in consciousness of the group, and are told implicitly that their group is superior because they have been a victim of other groups" (Wong). Although the classroom dialogues presented here are the beginnings of discussions that probed more deeply issues of diversity and unity, Carlos and his students attempted to meet what Cornel West calls the "political challenge . . . to articulate universality in a way that is not a mere smokescreen for someone else's particularity." West urges that "we . . . preserve the possibility of universal connection. . . . Let's dig deep enough within our heritage to make that connection to others" (331).

Students in both classes rated the approaches highly and commented in written evaluations that they learned a lot about themselves and others. One student in the listening class wrote, "We got to know each other which is something that is not used in other classes." Students said they welcomed the opportunity to learn more about their own and others' ethnic groups, an experience most of them did not have in elementary or high school. An African American student from the reading class wrote, "All my life I only read about white people and the way they see the world. This class was refreshing because it dealt with minorities. I learned a little more about my own ethnic group and I also learned a lot about the other minorities' ethnic groups." Both the listening and reading approaches created engaged writers and writing. When both classes wrote on the same topic before and after the course, the reading class using published text, the listening class using its own, three outside evaluators found no significant differences in the level of improvement in the two classes.

Although methodologically different, the listening and reading approaches both enhance students' multicultural literacy. As Rick Simonson and Scott Walker suggest in their introduction to *Multicultural Literacy: Opening the American Mind*, whose title itself responds to titles by E. D. Hirsch and Allan Bloom, "At a time when one in four Americans are people of color, none of us can afford to remain ignorant of the heritage and culture of any part of the population" (xi).

Decolonizing the Classroom: Freshman Composition in a Multicultural Setting

Esha Niyogi De and Donna Uthus Gregory

> *Whenever marginal peoples come into a historical or ethno-graphic space that has been defined by the (modern) Western imagination . . . their distinct histories quickly vanish. Swept up in a destiny dominated by the capitalist West . . . these suddenly "backward" peoples no longer invent local futures.*
> —James Clifford

While James Clifford's observation may seem remote from American classrooms, in which even immigrant students are already socialized well enough to gain college admission, we find that it illuminates two critical elements intrinsic to current debates about multicultural education. One is that Westernization seems inevitably to erase individual histories and, with them, the capacity to imagine a future in non-Western terms; the other is that students' relative distance from "the modern world" is the most salient predictor of their success or failure in Western cultural endeavors. For this modern world is constituted at its core by Western epistemic practices—that is, by supposedly superior Western ways of knowing the world and speaking about or constructing it. Having taught in the highly diverse freshman classrooms at the University of California, Los Angeles, we have seen that understanding how colonization occurs on a global level helps us better understand how it occurs in the classroom. Students whose thinking differs substantially from or lies on the margins of the epistemic practices dominant in a Western metropolitan academy are liable to be "colonized" by the theoretical methods they encounter on entering, but they are poised (often unconsciously) to resist and subvert those methods in a characteristically anticolonial way. Our readings of power

118

conflicts displayed in freshman writing have helped us formulate new pedagogies for multicultural students' needs.

Writing teachers widely recognize that culturally diverse students who succeed in the United States university do so because they have been successfully socialized into Western argumentative discourse. This socialization often occurs at the expense of students' culture-specific ways of interacting with reality (see the essays by Guerra, Soliday, and Gilyard in this volume). An emphasis on the teaching of argument tends to render multicultural students monocultural, an end few of us would celebrate. To obviate such unilateral socialization, writing teachers often turn to pedagogies that include both expressive and argumentative writing. Maxine Hairston suggests this kind of pedagogy and discusses several issues related to these concerns. She argues that the way to address multicultural students' needs is to help them "articulate and understand" their culture-specific experiences of the world; toward this goal, freshman composition teachers could have students write expressively on personal topics and argumentatively on common themes or texts. We agree with Hairston that instead of undermining students' self-confidence, values and preferences, teachers ought to empower them by enabling them to bring their "picture[s] of reality" to the classroom (190). But we are skeptical that her methods, which seem broadly typical of concerned writing teachers, can bring about that empowerment.

The means of fostering "genuine multicultural growth" that Hairston proposes (190) will fail because they do not analyze what it means to teach students to think in Western culture, in Western cultural terms. The proposals will fail whether students work with argumentative or narrative writing. Hairston's view, as well as the many others like it, ignores both what cultural anthropologists tell us about translation from other cultures and what postcolonial critics tell us about the peculiarities of Western culture. In brief, Western languages intimidate non-Western peoples and engulf their meanings, just as cultural practices dominant in Western societies tend to engulf the voices of those who are marginal and lower-class in that society. Dominant Western languages intimidate and appropriate largely because of their epistemic powers, which involve a refusal to acknowledge the rationalities of "lesser" languages.

In this paper, we first discuss how two anthropologists address colonization as a largely intellectual process by which one culture establishes and maintains unequal power relations with another. These anthropologists' discussions of how Western cultures and languages colonize non-Western ones provide a compelling model for understanding the multicultural classroom. By recognizing that students' relative mastery of Western epistemic practices mirrors this global dynamic, writing instructors can recognize how more local factors—such as whether students come from educated families, rural backgrounds, or ghettos—similarly distance students from what writing instructors consider to be competent, coherent prose. In this light, we redefine *multicultural* and show why instructors must take account of each student's relative proximity to Western epistemic discourse. Next, we describe and analyze several student papers. Finally, we offer some pedagogical strategies that resist colonizing students and that aim to let a multiplicity of student rationalities enter into dialogue with argumentative discourse.

Cultural Translation, Colonization, and Freshman Writing

Recent discussions by cultural anthropologists concerned about the ethnocentricity of Western views of rationality are relevant to debates about writing in multicultural settings. Talal Asad argues that languages are unequal in their powers to translate from other languages, in that some tend to incorporate and reinscribe the other cultures' meanings while some adapt and alter themselves to other languages. He says that "the languages of Third World Societies . . . are 'weaker' in relation to Western languages (and today, especially to English)." What this means is that the weaker languages "are more likely to submit to forcible transformation in the translation process than the other way around" (157–58). To illustrate, Asad discusses the radical transformation of modern Arabic as English and French texts are rapidly being translated into it.

In important ways, the issue turns on knowledge—on ability of Western languages to "produce and deploy *desired* knowledge more readily than Third World languages do." Societies that use "backward" or subordinate languages, such as those from the Third World, desire to consume and produce this superior knowledge and to imitate the powers the knowledge represents. But this knowledge has a price, for Western ways of knowing are enmeshed with Western economics and ideology. As Asad puts it, "Industrial capitalism transforms not only modes of production but also kinds of knowledge and styles of life . . . and with them forms of language" (158). Thus by importing knowledges and the practices that produce them, non-Western languages also incorporate other Western cultural practices, at the expense of their own. This is why the colonizing process inevitably involves a construction of subjectivity and, with it, a structuring of motive and desire: once a culture has been colonized in Western modes of productivity and exchange, a member of that culture cannot do other than try to master the "higher" culture's language, from which material powers flow.

The second anthropologist, S. P. Mohanty, draws on Asad's arguments by addressing how anthropologists read non-Western cultures. He shows how Western anthropology—and by extension, the Western intellectual enterprise—has been ethnocentric in its conception of rationality, refusing to recognize the rationality of other cultures. Anthropologists, he argues, tend to interpret other cultures' practices in Western terms. These terms reflect Western rationality—its analytic categories, evaluative schema, taxonomies, favored modes of representation, and the like: in brief, its epistemic practices.

Mohanty demonstrates how a Western intellectual makes sense of what appear to be illogical or incoherent ideas in a culture under study (7). One way is to take assertions made in the unfamiliar language out of their context, isolate them, and then analyze them according to Western analytic frameworks (9). This appropriation of another culture's meanings into one's own is what Mohanty characterizes as colonization. This colonizing, which has real political consequences, is fundamentally intellectual. It is analogous to writing teachers' asking culturally diverse students to incorporate their experiences into an appropriately structured academic argument (see Blalock in this volume).

Mohanty offers an alternative to this kind of translation: Walter Benjamin's concept of successful translation. Paraphrasing Benjamin, Mohanty says that "a successful translation of a significant text depends on our very ability to transform *our* language—i.e., our modes and habits of thoughts and action" (11; emphasis ours). That is, to avoid colonizing other people we must make our discourse and our logic more flexible. Toward this end, Mohanty wants a decolonizing anthropology, a revised set of practices that would include this flexibility, allowing for successful translation (11).

We writing instructors are in important respects like the anthropologists Mohanty criticizes. In our written and oral comments on students' drafts, we aim to elicit writing that is more coherent and logical, according to the definitions we hold as well-socialized members of academic culture. We translate and transfer, or enable the student to transfer, the incoherent sections into what we recognize as clear, coherent, logical, or appropriately academic discourse. In doing so, we encourage our students to write about their experiences and views within what we recognize to be the parameters of logic and the modes of representation. At the same time, we denigrate students' rationalities as self-expressive but not logical. When we assess only their mastery of academic logic, we further the inflexibility, or dominance, of academic English. In short, we contribute to the colonizing process or do nothing to prevent it.

When we adapt students' representations of their experiences, meanings, and knowledge to suit academic logic, we fail to supply a successful translation, in Benjamin's sense: one that leaves intact the peculiar coherence of the original utterance. One reason for this failure is our obliviousness to the "institutionally sanctioned power relations between interpreter and the interpreted"—in this case, the instructor and the student—"that determine the politics of meaning" (Mohanty 10).

A Note on *Multicultural*

Are some students more vulnerable than others to being forcibly translated into, or colonized by, academic discursive practices? We think so. Our usual ways of understanding the term *multicultural*, which generally involve race and ethnicity, are insufficient to account for the factors that contribute to a student's subordinate intellectual standing in a United States metropolitan academy. For instance, a rural white student may be further removed from university discourse than a Chinese American student whose parents are college-educated professionals. An African American male student raised in Minneapolis, son of a Presbyterian minister, could bring into the classroom a discursive framework closer to the standard academic one than could a white female art major born of New Age parents from Malibu. Likewise, a Taiwanese American woman with urban parents may have more in common with a young Ethiopian woman who grew up in Stockholm, spent three years in France and then three years in a California high school than she does with her Chinese counterpart, recently immigrated from Beijing. Moreover, none of these three students has the same relation to dominant Western epistemic practices as does a rural Vietnamese student who had received little formal education before she arrived in the United States at age eleven and encountered MTV. Finally, a Latino student who grew up in an urban ghetto will have a more distant relation to academic discourse than a Chicano who attended prep school.

A student's culture is not a single condition (or even a hyphenated one). Instead, it is a heteroglossic pastiche, a complex interplay of class; gender; geographic region; nationality; urban, suburban, or rural affiliation; and major socializing forces like popular culture, politics, and religion. All these determinants contribute to the student's relative proximity to the rigors of academic thinking and writing. Together, they determine the degree to which a student speaks and writes a language akin to the formal academic or tends to subvert that language and thus needs to be translated into it (and therefore colonized by it). A writing pedagogy that aims to decolonize the classroom must recognize in students' writings forces more complex than race and ethnicity, which increasingly are of little help. Below, we examine four papers written by four students, uncovering and analyzing how these papers disrupt and subvert their efforts to translate themselves into sound argumentative essays.

Four Student Papers

When we think about teaching in a multicultural setting, we immediately confront problems with traditional argumentative assignments. The first time Esha De taught freshman composition in a highly diverse classroom at UCLA, she was struck by two interesting patterns of interruptions in student first drafts. First, she found in argumentative responses occasional lively digressions that broke into the students' formulaic essay structures. Interestingly, she noted similar digressions in essays written by high school seniors for the University of California placement examination. Second, she found in some first drafts of more expressive essay assignments evidence of anxious efforts to make argumentative connections, efforts that inevitably interrupted the coherence of the piece. Let us look at samples of each.

One industrious student, Yeung (all student names are fictitious), handed in the first draft of an argumentative paper analyzing Theodore Sizer's view that American high school education produces mechanized minds. The assignment was highly structured; it supplied stringent guidelines for "focusing the argument and formulating a thesis statement, supporting the thesis with evidence, outlining and drafting the paper, and segmenting ideas into coherent paragraphs." The monotone of Yeung's draft and its few, superficial examples, mostly from texts the students had read in class, were interrupted by a brief, relatively impassioned excursus (totally unrelated to the point being made) extolling ambition and perseverance and pointing to their ultimate rewards in high social status. This paragraph not only conveyed a vigor that the rest of the essay lacked but also read more coherently than the other sentences. An Asian immigrant herself, De sensed the cultural underpinnings of this digression. It was no surprise to her that in a subsequent class discussion on the differing perspectives on education in different cultures, Yeung joined the other Asian students in averring that, for them and their families, education was a means to high status. The digression gave vent to the student's culture-specific response to Sizer's topic, education, when the analytical assignment had failed to do so.

While reading essays written for the University of California Subject A examination (a composition placement exam taken by about ten thousand high school seniors a year), De encountered several essays similar to Yeung's. Examinees were responding to a passage from "Home of the Free," an essay in Wendell Berry's *The Gift of Good Land*, in which Berry sharply criticizes contemporary American techno-comfort and praises the satisfactions intrinsic to physical labor, specifically, the labors necessary for life. Students had to respond to the following prompt:

> What does Berry think should give people "satisfaction"? What do you think of his views? To develop your essay, be sure to discuss specific examples drawn from your own experience, your observation of others, or of any of your reading—including, of course, "Home of the Free" itself.

Examiners looked for strength and sustainment of focus, coherence at all levels, and use of appropriate, well-developed examples—in short, the quintessential analytical argument. We describe two failing responses to this prompt, one by a European American, the other by a Southeast Asian American. The first begins to answer the question, albeit rather incoherently. But the writer progressively abandons this endeavor; as she does so, her writing grows significantly more imaginative and eloquent. The essay ends abruptly, with an aborted effort to reclaim command of the topic. The following is the full essay:

> Even though I am young and I haven't lived or experienced quite as much as Berry, I can relate to his viewpoint. I've seen many of my peers feeling really good about their test or home-

work grade, when all they really did was copy. It's just exactly what Berry says we are being satisfied with the wrong things. What better satisfaction is there than to know that we worked hard on a certain project that may have not come out quite as well as you wanted, but that you did. As I see time passing by and technology growing, I see our knowledge shrinking. I'm not saying technology is bad, but when we depend on it to do everything for us, then there is a problem. We need to know how to work with or without special help from different things or different people.

I have always seen the world as a big book. A book that leaves many unanswered questions in my mind. Questions that may seem dumb to many people, but not to me. Like for instance how can a seed become an apple tree with the right amount of water, sun, and soil. How can a wildflower grow in a desert where there is hardly any water. Sure we think we know just exactly how these plants grow, but the truth is we know only part of it. For me not knowing everything or as much as I can is a challenge. A challenge I want to satisfy. Sure sometimes we get lazy and the world seems to be a pain, but what would we do without the sun that brings the summers, or the rain that brings the beautiful flowers and trees of spring. If we just learn to work hard for ourselves and for everyone else, this world would be greater than what it is now.

From the examiner's standpoint, there is a progression from an inept logical response to the question to a digression from the topic, one replete with inappropriate examples. In the first paragraph, the writer attempts to formulate Berry's concept of satisfaction as involving hard work. In the second, she takes issue with Berry on the value of technology. For the student, however, the theme of the quest for knowledge and recognition of the hard work this requires appear to provide an underlying logical structure.

In some ways, the other examination sample is even more dramatic. The second writer, an Asian American, has greater command of the conventions of analytical writing than the first, for he does think of several conventional, though highly simplistic, examples that support his agreement with Berry. Noteworthy among them is an awkwardly worded narrative wherein the writer deplores the mechanized comfort of an airplane flight in comparison with the "satisfaction" immigrants once derived by "walking from Florida to California." Halfway through, the essay takes an unexpected turn and plunges into a parable.

Briefly, the story runs thus: a group of monks is asked to seek and name the nine billion names of God. They begin doing so with great ardor until they are interrupted by a team of scientists armed with a computer. The scientists take over the task and soon accomplish it to perfection, tabulating nine billion divine names. The story, which rambles on for a page and a half, closes with a flair of eloquence: "The computer was doing what the monks would have done in a million of years. When the last name of God was found, the scientists looked up in the sky and the stars disappeared." In moving tangentially from his wooden, albeit "logical" examples to this parable, the writer was responding with intuitive accuracy to Wendell Berry's quest for satisfaction. Once again, because of her Asian background, De recognized in this essay resonances of Buddhist and Hindu mysticism. This essay failed the test. Examiners decided that its one strong example (the parable), although compelling, was not logically elaborated and not tied in with the thesis.

When we look at expressive essays, we encounter a different kind of interruption, a sudden effort to introduce argumentative structures. This phenomenon surfaced in the work of a female Vietnamese student, Ling. Her typical argumentative paper was not only awkward (five to six paragraphs, simple sentences strung together, weak rephrasing of ideas she had encountered in class) but also ungrammatical to the point of incoherence. The two best pieces she produced were free-ranging expressive writing. The best by far, a near-lyrical piece on the sense of loss her family feels for those they left behind in Vietnam when they boarded the boat to the United States, lapsed into incoherence at least twice. Both times she was attempting to establish more traditional logical connections between her vignettes and her musings. The first two paragraphs of her essay read thus:

> After reading "Letter to My Mother" by Tran Thi Niga, I find the like story similar to the one with my mother. My mother, too, then, my mom still write to my grandfather and hoping that he would join us here one day. It is so difficult to come to the United States right now because officials have begun the repatriations. "The plight of the Vietnamese boat people are forced to return to the impoverished and politically unstable nation." My mother know that it is impossible for my grandpa to live here with us but in her heart and in ours that we, too, hoping one day he would join us here.
>
> My family have been living here for eight years. All my relatives on my dad's side are here with us. When I was a little girl, I re-

member that I was very close to my mom's side because they are good to me and my family. I am very fond of them because they are not only good to us because we are their relatives but they are also nice and kind to our who neighborhood. When my mom told me that there's a chance that I might not see them again, I was crying for days. We are Vietnamese people in plight. We has unstable life. How could I not ever see the people that I love so dearly again. Now when my mom told me that she wants my grandfather to move here and live with us, I remember I was filled with joy. They are more strict to let the boat people live here. My hope for reuniting with my grandfather are out of the question. It is an impossible dream now.

The quotation dropped into the first paragraph, which turned out to be an excerpt from the campus newspaper, was Ling's tentative attempt to support her previous assertion with explanatory evidence. It is significant that this official-sounding quotation interrupts a fairly coherent semantic sequence in the second paragraph. It is as if the conventions of logical analysis Ling were learning in the composition class were appearing as disruptive forces in her expressive writing.

These digressions—some of which move centrifugally away from the model of logical argument while others move centripetally toward it—together uncover a cleavage in the multicultural student subjectivity (see Guerra in this volume). The interruptions suggest that when students enter the "space" of academic discourse, as Clifford would put it, they encounter a hegemonic language at odds with their customary semantic moves. The conflict that results from this unequal encounter, we could say, erupts into the student texts we have been examining and unsettles their boundaries. In each instance, the student's writing tries to submit to the monologic imperative, gravitating toward voices that have already been constituted by other cultural negotiations. But the first drafts drift toward carnivalistic multiplicity instead of a monologic adherence to the structure of logical argument and analysis. What we witness, then, is Mikhail Bakhtin's polyvocal subject in conflict with the hegemony of a covertly colonial academic voice (*Dialogic Imagination* 269–300).

Foucault and the Classroom Examination

If Bakhtin helps us marshal the anthropologists' notion of intellectual hegemony to read student writing examples, Michel Foucault shows us how academic, epistemic practices "discipline" or colonize our students (just as they have colonized us). Foucault adds to our discussion of the grounds of a multicultural pedagogy the awareness that Western power is rooted in mechanisms of knowledge production that have been institutionalized in the academy. Foucault's discussion of the examination in *Discipline and Punish* (184–92) helps us theorize the role our student essays play in the larger structures of knowledge and power.

The Sizer and Berry prompts ask for a focused thesis with relevant evidence. Following Foucault, we would observe that such a prompt, the standard argumentative format, exhibits a hierarchical structure resembling a scientific taxonomy. In its simple form, the overarching claim or main point represents a generalization from particulars: it stands in a hegemonic position in relation to the other points, organizing them and giving them focus. An outline of this kind of argument, which the prompt also requests, explicitly displays the hierarchical array of relations among the main claim, the subclaims, and the evidence—the argument's taxonomy. This tendency in college English assignment expectations resembles a general tendency in Western epistemic operations. It reflects the practices inherent in most examinations: ranking and scaling, identifying the best performance, and arraying others below it (see Gleason and Hamp-Lyons in this volume).

Indeed the ranking process in the Subject A examination makes these practices very explicit. The "norming process" serves graders with stringent criteria for rating essays and elaborate procedures to ensure that the norms are maintained. Eight graders are arrayed at each of twenty tables, every table headed by a leader who checks each grader's work. The table leader reports to the room leader, who ensures uniformity from table to table. The room leader in turn is responsible to the examination supervisor. This hierarchy, with its layers of surveillance, replicates Foucault's analysis of disciplinary practices, even recalling his discussion of Jeremy Bentham's panopticon. (Ellen Quandahl discusses Foucault's relevance to writing pedagogy in detail.)

The astonishing entrenchment of hierarchies at every level of knowledge production, starting with the basic essay, indicates two things. It illustrates in simple form Asad's contention that other cultures import Western epistemic practices along with Western linguistic forms and Mohanty's depiction of how Western intellectual disciplines translate, and hence distort, the meanings of other cultures by incorporating them into our discursive practices. In addition, it shows how the writing classroom is often complicit in the web of practices by which West-

ern intellectual culture colonizes the others. When we teach traditional argumentation, then, we subject our students to Western intellectual hegemony in the fullest sense. We teach them an inflexible
language into which they in turn will ultimately incorporate the meanings of other cultures. And thus, in effect, we engulf the other culture
with them.

Pedagogy: Encountering Academic Argument

Now that we have examined some colonizing processes embedded in
our traditional writing pedagogies, what alternatives to the analytical
or argumentative assignment might we explore? If the solution, as we
suggest, does not lie in expressive writing, then where might it be?
It should lie in acknowledging our diverse students' local, culture-
specific logics, especially those that are remote from the standard discursive methods practiced in the metropolitan academies of this
country. Teachers should not be driven to interpret student first drafts,
that is, to translate them into academic prose; instead, they should
help students achieve a second-order critical perspective. Mohanty
leads us to see that students need not achieve such a critical perspective only in Western academic terms; rather, they can articulate a critical ability from within their own cultures and languages.

Teachers can enable students to exercise their own logic, bringing it
into dialogue with academic logic, by making classrooms sites of dialogic translation between academic and other modes of reasoning. We
have been able to do so in our classes using both simple and more
elaborate strategies.

In a relatively simple class exercise, we assigned students three brief
narrative fragments to read. The first described a looting incident followed by police intervention during the spring 1992 civil unrest in Los
Angeles; the second, an excerpt from an early-twentieth-century Welsh
novel, portrayed a bleak scene following a coal-mine disaster brought
on by the owners' neglect; the third, drawn from John Steinbeck's *The
Grapes of Wrath*, gave a lyrical account of an epic trek of "people in
flight [down] the migrant road" (160–61). Students identified thematic resemblances between these passages, which ranged from the
"human will to survive" to the "predatory character of capitalism."
Where some students saw solitary struggle, others saw group solidarity in the face of great odds. Next, students worked in groups to reflect
in writing and verbally on the following questions: "Why did you think
of these connections? How and why do your themes differ from those

generated by your group members?" Throughout this group work, the instructor was an active mediator and participant. During group discussions, many students tended to rationalize their responses by characterizing themselves and their ways of seeing things, leading to several uninhibited exchanges of personal memories and anecdotes. When the students finally turned to the analytic essay assignment, they were able to dip into a repository of associations and memories that contextualized and substantiated their initial rationalization of the passages.

The initial task of logically linking the passages illuminated student responses that might otherwise have been appropriated by the normalizing processes of producing a focused assignment in response to a prompt. When students began to connect words and images freely, they were actively patterning reality in a way that was meaningful to them. That is, by generating logical language from the students, the process engaged their inner voices in meaningful dialogue. Subsequent group discussions illuminated the contexts—first the particular contexts of individual students but eventually the group's broader cultural contexts—which informed the students' inner dialogues. The process legitimized the students' language and its logic (in short, the students themselves). (See Campbell and Troutman in this volume). This lesson sequence helped situate the students as subjects vis-à-vis argumentative writing and not as objects disciplined by it.

Similarly, we have used exercises that challenge students to articulate their own logic. We give them two or three short texts and ask for a response. Here are two examples of our prompts:

> 1. Think of a friend and imagine that she has read this text or that you've told her about it. Have your imaginary friend compose a rap piece describing her reactions to it. Videotape your performance of the piece (or have a friend perform it) and bring the tape to class together with the written transcript.
> 2. Draw some connections between the readings. Then make up a story linking the strands. This story could take any form you like: a parable, a ballad, a cartoon strip, a fairy tale, a letter, an e-mail message.

A more elaborate form of this question could ask students to work in groups, using the connections they draw as the basis for composing in one of the more complex forms, such as a screenplay, a sitcom, a music-video production, or a ritual.

These assignments represent the first stage of a semester-long pedagogy. Later, we ask students to analyze their productions according to typical academic criteria such as structure, topics, and relations among topics. At stage three, they compare the analyses with the original productions, addressing the following questions: How has the analysis changed the original? How has the original not been captured by the analysis? What are the different powers of the two? What gives you the greatest sense of competence to act in the world? Explain why. At this stage, the teacher enters into regular conferences with the student (or the group). Thus teachers and students prepare to be coagents in translating cultural constructions.

Both assignments described above make the students the primary translators of the texts to which they respond. A typical analytic assignment would deny them this role. Instead, it would force them to disrupt the peculiar coherence of their own culturally specific responses, displacing both their logic and their expressivity with the standard criteria of focus, development, and evidence. At the same time, the teacher would be poised to retranslate their language into the standard terms of university discourse; the teacher's translation would replicate the inflexible taxonomy of the stronger language, engulfing the student's language. The assignments formulated in this essay aim to avoid this engulfment. At the first stage, the assignments do not provide guidelines about interpretation and organization. Instead, they aim to elicit interpretation and organization from students. Only after the students have formulated their responses do the assignments expose them to standard analytic strategies. Students can then begin to deal with these strategies instrumentally; they are better prepared to use the strategies to elucidate their own logic, not restructure it.

The second, more elaborate assignment we outline above takes a step beyond the first in empowering student translators to use their own logic—something even more radical contemporary writing pedagogies do not attempt to do. Whereas the first assignment prompts students to represent the text's meaning in their terms, the second assignment requires students to produce meaning—to produce a "transformed instance of the original." It does what Asad recommends: it captures the peculiar *intentio* of the translator's putatively weak language. It does so because it enables the translator to move beyond the externally imposed logic of "representational discourse" into the realm of production and performance (Asad 159). Later, when the students retranslate their productions into standard analytic language, they are poised to mold the mechanisms of this language to their own peculiar intention—that is, to their own logic. Through this two-step process, they tend to gain control of their expressivity and of the standard mechanisms of analytic discourse.

Now the students are poised to bring the two into dialogue with— and into modification of—each other and in so doing to empower themselves to use their culturally specific logic. At this third stage, the teacher enters this dialogue. Together, student and teacher critique the relative powers of the two types of composition as culture-specific constructions, neither of which is norm or deviation, each of which has its own assumptions, coherence, and characteristic ability to empower the writer.

Through this three-step assignment, teachers help students resist colonization by academic discourse. These assignments do not subsume the expressive under the argumentative, and they provide students with the equivalent of two legitimate logics—two means of critiquing cultural productions. They help establish students as dialogic translators learning to move between their own languages and academic language without forfeiting their power of expression in either one. These students will be translators whose identities and abilities to imagine a future will not be engulfed by the stronger language of academia but will be enabled and elaborated by it.

Writing Identities: The Essence of Difference in Multicultural Classrooms

Wendy S. Hesford

> *I didn't want the white kids at my school to see me as black. I feared that they would associate me with negative images of blacks. I began to listen to white music and to dress as the white girls did. . . . I began to "talk" white, "act" white, and I even tried to disassociate myself from my culture as much as possible. . . . I strongly believe that if the curriculum was structured so that it was an Afrocentric curriculum, then black students would do just as well as their counterparts, because they will see the value in their culture.*
>
> —Nicole

> *In reading Adrienne Rich's "When We Dead Awaken," I found myself in a familiar position. Her goal in writing the essay was directed towards women, and I did not feel right reading it. The essay takes a stand in which, as I interpreted it, I was the aggressor, the one at fault. I felt responsible for the acts of men before me and felt obliged to feel guilty. At once, my response was revulsion and embarrassment, and a residue of those emotions stays with me with each rereading. Yet, I no longer feel that Rich was utilizing male readers as targets, but seeking to have them see differently.*
>
> —Gary

I begin with these two excerpts from autobiographical texts of first-year college writers because they depict some of the ways students negotiate with and against the social discourses of academe (see De and Gregory in this volume). Students write with the academic grain by using language that embodies the academy's conventions and expectations and against the grain by challenging and displacing the academy's authority through constructing disruptive subject positions and discourses. That they write with and against the grain signifies the contradictions of writing autobiography in academic settings, where more often than not teachers reward students for writing texts that preserve myths of objectivity and the impartiality of scholarship. As these students' texts suggest, autobiographical writing involves the complex negotiation of identities, which are themselves constituted by social discourse and in a constant state of struggle.

In this essay, I argue for the primacy of students' autobiographical texts in a multicultural composition curriculum and urge writing teachers to recognize the identity negotiations and interplay of social discourses articulated through the processes of writing and reading autobiography. My readings of students' texts are intended to show the complications in using autobiography in multicultural settings and to offer a way of teaching that embodies a recognition of these complications. The social-dialogic method of reading that I propose contrasts and challenges expressionist readings of autobiography. Expressionist readings, which have dominated the field of composition for some time now, assume that the personal voice can be achieved apart from the individual's participation in social-material realities. My approach to reading and teaching autobiography, which is informed by the social-dialogic theories of language outlined by Mikhail Bakhtin, C. H. Knoblauch, and others and by the postmodern feminists such as Michele Barratt, Judith Butler, Diana Fuss, and bell hooks, presumes that there is no true, private, hidden, or unchanging self or essence that writing or reading autobiography makes visible. Indeed, to construct the true self or the personal voice as lurking somewhere deep within, as expressionists do, is to ignore how discourse communities define which voices are the most personal or real (Henning 680). If we do not recognize how students must negotiate their identities in response to perceived power relations and teacher expectations, we risk dismissing the complexities and struggles involved in writing autobiography within the academy. (For additional critiques of expressionism see Berlin, "Rhetoric and Ideology"; Bernstein; Catano; John Clifford, "Subject"; Flannery; Hill; Jarratt; LeFevre; and Neel.)

I do not mean to suggest by focusing on a critique of students' constructions of readers and of themselves as writing subjects that composition teachers need not revise their curricula to include voices subsumed within or repressed by the traditional canon (one could argue that students' voices are among those marginalized). But there is danger in thinking that new content is liberating for students in and of itself—add more spices, stir, and everything will be fine. Curricular-reform initiatives in composition that are preoccupied with the integration of new material (namely, the published autobiographies of writers from diverse backgrounds) may universalize students as readers and writers and cultivate simplistic pluralist notions of voice and free expression without openly acknowledging principles of power, access, and privilege operative in the classroom (see Jamieson in this volume). Indeed, pluralistic principles often neutralize opposition and can lead to classroom practices that may actually serve as a way of regulating diversity; in simply pluralizing voices, as Elizabeth Ellsworth points out, one "loses sight of the contradicting and partial nature of all voices" (312).

The add-more-spices-and-stir approach to multicultural education also has racist connotations in that it tends to exoticize difference. If we are to take seriously the status of students as writing subjects without simply positioning them as objects in a pedagogical situation, then we have to look beyond the idea that multiculturalism is a set of plans or content to be implemented. We can improve our curricula if we also learn to focus on the discourses of our students, who have been virtually absent from most institutional conversations designed to support multiculturalism (see Miller in this volume). The interplay of social discourses in the two student excerpts above illustrates some of the ways students negotiate their identities discursively.

Nicole (all students' names are fictitious), an eighteen-year-old African American woman in my introductory writing course, wrote about her experiences at a private, predominantly white high school. The assignment Nicole responded to encouraged students to recognize the partiality of their voices and to explore how their education has been shaped by the forces of culture and history. In "Up by What Bootstraps?" Nicole constructs difference by pointing to white privilege in her high school. But as a high school student, the excerpt suggests, she attempted to conceal racial differences through accommodation. As a response to contradictory social messages (she was both an insider and an outsider at her school), she began to "talk" and "act" white. Although Nicole became part of the community because of her class privilege, as an African American woman she is alienated by the institution because of race's role in the construction of knowledge and power. Nicole exposes institutional racism and examines how the language of race expressed at the level of group consciousness can serve the voice of black liberation.

Nicole's text suggests how the language of race can function as what

Mikhail Bakhtin calls a double-voiced discourse. Bakhtin claims, "The word in language is half someone else's. It becomes 'one's own' only when the speaker populates it with his own intention, his own accent, when he [or she] appropriates the word, adapting it to his own semantic and expressive intention" (qtd. in Higginbotham 267). Nicole foregrounds the complexities denied by expressionist constructions of difference by acknowledging race as a shifting cultural sign that has historically served the voices of black oppression and black liberation. Thus, the essence of difference in Nicole's text is not a result of "natural" forces, as it is often constructed in expressionist pedagogies of autobiography, but an effect of social struggle.

The assignment that Gary, a nineteen-year-old European American, responded to encouraged students to explore their processes of interpreting Adrienne Rich's essay "When We Dead Awaken: Writing as Revision" and their positions as readers. Gary's response reveals his feelings of displacement as a reader and his preoccupation with what he interprets as Rich's positioning of the male reader. That Gary should base his response solely on an understanding of difference as "difference between," a conception that invokes sexual difference as the primary category of analysis, should come as no surprise; after all, Rich constructs difference similarly in her essay. One could argue, for example, that Rich essentializes gender difference through the construction of women as a universal and stable category. By the final paragraph, however, Gary has convinced himself that since he is not the intended audience, the best he can do is to try to put himself in Rich's shoes and "read as a woman":

> I do not delude myself into thinking that the essay was written to me; I have to make myself a part of it by restructuring my thinking toward it. . . . Many factors come into play for me in finding my natural aversion to the essay. In trying to read what she says from the point of view of a female poet, I may be able to get a sense of what she declares to be true.

Operative here is the deconstruction of readership through the simultaneous displacement and redeployment of essence. Gary deconstructs himself as a male reader by hypothesizing himself as a female reader. But what does it mean for Gary to read like a woman? Does his hypothesis allow him to forego his responsibility to consider how he is implicated in all this? Is Gary's reconstruction of himself as a female reader another kind of essentialism? Is it a response to a struggle with me because I, as a self-defined feminist, might expect him, as Rich does, to see differently? Unlike Nicole, who recognizes existing power relations and her own disempowered position and who attempts to enter the predominantly white discourse community by adjusting her language and behavior, Gary attempts to enter a feminist discourse community by erasing his historically empowered position.

Dialogism and Diversity in Composition

I turned to these two student texts (and numerous others) while revising my course Gender, Race, Class, and Language to address more adequately issues of authority and power within academic discourse communities. The class is an elective writing course cross-listed in women's studies that counts toward the Oberlin College's newly legislated cultural diversity requirement. To graduate, entering students must complete at least nine hours of course work dealing with social and cultural diversity, including courses that emphasize methods of analyzing and interpreting cultural differences. One of my primary goals in the course is to engage students in an analysis of discursive constructions of identity and difference through writing, reading, and analyzing autobiographical texts.

The curriculum includes readings that address social constructions of race, gender, ethnicity, and sexuality, including *The Woman Warrior*, by Maxine Hong Kingston, and *Yours in Struggle*, by Elly Bulkin, Minnie Bruce Pratt, and Barbara Smith. I encourage students to read the autobiographical works and the theoretical works in a number of ways. I ask them, for example, to think about their positions as readers and to consider these questions: What readerly roles does each writer seem to construct for you? How does your position as a reader manifest a partial view? How does each writer define identity and difference? Does the writer resist or challenge commonsense definitions? If so, how? Does the writer problematize the belief that one's achievements flow naturally from individual abilities? How does each writer's position recognize the way gender, race, class, and sexual orientation affect an individual's prerogatives and privileges? How does each writer frame relations among people across differences?

Early in the semester, students write autobiographical texts that concern the role of storytelling in their families and their histories as readers and writers. At the end of the semester students interrogate their constructions of themselves as autobiographical (negotiated) subjects, by examining how they negotiate their identities as writing subjects in earlier pieces. I invite students to use their writing as data, to use course readings as theoretical and methodological filters, and to consider questions such as the following: How are gender, race, class, ethnicity, or sexuality embodied in your writing? Did you construct difference as difference between men and women or between whites and blacks? If your construction of difference is not predicated on such binarisms, how would you define it? Each time students reread their autobiographical texts or reflect on their process of writing them, they engage to some degree in the reexamination of the autobiographical self or selves. In short, critically reflexive texts enable students to investigate the social forces that shape their personal voices, and they further the possibility that experience is open to contradictory and conflicting interpretations. In fact, from these student biographies and reflections, I have learned that students move quite readily among contradictory social discourses and subject positions and in so doing complicate expressionist notions about unified selfhood. One way they do so is by constructing autobiographical works of multivoiced elements that can be read as "historically or imaginatively [situated] in a field of other persons' utterances" (Don Bialostosky, qtd. in Clark 16).

Bakhtin's concept of dialogism helps us understand the interplay of social struggles and discourses invoked by autobiographical transactions in the multicultural classroom. According to Bakhtin, "meaning is formed in a dialogically agitated and tension-filled environment . . . where competing ideologies, languages and values are operative" (*Marxism* 276). Although composition teachers often want to achieve a unitary literary discourse (which serves to shelter some cultural groups from the full force of dialogism and to repress the perspectives of many unofficial discourses), multicultural education is about teaching students how to investigate those official and unofficial discourses and the power relations they enact. Multicultural literacy is not about initiating students into the logic of dominant discourses or simply celebrating a diversity of voices, as some recent multicultural composition textbooks imply (McLaren). Writing pedagogies designed to promote multicultural literacy should not be based on appeals to an uncritical mass of differences. Rather, they should seek to enable students to recognize the limits of their self-positionings and worldviews, to practice critical citizenship, and to develop critical awareness of the power of discourse instead of being subsumed by it (Giroux, *Border Crossings*).

To meet these goals, teachers of writing across the curriculum need to focus on how language shapes identity and knowledge. It is particularly important that the pedagogical process enable students to explore the self as a discursive and cultural construct in courses that rely on autobiographical experiences. But "to be constituted by discourse" is not, as Judith Butler observes, "to be determined by discourse, where determination forecloses the possibility of agency" (143). The writing subject in all his or her multiplicity can construct subject positions, however transitory, that can subvert, diffuse, or dislocate individualist concepts of selfhood and dominant forms of social discourse. Although postmodern feminist perspectives, which foreground relations between the discursive and the material and recognize the fracturing of identity in the writings of the disempowered, have emerged in composition, pedagogies of autobiography are steeped in expressionist rhetoric. For example, relying on the bifurcation of expressive and social discourse, the former associated with the feminine and the latter the masculine, a number of feminist scholars have created pedagogies predicated on assumed differences between the discourses of men and women. (See Caywood and Overing; Flynn; and Tedesco for early examples of difference-between pedagogies of autobiography.) While I do not deny their work's importance in contesting patriarchal views of teaching and in legitimizing autobiographical discourse, I want to suggest that a gynocentric counterpedagogy that simply shifts the terms of engagement and alliance cannot meet the objectives of multicultural education in the 1990s. A countermodel that privileges gender differences over other differences will misrepresent the complexity of autobiographical transactions between writers and readers in the multicultural classroom. (See Bernstein; Dingwaney and Needham; Jarratt; and Ritchie, "Confronting," for extensive critiques of appropriations of expressionism in feminist composition.)

I am not suggesting that we abandon gender as an identity category; I do say that we understand identity categories and concepts of difference as culturally, politically, and pedagogically shifting. We do not have to assume that the category "women" has a natural composition. As Fuss observes, it can be understood as a sign that is "historically contingent and constantly subject to change and to redefinition" (20). Identity can be understood as "a story, a history. Something constructed, told, spoken, not simply found" (Stuart Hall, qtd. in Giroux, *Border Crossings* 128). Even though a writer might construct the self as moving from one stage of development to another, she or he is not passively transmitting an earlier self but rather constituting it in language. The autobiographical writing process can be construed, then, as intrinsically dialogic, and the autobiographical subject can be read as always already in the process of becoming. I call for a multicultural pedagogy that focuses primarily on social aspects of language and identity construction to expose the inequalities that disempower and marginalize writers and to build classroom communities that enable students to construct positions of resistance.

The Politics of Difference and Essence in Pedagogical Terms

To formulate a pedagogy of autobiography that meets the needs of multicultural education, we must openly acknowledge essentializing practices. For instance, we must recognize how when used strategically essentialism can function as a form of resistance and how when it is used from dominant positions it can disguise differences and privilege certain identities. Feminists have long wrestled with the politics and interplay of essence and difference. Fuss, for example, puts forth a theory about the essence of difference that attempts to give agency to individuals at the same time it places them within discursive configurations. Like a number of postmodernist feminists, Fuss argues against a naive essentialism—an appeal to pure or original femininity that universalizes women's experience—and instead constructs essence as an effect of discursive practices and cultural systems of representation. Fuss does not counter essentialism so much as displace it. She recognizes that the disempowered in particular "need both to theorize essentialist spaces from which to speak and, simultaneously, to deconstruct these spaces to keep them from solidifying." "Such a double gesture," Fuss continues, involves "the responsibility to historicize, to examine each deployment of essence, . . . each claim to identity in the complicated contextual frame in which it is made" (118).

While Fuss recognizes, theoretically at least, the double discourse of essentialism, she has been criticized from a pedagogical standpoint for using marginalized voices to expose the negative effects of essentialism in the classroom. Fuss claims that essentialism can silence students when, for example, some students claim that only women can speak for the feminine experience. When used in this way, she argues, essence circulates as a privileged signifier that often depoliticizes oppressions, blinds students to other modes of difference, provokes confusion, and dead-ends class discussions (116–17). In "Essentialism and Experience" hooks criticizes Fuss for constructing the marginalized other as the essentialist and not sufficiently addressing how systems of domination are already in place in classrooms, namely, how teachers and students espouse expressions and critiques of essentialism from locations of privilege. hooks's response to Fuss raises important pedagogical questions: How is essentialism expressed from locations of privilege in multicultural settings? How is the other constructed? How is essentialism put to use strategically by marginalized groups? How do students conceal, display, or displace essentializing practices?

I have noticed that students newly introduced to feminist concepts or multicultural curricula are often enthusiastic essentialists (Gayatri Spivak makes a similar claim [Spivak and Rooney]) and often appear to shift from narrow-fixed essentialist positions to strategic essentialist positions as the semester moves on (as Joy Ritchie argues ["Confronting"]). However, I have also observed that these are not clear-cut developmental shifts. Any given expression of identity or essence may be embedded within a variety of conflicting subject positions and discourses. Thus I am less interested here in tracking developmental shifts than in interrogating the interlacing subject positions and essences negotiated within particular student texts. While some postmodern feminists might claim that my invocation of the concept of essence is itself a political-pedagogical faux pas because of the term's strong associations with expressivist views of identity, I believe that composition teachers need to explore the uses and limits of essentialism through its contradictory, strategic, and ironic positions within language. Indeed, I argue that the autobiographical subject cannot be written as a fundamental essence (text equals body); it can only be written as a strategic positioning.

With these theoretical concerns as a descriptive device and the above pedagogical questions as guidance, I turn to the autobiographical texts of three college students. My analysis of these texts is intended to further alliances between postmodern feminist theories of identity and a social-dialogic practice of reading and teaching autobiography, not to provide a universalized or prescriptive pedagogy. Although my examples come from three first-year women of color, my intent is not to enforce a gynocentric difference-between pedagogy or to advocate that students of color be placed in the roles of representative educators of difference. Nor do I mean to suggest that critiques of essentialism should be explored only in relation to women's writing, for as my opening analysis suggests, discourses of essence certainly interpolate the texts of college men. I focus on these three texts because they are compelling responses to some of the pedagogical questions raised earlier and because they clearly demonstrate that the student positioned as the marginalized other and newly introduced to a feminist multicultural curriculum does not necessarily construct a naive essentialist (or expressionist) position. In contrast to Fuss's pedagogical observations, I have found that invoking autobiographical experiences can lead to productive class discussions if students critique concepts of identity and difference and the relation between these concepts and material realities.

Autobiography and the Language of Location

Students investigated the ways in which identities and differences are negotiated and produced in their everyday lives on campus for a unit I called The Politics of Location and Experience. Before writing an essay, students read Ruth Perry's "A Short History of the Term *Politically Correct*" and other essays on the politics of language. Maria, an eighteen-year-old student from Puerto Rico, wrote about the essentializing practices of political correctness that she saw permeating certain discourse communities on campus. Maria considered the conditions under which she first heard the term *PC language* and whether her understanding of it had changed since then. She also examined who enforces politically correct language at the college and explored its effects on her and the community. The title of her essay, "Here I Stand" (which invokes the political oratory of Martin Luther King, Jr.), affirms Fuss's observation and Spivak's claim that the "clearing of a subject-position in order to speak or write is unavoidable" (qtd. in Fuss 32). This clearing does not, however, result in the construction of a fixed self but rather provides a context for the textual staging of the negotiation of several subject positions. In fact, Maria's essay prompted me to discuss with students the strategic use of essentialism and can now illustrate ways in which students stage essences and negotiate differences in their autobiographical texts.

"Here I Stand": The Staging of Essence

Early in her narrative, Maria writes about how essentializing practices of political correctness contribute to the censoring of her voice and simultaneously alienate her from her peers and her culture:

> I have lived quietly these past few months at [college] standing silently in a corner, absorbing, listening, admiring yet not being able to speak. . . .
> "Maria, your culture is so oppressive."

> "Why do you wear make-up? Men don't. . . ."
>
> "Don't say freshman."
>
> "I feel sorry for your sister. Why did she have to stop working when she gave birth to the baby? Why didn't her husband stop working instead of her? So disgusting, such a backward country. I feel pity for the women." I didn't have the courage to respond and defend my Puerto Rican pride, my own culture, my own self. Now I want to stand up and do more than just listen. I want to scream and make everyone realize that I am not an ignorant marionette sitting in a corner. I want them to hear what I've got to say and understand for once that my ideas are as important as their own. . . . Do they have any idea about how they make me feel, of the times I cry myself to sleep thinking of the ways to make myself less ignorant, less Puerto Rican, more like them? . . . How could I be expected to rebuild all that which I have been constructing all my life. I don't want to change at this point in my life where I need my true self more than ever. I need it for courage, strength, and assurance and for everything they try to take away from me.

In this passage, Maria reports having been subjected to essentializing assumptions that include the construction of Puerto Rico as a "backward country," and preemptory assumptions about gender relations. One of her first responses to this criticism is a desire to assimilate. But later she replies to the essentializing practices of others by essentializing herself; instead of undermining the concept of essence, she uses it to her benefit.

> Now I sit here and contemplate my thoughts once more. . . . I feel stronger and with all I've got at this moment I break the strings which held me down to that infernal corner. I move away from it and declare myself free. I wont let anyone ridicule, ignore or shush me anymore. . . . I won't feel pressured or suffocated anymore for I am going to take control of my life. Now, tell me, with all I've got, "Ain't I a woman!"

By appropriating the words "Ain't I a Woman?" from the title of Sojourner Truth's speech at a women's rights convention in Akron, Ohio, in 1851, Maria, in some sense, essentializes her own experience as a woman of color. Even though her use of Truth's language partially erases difference among women of color, she draws from a speech that revealed how whiteness hides its partiality, exposed the racialized configuration of gender, and subverted the essentializing practices of white middle-class feminists who universalized women's needs on the basis of their own experience.

Maria does not invoke the Black English Vernacular of Truth's speech as recorded by Frances Gage (the version that the class read), which would further subvert this universalization by exposing sociolinguistic differences. But by situating her words historically in the field of Truth's utterance, Maria implicitly invokes the double discourse of essentializing practices. That essentializing practices, when expressed from locations of privilege, can serve not as a silencing force but as a strategic response to domination suggests that the double discourse of essentialism lies in recognition of the motivation behind its invocation (Spivak and Rooney). Truth's language functions for Maria as an enabling constraint: as internally persuasive discourse, it is "'open' in each of the new contexts that dialogize it, [and thus] this discourse is able to reveal ever newer *ways to mean*." This is true, of course, for all the voices invoked in this article: none are static; all shift as they "enter into interanimating relationships with new contexts" (Bakhtin, *Dialogic Imagination*, 345–46). On the one hand, we could read Maria's textual staging of essence as a strategic response and position of resistance. On the other hand, we could also read it as an act of appropriation that decontextualizes the original intent of Truth's words. Either way, Maria's text reveals how essence, difference, and agency are situated in particular historical and discursive contexts.

"A Change in My Textual Voice": The Autobiographer as Agent

Angela, an eighteen-year-old African American woman, uses race and gender as analytical categories in her autobiographical essay "A Change in My Textual Voice." She examines the shifts and nuances of her academic voice, focusing on a paper of hers about Charlotte Perkins Gilman's "The Yellow Wallpaper," written for another English class, in which she reiterated her professor's interpretation instead of developing her own. The professor, a white male, assigned her to critique "The Yellow Wallpaper" using a psychoanalytic approach—a discourse with which she did not feel comfortable. Her professor's interpretation, as she represented it, positioned Gilman's nameless narrator as a passive victim and the "woman" in the wallpaper as Freud's internal partner or thought monitor. But Angela instead inscribed the narrator herself as agent and the woman in the wallpaper as a victim:

> My professor believed that the narrator wanted so bad to get out of the room that she began to believe that the "woman" in the wallpaper was there to help her, not hurt her. But I thought the "woman" in the wallpaper represented her desperateness to escape. By helping the trapped "woman" get out of the wallpaper she would be helping herself escape.

The subtle transfer of agency here is important, for the woman in the wallpaper is now read as an expression of the entrapment of the narrator in a male "text," not as a projection of the narrator's madness or the internalized other. The following passage further displays Angela's awareness of the consequences of men's control of textuality:

> It bothers me that we live in a male dominating world, not only that they're males . . . but white males. . . . I'm not a feminist or a world renowned writer, but I shouldn't have to censor my writing to get by. Because voicing our opinion threatens the power that men have over us . . . we can not go outside the realm of expected "womanness." . . . Writing to please someone else not only hinders your writing in terms of style, language and creativity, but it also destroys your self-esteem.

The irony, of course, is that even though Angela did not manage to read against her professor's text in her English paper, she now places him as antagonist in her own text. Writing her autobiography is an act of resistance.

Later in the piece, Angela broadens her analysis of her reading and writing situation: "These views that men have about how women should write are not only expected from male audiences, but trickle down to the expectations of female audiences." Consequently, she continues, "writing for female audiences becomes just as hard as writing for male audiences because the expectations are the same but for different reasons." For Angela to write with authority she must not only construct a stance oppositional to white men but also, because of asymmetrical race relations in the classroom and educational institutions, deliberately negotiate her relation to other white women. How then am I, a thirty-five-year-old, middle-class, Anglo-American woman, implicated in Angela's construction of otherness? The same question can be asked in connection with all my students' texts: Is my identity (in, e.g., racial identity, age, class, or gender) an enabling constraint? How am I constructed as a reader of texts? Am I perceived as a trustworthy audience?

My position as a reader shifts from writer to writer, from text to text. Like the students in the class, I am not free of internalized oppressions and social discourses about race and gender. Not only must I continually reflect on internalized discourses, but I must also realize that pedagogically I can function as an enabling reader who bears witness to a writer's struggle. I can serve as a point of counteridentification, or I can function entirely as a constraint. In my class, Angela struggled to negotiate her identity as a writer against the grain of both dominant and subdominant discourses appropriated by the other (that is, me, as well as other white women in academia). She is forced to be other to those who are others themselves, or as Michelle Wallace would put it, she is "the 'other' of the 'other' in public discourse" (53). This situation is complicated, of course, by the fact that writers are always made other to themselves through writing. It is the simultaneity of her struggles with the hegemonies of dominant and subdominant discourses, however, that characterizes the identity negotiations and dialogism of her autobiography. (See Henderson for more on the dialogics of black literary traditions.)

"Another Look at My Faith": Strategies in Context

Students of color often utilize the categories of gender, race, and ethnicity in their analyses of their struggles as writers; white students less readily address their whiteness as a contributing factor. But rarely do any students seem consciously to take on the category of class. Many of the students at Oberlin College, where I used to teach, are from upper middle-class families, yet they tend to identify themselves as middle-class, which, of course, leaves certain assumptions about class and culture unchallenged. Constructs common to upper- and middle-class experiences and ideology do surface, however, in their writing. Many students construct the private and the public as two distinctly different spheres. These constructs are also complicated by cultural differences.

A nineteen-year-old Chinese Malaysian student named Kim, for example, at the onset of the semester expressed difficulty with the autobiographical focus of the course. She said that because she came "from a culture that clearly distinguishes the private and public," she felt uncomfortable revealing such "personal material [to] outsiders, least of all strangers in a classroom." She continued, "Perhaps part of my reluctance is also due to the view that I have of a classroom—a formal setting where 'academic' knowledge is passed on from teacher to student." These excerpts not only reveal how cultural ideology structures students' assumptions about autobiography but also suggest some of the tensions inherent in using autobiography in multicultural settings.

First of all, the excerpts suggest that even well-intended pedagogical practices may silence and alienate some students while privileging others and that appeals to identity and to its way of shaping social discourse are not universally favored critical acts. In short, autobiography cannot simply be exported from one cultural or institutional context to another. In multicultural classrooms, we must be careful not to become imperialists in search of universalizing practices. Rather we should acknowledge struggles with and differences within the pedagogical situation itself. At the same time that Kim reinscribes a private-public dichotomy, she also complicates expressionists' long standing claims for authenticity in the genre when she suggests that to participate she will have to invent herself, to engage in what some postmodernists have termed the inevitability of fiction in writing the self (see S. Smith).

Kim decided to stay in the course though she was "not sure what would come out of it" and though she knew that writing autobiographies would probably make her "feel sad [and] homesick," as she had felt during her first year of college. A central theme of Kim's work was mediating her "dual identity." Her writing for the entire semester focused on competing languages and discourse communities in her life—she speaks English and Malay fluently and can converse in several Chinese dialects. In her final paper, "Another Look at My Faith" (an assignment that the students themselves designed), she experiments with dialogism in ways that challenge the conventional linear, reflective, and progressive autobiographical form. Tensions among discursive postures emerge from the beginning. These postures include the persona of the reflective autobiographer; the autobiographer as poet speaking to God; the "official" language of religion, appropriated by the writer; and the writer's unconventional presence, which serves as a disrupting force. In the following excerpt, Kim disrupts her prior unconditional allegiance to the authoritative language of patriarchal religion by positioning a section of I Corinthians among contradictory voices:

> The church elders gave us a simplified version. They said that when we gather to worship, the angels are looking down from

heaven on us. How can we show them that the glory of God, man, is equal to the glory of man, woman? As such women in church have to cover their heads; it is <u>because of the angels</u> and not because we are not equal to men. But notice the language used, <u>man did not come from, but woman from man; neither was man created for woman but woman for man</u> . . . <u>the woman ought to have a sight of authority over her head</u>. All these verses insinuate that the woman can only find fulfillment in a man, because she is <u>created for him</u>. She is also to be submissive and subservient to him as he <u>has authority over her</u>. Her relationship to God is second rated as she is only the <u>glory of man</u> and not the <u>glory of God</u>. Also, she has to direct her questions to her husband (indicating that she has to have one) and not to God as she cannot speak directly to him while in church. She has no voice in church.

The juxtaposition of these discourses traverses the scripture's insistence that the word not be taken in vain. Kim plays with the borders of this authoritative language by using different frames and contextualizations, breaking it apart and using typographic cues such as bold underlining to objectify it even further. Here the conscious embedding of narrative utterance—the interfacing of official and unofficial discourses—establishes the writer's authority and agency.

Another central feature of Kim's autobiography is its critique of the totality of cultural metanarratives, namely the common representation of Asian women as silent and docile. Kim battles for female subjectivity by confronting this stereotype and creating a position of resistance within a culturally specific context, namely, the church. Kim constructs herself as a moving site of opposition and contestation and situates her textual self within, alongside, and against oppressive and totalizing social practices. In the following passage, she directly challenges the Orientalist ideology and the authoritarianism of patriarchal religious discourse, both of which reduce Asian women to an idealized essence:

> I forgot to bring my veil to church today. I refused to wear my veil in church today. I feel scared, I know that I'm going to get into trouble, especially since I am a group leader. I can feel them watching me—"she has been Americanized." My head feels so bare. . . . It feels good to stand before God. I was right, here comes Mr. Daniel. ". . . as a youth leader you should be setting the example for the younger ones. . . ." I am.

For Kim, as for all the students discussed here, authority and agency lie in the movement among institutionalized, unsettling subject positions, in the subversion and diffusion of hegemonic forms of social discourse, and in the construction of positions of resistance—which, however transitory, are "strategies in context" (Ellsworth 317).

If differences are situated within particular social and discursive configurations, then writing identities in the multicultural classroom is not about finding a true essence or writing a real self; it is about recognizing that these autobiographical essences and selves do not originate with the subject alone. Instead, as Norma Alarcon suggests, these voicings of the self can be seen as social "discourses that traverse consciousness and which the subject must struggle with constantly" (365).

Autobiography, if framed dialogically, can help students and teachers address diversity in ways that do not merely celebrate or appropriate differences but that recognize each student's complex identity negotiations and discursive positions. It is precisely the embedding of multiple social discourses and interlacing subject positions that make autobiography so promising a catalyst for multicultural literacy, especially if students are brought into the process of critique. If students become engaged in a social-dialogic analysis of their autobiographical texts, they too can begin to discover "mutual implication," that is, the relations "between the self and the cultural heritage within which selfhood has meaning" (Spellmeyer, "Common Ground" 269). To make such reflexive acts and exchanges part of the multicultural classroom is to enable students and, I hope, teachers to recognize how they locate themselves discursively and to help them participate more critically in the exchanges that determine and maintain these locations.

NOTE

Many people have helped me think through this project. First, I would like to thank my students for all they have taught me. Second, I need to thank my feminist writing group, namely, Ann Cooper Albright, Sibelan Forrester, Camile Guerin-Gonzales, Wendy Kozol, and Yopie Prins. I would also like to thank Matthew Cariello and the editors for suggestions during this essay's final stages.

Composition Readers and the Construction of Identity

Sandra Jamieson

As our composition classes and teaching loads have continued to grow, textbook readers have become the most popular tools for teaching advanced literacy skills. These collections, which present essays and fiction within frameworks of explanatory text and assignments, are designed to teach classes practically by themselves, providing teachers with what appears to be a wide choice of material and allowing students to read additional essays at home if they wish. While some teachers use supplementary readings or use the anthologies for only part of their courses, many others depend on the readers to structure their courses and to provide most of the readings and assignments. The anthologies are therefore continually being published, and new types appear every five years or so in response to movements in the field, such as the spread of the process approach and of writing across the curriculum (WAC). The increasing centrality of readers in writing programs and courses since the mid-1970s has led some scholars to consider their content and message, much as Richard Ohmann did for rhetorics two decades ago. Kristine Hansen has found that many essays in WAC texts are not drawn from across the disciplines at all, and Nancy Shapiro has critiqued readers' emphasis on narrative prose. A more insidious problem is the image presented in readers of who writes and what they write about and the potential effects this image has on our students. Many teachers have criticized traditional readers for lacking serious essays by women and people of color and emphasizing "classics" such as George Orwell's "Shooting an Elephant" and Bruce Catton's "Grant and Lee" (which are among the pieces in the textbook canon that Robert Perrin has identified).

Initiatives such as the Conference on College Composition and Communication's 1989 resolution supporting a "policy that represents the inclusion of women and people of color in the curriculum at all levels" have encouraged a revision of the material in what I call traditional readers and the development and adoption of the multicultural reader ("CCCC Secretary's Report," 365). To a great extent, composition texts now reflect the makeup of our classes, providing the female role models that feminist writers such as Elaine Showalter and Joanna Russ have long called for and the positive role models for people of color that James Baldwin recommended in 1963. Although most readers since the 1960s have been somewhat multicultural, more recently they have begun to emphasize multiculturalism. Traditional readers, such as *Patterns of Exposition* (Decker) and *Norton Reader* (Eastman et al.), have incorporated more pieces by men and women of color and white women, creating an alternative canon of writings "from the margins." Publicity materials proclaim the numerical increases but stress that the structure and principles of the collections remain unchanged (see Jamieson, Rev. of the *Norton Reader*). The apparently more radical response has been the birth of multicultural readers, with titles like *Rereading America, Intercultural Journeys through Reading and Writing*, and *Emerging Voices: A Cross Cultural Reader*, organized by theme rather than rhetorical strategy (although frequently indexed under rhetorical categories also) and featuring what prefaces describe as "a wide spectrum of writers" designed to "educate" their readers from the "mainstream" and "empower" readers from the margins. For all their differences, though, these readers share many characteristics and problems with their forebears.

Most modern textbook readers, whatever their format, reflect the work of composition and education scholars who emphasize the importance of providing models for students. They also draw on scholarship developed from the work of Paulo Friere, which demonstrates that when students feel they have a stake in the issues they read about, they become more engaged and show more involvement with and effort on writing assignments. Thus the collections feature more readings about personal identity, a strategy intended to unite both trends by focusing on an issue that most students care a great deal about (identity) and providing model writers for them to identify with as they practice the personal essay. Many composition teachers find this approach appealing because of our egalitarian tendency to try to compensate for all the omissions of the modern academy in our composition classes, perhaps thus challenging the social hierarchies that cause students to be differently skilled as writers in the first place. Whether we are committed to the politics of diversity or simply want texts our students will enjoy, multicultural texts seem to make sense.

In this essay I examine the unexpected and unintended result of the education these texts provide: the beliefs and attitudes they teach along with reading and writing skills. I do not intend to single out specific texts as good or bad; the examples I use could have been drawn from many readers on the market, and I do not recommend one over another. Instead, I recommend careful analysis of any reader under consideration or in use. My purpose is to explain why I consider that analysis important, to suggest what requires particular attention, and to propose some pedagogical strategies to counter problems in writing texts. I hope that my questions will create openings for more questions and that my descriptions of the problems will alert teachers in mono- and multicultural classrooms to other potential problems, both local and general. Then we can each begin to generate questions and solutions appropriate to our own teaching environments.

Models of Writers and Writing

To fully explore the ways these texts empower—or fail to empower— we must first consider the larger role of language in our sense of who we are and in the ways we represent ourselves and others. As David Bartholomae has argued, students must invent an academic audience before they can write for it because they don't yet know who it is or how to join its conversations ("Inventing" [1986]). They must also *rein*vent themselves as writers who have something to say to that audience and a voice in which to say it. Readers are crucial in this process of reinvention because they provide students with models of writers and writing. Such models are especially important for students who have been taught to formulate less ambitious life goals; without more ambitious goals, they cannot be expected to hold the higher-order writing goals described by cognitive development theorists. Students who don't believe they have places in higher education cannot insert their written voices into the academic discourse community or represent their thought as valid. So our task as writing teachers would seem to be to help our students learn to reinvent themselves first as the academic writers they need to be to write for the academy and later as the business, technical, or professional writers they may become. This, then, is also the first task of readers.

If writing is connected with one's sense of self, students' writing processes begin long before they enter college, at the moment when they first begin to think of themselves as writers—or not writers, in many cases. Regardless of writing ability, they must retrace their steps to that moment if they are to become more effective writers. They must understand how they came to think of themselves as writers if they are to learn how to overcome their writing blocks and error patterns and modify their concept of what it means to write for their new scholarly audience. If they are to learn writing as a recursive process, they must also understand how they came to think of themselves as readers so that they can learn to reread and edit their writing effectively. And reading assignments can help, as proponents of multiculturalism and personal narrative essays attest.

However, there are many dangers here. If we become consciously involved with our students' sense of themselves, we risk influencing those senses negatively because of our beliefs and prejudices. I. Hashimoto warns us that much pedagogy tends to construct our students as failed writers so that we can "save them" (72), but this is probably the most obvious criticism, and once it has been pointed out we can easily see how it forces students to occupy the position of failed writers in relation to the academy and to their writing classes before they can learn. And we have all seen students who never lose that sense of themselves. Judith Butler's analysis of the feminist movement in *Gender Trouble* and Shelby Steele's analysis of African Americans' inheritance from the civil rights movement in *The Content of Our Character* warn of similar dangers. Although Steele's argument is flawed by, among other things, his emphasis on the individual and his failure to consider the role of ideology, his discussion of the limitations of constructing oneself as a failure or a victim is powerful. Steele asserts that for African Americans to claim the victories won by the civil rights movement, they must embrace the notion of themselves as "the victims" (14) and represent themselves as such to whites, who were reconstructed in that era as "the guilty" (8). Steele argues that such a polarity prevents any real progress because members of each group must remain in their preassigned roles to achieve anything, but the victim role necessarily limits the achievements of African Americans. Butler gives a more theoretically sophisticated argument but makes a similar point. She draws on Michel Foucault's analysis of the juridical process and the subject it creates "before the law" to explain how feminism has had to create a "universal" woman in order to be her representative (2, 4). Like the universal black "victims" on which claims of racial entitlement are based according to Steele, feminism's "woman" must reconstruct herself primarily as a victim of a universal patriarchy— despite her race, creed, or nationality. Doing so has won her certain rights and freedoms, but at the expense of her larger freedom to define herself. By constructing "woman" within the terms of the old binary structure responsible for the very hierarchy that oppresses her, feminism has inevitably mystified that structure and prevented analysis of so-called Third World women in terms other than those of the West or analysis of women of color in terms other than those of the predominantly white, middle-class "woman" of modern feminism.

As we intervene in our students' struggle to represent a self, we must be careful to avoid such limiting images. When we select what we consider to be representative models for our students, we must beware that we do not determine their suitability on the basis of subtle stereotypes. This is much easier to say than to do, as examination of contemporary readers reveals. In the rush to produce multicultural and more representative texts or in response to the publisher's economic imperative to appeal to the widest possible market, many textbook writers have paid insufficient attention to the images these new inclusive "models" represent, to the importance of their messages, and to the effect of their contexts. More important, these textbook writers also seem to ignore the complexity of identity construction and the role of language and ideology in that process. Because most readers are produced by composition theorists and experienced teachers, few of us question their choice of readings or ask whether the models they provide are equally empowering for all students. I contend that the inclusions and juxtapositions of these texts help create student writers who are differently skilled according to race, nationality, and gender and that if teachers do not actively intervene in the identity construction that composition textbooks unwittingly perpetuate, we will undermine whatever liberatory pedagogy prompted us to adopt these books and whatever politics encouraged us to rethink the issues of race and culture in the first place. I hope my examination of the writings and writers modeled in a variety of textbooks will help us develop teaching materials that will be equally beneficial for all our students.

Ideology and Writing

The first question we need to consider is, What kinds of essays are most frequently included in composition readers, and what role do these essays play in our students' reinvention and representation of themselves? Nancy Shapiro's 1991 review essay on readers answers the first part of that question. Shapiro found that the overwhelming majority of the pieces in readers—even most so-called WAC readers—are personal narratives rather than the various forms of academic writing that students will be asked to produce for other classes. As I observe above, personal narratives seem to meet the needs of a multicultural curriculum by allowing students to interact with the experiences of cultural "others" and encouraging a student-centered pedagogy through which the students learn to value their own knowledge and feel validated by the university that has asked them to write about themselves. But the effect of personal narratives runs deeper than that. The power of the personal narrative is its realism; a successful personal narrative engages its readers in a one-to-one correspondence with the narrator. We visualize what the narrator saw and feel what the narrator felt. What better way to help our students enter a multicultural world?

Louis Althusser's analysis of the role of realistic literature in transmitting ideology and reinforcing social hierarchy should give us pause, though. His discussion of ideology provides us with valuable tools with which to analyze readers and their effects on our students. Althusser asserts that social systems are maintained through two structures: the "Repressive State Apparatus" and the "Ideological State Apparatus" (ISA). The former is the overt system of control achieved through such organs as the military and the police, which clearly serve the interests of the dominant group (143–47). The ISA achieves a more complex and subtle form of social control through ideology, which we can define as a system of beliefs and assumptions about how and why things are. Because schools, the media, the legal profession, government, and so on are run by people with the same kind of education (which was designed by and for the dominant class and hasn't changed its basic values even if it has changed its pedagogy), they tend to teach the same beliefs and assumptions, which are then reinforced by everything from self-help books and religion to everyday conversations. This dominant ideology ranges from beliefs such as that democracy is good and that the family is important to acceptance of the notions of reward and punishment and the image of the individual. It rests on notions of hierarchy—that some things are better, more valuable, or more important than others and that everyone is qualified to make that determination. Dominant ideology thus reinforces the social hierarchy originally established by the Repressive State Apparatuses by teaching us to accept that hierarchy and our roles in it (it teaches us, for example, that if we are college-educated, we deserve higher-status jobs than those who did not finish high school; if we can write, we can contribute more to society than those who are illiterate; if we have stable incomes, own houses, and belong to nuclear families,

we will be better parents; and so on). Ideology thus shapes our beliefs and values and prepares us to accept our role in a hierarchical
(classed) society.

Althusser asserts that ideology is both "real" and "imaginary." Because most of our decisions and experiences are grounded in the beliefs, images, and social structures of the dominant ideology, that
ideology feels "real," causing us to imagine that it reflects rather than
shapes reality. To work effectively, then, the dominant ideology ("the
system of . . . ideas and representations" of the group that dominates
society and controls the Repressive State Apparatus—however indirect that control may seem) must continually reinforce this imaginary
side (158). If it does not, people might begin to question the status quo
and their own positions in the social hierarchy. Dominant ideology
serves this function in our classrooms, for example, through the
widely accepted idea that Standard English (the dialect of the dominant social group in America) is better than other dialects and that
those who use it are more educated or intelligent.

Realistic literature, especially descriptive and narrative prose, plays
an important role in the work of the ISA by helping to shape what we
perceive as "real" and making it seem so "natural" that we act accordingly and thus help reinforce the "imaginary representations" of social
relationships in others (164–65). Personal narratives epitomize this
function because they encourage us not to question their "truth," or
doubt the coherency of the "I" presented by the narrator. This last
point is crucial, because the coherent "I" narrator is the one Bartholomae says our students must invent before they can write ("Inventing"
[1986]). But first, Althusser would argue, they must learn to see themselves more broadly as "subjects" occupying a fixed subject position
from which to perceive their experiences. Althusser argues that the
function of ideology (171) is to create individuals who imagine themselves to be freethinking "subjects" so that each one will "(freely) accept his subjection . . . all by himself" (167–68; 182).

Literature helps create such subjects by addressing itself to a particular imaginary reader to whom the text is most intelligible and
who we must unconsciously "become" to read the piece. The most obvious examples include the use of *we* to refer to the reader and the
author and *our country* to refer to the United States, but on a more
subtle level the process occurs whenever writers assume that they and
their readers share values or a notion of reality and whenever writers
represent people according to the dominant ideology (strong men,
nurturing women, and so on). If a representation is repeated enough
times, we will come to "recognize" it as "obvious" or "true" and take it

for granted. We will, for example, recognize a caregiver named Mary as "a woman" (because we believe that Mary is a woman's name, that nurturing is a female characteristic, and that women have more female characteristics than men). Similarly, we might initially suspect a nonnurturing woman of being less "womanly" or even "unnatural"— regardless of our political beliefs.

Althusser calls this process "interpellation" (170). The text, he says, literally "hails" its readers, who respond just as we turn when we are hailed on the street whether by name, or even as *Sir, Miss,* or *Ma'am* (173–75). Because ideology always addresses me as the same person, I come to recognize myself as that person; thus I recognize myself as a woman, as white, and so on, and along with these identifications come all the dominant representations of what it means to be a white woman and how one "naturally" behaves, which is "obviously" different from how those in other categories, such as women of color or men, behave. I therefore come to see myself as a noncontradictory unified subject; although I might seem a totally different person to, say, my students and my friends, we accept that difference as natural and perceive me to have only one "real" identity (because it is "natural" to be a subject with one unified identity). Our language doesn't even allow me to think of myself as many selves, rather, "I" am one self who behaves differently in different situations. Catherine Belsey cites Emile Benveniste's challenges to the "obviousness" of the unified subject to further explain this point. It is through language, they argue, that I constitute myself as a subject because language allows me to make the I–not I distinction. Benveniste states, "Language is possible only because each speaker sets himself up as a *subject* by referring to himself as *I* in his discourse" (Belsey 47). It is, then, a relatively simple step for ideology to reconstitute this "I" as the signifier of a unified subject. Thus we come to believe our real identity (as "I") to be fixed and basically unalterable, providing the foundation of our sometimes-contradictory actions, unifying them, and giving them larger meaning. This belief is important because only unified subjects can imagine themselves as larger than their parts and, thus, as able to escape ideology and be the originators of "meaning, knowledge and action" (Belsey 51). If we did not believe ourselves able to transcend ideology in this way, we would see that we are subject to it, resist its image of reality, and denounce it as indoctrination.

Ideology, then, speaks to us as if we were particular individuals occupying a given place in the social hierarchy. Through repetition, we come to "recognize" ourselves as the persons hailed and so act as if we were "really" those persons. Because ideology has taught us that we are unified subjects with free will, we do not imagine our identities to have been created in this way. Our actions and choices seem to be the result of some fixed character or unfettered choice rather than the product of ideology. My concern in this essay is with the specific actions of reading and writing and with the ways the readings and assignments in textbook readers might influence our students' reinvention of themselves as academic readers and writers. If ideology causes some people to imagine themselves as "bosses" and others as "workers," we should be able to see this process in action by looking closely at the readers and writers addressed in textbook readers. Students already have a sense of where they are placed in the social hierarchy when they enter our writing classes, so we must ask whether our texts challenge that hierarchy and help our students reinvent themselves as equals or whether the texts reinforce that hierarchy and thus help preserve the status quo.

In English-speaking societies (as in many others), white men are positioned—and thus addressed—differently from men of color, white women, and women of color. To return to Althusser's hailing metaphor, not everyone turns around when someone calls out, "Excuse me, Sir." The phrase speaks to those who have already come to think of themselves as male ("Sir") and worthy of respect ("Excuse me"). Middle- and upper-class white men who believe that "Excuse me, Sir" might refer to them act on that image of themselves and turn around, and when the phrase does refer to them, the image is reinforced. Age, nationality, regional origin, religion, ethnic origin, and physical ability are among the other elements of the identity we "recognize" as ours and respond to. And, of course, part of the definition of these elements is their hierarchical status, so that in "recognizing" ourselves as the identities ideological apparatuses call us into, we also recognize our place in society, as the example shows. Because this "recognition" of "ourselves" is based on a system of beliefs about what it means to occupy specific social positions and because the non-contradictory unified subject is simply a convenient fiction, we are not really recognizing ourselves, Althusser points out; we are "misrecognizing" ourselves as the subjects ideology is calling us into or interpellating us as. He says, "The 'obviousness' that you and I are subjects—and that that does not cause any problems—is an ideological effect, the elementary ideological effect" (172). Because the notion of an individual subject is created by ideology, our recognition of ourselves is always really a misrecognition.

In the United States, perhaps more than in any other nation, the image of the autonomous individual dominates our beliefs and makes it possible for us to imagine that social hierarchies are just and natural.

Those images are challenged by the assertion that ideology creates an imagined self for each of us. If we want to make our students question social and racial hierarchies, then, we need to look at how these hierarchies are constructed by language. We might expect textbooks designed for language instruction in multicultural college classes to resist simple stereotypes and traditional ideologies, but if we find instead that they reinscribe and reaffirm the image of the autonomous individual, we must conclude that they unwittingly serve to perpetuate the status quo. If they represent "individuals" of different races and genders in ways that reinforce the hierarchical location of those groups, we must conclude the same thing. If they also obscure the workings of language, they will, of course, be even more effective. And they do. The failure of textbook readers to treat language as anything other than a tool for learning or a vehicle to express our thoughts encourages students and teachers to ignore its role in shaping those thoughts and our notion of our unified identities and membership in discourse communities.

The Implications of Writing Assignments

Language, as part of the symbolic order Jacques Lacan describes, constructs a fragmented self, and literature produces a similar fragmentation between the reader, the reader the text addresses, the social relations the text portrays, and the social relations the reader experiences as real. But this fragmented self is hidden from most students by the imaginary readers the texts address and the model individuals the texts present. When the experience narrated could lead to a discussion of the issue of the unified subject or call into question established patterns of belief, the introductions, commentaries, and questions for further writing close the piece off from such discussion and focus students' attention on style or use the piece as a jumping-off point for writing about tangential issues instead. An example of this can be seen with the questions following E. B. White's immensely popular essay "Once More to the Lake." In all the readers I have studied, the questions distract attention from the fascinating shifts in perspective as the father actually confuses his own body with his son's (such as in his description of how he felt while they were fly fishing: "I looked at the boy, who was silently watching his fly, and it was *my* hands that held his rod, *my* eyes watching. I felt dizzy and didn't know which rod I was at the end of" [G. Miller 80–81; Eastman et al. 48–49]). Instead of raising issues of identity and identification, texts ask students to "pick a particular event from [their] childhood, make a list of what [they] remember, then, in a paragraph, narrate [their] experience" or "write an account of an experience, real or imagined, in which [they] return to a place [they] haven't seen for a while" (G. Miller 87; Eastman et al. 52).

The ideology of what a composition reader should do is so firmly entrenched that, instead of asking students to engage with the content of the piece as they would in other classes, suggestions for further writing such as these ask them to place themselves at the center of the text and use its style to write about something they might believe to be a similar experience. A stunning example is the suggestion following Jonathan Swift's "A Modest Proposal" that students "select an activity which offends [them], such as people who throw trash from their car windows or surly and rude salesclerks [and] offer an exaggerated alternative to improve the situation" (Lester 361). A similar assignment suggests, "Write your own modest proposal for something, keeping in mind Swift's technique" (Eastman et al. 529). Instead of being asked to consider issues raised in the text, such as the hypocrisy with which we treat poverty, exploitation, and death, students are invited to use satire to expose trivial issues—thus littering and homelessness can be easily equated. Although such supposedly student-centered writing can have pedagogical value, there are several dangers in asking students to write about themselves in response to another text. Such an assignment renders their own experiences and observations more important than those of the author of the piece they have just read, and thus does not encourage them to engage with the emotions or experiences of others—one of the goals of multiculturalism. In addition, the influence of the reading on students' narratives remains unacknowledged.

The potential influence of a text's ideology on student narratives written in response to such assignments can be seen most clearly in the example of "Once More to the Lake." This essay addresses itself to a reader who shares the narrator's fear of change, his romanticization of the American dream and the image of the family, and his representation of "girls" as sexual objects. Sitting with his son on the dock with the "American flag floating against the white clouds in the blue sky," the narrator fears that the newcomers to the lake will be "common" rather than "nice" (G. Miller 82; Eastman et al. 49, 50). He implicitly connects fear of the loss of land, space, freedom, plenty, paternal authority, and American values with fear of death, of castration, and of the loss of sexuality, certainty, and self. And it is change, especially the intrusion of "common" people into his "cathedral-like" lake, which represents that fear (G. Miller 79; Eastman et al. 48). In order to enter into the narrative or even make sense of it, the reader addressed by this text must identify with and recognize *him*self as an American nostalgic for a golden age and fearful of change. Then, still in that identity, she or he must narrate a "similar" formative experience. Reconstructing one's past in these terms reinforces the sense of self created by the text—the students must "become" the text's implied reader in order to read it and must remain that person as they narrate formative events from their own pasts. Literally, then, they reinvent themselves as the person the text called on them to be. Moreover, the student proposing a solution to the problem of littering comes to see herself or himself as a unified individual who is the origin both of understanding and of action in accordance with that understanding. Perhaps this helps explain the enormous popularity of these two essays.

Ironically, we do not find student-centered assignments where they might encourage students to articulate their frustrations and explore their locations in the social hierarchy: after pieces dealing with racism, sexism, and anger. Such pieces are approached in ways that minimize these elements; one example is Maya Angelou's recently canonized "Graduation," which describes the pain and humiliation the narrator and her fellow students felt while listening to the racism of their white graduation speaker. Some textbook writers, such as the *Norton Reader*'s, simply decide not to follow it with any questions (a decision Eastman et al. repeated for "Mommy What Does 'Nigger' Mean?" by Gloria Naylor, and "Letter from Birmingham Jail," by Martin Luther King, Jr.—although they include several questions for "focusing reading" after less controversial pieces). Other texts ask students about tone or style but do not give them space to discuss the institutional racism at the heart of the piece or the anger just below the surface of many multicultural classes. Some textbook writers, such as Janet Madden-Simpson and Sara M. Blake in *Emerging Voices*, ask what Angelou has learned about herself, "how effectively she learned it," and "what Mr. Donleavy's speech teaches his audience" (298), but they avoid the larger issues the piece raises about differential spending on education and the effect of racism in America. Such questions differ from those following other essays in that they fail to generate student-centered writing on their reaction and relation to the issues raised by racism or sexism, even though student-centered assignments are the norm after other essays.

Writing Identities

In all the texts I have studied, the writing assignments following essays by white men, such as "Once More to the Lake," ask students to write from the same identity as the one they were required to adopt to read the piece (in general, an identity just like the author's). In sharp contrast, almost no assignments following essays by white women and by women and men of color ask students to adopt the voice of the narrator (or even the implied reader, if that is different). Instead, these assignments ask students to step back from the text and discuss it from another perspective or identity.

Because we must imagine ourselves as unified subjects in order to represent ourselves in any form of writing, it is particularly effective for the texts designed to teach students to write within the academy also to offer them a carefully defined identity from which to write. Many students in composition classes, especially since the 1960s, are there because they write in a voice that is unfamiliar to the academy and speak from a position that might challenge the status quo by revealing the arbitrariness of its hierarchy. Instead of changing its basic values and standards (such as Standard English) to accommodate these new students, academic ideology maintains that we have to change the students: help them to reinvent themselves. Composition readers have been used for this purpose since their introduction in fifteenth-century England (originally to help regulate the language of French mercantile traders, later to help assimilate Huguenot refugees and working-class students, and then as part of the colonial expansion; see Jamieson, "United Colors"). But this reinvention is complex. It must produce students who share the values and beliefs of the dominant culture without sharing the personal expectations of the dominant class. It must, in other words, create educated people who reaffirm the social hierarchy even as they prepare to accept lower positions in it than others with similar educations.

Thus if the pieces collected in readers can help reinvent students as "individuals" who "willingly" adopt identities that reinforce the structures of the dominant culture, those texts will be particularly effective at teaching students whose "difference" might otherwise have challenged those structures. To read a text, students who do not recognize themselves in the position of the reader the text seems to demand must learn to become that individual and allow themselves to be addressed by "him." Once they read the piece, they must adopt identities as writers to respond to it.

Although the issue of authorship is obscured in most textbooks and has been called into question by Foucault ("What Is an Author?") and others, the name and brief biography of "The Author" always precedes the text in composition readers, establishing the notion of the autonomous author. The emphasis on each author's race and gender provides models of *who* can write in the academy, *which* styles of writing are permitted, and *whose* interpretations are accepted. In a classic example of mixed messages, the texts created for use in contemporary composition classes reinforce beliefs about who is authorized to write and who is not, while at the same time telling the students that they are all to become writers and appear to give them the skills to do so.

An example of this occurs with the inclusion of Langston Hughes's piece "Salvation," which, along with Swift's and White's, was one of the eight most often reproduced essays in readers published before 1990 and which was the most consistently included text by an African American in readers published since the 1960s (Jamieson, "Rereading" 131–33). The "writer" addressed by this essay might at first appear to be like Hughes (although not necessarily African American). As with "Once More to the Lake," the textual apparatus requires students to replace Hughes's experience with their own, to write from a vaguely similar situation and, maybe, with a similar purpose. They are asked to "describe an experience where group pressure forced [them] into doing something [they] did not believe in" (McCuen and Winkler 97) or "narrate an incident from which [they] learned something" (Lester 69). But if they turn back to the introductory sections explaining how to write narratives, the students will learn that they must not write as Hughes did; instead they must have a "clearly defined point" rather than simply "tell what happened." A narrative must "clearly reveal its intentions" and state its "reason for being" (G. Miller 60). Despite being one of the most frequent examples of narrative style offered by readers, "Salvation" does not do what readers tell us "good" narrative writing should.

We find a similar pattern with the anthologized portion of Martin Luther King's "I Have a Dream" speech. Although it is generally included in sections on persuasion, it does not fit the definitions of persuasive writing in the introductions to those sections. These introductions warn students to avoid repeating themselves, to make statements and then back them up carefully and logically, and to provide premises and justify all claims, injunctions that King's piece does not observe because it is not a piece of persuasive *writing*. King's and Hughes's pieces seem to serve as models of what not to do, and students who imitate their styles in other classes will be told, "This is not how we write in the academy."

It could be argued that in the context of the readers, these texts address (and thus "hail") a white audience, especially since the questions following them, unlike those for other pieces, don't invite students to adopt the voice of the writer. But the emphasis on the race and gender of the author before each piece suggests that some students were intended to identify with, and thus "misrecognize" themselves as, Hughes and King, and see themselves as African American writing subjects. If they do, they will learn that, although their stories and beliefs are interesting and they are encouraged to give them, the writing styles identified as "theirs" are not appropriate for the university. The only logical conclusion for students who have reinvented themselves after the models presented to them is that they cannot write for the academy, despite their admission into college. Once they have been called back (reinterpellated) into their racial identities, it is hard for them to unimagine those identities again. The other possibility, that they reject the notion of the individual altogether, would require analytical skills that we rarely teach; it would require them to reject "the obvious," as Althusser points out (172). Their real choices are to accept the standards explained by the text and internalize the lesson—that people like them fail to meet those standards despite the importance of their message—or to reject the standards and rules and write as these models do. In the former instance students will come to accept the values of dominant culture and thus accept their own status as inferior; in the latter their writing will "fail," and a judgment of inferiority will be conferred on them and recorded on their transcripts.

We see the same hierarchical structuring occurring in *Models for Writers*, a collection offering "sixty-five short, lively essays that represent *particularly appropriate models* for use by beginning college writers" (Rosa and Eschholz v; emphasis mine). In it we find one Latino, one Native American male, six African Americans (three of them women), thirteen white women, and forty-four white men. Among the so-called models who are not white men, we find Shirley Chisholm explaining that she would "rather be black than female," Susan Jacoby re-posing the question "What does a woman want?" and Rachel Jones explaining "what's wrong with black English." As in all readers I have seen (traditional, like this one, and multicultural), the essays by women and people of color are *about* women and people of color, often placing the two identities in competition. Their discussions explain what it's like to be a woman or a person of color, so their imagined audience must be people who do not know that, that is, white men—or white women and people of color who imagine their experiences differently and so are assumed to need this instruction in what it is "really" like. In contrast, among the representatives from the dominant group, Jason Salzman discusses "the suicide pill option"; Michael

Korda asks, "What makes a leader?"; Robert Veninga and James Spradley inform us "how the body responds to stress"; and so on. The content of the models considered "particularly appropriate" for white male writers is clearly different from that presented as "appropriate" for people of color and women, who are shown writing about themselves or issues of race and gender while white men are seen discussing apparently universal and academic topics. This hierarchy has remained largely unchanged in the new readers I have seen, both traditional and multicultural.

Joanna Russ argues, "Women need models not only to see in what ways the literary imagination has . . . been at work on the fact of being female, but also as assurances that they can produce art without inevitably being second-rate" (87). But the models provided by composition readers consistently present very trivial "ways the literary imagination has . . . been at work" in women's writing, and most of the writing by white women and people of color is nonacademic (as in the example above) and, by the standards carefully described in these texts, "second-rate." If we accept that academic topics are more important, the lesson we internalize is that white women and people of color are permitted to address only second-rate topics and thus must be second-rate and occupy a lower position in the social hierarchy as people and as writers.

Florence Howe describes her "women students [who] constantly consider women writers (and hence themselves, though that is not said outright) inferior to men" (qtd. in Russ 89). Most teachers have heard similar admissions from African American, Asian American, Latino or Latina, Native American, and working-class white students, although the assertion usually simply takes the form "I can't write" because the "*I*" they imagine has not been represented to them as a writer. Students entering college and trying to write for the academic discourse community need to construct adequate definitions of an "I" who does write, and they need to find images of that "I" in what they read (which, of course, allows them to be called into specific identities all the more effectively). If they look in what is often their first university textbook, the composition reader, and do not find "themselves," or, worse, find what they misrecognize as "themselves" in the examples of what the text calls incorrect writing, they have only two options. They may try to "become" the subject the text seems to address, or they may simply accept that they are not that subject and thus accept the apparently obvious conclusion that they are not the legitimate subjects of the academy either—that they literally cannot write there. Some students are able to understand their absence instead as part of what

Mike Rose terms a "language of exclusion" or as the result of a larger politics they seek to change, but these students seem increasingly rare.

The Role of Victim

In contrast to, say, Toni Morrison's images of African Americans as complex characters who act and influence their environment (for better or worse), readers present simplistic images of people of color as disempowered and lacking any agency (Angelou's fellow students may be cheered by James Weldon Johnson's poem, but they cannot change their situation, they can only respond to it). In the readers I have studied, I have not read one piece by a writer identified as a person of color that does not deal in some way with racist victimization. It may conclude with an overcoming of sorts as do Angelou's "Graduation" and "Momma, the Dentist, and Me" or an assertion of identity like that in Toni Cade Bambara's "The Lesson" or King's "I Have a Dream," but the writer is still constructed as a victim. Moreover, that writer is too often a child (as in three of the four examples above) and thus lacks power and mature agency. He or she is often a victim of language or linguistic complexities, as are Langston Hughes in "Salvation," Richard Rodriguez in "Aria," Maxine Hong Kingston in "Girlhood among Ghosts," Ernesto Galarza in "Growing into Manhood," and Dick Gregory in "Shame," and thus cannot prevent the problem, protect himself or herself against it, or even, for that matter, comprehend it as an adult would. Because the questions and assignments after these texts never challenge this notion, this is the writer our students of color are forced to "misrecognize" and reinvent themselves as if they are also to represent themselves as part of a racial group. Thus negative self-images are perpetuated and the students "recognize themselves" as unable to overcome or even theorize their victimization but also unable to write about anything else.

In addition, by reconstructing people of color as "other," with special needs and unique problems that "we" can seek to solve for "them," these texts mystify the implicit structures of racism that most white students and teachers have been taught. In a fascinating development, at least a dozen of the 1992 readers I examined featured a new inclusion whose appearance made its author the most rapidly canonized to date. This newly embraced author was Shelby Steele, and the extracts were taken from *The Content of Our Character*. What is significant is which pieces editors decided to extract and what effect these pieces have in juxtaposition with the pieces around them. The selected extracts are all narratives of incidents in Steele's life interspersed with his conclusions about the events and unsupported generalizations about black complicity in systems of white racism. They might make some white students question the status quo as one assumes the editors hope, but I suspect few black students would be comfortable discussing them in a racially mixed class (even if they were not asked to verify the experiences). And, as with the models described above, essays written in that style would be unacceptable in most classes because the generalizations are based on the author's experience and make no reference to other case studies or research.

While using personal experience to formulate theories is one way students can learn the rhetorical strategies required in academic papers, if we do not then encourage them to research other articles on the same subject, cite documented studies, and test their theories against other statistical, sociological, or psychological analyses, we leave them unprepared for the real requirements of the academy. None of the texts I have seen comment on Steele's lack of supporting evidence, although the more conscious ones ask questions such as whether "bargaining [is] an available and acceptable alternative for all African Americans" as Steele claims (Columbo, Cullen, and Lisle 358). If the content remains unquestioned, students will do what they have been taught to do all their lives: they will read to learn. And what they will learn is that African Americans have a hidden investment in victimization and poverty and do not advance because they depend for power on their collective status as victims. The sections in which Steele qualifies these claims and suggests solutions are never anthologized, nor is most of his analysis. Thus he seems to be presenting facts about the world rather than theorizing about it. Many readers encourage the students to learn from the extract instead of simply responding to it. These readers ask questions such as "In what ways and for what reasons do blacks understand that they are innocent?" (Layton 557) rather than "In what ways and for what reasons *does Steele claim* blacks . . ." That Richard Rodriguez is also included in most of these texts and appears to echo Steele's position on affirmative action and the need for a strident individualism to counter the damage done by liberal social programs seems to support this lesson further. Steele's assertions overwhelmingly support the image of the victim of color presented throughout these texts and support the ideology on race increasingly presented in other areas of culture. His theory that "there is an unconscious sort of gravitation toward [victims], a complaining celebration of them" (15) is also implicitly supported by the editorial decisions (whether or not they are motivated by what he calls "white guilt" [80]) to select other extracts by people of color narrating their victimization. Thus Steele's lack of corroborating data can be ignored because the composition readers themselves appear to provide it and support his assertions.

These victim narratives also allow white students to ignore what Peggy McIntosh calls "white privilege." She argues that white Americans have been taught "about racism as something which puts others at a disadvantage, but . . . [not] its corollary [aspects], white privilege, which puts [whites] at an advantage" ("Unpacking" 10; "White Privilege" 1). Essays like these allow white students and teachers to continue to avoid the painful reality that they benefit from being white, even if they strive to overcome the racism that their culture has inscribed in their attitudes and practices. These essays therefore support the dominant ideology that racism is the problem of "others" who have made themselves victims and support the more liberal ideology that they have been rendered victims by a corrupt system but can be helped by good whites who are somehow above that system. Both ideologies reinscribe the traditional hierarchical model reaffirming the supremacy and innocence of those of us who are of Anglo-Saxon ancestry and justifying both our position at the center and the notion of people of color as helplessly balanced on the margins.

Although Steele's argument is seriously flawed by his failure to consider ideology or structures of power, his description of the paralysis resulting from "misrecognizing" one's subject position and thus allowing oneself to be interpellated as victim is, in my opinion, accurate. It is therefore doubly ironic that so many multicultural and traditional readers have decided to include Steele as the only apparently theoretical voice in their collection of victim narratives by people of color. His discussion reinforces the identities presented and addressed in the rest of the text, helping to construct the very victims that he rejects. Once these powerless and marginalized student writers have been created, Steele's essay tells us (the white, male readers the textbook has forced us to become as we read) to blame the victim for this state of affairs, allowing responsibility to shift from the hegemonic structures governing these texts to people of color themselves. Not only is the hierarchical model reinforced, but those who benefit from it are absolved of responsibility.

Students who do not become the traditional writers of the academy and adopt its interpretive schema are accused by many of our colleagues in other disciplines of "not being able to think." I would argue that in fact the real problem is that many of these students have thought carefully about what is expected of college writers. Struggling to "reinvent" themselves, they have modeled their writing and their academic identities on the readers and writers their textbooks seem to tell them they should be: the models in their textbooks who are most like them (i.e., who they misrecognize themselves as). But the writers that they have reinvented themselves as, like their models, are deemed inappropriate for the academy. As a result, students who "misrecognize" themselves as the apparently white male writers in their readers and write accordingly occupy a stronger position as fledgling members of the academic discourse community, while those who "misrecognize" themselves as the white women and women and men of color presented to them are placed in a weakened position vis-à-vis academic discourse. Thus the essays and questions in composition readers help teach students what values are acceptable in the academy and to construct reading and writing identities that frequently contradict and subtly undermine whatever more egalitarian pedagogical strategies we composition teachers may have adopted. They demonstrate how effectively the academy, as what Althusser calls the "number-one . . . Ideological State Apparatus" (153), and we, as composition teachers within the academy, can modify the appropriation of discourse in response to social conflict. They also reveal just how much is at stake when representatives of the status quo raise the overused charges of political correctness against pedagogical strategies that might reveal the workings of language and the hierarchical construction of the subject and thus challenge that status quo.

Effective Intervention in Students' Identity Formation

But if we can unwittingly cause students to "misrecognize" themselves as failed or nonacademic writers, we can also deliberately select texts that construct them as equally empowered writers. Although there are no totally unproblematic readers on the market, we can balance our assignments and encourage students to analyze the texts we select. The following suggestions are certainly not new, but what is important is that they be selected specifically to counterbalance the effects of textbooks and readers in use in our classroom rather than simply as effective writing pedagogy. That is, in addition to helping us teach writing, these strategies can help us effectively intervene in our students' processes of identity formation. To decide which ones to select, we must be hyperconscious of the texts we use in our classes and their implicit ideologies.

Assigning narrative writing before the students read a narrative essay and inviting them to compare their narrative strategies and concerns with those in the reading prevents students from being reconstructed with the voice of the writer of the text and also helps them learn comparative reading and writing skills. Selecting supplemental "victim" and "success" narratives by white men *and* men of color and inviting students to analyze the writers' voices and strategies teaches them analytical reading and writing skills and subtly challenges dominant stereotypes. Assigning additional readings such as those in the annual collections published by Graywolf Press (Rick Simonson and Scott Walker's *Multicultural Literacy* and Walker's *Stories from the American Mosaic*, for example), pieces from Henry Louis Gates's *Bearing Witness*, and essays by white women and people of color from journals and the popular press can balance even the most unbalanced reader.

A more radical step is to teach students to see the patterns of oppression and inscription in their textbooks, perhaps including all of or brief extracts from Frantz Fanon's *Black Face, White Masks* (145–46 or 165 are especially useful), Peggy McIntosh's "White Privilege and Male Privilege," Ward Churchill's *Fantasies of the Master Race* (consider 1–4, 17–19, or 24–29), Edward Said's *Orientalism* (perhaps 1–4 or 20–21), or David Mura's "Strangers in the Village" (esp. 141–43). The last might also help begin to address the anger that such an analysis will inevitably produce—anger that Mura says tends to be repressed into depression and reduced self-worth and must instead be rechannelled into analytical skills (a sentiment also voiced by Fanon and many other activists and theorists).

I suggest, then, that after determining the academic and political goals of a class (including the goal of "not being political"), we first ask, How will this reader teach the writing skills central to this class? and What reading and writing subjects does it call into being? We might also ask, What model of diversity does it present—inclusion of the other in the mainstream, understanding of the other, or challenging the notion of social hierarchy? If we accept that we and our students will always be engaged in the process of creating and re-creating selves to write from, then the danger remains imminent that we will "misrecognize" the selves that others (and ideology) address as "real." This danger is compounded by the fact that in other realms ideological structures encourage us to desire the security of believing ourselves to be "concrete, individual, distinguishable and (naturally) irreplaceable subjects" (Althusser 173), so we are always susceptible to such representations of ourselves—especially those students who are engaged in the process of absolute reinvention in an effort to be successful college writers. Our task as writing teachers becomes to ask what identities are most likely to enable our students to satisfy the academy's demands in their writing without ceasing to be aware that they are doing so. They must remain able to move in and out of several "identities" rather than submit to the one, unified individual demanded by the ideology of the dominant culture, especially where that individual identity is one of a disempowered nonacademic writer. To achieve this goal fully, we must call for or create collections of readings that fulfill Foucault's demand that education be "the instrument whereby every individual, in a society like our own, can gain access to any kind of discourse" (*Archaeology* 227). In this way we can fracture the hierarchical model that keeps our students diversely skilled, and give them all the prospect of learning to become successful academic writers. Only then can we fulfill the dual demands of the composition class and the multicultural campus, instead of unwittingly undermining our good intentions with our choice of texts.

"But Isn't This the Land of the Free?": Resistance and Discovery in Student Responses to *Farewell to Manzanar*

Virginia A. Chappell

> *Teachers who know the ways of interpretation should interpret the texts of their own classrooms, and . . . teachers who understand the value of story should see and tell the stories of themselves and of their students.*
>
> —Glenda Bissex

My story begins in naïveté, but it is not politically innocent. It is about using multicultural course materials in a predominantly white educational setting. I decided to use *Farewell to Manzanar* in my first-year composition classes because I wanted to complicate my students' worldviews. I wanted them to think deliberately about racial and ethnic identity and about freedom. Written by Jeanne Wakatsuki Houston and James D. Houston and first published in 1973, the book is Jeanne's autobiographical account of a childhood defined by life at Manzanar, a World War II "relocation" camp for Japanese Americans. The book's primary concern is the identity issues that Jeanne's family's internment raised for her both at the camp and during her adolescence immediately afterward. Evocative of turbulent emotions and a starkly beautiful California landscape, the Houstons' highly readable narrative is not bitter or condemnatory. Its starting place is political, but its course and ending place are primarily personal: by telling her story Jeanne becomes able to issue the "farewell" of the title. "Everybody knows an injustice was done," Jeanne reports that her husband told a friend as they began working on the book, but "how many know what actually went on inside?" (ix). They have written "not political history," Jeanne says, but "a web of stories . . . tracing a few paths . . . that led up to and away from the experience of the internment" (x). Political judgments are left to the reader.

As I first planned classes about the book in spring 1989, my pedagogical purposes were twofold: I wanted to foster imaginative engagement with a coming of age radically different from my students', and I wanted to use the book as a focal point for extensive collaborative work on source-based writing. I designed a variety of assignments centered on the historical circumstances surrounding the internment and the process of the United States' officially coming to terms with it. At the time, the Japanese American redress movement had some visibility in the national news media, and students could find relevant materials in fairly recent periodicals and books. The previous summer, the Civil Liberties Act of 1988 had authorized reparations to those who had been interned, but funding was still pending in Congress. (The first appropriation was approved in November 1989, and payments began with the 1991 federal budget.) In addition, in October 1988 the United States Supreme Court had refused to review a case challenging the constitutionality of the internment; the plaintiffs had argued that evidence the government had previously suppressed "demonstrated that racial animus, not military judgment," had motivated the internment ("Certiorari").

Clearly, issues of race and constitutional rights become unavoidable as soon as one begins to gather information about the camps or the redress movement, so assigning my students this kind of text and this kind of research was not innocent of politics. Indeed, one way I intended to complicate their worldviews was to give them an opportunity to study and write about the United States government, their own democracy, making a mistake and to consider what role individual citizens might have in preventing a recurrence of such error. Nevertheless, the naïveté with which the story begins is my own. The class was reluctant to talk about race, and I was surprised.

When I envisioned our initial class discussion, I had expected that some students would find it disconcerting to confront the story of the internment, of what I took (and still take) to be a racially motivated act with dangerous implications, a government action that defied the fundamental protections of habeas corpus and due process. I was not prepared for resistance. Although I expected students to be dismayed, I did not expect them to deny that the relocation was racially motivated. Nor did I expect them to condemn Japanese Americans for obeying Executive Order 9066 and allowing themselves to be shipped to the camps. I did not expect them to question Henry Steele Commager's report that "the record does not disclose a single case of

Japanese disloyalty or sabotage during the whole war" (Houston and Houston xiii). I did not expect the wry comment from the back of the room about Japanese "coming over here and buying up American industry like mad."

My purpose in this essay is to reflect on how that first Manzanar unit and two subsequent ones unfolded and on my efforts to remediate my naïveté, to project respect for my students (themselves naive), and to foster inquiry that would expand their worldviews. The experiences of these classes suggests that pedagogy calling for serious, productive inquiry can capitalize on resistance even while providing a valuable antidote to it. I found much of my students' resistance rooted in naïveté and inexperience, which psychologist Fletcher Blanchard has termed interracial incompetence (B2). I, of course, wanted to move them toward interracial competence, a stance that would enable them to respect race, appreciate difference, and recognize the central role that race plays in contemporary life. My approach enacts Henry Giroux's critical pedagogy as it encourages students from the dominant culture to become "border-crossers" who can—and will—explore diverse cultures and histories even though that study threatens to complicate the complacency of their political, economic, social—and racial—identities (*Border Crossings* 170–75).

The project did not begin as a formal research study and is not structured as one. Rather, I offer my account as informal teacher research, a case study of critical reflection guided by Ann Berthoff's injunction that teachers be "REsearchers" (30), putting theory in dialogue with practice to "define what our purposes and aims are and thereby how to evaluate our efforts in reaching them: what and thereby how" (32). James Britton says that "every lesson should be for the teacher an inquiry, some further discovery, a quiet form of research" (15). It has been my custom for some time to keep a teaching journal, writing in it while students are writing in class and maintaining it as a personal record of problems and ideas. My story here is based on my notes from three semesters of planning, teaching, and evaluating work about *Farewell to Manzanar* and the internment and on stacks of my students' journals, essays, and in-class writings, photocopied and saved with their consent. Nearly every student agreed to participate; I collected materials from sixty-seven students out of a total of seventy-one. I see my work during the teaching and now in writing about it as the "reflection-in-action" advocated by Donald Schön. This stance of inquiry is a means by which practitioners can "cope with the troublesome 'divergent' situations of practice," as Schön puts

it. "When someone reflects-in-action," Schön writes, "he becomes a researcher in the practice context. He is not dependent on the categories
of established theory and technique, but constructs a new theory of
the unique case" (qtd. in Gere 118).

My reflecting began with freewriting in my journal as I tried to make
sense of our troublesome first discussion of the book. I had asked the
students to bring *Farewell to Manzanar* to class but not to read it yet.
To start us off, I presented them with a scenario in which some disaster would make their families move somewhere with nothing but what
they could carry in their hands and on their backs. Stressing that they
and their families would not be coming back, I asked them to free-
write about what their family members would do as they got ready for
the bus that would come for them the next morning. After they wrote
for five minutes or so, I asked them to consider what might cause this
situation. Most wrote about a storm or nuclear accident, a few imagined being involved in a witness-protection program, and a few recognized what lay ahead and wrote about the internment. Our discussion
of these freewrites turned gradually to the circumstances of Japanese
Americans' evacuation from the West Coast in 1942 and to the book itself. As in subsequent classes, a few students voiced dismay over the le-
galized discrimination evident in the Houstons' chronology, which
begins with 1869, when the first Japanese to settle on the mainland arrived in California, and ends with 1952, when Congress granted the
right of citizenship to Japanese aliens (xi–xii). But members of the
class seemed equally uncomfortable at the prospect of questioning
Roosevelt's decision to authorize the evacuation. Many (not all) wanted
to reason away nascent disillusion by suggesting that the relocation
was probably, regrettably, a military necessity. These efforts tended toward awkward generalizations about race and difference that some
observers would have labeled racist.

Rather than try to challenge or correct the generalizations and ratio-
nalizations, I asked questions. I pressed for clarification about "military necessity" and what might justify the removal of legal residents
and citizens from their homes. How would we recognize reliable answers about the military and political decisions behind the internment? Whom could we trust to assess the extent to which Japanese
Americans posed a threat to United States security or needed protection from other citizens? Revising my sense of the students' cultural
and political awareness but not my goals for enriching it, I decided to
let the Houstons' book and the materials students would find in their

research speak for themselves and thus chip away at, or perhaps even dissolve, the students' resistance to dealing with the internment in racial terms.

Teaching often resembles jazz improvisation. I was operating here on the basis of what Britton describes as "off-the-cuff decisions that can only reliably come from inner conviction, that is to say by consistently applying an ever-developing rationale" (15). My journal entry from later that day articulated a classical liberalism:

> I don't want to squelch discussion. I don't want them to think they have to say what I want them to. If I truly believe in free speech and a free marketplace of ideas, then I have to let them explore their ideas without their feeling foolish or condemned.

Terry Dean urges the use of culturally oriented topics in multiracial classes to validate the students' diversity. He cites James Cummins's argument that the "valuing of culture within the school . . . leads to academic success because it reverses the role of domination of [minority] students by the school" ("Multicultural Classrooms" 27). But my classroom was monocultural, the overwhelming majority of the students representing mainstream culture. (Of the seventy-one students in these three classes, five were students of color—a low percentage for this college—one in each of the first two classes, three in the last.) James Berlin describes a writing course that uses the theory and methods of cultural studies to encourage students to resist and negotiate cultural codes ("Composition"). But I had students who were starting off by resisting challenges to the validity of their cultural codes. Here is more from my notes about that first discussion:

> S_1: Did they catch anyone siding with the enemy?
> Me: No, no one.
> S_2: How do they know? It's a hard thing to prove, you know, spying.
>
> S_3: Why were they put in camps and the German Americans weren't?
> S_1: This [Pearl Harbor] had been an attack on our land, that's different.
> S_4: They [Germans] had been here longer and had mixed with other groups.

S₅: This doesn't shock me that much. I read a lot of history about Germany and it was so much worse there.

"A way of teaching is never innocent," Berlin tells us. "Every pedagogy is imbricated in ideology, in a set of tacit assumptions about what is real, what is good, what is possible, and how power ought to be distributed" ("Rhetoric" 492). What is real, good, and possible in a composition or literature class, let me assert, is reading and inquiry that expand students' imaginations and thus their understanding of the world. This is hardly a radical position. Long before multiculturalism became a bone of academic contention, Louise Rosenblatt, the first exponent of reader-response criticism, declared that a democratic society could benefit from the potential of literary study to enhance social sensitivity and imagination. Indeed, her comments in the 1938 edition of *Literature as Exploration* seem prescient in relation both to the internment, then only four years in the future, and to my students' initial reluctance to take a hard look at it some fifty years later: "Many of our greatest political blunders or social injustices are the result not so much of maliciousness or conscious cruelty as of the inability of our citizens to translate into human terms the laws or political platforms they support" (218). More recently, as part of a different conversation, Amy Ling speaks of literature's potential power to broaden readers' perceptions of race. Endorsing Ellen Messer-Davidow's proposal of perspectivism for feminist literary theory, Ling writes:

> Perspectivism would validate, respect, and encourage every perspective so that WASP males, Jewish males, black males, and white females would need to stretch themselves out of their own skins to understand Maxine Hong Kingston, Lin Taiyi, or Han Suyin, as I have always had to stretch outside of myself to understand James Fenimore Cooper, Bernard Malamud, and Richard Wright. This is what I have always believed reading literature is really all about—getting inside other people's skins and experiencing their lives. (153)

My resisting students may have been naive in their limited perceptions of racial and cultural difference. But in that first class, I was naive not to have stopped to consider how the news of the internment might sound from inside their skins. Most had skins of the same pinkish tone as mine, but they had not had the time, never mind the opportunity, to experience literature and interracial relationships as I had. I had spent three years in Asia. I had lived in Seattle during the 1970s and 1980s, when the air was full of conversations about Asian American identity as Japanese Americans began breaking silence about the internment, producing essays, poems, fiction, and drama in the process. I needed to remember, and tell my class, that I myself did not hear of the internment until after I graduated from college and moved to the West Coast. I reminded myself that I hadn't really understood what had happened until I met and had long talks with someone who had been interned. I encouraged students to free-write about their reaction to hearing about the internment. What had I felt when I found out? A sinking, suspicions-confirmed anger. But it was a time when I felt alienated from much of government policy, so another betrayal did not surprise me. In the Midwest in the late 1980s and the 1990s, the news did surprise a lot of students, and their efforts to rationalize the policy dismayed me at first. Trying to come to terms with their responses, and mine, I wrote in my journal:

> Why don't they want to hear about it? Why is talking about race so disturbing to them? It's not that they're prejudiced, they say, and it's true. It's just that . . . what? That their lives have been lived in overwhelmingly Caucasian, middle-class contexts—neighborhoods, schools. They want "civil rights" to be over, taken care of, not their fault. They don't want to think of themselves as privileged—they want to think they, their parents and grandparents, have earned it [their privilege].

They also don't want to feel that a teacher may be foisting a political agenda on them, one they might have to adopt if they want a good grade. And who can blame them? It's just that some politics are more visible than others. A student from the following spring's class wrote in her journal:

> Thinking about these hardships [at Manzanar] I begin to wonder how I would have reacted to the Japanese during this time period. To be honest I don't know of many people of Asian descent. That's not to say that I don't want to know them, but there just haven't been many opportunities for me to know them. Coming from the area I live in, it is likely that the feelings towards the Japanese during this time would have been *extremely* hostile. It is a good thing that I wasn't around during this time. It leaves one *less* page of "bad" history in my text.

I take as a pedagogical touchstone a maxim from Jim Reither: "To 'teach writing,' is . . . necessarily to ground writing in reading and inquiry." It has become clear to me that the dissensus created by my students' resistance in the Manzanar classes actually stimulates inquiry. The resistance creates an ideal (if touchy) starting point for the research work I want them to do. Having them grapple with new and disturbing material asks them to engage in the kind of academic inquiry that Reither describes as a collaborative, social process resulting not only *in* but *from* social products (625). Discussion establishes a community of researchers with a shared interest in finding out what happened. This finding out, the students discover, involves examining a variety of perspectives about what happened, such as John Hersey's condemnation of the attitudes and policies that created the camps and Eric Sundquist's more measured appraisal of the political and social climate in which the camps were created. Reading and writing about Jeanne's story and the internment give students an opportunity to form rationales for (and sometimes to revise) the politics implicit in their initial, largely uninformed responses.

The department's syllabus for this course, the second of a two-semester sequence required of all first-year students, calls for a paper based on library research related to a literary work (usually a novel). Questions that will become the focus of this research emerge quickly in students' journals, in which I ask them to record their chapter-by-chapter responses to *Farewell to Manzanar*. When they begin reading, expressions of anger and shame are common. "It almost made me embarrassed to be an American," wrote one of the many students who said they had just learned of the internment in this class. Another wrote:

> At the end of the first chapter I was in shock. All of her father's rights had been taken away just because he was a Japanese fisherman. I felt ashamed.

The news of the camps clashes with students' perceptions of their country's role in World War II and in foreign affairs in general. As one put it:

> We were supposed to be upholding justice and saving others but we were really just as bad as they were. . . . I feel betrayed and angry.

Such expressions of distress are often followed by insistent questioning—How could this happen?—a response indicating a desire to staunch disillusion with "facts." Many students set a goal, in the words of one, "to uncover who was involved, who led the relocation and were they aware of the real situation in the camps?" Similar desires to get at "the truth" are voiced by the smaller number of students who seek to maintain a cooler, "let's look at this objectively" stance. One wrote that as he learned more about Jeanne's story, he felt disappointed by the government's actions; yet, he said, if he tried to "be objective, and look at both sides equally," he could "understand the fear" that Japanese Americans might engage in sabotage. Another commented:

> It's not as if [the internees] were tortured physically or even intentionally. . . . Is it possible that the camps were truly for their own good as well as [the good of] other Americans?

As the students move further into the book, another phase of resistance emerges in the protests of many (again, not all) against the internees' acceptance of their fate. "I think it's amazing that the people could remain loyal [to the United States] even though they were held in camps," one wrote. Another set an early goal to "write about the reasons why the Japanese were so passive." Sometimes the students' surprise at Japanese Americans' compliance verges on blaming the victim and reifies notions of Japanese as other. One woman wrote:

> It makes me angry that these people are *so* passive about all of the hatred they are facing. They never get angry or upset that they are being persecuted because of something they can not control. I feel like they have little respect for themselves, only respect for their country [i.e., Japan].

We discuss in detail that most camp residents were citizens: native-born Americans of Japanese descent. But in many students' informal writings the one-word description *Japanese*, representing the larger—perhaps more exotic—category, persists. A striking example of this exoticism is one student's angry supposition that Army surplus clothing replaced the silk kimonos she imagined the internees wearing when they arrived at camp. Some journal entries and later some papers speak admiringly of the dignity and resourcefulness that Jeanne describes as sources of strength for her family and neighbors at camp.

Students keep their journals in double-entry or dialectical notebooks, and I require what students call "left-margin work," glossings and annotations of previous journal entries in a process described by Berthoff and Jim Stephens. As a result, the pages they give me to read sometimes demonstrate complicated and changing responses to the book. The student whose shock and shame about Mr. Wakatsuki's arrest are cited above recorded a struggle against too simple a response. After reading the first chapter, he wrote, "I don't understand how the Japanese Americans could be so accepting to being moved around so much. They did not even put up a fight." He went on to explain that he meant a legal fight or nonviolent protests and added in the margin, "The first idea that I have on why the JA's didn't fight is because they were scared of what the American people would do." Further in the journal, he acknowledged that it was "easy for [him] to say." He wrote, "I hope I would fight!!! and stand up for my rights!!!" Later he added another marginal note, "I'm not in that time or place. I'm also not a JA."

Across the three classes, a few students were already familiar with details of the internment, but most were unaware or only vaguely aware of it. Several students had read *Farewell to Manzanar* in high school, one had seen the television movie based on the book, and one had grown up in the Owens Valley, where the camp was located and where a memorial monument stands. The lack of common knowledge about the internment piques the ire and curiosity of many. It is clear that they have been trained not to believe everything they hear. "It's hard for me to believe that this was never taught" is a typical protest. Some students voice caution against passing judgment on the internment because they have not heard "the other side of the story." Students with military or ROTC backgrounds seem particularly inclined to circumspection. "I've heard it was an injustice, but being in the military I can see why [it was done], kind of," one wrote. "What if we really did find [out about] an attack from within? Would we know?" In another entry he expressed concern that he had only Jeanne's story to go on and had "no input from the American side." Other students wonder why the public and press did not protest, and a few in each class set out to discover how the media treated the internment during the war. "I was surprised to learn that not many people have heard about the Japanese treatment," wrote one Asian student. "Is it because it's not important, or is it 'accidentally' overlooked? I'm curious to know *why*." The following is from the introduction to a paper by a student to whom the subject had been entirely new:

> Though in my heart I didn't want to believe it, my mind told me that yes, my country was guilty of the rash and unjustified treatment of Japanese Americans during the war. It was in some ways even more devastating to learn that the U.S. has in no way, if [it

were] even possible, compensated the 110,000 people it interned. The third and final blow to my young and nationalistic mind was the realization that somehow I, as well as countless others, have been kept in the dark about the internment due to its absence in the majority of American history texts.

I assign two papers in connection with Manzanar, both of which leave the students largely free to choose the topic. For the first I ask them to choose a short passage from the book and explain how it illuminates a larger issue in Jeanne's story; for the second, I ask them to argue a point that is based on their research into the book's historical context. In the first paper, students usually take up some aspect of the conflicting pressures on Jeanne to become Americanized and to maintain traditional Japanese values. The most popular topic for the second paper is reasons for the internment, official and unofficial, then and now. Also popular are papers looking at the court cases challenging the constitutionality of the internment, a topic that for some grows out of puzzlement over Japanese American cooperation with the evacuation orders. To facilitate and motivate their research for the second paper, I organize a series of collaborative activities designed with three goals in mind: to put a substantial amount of information about the internment on the table for discussion; to help students learn to read rhetorically; and to teach them principles for evaluating their sources.

If a research project exists merely to generate papers, it becomes a performance, not an inquiry. When students work together to assemble material on a large topic that none could handle alone, each question investigated gains salience because of its relation to a larger but immediate conversation. So that tracking down library materials does not distract students unduly from the important rhetorical issues with which I want them to become familiar, I simplify the search process by putting a broad range of relevant books on overnight reserve and listing them in a handout. Although bibliographic purists might object that this shortcut eliminates potentially valuable search-and-retrieval experience, I contend that for this project it puts the emphasis on more significant and revealing searches among and within the books, which remain relatively available to everyone.

To introduce the class to some of the important events and concepts in discussions of Manzanar, I assign small groups to investigate aspects of the internment and the redress movement from different angles. These task forces, which develop their own internal senses of responsibility and loyalty, report their findings to the class to help others sift through the mass of information available. The groups give reports on the meaning and relevance of terms and concepts such as *due process*, *habeas corpus*, *no-no boy*, *loyalty oaths*, and *8-8-88*, which is the date Congress authorized reparations for former internees. I choose some of the items to bring forward essential background information. Others are generated by students in a brainstorming session on question analysis, a process that helps them narrow research topics and then determine which academic disciplines (e.g., history, sociology) have addressed the issues that interest them. (See Oberman on question analysis; Reither and Vipond on organizing courses as collaborative investigations.)

To my mind, a corollary to Reither's call to ground the teaching of writing in reading and inquiry is that the library is the ideal venue for such teaching: for teaching rhetoric. Doug Brent's constructivist model of rhetorical reading speaks of "the transaction between reader, writer, text, and situation not as a passive uptake of information but as a persuasive transaction" (72). He argues that we should help novice researchers "get research back inside the rhetorical act, a place where more experienced readers (whether or not they know it) routinely place it." As Brent emphasizes, students "must learn how to be persuaded by texts" (105). Important to learning how to be persuaded, Christina Haas and Linda Flower suggest, is learning how to make "an active attempt at constructing a rhetorical context for the text as a way of making sense of it" (167–68). Libraries can supply abundant materials through which students can practice both being persuaded and resisting persuasion while they work on learning to persuade others.

Rhetorical reading, a strategy unfamiliar to many first-year students, becomes a critical issue when students are researching their Manzanar papers, and the reality of the historical controversy increases their investment in the project. Examining a source's rhetorical context—its author's background, its intended audience, and its publication date—is no longer just an academic exercise. For example, a student who uses the seemingly authoritative United States Army *Final Report* as the only source about the internment will tell a story quite different from that of a student who uses the 1983 report of the congressional Commission on Wartime Relocation and Internment of Civilians (CWRIC), *Personal Justice Denied*. To demonstrate efficient techniques for discovering not only the context for a given source but also what else may have been published on the same topic, the second time I taught the book I assigned additional task forces to use library reference tools to report on the backgrounds of authors who figure into discussions of internment or redress. In the most recent class, teams participated in a workshop at the library on evaluating sources and investigating the background and reception of Michi Weg-lyn's *Years of Infamy*. (See Chappell, Hensley, and Simmons-O'Neill for a fuller discussion of workshops on evaluating sources.)

To help the students evaluate the claims in sources they find for their final papers, we practice rhetorical analysis on Manzanar-related materials in class. The materials come from firsthand accounts, from later commentaries, and from the comments of two officials who helped bring about and never renounced the decision to relocate the Japanese Americans. In one activity, students in small groups gloss passages by writers protesting the internment, then formulate brief summaries of how the passages complement one another—a technique from Berthoff and Stephens. The commentaries come from James Michener's introduction to Weglyn's book and from Hersey's essay "A Mistake of Terrifically Horrible Proportions." The firsthand accounts are from William Hohri, a leader of the redress movement who graduated from Manzanar High School in 1944, and from Ansel Adams, who visited Manzanar in 1943 and published a book-length photo essay on it, *Born Free and Equal*, the following year. (Armor and Wright reprint many of the photographs from the Adams book, which is difficult to find because many copies were burned publicly soon afterward.) In a separate assignment, the collaborative groups analyze arguments defending the evacuation. These are found in 1984 letters from John J. McCloy, who was assistant secretary of war in 1942, and Karl S. Bendetsen, the army colonel who directed the operation (Daniels, Taylor, and Kitano 213–16). Both men opposed redress in testimony before the CWRIC. Bendetsen's letter, the more adamant, insists the relocation was necessary and justified, and he protests the use of the term *internment* because, he asserts, camp residents were free to leave.

The many pages of student work resulting from these assignments have remediated my naïveté and complicated my worldview by opening to it the tentative, naive formulations of young white adults attempting to articulate their understandings of racial and cultural difference. In the provisional, often revelatory journal pages that students submit, I read guileless treatments of Japanese Americans as exotic others or as surprisingly like "regular people," but I also read comments that substantiate Rosenblatt's, Ling's, and my own confidence in the power of text and imagination to move us outside the limits of our own skins. Students comment that reading *Farewell to Manzanar* shows us "the people behind the facts of history" or that now they understand "what it must have been like" for Japanese Americans. One student wrote that she had not realized the implications of the initial exercise about packing up until she began reading the book. Another wrote that the book showed her the "human cost" of the internment. Students often praise the Houstons for not condemning the government and marvel that Jeanne is not "bitter." Seeing students relax their resistance as they move through the book leads me to infer that the Houstons' show-don't-tell narrative helps many of them extrapolate from Jeanne's story the larger story of the internment, the racial motives behind it, and the necessity of eternal vigilance even in a democracy.

Resistance to considering racial difference and prejudice as motivating factors gradually erodes as students begin their research and read more of *Farewell to Manzanar*, particularly the chapters in which Jeanne has to face prejudice at school after the war. Some of the journals reveal a discovery process articulated through questions. Apparently tracing her thoughts on paper, one student wrote in her journal:

> Why would the U.S. government be threatened by the average citizen trying to earn an income? What does it matter if they were living all together or not? What could the Japanese gain by having someone pose as the average citizen? Why just the Japanese, why not the Germans . . . too? Is it because you can visibly tell that the Japanese were the enemy?

One of the more politically sophisticated students speculated that the public at large did not protest the internment because either "the government disguised what was going on, or the prejudice and anger over Pearl Harbor would make a cover up unnecessary."

This student's journal chronicles the development of her thinking along lines that would gratify Rosenblatt and Ling. She notes that early in her reading she found herself wondering, "Didn't the Japanese in the camps have it better than others in some ways?" She continues:

> I couldn't get past this way of thinking at first. . . . It wasn't until I compared their experience to something else that I realized how wrong I was. After attending a lecture . . . by a man who felt women were somewhat inferior to men, I started thinking about that statement that he and so many other chauvinists bring up [about] women's positions in society: "So what if they are discriminated against sometimes? At least they don't have to serve in the military." The stupidity of this argument brought home the

fallacy of my idea that just because the Japanese in the camps were spared from combat the other injustices against them were not as great.

In her next paragraph she moves past the boundaries of her limited perspective, of her own skin:

> It is easy to use such an excuse to explain away the circumstances of the whole internment. . . . I found that the only way to overcome such ideas is to stop separating yourself from the situation and maybe try to bring it closer to home for *you*.

By the time they began writing their research papers, most students in all three classes were writing and talking about racial prejudice in connection with the internment. Some angrily saw it as the primary factor; others acknowledged it but analyzed legal and military matters as well. Race was most current as a topic for discussion the second time I taught *Farewell to Manzanar*. While drafting his paper on the book late one Saturday afternoon, the "young and nationalistic" student quoted above telephoned Jeanne Houston and asked her why the internment happened. She told him, "We were interned because we looked like the enemy." She had just returned from a speaking engagement about the book and must have spent considerable time answering his questions and relating the internment to long-standing anti-Asian attitudes on the West Coast. When he told the class about the conversation, it made a significant impression. Here is part of the introduction to his paper:

> At first it seemed crazy to me that the US would have sanctioned such an anti-democratic event, but as the reality of the situation set in, I almost forcibly made myself believe that not only did the internment occur, but the US tucked its tail and ran away from the responsibility. As these feelings of confusion and anger welled up inside of me I sat down and began to write a cynical response both to the book and to America. Then I phoned Jeanne W. Houston.

Just as Houston's response to my student remediated his naïveté and cynicism by broadening his perspective, his response to her helped remediate mine. "[For] a white male," he wrote, "this [looking like the enemy] was somewhat difficult . . . to understand, but somehow, though not fully comprehending the racism, I connected with the emotional damage, trauma, and rejection the Japanese American felt during this shameful period of American history."

A genuinely multicultural pedagogy must provide room for respect not of bigotry, not by any means, but of monocultural students' inexperience and naïveté. Research in psychology has found considerable elasticity in college students' privately held views about racism. Blanchard reports that in brief survey encounters, students walking between classes voiced opinions about racism that reflected whatever views a third person, an undercover member of the research team, offered just before their own responses. He attributes the malleability to naïveté, that is, to a lack of knowledge about racism and an uncertainty about how to respond to it. The problem's cause is continued racial segregation, he suggests: "Few of the many whites who have reached an honest commitment to egalitarian values have had the opportunity to acquire the full range of interpersonal skills, sensibilities and knowledge that might allow them to fulfill that commitment." Only the few are "genuinely mean-spirited," he says; the many are naive, inexperienced, and well-intentioned (B2).

Unfortunately, monoculturalism is pandemic. Though probably most prevalent among Americans of European descent, it is not limited to them. Education that attempts to counter monoculturalism (here my classical liberalism gives up any remaining pretense to innocent impartiality) must itself embody the values of respect and justice that it means to promote. Giroux's writings on education describe students' responses to enculturation as a process involving accommodation (unquestioning acceptance of conventions), opposition (movement against the dominant ideology that nevertheless reinforces it), and resistance (also a counter to the dominant ideology, but one that leads to emancipatory critical consciousness). Giroux advocates a critical pedagogy to move students from accommodation to resistance. Resistance, then, may culminate in "civic courage," by which he means "the willingness to act *as if* [one] were living in a democratic society" (*Theory* 201). I do not propose that the Manzanar classes present a single paradigm of resistance or discovery, but the initial responses of resistance and their gradual ebbing demonstrate an interesting twist on Giroux's theory. Confronted with challenges to their cultural assumptions, assumptions that support mainstream ideology, students imbued with the dominant culture may *begin* with resistance. Invitations to engage in inquiry may then lead students from resistance to an accommodation that itself may be a step toward civic courage. That is, the students' writing overall suggests that in response to the challenge of understanding the internment—its causes and its lasting effects—they revised their conventional conceptions of the dominant "land of the free" myth to accommodate the racial difference and governmental error they learned about.

I intend the pedagogy and materials I describe to take issues of race beyond the comfortable notion of cultural diversity that Giroux says typically limits "liberal" approaches to difference (*Border Crossings* 171). A major part of my point is that when studying the World War II internment of Japanese Americans, one cannot escape race and racism, because they are central to political, social, and economic realities. Indeed, this study is valuable because of the central role of race and racism in it.

Racial difference is not a nostalgic precursor of the melting pot. There is no melting pot. Furthermore, there is no denying the complicity of complacency in the material and spiritual suffering of marginalized people. Nevertheless, marginalizing the complacent in the classroom is not a helpful response. In *Border Crossings* Giroux describes and advocates a "border pedagogy" based in part on the need for teachers to be "able to listen critically to the voices of their students" and thus become border crossers themselves. We do this not only by making "different narratives available to [our]selves and . . . students" but also by "legitimating difference as a basic condition for understanding the limits on one's own voice" (170). I wish to extend this concept: a pedagogical practice that, in Giroux's words, "takes seriously how ideologies are lived, experienced, and felt at the level of everyday life" (176) must provide for listening to and negotiating with inexperienced students who may fit Blanchard's description of "interracially incompetent" (B2). Building toward a true multiculturalism means using culturally diverse materials not as dogma or indoctrination but as part of a larger process of educating students about the power of reading and writing as tools of critical inquiry. Our multicultural land of the free has many voices, many ears, many opportunities for change.

NOTE

I want to thank three classes of English 002 students at Marquette for their cooperation, their insights, and even their resistance and to express special appreciation to Claude Morita, who first taught me about both the internment and the redress movement.

Cross-Talk: Teachers, Texts, Readers, and Writers

Cecilia Rodríguez Milanés

Let's start from the premise that none of us is pure. I am no more purely Latina than you are purely African American or midwestern white middle class or Seminole or radical feminist lesbian or physically challenged Jew. Neither are we pure in gender. No one has to be reminded how inconsistent we are in playing our prescribed or voluntary roles; robots are consistent but boring.

Next, we are all readers of the world; we read texts, signs, weather, stars, traffic, foreign policy, people, animals, rivers, and anything else that can be interpreted, including ourselves (see Freire and Macedo). Some of us are better or more practiced readers than others. In many ways, illiterate people are more astute as readers of the world than highly educated folks are. Since there is no single, best interpretation or reading, no one can be an expert reader of any one text every time. We may pose a beautiful, complex, practical, and fantastic interpretation of any given text or sign—once; we can approximate this reading every time afterward more or less successfully, but it never is the same. No, it never is like the first time ever again.

Finally and perhaps best of all, we influence one another: each time we talk or see one another on television and on movie screens; each time we buy a compact disc we didn't record or eat Chinese food we didn't cook. Every single time we greet one another, we affirm that everyone is other to us. Identical twins are other to each other. Some of us are more obviously ethnic or other. Race, class, ethnicity, tribal affiliation, sexual orientation, and even physical ability can be and have been disguised, but for some, markers such as these reveal us—parts of us, anyway. In some ways, they protect us; in other ways, they can be used to objectify or commodify us.

Most people considered mainstream today would not have been representative in 1912, when 40% of the whites in the United States had been born elsewhere and 99.2% of the blacks were United States born;

yet still African Americans are not viewed as mainstream Americans (Morrison 496). When the Irish arrived in New York City, the dominant culture's sign read: "No dogs or Irish." When the Italians arrived, it changed to "No dogs or Italians." Each successive group arriving on the shores of the United States attempted to adapt, accommodate, and strip itself of the difference markers that betrayed them. White European immigrants were marked by accent, stature, color (hair, skin, and eyes), facial bone structure, and dress. American Indians, the only indigenous Americans, were efficiently decimated by plagues and continual wars and forced to melt into the mythical American pot by rape, assimilation, and destructive, deceitful, and devious governmental policies and programs. Schooling has been an effective tool of assimilation. But my people have a saying—"*la sangre llama*" or "blood calls you." And all our bloods are intermingled; just ask anyone looking for a bone-marrow transplant. History, memory and rememory, ancestry, and DNA surge through our veins. But some of us are more attentive to blood, culture, and difference than others are.

So if everyone is multicultural, we may come to the conclusion (or understanding) that difference is only natural. Making the leap to viewing difference as empowering, then, isn't so arduous or perplexing. If all this is so, our work as teachers, civic activists, politicians, parents, and readers and writers of the world should be relatively easy. Yet most of us know how very difficult it is. Teachers who use multicultural literature and discourses at the center of their curricula and pedagogy are keenly aware of this challenge, especially when they receive their student evaluations. I would argue that the mainstream culture, ideology, and educational system pays lip service to multiculturalism, rendering it fashionable, frivolous, and dismissable. Perhaps we multiculturalist educators should be grateful for such treatment, particularly if multiculturalism, following its "add and stir" or "We're all different; I'm OK; you're OK" trend, continues to evolve into a theme park, coming to your state soon. But multicultural education, in contrast, demands contextualization of cultures and their texts, close attention to the influence of each culture on ourselves, our society, and our perspective. Perspective should be foremost in the mind of the multicultural educator. How can we convey to students a perspective that encourages engagement with others (where transformative power is centered), the understanding that people will always be different from us and that difference is to be respected and appreciated?

Each contributor to this section is teaching and writing to answer that question. These multicultural teachers discuss the multicultural literatures they teach in classrooms made up principally of multicultural students. The work of multicultural education and empowerment, as described in these essays, is exceedingly hard but deeply satisfying. It is rewarding to note that each teacher strives for that perspective of tolerance, advising us to be conscious about what we do when we teach and when we read and respond to writing. Post-structuralist pedagogical theories show the need for this kind of self-reflexive teaching (see Cahalan and Downing; Miller and McCaskill; and Trimmer and Warnock). We still need to consider, however, the roles of reading and writing in courses shaped by multicultural theory and curricula.

The concentration on writing in this volume helps fill that gap. The five pieces in this section blur the boundaries between reading (inter-pretation/criticism) and writing. The contributors' emphasis on the correlation of reading and writing and their tendency toward or pref-erence for using autobiographical or expressive writing is encourag-ing. I've found that cross-genre writing, especially autobiographical narrative, elicits engaging, remarkable writing from students—work that requires the writer's power to draw in the reader and inspire a connection (see Freedman).

In the first essay, Carol Severino describes how a Latino teacher used a traditional teacher-centered approach in one class and a more student-centered workshop approach in another. Severino shows how the different curricula and the teaching strategies that use the stu-dents' culturally based texts help students discover both cultural dif-ferences and similarities and build multicultural literacy. I would have liked to hear more about this teacher's role as a man of color, an ex-amination of the effect and traces of his otherness in these multi-cultural classrooms. None of the contributors discuss this issue in depth, though Esha De and Donna Gregory briefly address it.

De and Gregory outline a theory and provide strategies to combat the colonizing and dominating power of Western academic discourse. To curtail this domination, they ask pointed questions to their stu-dents about the students' work. The pedagogical section of their essay splendidly illustrates how careful planning and consistent theoretical underpinnings can transform the multicultural classroom into more than a trip to a cultural smorgasbord. Their assignments demand cre-ativity and analysis. It is not clear, however, if the plan worked; they do not give examples of what they consider successful student writing, al-though they show where the students' non-Westernized discourses clash with Western essayist prose. A problem arises when the authors posit an exaggerated dichotomy between "non-Western" and "aca-demic." Surely there are dominating non-Western rhetorics or dis-courses that erase, silence, or thwart their own non-Western dialects, languages, and ways of imagining the world.

Wendy Hesford argues for the use of autobiographical writing by students, but like De and Gregory she urges us to note the interplay of conflicts and negotiations between the selves students present in their texts. Hesford convincingly poses the postmodern self and writer as a productive, though shifting, stance from which to deconstruct the designs language and culture have on us. This essay also provides excellent questions we may pose of students about their own and others' texts, for example, asking them to think about their positioning as readers and the readerly roles authors construct for them. Hesford gets students to recognize displacement, alienation, or ruptures in each reading.

Autobiographical writing in Hesford's class includes assignments that examine the role of storytelling in the students' lives and in reading and writing autobiographies. Hesford wants students to uncover and analyze the social forces that shape their voices; she presses them further to consider the possibility that experience is not only highly subjective but also subject to "contradictory and conflicting interpretations." While I am quite fond of this view, I wonder how the students felt about it. Even though many of us embrace a postmodern epistemology, most students I teach are terrified of their powerlessness and of postmodern explanations. I'm concerned that Hesford's adamant opinions about the shifting nature of identity will be maddening for already uncomfortable students.

Sandra Jamieson's essay on text selection clearly illustrates the need to be clear and self-reflexive about the theoretical underpinnings of one's pedagogy. She exposes the insidiousness of the textbook industry's adoption and co-optation of multiculturalism and how it endeavors to fix us in identities. If you ever felt uneasy about using these multicultural collections, Jamieson's close examination may confirm your suspicions, especially when she deconstructs text selection within some of these anthologies and the discussion questions that accompany the readings. I have always found these follow-up questions to be insipid, but I never imagined their deviousness in moving teachers and students away from critical thought—even when the readings themselves are powerful and persuasive. The message is plain: these anthologies may be very useful if we are attentive and cautious; we must make them serve our needs as multicultural educators.

The last essay in this section is a teacher story. Virginia Chappell relates her experience teaching *Farewell to Manzanar* in classes of predominantly mainstream students and reveals various dynamics of otherness that emerge from the reading. Her story illustrates self-reflexive teaching in process. It "begins in naïveté," provides a "thick" description of the classroom, and ends with her realization that, in

James Berlin's words, "a way of teaching is never innocent" ("Rhetoric" 492). Though she shares a "pinkish tone" with most of her students, Chappell's discussion of her life experience reveals a political "dissensus" that sets her apart as other and threatens some members of the class. I have found that my own otherness plays a definite, tangible role in the classroom for both mainstream and nonmainstream students. When, for example, I read Chappell's declaration that she was not prepared for her students' resistance, I was alarmed. Any pedagogy based on liberatory or transformational foundations leads to resistance, especially given most of our students' previous schooling.

Let me be clear: no one has any special or privileged authorization to teach the texts of any group—mainstream or not. I teach predominantly mainstream students texts deemed "minority" not because I have innate, exclusive insight into the writings of people of color. I teach to show that anyone can, and all should, do this work, as long as one has a sensitivity and a sensibility about the cultures one teaches. Developing them relates to the perspective I mention above. Other theorists can shed light on how that perspective develops.

Reed Way Dasenbrock has articulated an interesting and useful way to think about our otherness to texts, particularly texts viewed as non-mainstream. Expounding on Donald Davidson's *Inquiries into Truth and Interpretation*, Dasenbrock describes the implications of Davidson's work for the interpretation of literary works:

> First, the central movement in interpretation is from an assumption of similitude to a location of and an understanding of difference. Second, this understanding of difference leads not to an inability to interpret but to an ability to communicate across difference. . . . what is essential is that we understand what others mean by their words and what they understand ours to mean. We can understand someone, even if we do not share a set of beliefs or a language, as long as we know what the other's beliefs are. What enables us to do this is our ability to construct passing or short-term theories to interpret anomalous utterances. Faced with an anomaly, with something that doesn't fit our prior theory, we adjust that prior theory, incorporating what we learn from encountering that anomaly into a new passing interpretation, its stress on how the interpreter changes, adapts, and learns in the encounter with the anomalous.

Humans have a delightful habit of trying to connect—to texts and people like and unlike them. Dasenbrock stresses that while we assume similarity, we inevitably encounter difference and that this encounter

"is productive, not frustrating, because it causes change in the interpretive system of the interpreter" (41). I would add that those of us
who are accustomed to being with and around people like and unlike
us are good at developing "passing theories" and are less uncomfortable celebrating, affirming, and speaking from diversity and difference.
Those of us who live or have lived in neighborhoods where obvious difference is the norm have come to see how diversity and difference are
the opposite of deficit; difference is, in Audre Lorde's words, "a fund of
necessary polarities between which our creativity can spark like a dialectic." We know the advantage of many perspectives, insights, and
ways of making and articulating meaning of the world. Lorde attempted to convince us that her otherness was our otherness and that
advocating the "*mere* tolerance of difference" was the grossest re-
formism and "a total denial of the creative function of difference in
our lives" (111; my emphasis). To theorize is to think, describe, and
imagine what it is like to be other. Good theorists are adept at posing
how to think, speak, and read like who we're not. Some of the less analytical among us would be satisfied to leave the theorizing to those
who say "You do your thing and I'll do mine" or "Who am I to judge?"
Sooner or later we recognize difference, although we learn to rank different groups through the schooling process.

So what's a multicultural educator to do? The contributors here have
given us engaging ideas we may apply to our own teaching, but if we
aspire through our pedagogy to transform passive recipients into active participants, if we want readers and writers of the word and the
world, then we should be especially attentive to the potential of difference and diversity to empower (and I use this word in the most radical
sense).

I end with the words of Audre Lorde, to whom I go for comfort and
strength whenever my teaching multiculturally for transformation
seems too difficult:

> Only within that interdependence of different strengths, ac-
> knowledged and equal, can the power to seek new ways of being
> in the world generate . . . courage and sustenance to act where
> there are no charters. Within the interdependence of mutual
> (nondominant) difference lies that security which enables us to
> descend into the chaos of knowledge and return with true visions
> of our future, along with the concomitant power to effect those
> changes which can bring that future into being. Difference is the
> raw and powerful connection from which our personal power is
> forged.   (111–12)

PART III

ESL Issues

Introduction

This section highlights key issues from contrastive rhetoric, the study of the discourse patterns and features of writers from different language backgrounds; this area is especially relevant to composition studies, which is also rooted in rhetoric. We have included this section to strengthen much-needed connections between native-language and second-language composition studies. In a multicultural (interethnic, intercultural, or transcultural) classroom and world, it no longer makes sense to separate as much as we have the study of first-language (L1) and second-language (L2) writing. Exploring relations with rhetoric, the common ancestor, is a way to bring the two communities into a dialogue.

The first essay, by Ulla Connor, redefines and reconceptualizes the field of contrastive rhetoric, expanding it to encompass the study of processes as well as products and the study of oral as well as written communication in the classroom. Tony Silva's review essay acquaints first-language composition teachers with the differences between writing processes and products of native and nonnative speakers of English, recommending specific teaching strategies for the ESL population. Muriel Harris focuses on the needs and expectations of international students served in a writing center. Ilona Leki's cross-talk balances the discussion by examining the limits of contrastive rhetoric and emphasizing the similarities between native-English and ESL writers, especially in writing for the disciplines.

Contrastive Rhetoric: Implications for Teachers of Writing in Multicultural Classrooms

Ulla Connor

The number of international students in the United States is growing. A record number—419,585—were enrolled in 1991–92, approximately half in graduate programs and half in undergraduate programs (Zikopoulos). If they do not arrive with sufficient English skills, they are required to take English as a second language (ESL) classes before full-time enrollment. Universities enroll many other nonnative English-speaking students, often citizens or permanent residents who are not subjected to ESL tests before admission. Because of extensive training in English and a long residence in the United States, many nonnative students speak and write English like native speakers. Others, however, struggle in courses that emphasize the use of English.

ESL students often mention that when they write in English, they translate words, phrases, and organization from their first languages. A Chinese ESL student at my university describes his writing process:

> While choosing Chinese words is second nature to me, extracting the proper English word is much more difficult. In casual communication, my inner thoughts are like free river flowing down directly from my mind to the paper. I can write whatever appears in my mind. When I wrote compositions, I come in to trouble. There are many good sources I could get from the Chinese culture while I write in Chinese; such as literary quotations, famous old stories, and ancient word of wisdom. These rich sources definitely influence my paper quality in Chinese. Unfortunately examples like this are very hard to translate to English. Sometimes I try to make a joke, but it loses its impact in translation.

In an eloquent memoir, *Lost in Translation*, Eva Hoffman—an editor of the *New York Times Book Review* who immigrated from Poland to the United States when she was thirteen—describes being unable to find the right words:

> The problem is that the signifier has become severed from the signified. The words I learn now don't stand for things in the same unquestioned way they did in my native tongue. "River" in Polish was a vital sound, energized with the essence of riverhood, of my rivers, of my being immersed in rivers. "River" in English is cold—a word without an aura. It has no accumulated associations for me, and it does not give off the radiating haze of connotation. It does not evoke. (106)

Contrastive rhetoric explores problems of second-language writers like those above. Initiated in the 1960s by the American applied linguist Robert Kaplan, contrastive rhetoric maintains that language and writing are cultural phenomena. Thus each language has unique rhetorical conventions. Furthermore, the linguistic and rhetorical conventions of the first language influence a student's second-language writing.

This essay is an introduction to contrastive rhetoric for teachers of nonnative English-speaking students. I begin with a short review of the Sapir-Whorf hypothesis of linguistic relativism, on which the principles of early contrastive rhetoric were based. Then I review findings from studies about cross-cultural differences in writing. Finally, I discuss recent cognitively based and context-bound studies of writing that reflect changes in composition theories, and I suggest implications for teaching.

The Sapir-Whorf Hypothesis

The Sapir-Whorf hypothesis of linguistic relativism and determinism, also called the Whorfian hypothesis, suggests that different languages affect perception and thought in different ways. The Whorfian hypothesis, therefore, dictates that one's native language influences and controls thought, consequently barring fluency in a second language. Psychologists maintain that this strong version of the linguistic relativity hypothesis, which states that language controls both thought and perception, has been proved false. Some consider the weaker form, that language influences thought, vague and thus unprovable. Herbert Clark and Eve Clark express this view: "What can one conclude about the Sapir-Whorf hypothesis? At present very little. . . . Languages can apparently be stretched and adapted to fit the needs of virtually any group of experts. . . . Language differences reflect the culture and not the reverse" (557).

But recently a new argument in defense of the weaker form has gained ground. The psychologists Earl Hunt and Franca Agnoli, through careful review of theories and experiments in linguistics and psychology, claim that the Whorfian hypothesis should be considered a hypothesis about language performance, not a linguistic hypothesis about language competence (i.e., the native speaker's knowledge of language and its grammar). According to Hunt and Agnoli, every language is translatable, but often a loss is involved—an utterance that is natural in one language may be completely unmanageable in another. This argument supports the weaker version of the Whorfian hypothesis. For example, Hunt and Agnoli maintain that it is not because the Chinese language lacks counterfactuals (statements contrary to fact, such as if-then constructions in English, e.g., "If I were rich, I would buy a boat") that the Chinese do not use them. Instead, it is because the Chinese language does not have the subjunctive form; counterfactuals in Chinese require an elaborate, time-consuming circumlocution. Hunt and Agnoli take their example from Alfred Bloom. The Chinese translation of the English utterance "If you weren't leaving tomorrow, you would be deportable" would read: "I know you are leaving tomorrow, but if you do not leave, you will be deported" (Bloom 18). Thus the Chinese sentence is awkward and difficult to produce and process linguistically. The relative cost of reasoning is greater in Chinese than in English.

Instead of focusing on universals of language and thought (e.g., all languages have basic color terms, pronoun systems, and word order), psychologists and linguists have begun to identify cultural differences. A similar trend is taking place in composition studies; cultural and language backgrounds are being shown to affect writing behaviors and written products.

Kaplan's Contrastive Rhetoric

In 1966, the applied linguist Robert Kaplan, echoing the strong Whorfian view that each language forces a worldview on its users, claimed that not only language but also writing is culture-specific:

> Logic (in the popular rather than the logician's sense of the word), which is the basis of rhetoric, is evolved out of culture; it

is not universal. Rhetoric, then, is not universal either, but varies from culture to culture and even from time to time within a given culture. It is affected by canons of taste within a given culture or a given time. ("Patterns" 2)

Kaplan analyzed some six hundred compositions written in English by international students. On the basis of the analyses, he hypothesized that in expository writing "each language and each culture has a paragraph order unique to itself, and that part of the learning of the particular language is the mastering of its logical system" ("Cultural Thought Patterns" 14). Kaplan describes English exposition as linear in that a paragraph begins with a topic statement, which is supported by examples related to the central theme. Although most English paragraphs fit this pattern and thus are deductive, Kaplan also acknowledges inductive paragraph development, in which the topic statement ends the paragraph, in this first version of Kaplan's theory.

Kaplan tentatively identified five types of paragraph development for five language groups. The classification was informed by his knowledge of the rhetorical theories of the language groups as well as extensive examination of ESL writing by students from those groups. According to Kaplan, paragraph development in Semitic languages is based on a series of coordinate rather than subordinate clauses. Parallel constructions are achieved when the first idea is completed in the second coordinate clause. What Kaplan calls Oriental essays use an indirect approach and come to the point at the end. The writer achieves circularity by looking at the topic from different perspectives. In Romance languages and in Russian, there is freedom to digress and to introduce material that writers in other groups would consider extraneous.

Although intuitively appealing to writing teachers and popular among ESL writing researchers, Kaplan's representations have come under much criticism. Detractors fault Kaplan's first theory of contrastive rhetoric for using overgeneralizing terms such as *Orientals* and improperly grouping languages that belong to distinct linguistic families; stereotyping English paragraph organization by depicting it as a straight line; generalizing about native language organization on the basis of students' second-language essays; and overemphasizing cognitive factors at the expense of sociocultural factors (e.g., schooling) to explain preferences in rhetorical conventions.

Since Kaplan's seminal research, much ESL research has compared ESL writing with native English speakers' writing. The most frequently studied languages have been Arabic, Spanish, Chinese, and Japanese, reflecting the backgrounds and numbers of ESL students in the United States. (For comprehensive discussions of these contrastive rhetorical studies, see Kaplan, *Contrastive Rhetoric*; Connor and Kaplan; and Purves, *Writing*.) Most of the contrastive studies point to differences in written products between native English speakers and ESL students. The differences echo Kaplan's findings with different languages, but the explanations for them do not always concur with Kaplan's first claim attributing the differences to cognitive factors. Instead, the reasons have to do with culturally embedded preferences for good writing, which result from many factors besides linguistic, rhetorical, and cognitive ones, such as schooling and writing instruction.

New Trends in Contrastive Rhetoric

Contrastive-rhetoric research is changing in the 1990s. The traditional contrastive-rhetoric framework has proved unable to account for the data; a new one is needed. Contrastive rhetoric is moving from a purely linguistic framework—involving structural analysis of products—to one that considers both cognitive and sociocultural variables.

Internal and external forces have necessitated this change. The internal criticism mentioned above has required contrastive rhetoricians to go beyond the traditional, linguistic parameters of analysis to consider discourse-level features as well as processes of writing. Equally important have been two major external forces: changing foci in first-language composition research and new developments in discourse analysis and text linguistics.

In native-language composition research, cognitive models have described writing as a discursive process of generating, organizing, and translating ideas into text (Flower and Hayes). But increasingly researchers view writing as interactive and social, involving more than the generation, organization, and translation of ideas (Nystrand). They see writing as interaction within a particular group, discipline, or scholarly community. Not only the writers' purposes but also the context, the situation, and the reader explain the decisions writers make. In addition, another external force—discourse analysis and text linguistics—allows for analyses that consider whole texts as dynamic entities (Enkvist; Brown and Yule; Connor, "Research").

These internal and external forces have produced four new developments in contrastive rhetoric: contrastive text linguistics; the study of writing as a cultural activity; second-language classroom-based contrastive writing studies; and contrastive-rhetoric studies of different genres for different tasks and purposes.

Contrastive Text Linguistics

Developments in text analysis in the 1970s and 1980s have had far-reaching consequences for contrastive rhetoric. Text linguistics is "the study of linguistic devices of cohesion and coherence within the text," or, more broadly, the analysis of texts "in their interactional and situational contexts" (Enkvist 26). It is concerned with the processes involved in the reading and writing of texts.

Several text-linguistic studies have contrasted various coherence and discourse patterns in different languages. Perhaps the most influential has been the work of John Hinds. He has shown that writers use certain text structures to achieve a coherence and thus enable the reader to make the right inference and that these textual patterns vary among languages and cultures. Hinds has described how Japanese, Chinese, Thai, and Korean writers favor an inductive presentation, or what he calls "delayed introduction of purpose," over deductive presentation ("Expository Writing" 98). The specifics lead up to what appears to be, and often is, the conclusion. This approach may appear incoherent to the English-speaking reader (although not to the native reader), especially since the concluding paragraph does not always constitute a conclusion in English rhetoric. English-speaking readers, Hinds says, expect most essays to be organized deductively, to move from the general to the particular.

In addition to achieving coherence through textual structures such as induction, writers need to be sensitive to different cultures' expectations of reader and writer responsibilities. In proposing a new typology of language based on "speaker and/or writer responsibility as opposed to listener and/or reader responsibility," Hinds has shown that, with respect to coherence, for example, Japanese writing demands more of the reader, while the Western rhetorical form places the expository burden chiefly on the writer ("Reader").

Study of Writing as a Cultural Activity

The 1980s witnessed a proliferation of research on the processes of becoming literate in one's native language and culture. Anthropologists, psychologists, and researchers in education have investigated these processes and their effects on learners' thinking and social behavior, making important discoveries about the embeddedness of discourse

and writing in culture and about the role of instruction in this embeddedness. Most significant, research reveals that written texts and their
uses vary among cultural groups. It also shows that people learn many
of the conventions and uses of writing through instruction in schools
or elsewhere.

Empirical research examining the relation between culture and discourse falls into three categories. The first is research in anthropology
and psychology that focuses on the functions of writing in society.
Sylvia Scribner and Michael Cole investigated the various kinds of literacy among the Vai in Liberia, and Shirley Brice Heath researched
varying oral traditions and their effects on literacy development
among groups of different cultures and class backgrounds in the Pied-
mont Carolinas (*Ways*).

The second major research direction is educational and deals with
the role of writing instruction in a language and culture. The International Study of Written Composition, planned and carried out during the 1980s by the International Association for the Evaluation of
Educational Achievement (IEA), examined the relations of culture,
writing, and the curriculum in schools in fourteen countries (Purves,
Writing). While it found some universal conventions and uses of writing, it also confirmed culture-specific uses and conventions in school
writing. The IEA study is directly relevant for contrastive rhetoric in
that it examined essay writing, the long-preferred domain of traditional contrastive rhetoric.

The influence of the research into the development of first-language
literacy is clearly evident in the third area of investigation, studies of
ESL students' backgrounds and their effects on second-language literacy. Joan Carson has conducted beneficial ESL research in this area.
In a discussion of literacy development in first and second languages,
Carson examines how Chinese and Japanese speakers learn to read
and write in their first languages and how that learning affects their
expectations and strategies in learning to read and write in English
("Becoming"). Carson is concerned with the influences of social context (the educational system) and cognitive considerations (issues of
the writing system) in language learning. She begins by describing
how Japanese children learn to read and write in a society that values
"the importance of education (and of literacy), the need to work hard
to succeed, the inherent values of the group, and the primacy of
shared social purpose" ("Becoming" 42). Thus Japanese children learn
to value language as a means of expressing social cohesion, not primarily as a medium for individual expression. In China, the situation

is a little different. Carson writes:

> Becoming literate in China involves learning to read and write
> in a society that values education, but that has only recently been
> able to develop among the masses a positive attitude towards lit-
> eracy. Schools reflect the traditional function of Chinese edu-
> cation, which is to teach moral principles reflecting basic societal
> values: patriotism, the collective good, group loyalty, and respect
> for authority. In this context, schools are controlled and regi-
> mented, with a focus on maintaining order and authority. As in
> Japan, language is not thought of as primarily a medium for
> expressing individual meaning, although in China clear public
> expression is valued as a tool for successful communication.
>
> (44)

Carson also discusses the strategies of learning required to master
literacy through writing systems in Japan and China (*katagana, hira-
gana,* and *kanji* in Japan; *kanji* in China). She notes that in Japan traditional methods of memorization, repetition, drilling, and testing are
used to teach a written language consisting of thousands of different
signs. In China memorization of characters and passages is also a
large part of literacy instruction. "There is a strong belief that the path
to lively and creative writing styles lies in internalizing others' styles,"
Carson writes ("Becoming" 53).

Finally, Carson explores possible consequences of Chinese and Japanese learning styles and strategies for ESL writing students. She concludes that at least two areas will be difficult for Japanese and Chinese
students. Accustomed to working for the collective good of the group,
these students may have trouble in group work in United States classrooms, where the emphasis is on improving the individual's writing.
They must also strive for originality and creativity because so much of
their education has involved memorization and reliance on others'
texts. In Carson's opinion, "knowing the educational background of
their students can provide ESL writing teachers with important insights into the ways in which ESL writers approach the often formi-
dable task of learning to write in English" ("Becoming" 56).

Classroom-Based Contrastive Studies

Research on writing as the social construction of meaning has shown
the value of examining perceptions and beliefs about literacy and

learning in mainstream writing classrooms (Hull et al.). Cultural mismatches manifest themselves in several classroom situations: conversation, collaborative groups, and teacher-student conferences.

Glynda Hull and her colleagues have shown that competence in writing classrooms means "interactional competence with written language: knowledge of when and how and with whom to speak and act in order to create and display knowledge" (301). Classroom talk is deeply embedded in culture. In Western culture, classroom conversations consist of a tripartite series of turns in which a teacher initiates talk, a student replies, and the teacher evaluates the response. Students from linguistically diverse backgrounds may not function well in this type of conversation.

Research by sociolinguists on the style and patterns of oral interaction also shows interethnic and cross-cultural differences that often impede communication. Ron Scollon and Suzanne Scollon studied interaction between Athabascan Indians and native English-speaking Canadians, observing frequent conflicts in communication (*Narrative*). They found differences in the amount of talk (Athabascans talk little; English speakers talk a lot) as well as in the expected role of the speaker and the listener (Athabascans expect the superordinate person to do the talking; Canadians expect the subordinate person to do the talking). The Scollons explain the consequences of these differences for the educational performance of Athabascan children. Although the research of writing experts like Hull et al. and sociolinguists like Scollon and Scollon points to the importance of understanding cultural variation in classroom behavior and conversational patterns, little published research in ESL investigates this issue.

Recently, however, there has been some research into cross-cultural influences in collaborative writing groups in ESL and other writing classes. This research also relies on sociolinguistic analyses of cross-cultural interaction among students in writing groups responding to one another's writing. The quality and quantity of these responses show cultural differences. Sara Allaei and I offer suggestions for classroom practice to handle some of the problems with collaboration and peer response of international students.

The third related area of research deals with teacher-student conferencing, in which cultural differences may also hinder communication. Lynn Goldstein and Susan Conrad examined the degree of active participation and negotiation in teacher-student conferences and the effects on revision and final written products. They found large differences in the extent to which the three students in the study participated in the conferences and negotiated meaning. Although the sample was small, Goldstein and Conrad speculated about the effects of culturally different role designations: "In our study, it is possible that the variation we have seen across the three students may result, at least in part, from these students using culturally diverse rules for how much teachers and students control the discourse when interacting with each other" (456). The study of conferencing seems another important direction in contrastive research with implications for both the classroom and the writing center (see Harris and Blalock in this volume).

Contrastive Rhetoric and Genre Analysis

Most contrastive-rhetoric studies have dealt with expository prose; only recently have some examined other genres, such as persuasion and argumentation. With the increased interest in having ESL learners write for many purposes and in many contexts, the specification of genre is important.

John Swales provides a useful definition of *genre* in contrastive-rhetoric analysis: "A genre comprises a class of communicative events, the members of which share some set of communicative purposes" (58). Thus research articles, grant proposals, and presentations are different genres. Swales criticizes contrastive-rhetoric studies for not distinguishing among genres. He faults Shirley Ostler's research, for example, for comparing student essays written by Arabic ESL students with published texts in English. According to Swales, researchers need to compare texts written for similar purposes in similar contexts.

Some genre-specific studies already exist, including Anna Mauranen's investigation of Finnish and English economists' metalanguage strategies in economic reports, my study of a Japanese and an American manager's negotiation styles in written business correspondence ("Contrastive Study"), and a comparison by Melinda Kramer and me of ESL and American business graduate students writing business case reports. Research like this helps untangle the combined effects of culture, the writer's background, and the specific situation. The research conducted so far has produced traditional contrastive-rhetoric findings that explain some characteristics of processes and products of specific genres (e.g., Japanese and Chinese tend to be more indirect than Americans; Finns and English speakers have different coherence conventions, the Finns leaving things unsaid that they consider obvious and the English speakers expecting them as clarification; and Korean students do not want to take strong positions in defending business case decisions). Future research should continue addressing the interaction among the various variables: native culture, genre, situation, and students' backgrounds.

Relevance for Teaching Nonnative English-Speaking Students

Ilona Leki suggests that contrastive rhetoric has several implications for ESL teachers ("Twenty-Five Years"). First, contrastive-rhetoric research helps students understand that preferences in writing styles are culturally influenced. Second, this awareness can benefit students psychologically: they can feel good about themselves knowing that their writing in English is not bad simply because it exhibits some rhetorical features of their first language. Third, contrastive rhetoric helps explain why and how teachers should teach the expectations of the English-speaking audience to ESL writers.

The new, broader definition of contrastive rhetoric has further implications for teachers of nonnative English speakers. Teachers need to be aware of cultural differences in their students' writing and understand their students' composing and revising behaviors. In addition, they need to be sensitive to differing interactional patterns across cultures and adjust collaborative writing groups and other classroom activities accordingly. Finally, to help their ESL students to become successful college-level writers, teachers need to be sensitive to the complex interactions among culture, genre, and discourse community.

Differences in ESL and Native-English-Speaker Writing: The Research and Its Implications

Tony Silva

In recent years ESL writing practitioners (teachers, testers, and program directors) have been advised to adopt practices derived from research on native English-speaking (NES) writers. This advice seems sound in general, for it would be foolish to ignore the many important insights generated by this research. But it would be just as foolish to assume that these practices will necessarily be appropriate for ESL writers; ESL writing practitioners' intuitions and empirical studies of ESL writers suggest that ESL and NES writing differ in salient and important ways. Consequently, it appears reasonable to suggest that to make informed and intelligent decisions about adopting or modifying NES practices, ESL writing practitioners need a clear and detailed account of the type and extent of differences between ESL and NES writing. I seek to provide such an account here; I review and synthesize the findings of empirical studies comparing ESL and NES writing and discuss their implications for ESL writing theory, research, and practice, as well as for mainstream or first-language theories of writing.

I offer a couple of caveats: First, though I focus on differences between ESL and NES writing in this paper, I believe there are many important similarities as well. Only by examining the differences, however, can we learn about and address ESL writers' special characteristics and needs. Second, I know from my experience as a second-language writer and second-language-writing teacher that L2 writing is extremely difficult. I am constantly amazed and humbled by the quality of the efforts of ESL writers in my classes. Therefore, when I point out differences and limitations of ESL writers vis-à-vis their NES counterparts, I in no way mean to denigrate ESL writers. Furthermore, it is important to keep in mind that many of the perceived limitations of ESL writers are developmental; that is, they exist because these writers are still learning English.

The ESL-NES Studies and Their Findings

I report here on all the empirical studies I was able to locate that focus on a direct examination of comparable adult ESL and NES writing; I exclude studies that did not involve both ESL and NES writers and those that involved unfair comparisons of ESL and NES writing—for example, impromptu writing by ESL students versus the published work of professional NES writers. The studies demonstrate some general patterns of subject characteristics, writing tasks and contexts, and focus. The ESL subjects were typically undergraduate college students in their late teens or early twenties who had fairly high levels of English proficiency. Native speakers of Arabic, Chinese, Japanese, and Spanish predominated (see app. for more detailed information on the subjects' native languages). Writing tasks were usually short expository or argumentative essays written in thirty- to sixty-minute sessions in class or as parts of entrance or placement exams. Most of the studies focus on written texts; only a few look at composing processes. Of those that focus on written texts, most examine either discourse or lower-level linguistic features; a few examine both.

Quality, Fluency, and Accuracy of ESL and NES Texts

Most of the studies imply that the texts written by ESL subjects were less effective than those of their NES peers, at least in the judgment of NES readers. This suggestion is explicit in the studies that report lower holistic scores for their ESL subjects (Campbell, *Writing* and "Writing"; Carlson; Connor, "Study"; Park; Reid; Xu).

Overall, ESL writers' texts were shorter in word count than their NES counterparts'. Seven studies report shorter texts for their ESL subjects (Hirokawa; Linnarud; Mahmoud; Ragan; Reid; Silva; Yau), and three report longer texts (Benson; Dennett; Hu, Brown, and Brown, et al.).

The studies report that ESL writers make more errors overall than their NES counterparts and (Benson; Hirokawa; Silva; Stalker and Stalker), more morphosyntactic errors (Benson; Campbell, *Writing*; Hirokawa; Hu, Brown, and Brown; Silva; Stalker and Stalker), more lexicosemantic errors (Benson; Dennett; Hirokawa; Linnarud), more spelling and punctuation errors (Benson; Hirokawa; Stalker and

Stalker), more errors in cohesive device use (Mahmoud; Scarcella, *Cohesion*), and more verb, noun-pronoun, article, and preposition errors (Benson; Silva).

Complexity of ESL and NES Texts

General textual patterns. The discourse features that have stirred the most interest are general textual patterns, typically in expository texts. Nathaniel Norment's work corroborates Robert B. Kaplan's claims about the thought patterns of ESL and NES writers ("Cultural Thought Patterns"). Norment reported finding distinct linear organizational patterns in the texts of native speakers of English, centrifugal patterns in those of native speakers of Chinese, and linear patterns with tangential breaks in those of native speakers of Spanish.

Michelle Burtoff reported distinct patterns of logical relations in the texts of native speakers of English, Arabic, and Japanese. She described the patterns as culturally preferred—as opposed to linguistically determined—and distinguished between preferred and strongly preferred patterns. She reported that her NES subjects preferred explaining how something happened, using specific detail and organizing information in a text to form a theme-rheme pattern (recalling Kaplan's notion of a linear pattern) and that they strongly preferred to reintroduce information from earlier in the text to develop another aspect of it. The native Japanese-speaking subjects preferred to explain why something happened, immediately repeating facts or ideas for emphasis, and to include only logically related information. They strongly preferred ending texts or segments of texts with generalizations, ordering information to form causal chains, as in Kaplan's notion of an indirect or circular pattern, and using adversative relations in clauses—creating a reason-counterreason pattern. Finally, Burtoff reported that her native Arabic-speaking subjects preferred explaining by example and organizing information in arguments of equal weight, a structure similar to Kaplan's parallel pattern; they strongly preferred writing short texts that included extensive subordinate arguments or information—that is, structuring information horizontally rather than vertically—and they used a variety of types of subordinate arguments, including serial and parallel.

Hiroe Kobayashi ("Rhetorical Patterns" and *Rhetorical Patterns*) and Kyoko Oi, who compared the written texts of native speakers of English and Japanese, reported that NES subjects tended to follow a general-to-specific, or deductive, rhetorical pattern, and native Japanese speakers a specific-to-general, or inductive, pattern. Finally, George

Xu, who examined the expository-paragraph structure of ESL and NES subjects, provided a counterpoint to the foregoing studies, reporting that, although there were differences (ESL subjects had fewer levels of generality per paragraph and fewer subordinate and mixed paragraphs—including both subordinate and coordinate elements), the differences were not statistically significant.

Argument structure. Six research reports compare the structure of arguments in English by NES and ESL writers. In a functional analysis of arguments written by native speakers of English and Arabic, Amal Mahmoud reported that the native Arabic speakers did less stating of conditions, less defining, and less exemplifying but used more warning and phatic communion. He reported that the Arabic speakers less often stated and supported their positions fully and were inclined to develop their arguments by restating their positions—as opposed to the NES subjects, who developed their arguments by stating rationales for their position. Mahmoud also claimed that the Arabic speakers' argumentative texts exhibited less paragraphing, less rhetorical connectedness (position restatements interrupted the flow), a looser segmental structure (introduction, discussion, and conclusion), less variety and more errors in the use of conjunctive elements, and less explicit formal closure.

Ulla Connor, focusing on coherence, reported that her ESL subjects' texts had less adequate justification of claims and were less likely to link concluding inductive statements to the preceding subtopics of the problem ("Study"). Oi reported that her native Japanese-speaking subjects used more mixed arguments (arguing both for and against) and argument alternations (between arguing for and arguing against) and more often ended their arguments in directions that differed from the beginning positions. She also reported that her Japanese subjects were inclined to be more tentative and less hyperbolic than their NES peers, using more hedges and fewer superlatives.

One part of a study by Driss Ouaouicha compares arguments written in English by native speakers of English and Arabic. Ouaouicha stated that the native speakers of Arabic provided more data but used fewer claims, warrants, backings, and rebuttals than their NES counterparts. He also claimed that the Arabic speakers less often fulfilled the task, used less ethos in their arguments, addressed the audience less often, and expressed more pathos.

Finally, in two studies Yeon Hee Choi compared arguments written by native speakers of English and Korean. In the first study, Choi reported that, although all the NES subjects' texts included the elements of claim, justification, and conclusion, some elements were missing in some of the Koreans' texts ("Text"). He found that the Korean subjects more often used indirect or inductive strategies—moving from evidence to conclusion. This point corroborates Kobayashi's and Oi's findings. In the second study, Choi noted differences in argument structure between the two groups—the NES subjects preferred a claim-justification-conclusion pattern; the native Korean speakers, a situation-problem-solution-conclusion pattern ("Text").

Narrative structure. Two researchers looked at narrative structure in the texts of ESL and NES writers. David Harris asked his subjects to produce an account of a short animated cartoon. He reported that his ESL subjects had less to say on most of the narrative points, more often began their accounts in the middle of the story, less often referred explicitly to the film, and more often omitted essential scene-setting elements than their NES counterparts did. Chantanee Indrasuta, comparing the texts of native speakers of English and Thai, stated that the native Thai-speaking subjects' texts exhibited more use of the first-person singular, less action, more focus on mental states, and more backdrop setting (in which time and place are not important) as opposed to integral setting (in which characters, action, and theme are closely interwoven—and thus setting is essential; *Comparison* and "Narrative Styles").

Features of essay-exam responses. Keiko Hirokawa compared ESL and NES subjects' essay-question responses on a final exam for a graduate course on second language acquisition. She reported that the ESL subjects used more undefined terms, unnecessary or irrelevant detail and information, and repetition; were less cognizant of expected essay forms (i.e., they more often used lists or short responses); and were less able to paraphrase concepts, identify the topic in the exam question and an appropriate strategy for framing an answer, and present a reasoned argument and strong support.

Textual manifestations of the use of a background reading text. Cherry Campbell looked at the differential use of a background reading text in the writing of ESL and NES subjects (*Writing* and "Writing"). Her ESL subjects' texts had fewer examples from the reading text; less backgrounding and foregrounding of examples; less information from the reading text in their first paragraphs and more such information in their last paragraphs; more documentation in footnotes and less documentation in phrases acknowledging the author or text; more acknowledgment of quotations and paraphrases; and less appropriate and consistent language, style, and tone. She also found that their incorporation of material from the reading text was less smooth.

Reader orientation. Robin Scarcella focused on differences in reader orientation, that is, material preceding the introduction of a thesis statement ("How Writers"). Her ESL subjects' orientations were longer than their NES peers'. She noted that the ESL subjects used fewer attention-getting devices and a smaller range of them. The only such device that the ESL subjects used more often than their NES counterparts did was historical context—of which they provided lengthier treatments. She also reported that the ESL subjects downplayed the importance of their themes, while NES subjects emphasized the importance of theirs. ESL subjects used fewer explicit statements and presequences (sentences signaling a theme to follow) and more clarifying devices (repetitions, paraphrases, and explanations); they more often overspecified their themes and thus underestimated their readers' knowledge by introducing information readers considered obvious. Similarly, Omar Atari reported that his native Arabic-speaking subjects preceded their topic sentences with broad statements about general states of affairs more often than their NES peers did.

Cohesion. The studies that compare the use of cohesive devices by ESL and NES writers indicate differences primarily in two areas: the use of conjunctive ties and the use of lexical cohesive ties. ESL writers used more conjunctive ties (Hu, Brown, and Brown; Oi; Scarcella, *Cohesion*) and fewer lexical ties (Hu, Brown, and Brown; Indrasuta, *Comparison* and "Narrative Styles"; Mahmoud). ESL subjects used less variety and more repetition in lexical ties (Connor, "Study"; Oi) and fewer synonyms and collocations (Connor, "Study"; Mahmoud).

Sentences. The studies comparing the sentences of ESL and NES subjects indicate a number of salient differences. The first has to do with sentence constituents: T-units and clauses. ESL subjects' sentences contained more T-units (R. Gates; Silva) but shorter ones (Dennett; R. Gates) and fewer but longer clauses (R. Gates; Hu, Brown, and Brown) than those of their NES peers. ESL subjects' sentences also exhibited more coordination (Silva) and less subordination (Hu, Brown, and Brown; Park; Silva), and they had fewer nonclausal and single-word noun modifiers in each T-unit (Dennett; R. Gates). In particular, the ESL subjects had fewer adjectives, possessives, and verb forms used as noun modifiers (R. Gates); fewer prepositions and prepositional phrases (R. Gates; Reid); and fewer definite articles (Oi). Young Mok Park claimed that ESL subjects used fewer free modifiers (nonrestrictive phrasal and clausal elements). Finally, ESL subjects used the passive voice less often (Carlson; Reid) and used more initial but fewer medial transitional devices (Mann).

Words. There is evidence of ESL-NES differences at the lexical level. ESL subjects used shorter (Reid) and vaguer (Carlson) words than their NES peers, and their texts exhibited less lexical variety and sophistication (Hu, Brown, and Brown; Linnarud). There are also data on the comparative use of metaphor. Sarah Webb reported evidence that suggested a second-language effect for ESL students of increased awareness of the metaphorical qualities of language and less use of imagery in their writing, but she did not find that they used metaphors to fill gaps in their second-language vocabularies.

ESL and NES Composing Processes

Researchers have reported differences between ESL and NES writers in planning, writing, and revising. ESL writers planned less at the global and local levels than their NES counterparts did (Campbell, *Writing*; Dennett; Yau). In assignments involving background texts, ESL writers consulted and relied on the texts more than NES writers did (Campbell, *Writing*). Writing was more laborious for ESL subjects than for their NES peers, primarily because of greater concern and difficulty with vocabulary (Dennett; Silva; Yau). ESL subjects did less rereading of their texts (Dennett; Silva) and made fewer changes on the basis of how their writing "sounded" than the NES subjects did (Silva; Yau). Joann Temple Dennett also stated that, unlike her NES subjects, her ESL subjects focused on content, structure, meaning, and communication value when rewriting as a separate activity but focused on grammar and conventions when rewriting as part of another task. Further, she reported that for her ESL subjects, but not for their NES peers, more rewriting corresponded to better writing mechanics.

This body of research suggests that in general the ESL subjects' writing was distinct from and often simpler and less effective, in the eyes of NES judges, than their NES peers'. The ESL writers' composing processes seemed constrained in some salient and important ways. Compared with the NES subjects, they planned and reread their writing less, wrote with more difficulty because of a lack of lexical resources, and exhibited less ability to revise intuitively by ear.

At the discourse level, the ESL subjects wrote shorter, less effective texts that contained more errors than those of their NES counterparts. Their texts exhibited distinct patterns of exposition, argumentation, and narration; their answers to essay exams and use of background reading texts were different and less effective. Their orientation of readers was deemed less appropriate and acceptable, and they exhibited distinct patterns and less facility in their use of coherence devices, primarily conjunctive and lexical ones.

At a lower linguistic level, the ESL subjects' texts exhibited a simpler style of writing than the NES subjects'. The ESL subjects' sentences included more but shorter T-units, fewer but longer clauses, more coordination, less subordination, less noun modification, and fewer passives. The ESL subjects used shorter and less specific words and generally exhibited less lexical variety and sophistication.

Before the implications of these findings can be considered, it must be recognized that, like any body of research, this one contains studies with limitations. Some of the most common limitations were small samples, inadequate descriptions of subjects or writing conditions, and a lack of reliability estimates or significance tests. These limitations require that we see the findings of these studies and any conclusions based on them as tentative and provisional—as conclusions to be handled with care.

This synthesis of findings has implications for theory, research, and practice. It contributes to theory in that it represents a modest step toward a viable model of differences between ESL and NES writing, a model that, in turn, could serve as a central element in a comprehensive theory of second-language writing. Such a theory could do much to enhance and legitimize current mainstream (L1-based) theories of writing by making them less narrow: less monolingual, less monocultural, less ethnocentric, less fixated on writing by eighteen-year-old native speakers of English in North American colleges and universities and more inclusive, more realistic, more generalizable, and ultimately, more valid. Just as a credible general theory of language cannot be based solely on evidence from English, a credible general theory of writing must be based on more than research on the writing of native English speakers.

There is also evidence of a need for more and better research comparing ESL and NES writing. For example, researchers must corroborate and enhance current findings and fill a number of gaps—especially in the area of composing processes. Future researchers should also do a better job of reporting subject variables (especially language proficiency and writing ability), make writing tasks and conditions more realistic, and analyze data more rigorously—particularly in coding reliability estimates and statistical significance testing.

But more and better research will be to no avail if it never reaches the readers who need it. Much of the research I cite here is neither highly visible nor easily accessible; much of it appears only in hard-to-acquire documents like doctoral dissertations. As a result, important, high-quality work in this area is dying on the vine, and progress toward a better understanding of ESL writing and writing instruction is impeded. Some efforts, for example, the creation of the *Journal of Second Language Writing,* have provided more outlets for publication, but this is not enough. If the potential of ESL writing studies is to be realized, publishers of mainstream books and journals on writing must pay more attention to second-language concerns, and ESL generalist publications must give more play to second-language writing issues.

These findings have important implications for educational practices, such as assessment, placement, staffing, and developing instructional procedures and strategies for ESL and NES writers. First, they make it seem unreasonable to expect that ESL students, even those with advanced levels of English proficiency, will perform as well as NES students on tests of written English, to expect that ESL students will meet standards promulgated by native English speakers for native English speakers. This conclusion suggests a need for different evaluation criteria for ESL and NES writers and raises such difficult but necessary questions as When does difference become deviance? What is good enough? Second, the findings suggest that ESL students, basic or skilled writers, have special needs different from those of NES students and thus are best served by having the option of taking credit-bearing, requirement-fulfilling writing classes designed especially for them—that is, by not being forced into mainstream, NES-dominated writing classes, which may be inappropriate for them. Third, the findings support the notion that ESL students' teachers, whether in ESL or in mainstream writing classrooms, should be cognizant of, sensitive to, and able to deal positively and effectively with their students' sociocultural, rhetorical, and linguistic differences. ESL teachers with substantial backgrounds in writing or NES writing teachers with ESL experience would seem to fit the bill nicely.

Finally, the findings have numerous implications for ESL instructional practices. In the most general terms, ESL writers seem to need, as Ann Raimes suggests, "more of everything" (250). However, more of everything should not necessarily entail more work—for the same compensation—for ESL writing teachers; reducing class sizes and having students complete fewer writing assignments over longer periods of time are also viable options. In particular, ESL more than NES writing teachers need to devote more attention both to process and to product, to strategic and textual concerns. They need to expand the composing process to include more work on planning—generation of ideas, text structure, and language—to make the actual writing more manageable. They need to have their students write in stages, for example, focusing on content and organization in one draft and on linguistic concerns in a subsequent draft. They also need to separate their treatments of revising and editing and provide realistic strategies for each that do not rely on intuitions ESL writers may not have.

ESL teachers must also treat textual concerns more extensively. At the discourse level, ESL teachers need to familiarize students with audience expectations and provide them with strategies for dealing with potentially unfamiliar textual patterns (e.g., exposition, argumentation) and task types (e.g., essay exams). Teachers should also devote extra attention to cohesive devices.

At the lower level, ESL writing teachers need to place greater emphasis on sentence structure. In particular, they should help students use subordination and noun modification to construct complex sentences; I recommend sentence-combining exercises employing sentences from the students' own texts. Teachers should also help students augment their lexical resources through reading (intensive or extensive) and providing lexical options, again, using the students' writing.

The research comparing ESL and NES writing strongly suggests that they are different in numerous and important ways. Those who deal with ESL writers must acknowledge and address this difference if these writers are to receive fair treatment, effective teaching, and thus an equal chance to succeed in their writing-related personal and academic endeavors.

Appendix: Native Languages of the ESL Subjects Involved in the Studies Examined

Atari: Arabic
Benson: Arabic, Farsi, Ga, Japanese, Spanish, Thai
Burtoff: Arabic, Japanese
Campbell (both studies): Chinese, Farsi, Hebrew, Indonesian, Korean, Lao, Spanish, Vietnamese
Carlson: Arabic, Chinese, Spanish
Choi (both studies): Korean
Connor: Japanese, Spanish
Dennett: Japanese
Gates: Farsi, Spanish, Thai

Harris: not specified
Hirokawa: Arabic, Chinese, Indonesian, Japanese, Thai
Hu, Brown, and Brown: Chinese
Indrasuta (both studies): Thai
Kobayashi (both studies): Japanese
Linnarud: Swedish
Mahmoud: Arabic
Mann: Arabic, Chinese, Spanish
Norment: Arabic, Chinese, Spanish
Oi: Japanese
Ouaouicha: Arabic
Park: Chinese
Ragan: Chinese
Reid: Arabic, Chinese, Spanish
Scarcella (both studies): Japanese, Korean, Romance languages,
    Taiwanese
Silva: Chinese, Spanish
Stalker and Stalker: not specified
Webb: Spanish
Xu: not specified
Yau: Chinese

Cultural Conflicts in the Writing Center: Expectations and Assumptions of ESL Students

Muriel Harris

When students learning English as a second language enter writing-center tutorials, they bring along not only their papers but also their culturally conditioned notions about what to expect in a nonclassroom instructional setting. Too often they enter a learning environment that seems bewildering, threatening, frustrating, or antithetical to their prior experiences. Similarly, tutors, having been trained in the theory and pedagogy of writing centers, are often just as bewildered and frustrated by these students, who may resist the roles tutors want to assign them. The tutor and the student, if they are unaware of culturally determined differences in how they expect the tutorial to play out, are likely to begin working at cross-purposes. When this happens, the outcome is not usually very productive. Without shared assumptions about what will happen, the tutor and ESL student can proceed on opposite tracks and spend their tutorial time trying to get the other person to move in their direction. But tutors—as well as teachers who meet in collaborative, one-to-one settings with their ESL students—can remedy this lack of overlap by becoming more sensitive to cross-cultural differences that may impede ESL students' ability to profit from writing tutorials.

To help us learn more about these possible conflicts, I focus here on differences between the theory and pedagogy of collaboration in the writing center and the assumptions and expectations of students from culturally diverse backgrounds who seek tutorial help with writing skills. With such awareness, I hope, we can help ESL students step more fully into—and profit from—the collaborative world of the tutorial.

Tutors' Perspectives on Collaborative Learning

The writing-center approach that tutors are trained to use puts the student in a collaborative, interactive, individualized setting. Collaboration is viewed as empowering because it returns ownership of the piece of writing and responsibility for learning to the writer. Tutors are there to guide, ask questions, listen, and make suggestions, but they are neither authority figures nor evaluators. As Art Young has written:

> Collaboration . . . is fundamental to who we are and what we do. . . . Writing centers have been places for collaboration from their beginnings; for tutoring, for conferencing, for the talk that brings clarity to purpose and ideas, for the listening that empowers those who would write and speak. Writing centers were founded on an alternative vision of the way many people learn and develop facility with language. . . . they were founded on the deceptively simple principles of human interaction, social negotiation, and contextual language development. (4–5)

Tutors, then, are trained to move writers into the active role of making decisions, asking questions, spotting problem areas in their writing, and finding solutions. Tutors are taught how to keep from seizing control and how to avoid identifying problems and offering solutions for students. Tutors may initiate tutorial talk about aspects of the paper, but they expect to be collaborators, not teachers. The tutor's goal is not to fix the individual paper but to help the student become a better writer. The tutor hopes that the writer will internalize the tutor's questions and use them from then on and will adopt as practices the strategies the tutor demonstrates. Tutors provide answers and information, of course, but that is merely one of the ways they help writers. But do ESL students share these assumptions? When they sit down next to their tutors and launch into the session, how likely are they to respond as tutors expect them to? If they are not inclined to share their tutors' perspectives, what do they expect will happen? What do they want to happen? What role do they expect their tutors to play? How willing are students from other cultures to enter into the kind of collaboration that requires them to answer questions as well as ask them? Or, acculturated to treating teachers as authority figures, can they enter into collaboration with tutors who, despite their age and level of education, situate themselves as peers?

ESL Students' Perspectives

To learn more about what ESL students expect when they come to tutorials, I asked eighty-five international students at my university to respond in writing to a lengthy list of questions. These students were enrolled in writing courses ranging from low-intermediate to more advanced composition, and the length of time most had spent in the United States varied from a few months to several years. Although a few had been here most of their lives, many retained citizenship in other countries, pending future plans. While immigrants or refugees are more likely to come to this country with little or no formal instruction in English, the majority of the ESL students answering the questionnaire had learned at least some English in their home countries, a factor that may have influenced their answers to questions about what they want to learn about writing in English. Their national origins reflect the ESL population in my university and are not particularly different from the general percentages for ESL students nationwide. Over sixty percent of the group were from East Asia—the People's Republic of China, Taiwan, Korea, Hong Kong, Japan, and so on—but there were also students from the Middle East, Europe, Central and South America, Africa, and the Indian subcontinent. Two-thirds were male.

To see how their written responses might differ from interviews, I did a trial run with six students, asking them the kinds of questions I planned to include in the questionnaire. Their answers in person were more minimal, more guarded, and less critical of anything American than their anonymous responses on the questionnaires. Anonymity and the privacy of writing seemed to free some of the students, and the fuller responses on paper were most likely the product of the students' being able to take the questionnaire home for a few days, reflect on what they wanted to say, and then write for a while. The written responses are indicative only of the group surveyed, but the comments should caution us to be wary about creating learning environments in which we assume students from other cultures share our perspectives and goals.

Tutors versus Teachers

Several questions about the differences between tutors and teachers and between classrooms in their home countries and in the United States invited these ESL students to describe their perceptions about tutors and teachers. Despite their cultural diversity, they were remarkably consistent in stating that teachers teach and tutors help. They described teachers as those who work with large groups, lecturing on general concepts and course content. Teachers are the experts and authorities on the subject, and their role is to deliver information. Tutors are "not as advanced," lower down on the ladder of authority, prestige, or knowledge. Tutors work individually with students to help them solve their problems and improve their abilities, give more detailed advice and answers, and deal with specifics. "A teacher can tell that you got a problem but is not to work with you to solve them," one student wrote. "Tutor works with you to fix mistakes or solve your problems." Thus these students view the tutor as the appropriate person to bring their problems to and as the person who deals with specifics, that is, with individual examples of larger principles explained by the teacher. This perception can impede tutors who want to help students gain greater insight into larger rhetorical issues of writing as well as mastery over various writing processes and can frustrate the student as well. Tutor and student may have different goals, but both perceive the tutorial environment as informal and helping; these ESL students see tutors as more understanding, more personal, more adept at helping each student, and easier to talk to than teachers. A number of these students noted that they feel freer to ask tutors questions. "Teachers tell you what to do, tutors give advice," wrote one student; "The teacher lectures, the tutor discusses," noted another.

ESL students, then, perceive tutors to be more immediately helpful, more approachable, more practical, and more personal than teachers are, but the students expect tutors to work on errors and difficulties in specific pieces of discourse, not on the larger, more abstract level of writing skills and processes. A few students also said that the tutor is supposed to help with writers' concerns. Typically, they indicated that the tutor should encourage and/or motivate the student. One Puerto Rican student noted that the tutor should "help and encourage students to 'keep it up.' That with a little effort, people can reach their goals and do well in college." Another Puerto Rican student saw the tutor as someone who "encourages the students to improve their work." Similarly, an Indonesian student wrote that the tutor's major responsibility is "to motivate the students to study the subject." There were several other similar responses, but all were from non-Asian students. The Asian students all responded that the tutor's job is correcting errors, showing mistakes, and "giving clear understanding," not providing motivation or encouragement.

While many students noted that in their countries students do not ask questions in class, all the students responded that they are willing (and eager) to ask tutors questions. None expressed any reluctance to do so, and many wrote that they see tutorials as their opportunity to ask the kinds of questions they hesitate to ask in class or cannot ask elsewhere. "I have many questions but few opportunities to do asking," wrote one student. Since all these students are enrolled in courses in which teachers set aside several hours each week for conferences, they apparently do not see that time as the appropriate opportunity. Asking questions is how they check their mistakes, give the tutor a better idea of what kinds of problems they have, and clear up their doubts. "I should know what I want to know, so I must ask a tutor," one wrote. Many echoed one student's succinct comment: "How else to learn?" Given this expectation, it may surprise some ESL students that tutors have long lists of their own questions to ask writers. Tutors, trained to work from the top down, from higher-order concerns such as clarity, focus, and organization to lower-order concerns of sentence-level correctness, might well want to open a tutorial by asking what the student liked best in the paper, what the main point was, which part was troublesome, who the audience is, and so on. For the student who wrote that he sees the tutor's role as "answering my questions about hard points like right verb tense," such broad questions about more general matters might be disconcerting indeed. Moreover, the student may well enter the tutorial prepared to ask questions, not to answer them.

While students from other cultures enter tutorials expecting to take an active role in asking questions, the students have a concomitant expectation that tutors deliver information, that tutors are in control of the situation and do the work of finding problems and offering solutions. Numerous responses on the questionnaires repeated the point that the tutor's task or responsibility is to help students—to point out weaknesses, to correct errors, to answer questions, to help improve their writing, to show students how to make their papers better, and to help them understand what they need to know. These responses all use active verbs, describing actions that the tutor is to take. ESL students expect the tutor to take control of the session—to diagnose and convey to the student what needs to be learned, much like a teacher is expected to lecture and deliver information. The tutor's responsibility is "to solve my problems" or "to explain my errors." A few students, however, did recognize that their role in the learning process is also active: "A tutor helps people to find their own style of writing and know how to check our mistakes" and "The tutor gives hints and lets the thinking to me." More generally, though, these students think their role is to listen, remember, and ask questions that will clarify their understanding. Thus there may be strained silence in a tutorial when a tutor asks and then waits patiently for answers to standard tutors' questions intended to give the student an active role, such as "How would you fix this paragraph?" or "What do you see as the problem here?" The tutor may interpret this silence as an indication that the student doesn't have an answer, but it may more likely be that the student is also sitting patiently, waiting for the tutor to fulfill her or his function of providing such answers. Some discussion is then necessary to help the student see that he or she really is being given an opportunity to learn by offering an answer.

Nonnative students' passivity in tutorials may stem from behavior learned in classrooms in other countries. When the ESL students I questioned described classrooms in their native countries, they noted that students listen and teachers lecture. Students are expected to accept what the teacher says and not to raise questions. The student's role is to study hard and to learn—sometimes by memorizing—what is presented. When asked to describe differences between American classrooms and those in their own countries, they often commented on the freedom in our classrooms to ask questions. One student wrote that "students in America are more involved in the learning process," and another wrote that in her country "the student is not so active." Yet another student commented that in his country students spend their class time copying down what the teacher writes on the board and their time outside of class memorizing what they have copied. (See Tateya for a description of the student as note taker in the Japanese classroom.)

These very different approaches to education should help us realize what a leap we are asking some students to make in the tutorial. Students who have not had lengthy conditioning to classroom discussion and question asking are less likely to take control in tutorials, even when invited, because they are not familiar with how to become the active learners that tutors want to develop. For ESL students, finding their own answers rather than being told what the answer is or what they must learn can be a new process. As tutors, we have to suppress any discomfort with ESL students who seem to want us to tell them how to fix their papers. There is a cross-cultural problem in the clash between ESL students who sit with pencil poised, waiting to write down what we tell them, and us, as we keep trying to return responsibility for revision to the writer. When the tutor asks, "What is the connection between these two sentences?" or "Is there a word missing there?" and the polite student waits for the tutor to answer the question, the two parties are acting out assumptions and expectations from very different worlds. If we want to break this mold, we need to backtrack and address the differences, to think about how to help the student adopt a mode of learning that can seem foreign and difficult at first—even impolite or disrespectful. Sometimes we can do so by stating at the beginning of the tutorial that we expect and look forward to having students answer their own questions and that answering will make them better writers. Judith Kilborn suggests an alternative approach for nonnative students who are used to hearing directive statements from teachers: When appropriate, tutors can begin their questions with "Please explain" instead of "Why" or "How." An answer to a relatively open-ended request might be more useful and enlightening for both the ESL student and the tutor.

We need not be hesitant about introducing ESL students to new learning environments. These students are already astute observers of how things operate in this country. Even if they are not comfortable embracing our approaches, they recognize some of the differences. When asked to compare student-teacher interactions in the United States with those in their countries, the ESL students frequently commented that the relations here are more informal, casual, or relaxed. In their home countries, students do not criticize teachers and students show more respect than these students see exhibited here. Repeatedly, ESL students commented on the freedom in American classrooms to challenge the teacher, to interrupt with questions, to sip drinks, to call teachers by their first names. Some ESL students are likely to change their modes of interacting with teachers and tutors in an effort to conform. They may, then, start acting more like American students, but we must realize that their adaptation may not be very deep. ESL students can still find it difficult to interrupt us, to slip easily into the informality of the tutorial setting. Other cultural factors may be at work as well. Xiaomin Cai, an Asian tutor in an American writing center, cautions us that Asian students prefer to be indirect and may agree or nod rather than challenge or confront those they disagree with. They may also pretend to understand when they don't, to save face.

Just as ESL students adopt some behaviors to cope with our culture, our behaviors may be irritating or offensive to them. For example, a number of students responding to my questionnaire expressed strong feelings of discomfort at American habits such as engaging in discussion after the teacher answers a question, smoking and joking around in class, even putting their legs up on tables or other informal means of slouching. One European student was angry about being called by his first name. He wrote that he expects us to use appropriate titles and expects in return not to be treated like a child and called by his first name. His discomfort was echoed by a student from Pakistan, where students also do not call teachers by their first names. We may not easily recognize such students and their resistance to behavioral norms and standards in American learning environments, but we can at least be aware that the ESL students who come to our writing centers may be trying to move from very different perspectives on the teacher-student relationship or are not comfortable with our assumptions or ways of interacting. A peer tutor in training recently commented to me that she wished the ESL student with whom she had been working would stop agreeing with her all the time. "He just needs to stop that and to concentrate on what is going on," said the irritated tutor, obviously unaware that all the vigorous head nodding and verbal affirmatives was likely the result of a deeply felt need to show respect, which was no doubt inculcated in his native country.

ESL Students' Attitudes

Because tutoring pedagogy emphasizes the need to establish a comfortable relationship at the beginning of the tutorial, tutoring manuals often advise starting a session with a few minutes of friendly chatter. This getting-acquainted time can have several benefits. It can send students the message that the environment will be collaborative and helpful and will not sustain whatever anxieties they entered with. As they relax, they will feel freer to ask questions, and tutors, as a side benefit, can learn some useful information about things that interest the students, about their levels of motivation, about classroom or time-management problems, even about their levels of verbal ability. Students who speak easily and comfortably but have some diction problems in writing will probably benefit from proofreading. But students who exhibit problems with verb endings or prepositions in speaking will probably require more than proofreading practice.

These benefits can also apply to ESL students. But I find they occasionally seem very businesslike when we begin a tutorial. Are they uncomfortable or reluctant to enter informal conversations because learning environments in their cultures are very formal? Do they even want to converse with a tutor in this second language with which they are struggling?

On the questionnaire I asked the ESL students whether they want to spend a few minutes in friendly conversation with a tutor before beginning to work together, and I encouraged them to explain their answers. Overwhelmingly, these students wrote that they very much do. Most explained that they are nervous at the beginning of a session and need to relax. As one student wrote, "Most of foreign students have the anxiety and fear about conversation. So it will soothe them or warm them up." Another student wrote, "I get nervous when I must speak in English at this time. Therefore, a friendly conversation can make me relaxed." John Parbst, a tutor, described using such off-topic conversation in a session with an ESL student who initially was too shy or nervous to speak. Over about twenty minutes of conversation, the student slowly relaxed and eventually became interested in talking. The few remaining minutes of the tutorial were focused and productive: "That five to ten minutes of a true exchange of ideas was better than the alternative: me talking at an uninvolved audience for thirty minutes" (2).

Some of the students also recognized that their sessions would be more effective if they could get to know the tutor first: "I like friendly atmosphere while learning as I always have a better result." Other students expressed a need to be comfortable with the person who would be their tutor—or at least comfortable enough to discuss their problems. Still others considered it important to break the student-teacher barrier through conversation, and a few welcomed the opportunity to chat with a native speaker because they rarely have occasion to do so. Two ESL students also recognized this as a chance for the tutor to do some diagnostic work: "[Conversation] can make more understand between tutor and students and make the tutor know what level the student is," and "The tutor can understand me more, e.g., how long have I been learning English." In addition, as Cai reminds us, there is an Asian preference for making friends before getting down to business; this practice can mystify or confuse American businesspeople when dealing with their Asian counterparts (L. Young). But a few ESL students did not prefer to open a tutorial with friendly talk, mainly because they did not want to waste time or because they felt uncomfortable chatting while other students were waiting to see a tutor.

The questionnaire contained an open-ended question that invited the ESL students to offer advice to tutors. Many of the students—from a variety of language groups—responded with a plea: ESL students, they wrote, need sympathy and understanding when they ask what they perceive to be dumb questions or when they think they are making foolish mistakes. "International students make silly mistakes that native speakers never will," wrote one student. "Don't be scared by the stupid mistakes that we made," noted another. "Please do not laugh at what you see. They already have had a feeling that their writing is not good," wrote another student. It is important, then, for tutors to remember that the ESL students elbow to elbow with us may feel inept or uncomfortable, that they see themselves as objects of ridicule. As we talk with them, we may be awed by their ability to function in an institution of higher learning in a second language, though we rarely say anything. Those of us who have tried to negotiate our way in foreign countries with a smattering of the local language know the humbling feeling of incompetence or childlike dependence that we sink into when we try even simple tasks such as finding the appropriate bus or purchasing tickets. ESL students have to negotiate far more complex tasks in English while learning the language. It is our responsibility to be sensitive to their discomfort and to help them restore their sense of self-worth as they go through this process. If nothing else, we can do more to allay their fears of being objects of derision because they make mistakes and have to ask questions that native speakers do not ask.

ESL Students' Expectations about Learning

The ESL students I questioned usually commented that what they most want from writing tutors is help in improving their writing. This response is not specific enough to be very informative. But I also asked them to characterize good writing in their first language, and their answers offer clues about what qualities they want their writing to have. Most of the students, from a variety of language groups, noted the significance of "good organization" or "well built structure." They cited grammatical correctness as important almost as often, indicating perhaps a rationale for ESL students' emphasis on eliminating sentence-level errors in the papers they write in English. If they continually request help with grammar, it may be that, in addition to having focused on sentence structure, mechanics, and spelling when learning English, they view correct grammar as integral to good writing. Some Asian students also cited the importance of clarity and vivid description in writing in their languages, and Asian and non-Asian students alike rated vocabulary, the use of "good and broad" words, as a major quality of good writing in their first language. Use of "nice words," "beautiful vocabulary," and "good choices of words" were frequent answers, which indicates that we need to pay more attention to ESL students' requests for help with vocabulary. We may dismiss these requests or put them on back burners when the student seems to be capable of adequate expression in a paper, especially when there are other problems to address. But we should listen more closely, understanding that perhaps vocabulary building is a pressing concern for the student, even if it is not high on our agenda. Similarly, we must respond to requests for help with synonyms when students express un- happiness that they are repeating words. The Chinese students I have tutored are particularly interested in synonyms; they often cite repeti- tion (sometimes of a word that has appeared several times in a three- or four-page paper) as something that detracts from the quality of their drafts. In our rush to help nonnative students master the ele- ments of American academic writing, we need to be sensitive to their goals as well.

Although work on grammatical correctness and vocabulary is not simple, obvious, or quick, working on rhetorical qualities of good writing is even more difficult because we are less aware that some are culturally determined, not universal. For example, while Americans value conciseness, directness, and clarity, work in contrastive rhetoric has shown us that these qualities are not necessarily valued in the discourse of other languages. We have learned about the Asian prefer- ence for indirection, which contrasts with the American preference for clear, overt announcement of a topic in an introductory paragraph (Eggington; L. Young), about the difference between languages in which the reader is responsible for making meaning from the text and languages, such as English, in which the writer is responsible for mak- ing the meaning obvious to readers (Hinds, "Reader"), and about some languages' higher tolerance for digression (Clyne; Kachru, "Writers").

The students who responded to my questionnaire generally seemed unaware that there might be differences between rhetorical values in American academic writing and writing in their first language, though a student from Switzerland noted that in the United States "content can be directly read out of the text passage" while in Switzerland "con- tent is more implied." Because most of the respondents did not indi- cate an awareness of the need to learn about rhetorical values of American academic discourse, a tutorial with an ESL student may be a tug-of-war, as the tutor may, for example, see a great need to have the student work on specificity while the student feels no such need but has a strong desire to learn how to use articles or prepositions. Cai notes that because Asian students are less likely to see the need to work on documentation, tutors need to help them understand its im- portance in American discourse. As Cai explains, in Asian cultures there is a strong sense of putting the group first, as opposed to the American sense of self that leads to a strong sense of ownership of ideas. Americans more easily understand the importance of citing sources, providing documentation, and avoiding plagiarism. Citing sources is less important to Asian students, says Cai, and may even, for some, be an unknown art, resulting in the ready mixing of ideas from various sources and the use of few if any citations. Furthermore, as William Eggington explains, in Korean prose writers may use a "some people say" formulation when taking a controversial stand, in order to protect their positions by enlisting anonymous support or to avoid appearing too direct when criticizing another's position. Student writing that features this approach might look as if it needs citation but may actually present the writer's own ideas. (For a further discussion of cross-cultural rhetorical differences, see M. Harris, "Individualized Instruction.")

While contrastive rhetoric has helped us identify some of what non-native students may need to learn about English, it is also useful to uncover what they feel is important and what they perceive as stumbling blocks on the way to better writing skills. Therefore I asked respondents to note the characteristics of good English that are difficult or puzzling for them. The responses most often were lists of items at the word or sentence level. Vocabulary was the most frequently listed item: "Sometimes I know the meanings of some words but I don't know how to use them"; "Sometimes, there are different words that can be translated by a same word in our language, but they will be used in different positions in English." The students also frequently cited verbs, colloquialisms and idioms, prepositions, and sentence structure. Larger discourse concerns appeared occasionally, though infrequently: "Be specific or concrete is difficult for Chinese," "how to develop my argument in American way," "how to express my ideas in an American way," and "use American language not [my] language." With this kind of knowledge we can be more aware of what the ESL student really wants—or expects—when she or he comes to a tutorial with a paper and asks that familiar question, "Can you please help me with my writing?"

ESL Students' Advice to Tutors

Finally, another area of concern for tutors working with ESL students is the students' response to American habits that help or interfere with tutoring. What pleases these students? What annoys them? Asked to offer advice to American tutors, the student respondents did so at length. They most often cited American friendliness as a characteristic they appreciate; many also respond favorably to American helpfulness. Other qualities of American tutors that the students cited favorably were enthusiasm, eagerness, energy, ability to make jokes and to speak humorously, willingness to offer encouragement, and ability

to motivate. A few respondents seemed puzzled by the American preference for informality, but some thought that an informal atmosphere
makes tutorials more "agreeable" or "happy." Among the American
habits that annoy them are showing impatience with students who
don't know answers or who catch on slowly, covering too much material in too short a time, "looking down on students," speaking too
quickly, using slang, approaching students as if they don't know English at all, displaying uneasiness in talking with ESL students or listening to "poor English proficiency." Other habits that annoy ESL
students may result from the tutors' lack of understanding about what
is acceptable to ESL students in tutoring situations or lack of awareness of cross-cultural differences. Exhibitions of American informality
in tutorials, such as drinking coffee or putting one's feet on a table,
may not bother most American students, but some ESL students listed
these acts as annoying. One ESL student, not used to the frequency or
type of compliments Americans bestow so easily, suggested that American tutors refrain from comments that may seem like insults to students from other cultures. "If I am look nice in my new coat, I very
much wonder if my tutor is mean I am not look nice before," explained
the student.

Mainly, though, in their advice to tutors, ESL students asked for
patience and some understanding of them and their cultures. The following responses (presented in their own words) indicate that the students are acutely aware of how different they are:

○ Tutors need to be quite patient because international students may
   come from a country with different cultural background.
○ Learning little background of the country and difference in writing
   will help much.
○ Please try to understand problems faced by international students.
○ Try to understand how hard they have to work to study in the for-
   eign country and language.
○ Be more patient since the way we think sometimes is so different
   from the way American people do.
○ Do not think of them as foreigners.
○ Try to enjoy getting to know different persons from different cul-
   tures; don't be frightened or look down to us.
○ Try to learn from those cultures.

Because my exploratory conversations with ESL students indicated
their concern for showing respect to and receiving respect from teachers and tutors, I included a question about how students, teachers, and

tutors show respect. The many lengthy responses made me realize that this is a topic that we as tutors do not consider much. Many of the ESL students expect that teachers and tutors, as a sign of their respect for the student, will be patient, polite, and helpful; will treat the student as an adult; will make an effort to understand the student; and will not laugh at the student's mistakes. The students indicated that they could show respect to their teachers and tutors by arriving on time, following instructions and having all assignments finished, having pen and paper ready to take notes, listening closely and paying attention to what the teacher or tutor says, working hard, and expressing appreciation for what is being taught.

The ESL students' responses to my questionnaire may differ in some details, but I came away from their pages of writing with a strong sense of their commitment to learning. Despite the different written accents in their English and the variety of their comments and suggestions, they all are determined to learn how to write in English. They come to writing-center tutorials (and classrooms and office conferences) ready to learn, and we are equally eager to help them become fluent in our confusing language. In the interaction that follows, then, we need to remain conscious of the assumptions we work under in the learning environments we create. Tutors, particularly new initiates to the collaborative environment that frees them from the red-pencil world of finding errors and telling writers how to correct them, tend to forget that many of the students sitting next to them, particularly ESL students, do not necessarily share their goals or methods. The writing-center commitment to working with individual differences in the tutorial should therefore extend to seeking out and understanding the expectations and assumptions of students from other cultures. When tutor and student are headed in the same direction, they are more likely to get there together.

Cross-Talk: ESL Issues and Contrastive Rhetoric

Ilona Leki

One of the few areas of second-language (L2) writing theory, research, or pedagogy that have interested first-language (L1) professionals, particularly in the light of the recent focus in the L1 community on multiculturalism, has been contrastive rhetoric because of its cross-cultural insights. And as Tony Silva says in this volume, such a reliance on work in L2 certainly helps to make L1 writing theories "less narrow":

> less monolingual, less monocultural, less ethnocentric, less fixated on writing by eighteen-year-old native speakers of English in North American colleges and universities. . . . Just as a credible general theory of language could not be based solely on evidence from English, a credible general theory of writing must be based on more than research on the writing of native English speakers.

Contrastive rhetoric is a liberating concept. Without it, mismatches in L2 student writing and teacher expectations impugn the students' ability to write or the teachers' ability to read (although the latter is much less likely except in hopeful but perhaps unrealistic calls for encouraging L1 readers to read with "a more cosmopolitan, less parochial eye" [Leki, "Twenty-Five Years" 133]). Contrastive rhetoric allows us instead to accept differences between our expectations and L2 students' writing by recognizing that the choices L2 students make in their writing originate in different and legitimate rhetorical histories. Instead of interpreting these differences as errors and looking for what is wrong with L2 students' writing, we can matter-of-factly note our different expectations and get down to the business of exchanging what we want or need from one another. The writers in this section point out and examine this liberatory side of contrastive rhetoric, and, as Silva remarks, "only by examining the differences can we learn about and address ESL writers' special characteristics and needs."

What more appropriate introduction to issues in contrastive rhetoric than Ulla Connor's essay about L2 students' struggle with English? Connor relocates the roots of modern contrastive-rhetoric studies in the work of Edward Sapir and Benjamin Whorf, which has been in disfavor in recent years because of its emphasis on language as a determining force in a society's view of reality. It is easy to see how readily certain linguistic facts can be overanalyzed within a Sapir-Whorf framework in a way that smacks of racism: If Chinese has no subjunctive or counterfactual forms, then Chinese people cannot think in hypotheticals; if Hopis have no linguistic forms for the future, they are unable to conceive of the future (and so unable to plan for it, living only in the present). Partly at issue is whether these conclusions that groups of human beings cannot grasp certain types of time-space-object relations are distortions or accurate extrapolations of Whorf and Sapir. Connor depicts modern contrastive-rhetoric studies as far more sensitive to societal, educational, and cultural factors in the study of difference.

Silva's essay is evenhanded and thorough in its review of the literature on L1 and L2 composing and appropriately measured in its conclusions. Although, as he states, research comparing L1 and L2 writing has not always been as rigorous as we might hope, close examination of all aspects of that writing and its contexts is the only legitimate grounding for pedagogical decisions about both types of students, attempts to formulate a model of L1 and L2 writing, and construction of a theory of writing. Certainly, a theory of writing limited to the writing of young Americans accounts for little.

One dimension we should consider when making pedagogical decisions about both L1 and L2 students is student expectations, the basic theme of Muriel Harris's chapter. Mismatched expectations are the source of great frustration and potentially of failures to communicate or to reach mutual understandings. Harris attempts to determine what ESL students' expectations are and how they conflict with the culture of the writing center, which holds a clear and distinct view of itself. In some sense, exploring conflicting expectations is the essence of contrastive-rhetoric studies and undergirds all pedagogical adjustments informed by contrastive-rhetoric research. The will to conduct this type of exploration is contrastive rhetoric's most admirable feature.

But contrastive rhetoric has also come under attack by L2 writing professionals. The criticisms have focused on methodology, including interpretation of research findings, and the potential pedagogical uses of contrastive rhetoric. The possible ideological implications of these studies make up another as yet little-explored area susceptible to criticism. Since the authors of this section have delineated many of the benefits of a contrastive-rhetoric approach, I take a more cautionary stance and explore the limitations of contrastive-rhetoric study by reviewing and extending criticisms of this research.

Despite a possible resurrection of the Sapir-Whorf hypothesis (see Connor's essay in this volume), contrastive rhetoric cannot show us the thought patterns of another culture. Rhetorical choices are not directly linked to thought patterns; they are made in response to social, political, and rhetorical contexts and histories. Contrastive rhetoric cannot even show us all the rhetorical patterns of another culture; it is unlikely that "a finite number of formal text shapes or rhetorical patterns exist in any language" (Martin 10). Even if a culture's writing could be reduced to a limited number of rhetorical patterns, different types of texts would likely require different rhetorical strategies. Yet the findings of contrastive-rhetoric research on a single text type (or a small number of text types) have sometimes been promulgated as discoveries about an entire cultural group's general rhetorical preferences. That this conflation is problematic seems especially obvious when we consider the degree to which much contrastive-rhetoric research has focused on the examination of L2 texts written by students in L2, the claim that students writing in L2 are directly reproducing L1 writing patterns, and the assumption that these texts represent the defining characteristics of a culture's writing. Imagine writing researchers in France or China trying to determine English thought patterns or even rhetorical patterns. How many writing teachers of native English-speaking (NES) students would be willing to accept descriptions of English rhetorical patterns based on essays by a randomly selected group of NES freshmen writing in a language other than English, even one as close to English as French, let alone Chinese? What would these texts tell Chinese or French researchers about English writing? Even if students writing in a second language were reproducing first-language rhetorical patterns, we could not know how well they were reproducing them, since, as Bernard Mohan and Winnie Au-Yeung Lo point out, students are still likely to be developing as writers. We mistake shadows for reality if we do not question the notion that the school writing of youngsters represents the rhetorical preferences of a culture in all contexts.

Aside from raising questions about expertise in writing, the claim that the problems L2 students may have in writing in English stem from differences in rhetoric requires closer examination. It can be argued that the school-sponsored writing examined in contrastive-rhetoric studies is contrived and, in certain respects, a genre unto itself (Biber 204). In what context other than an L2 writing class might Chinese students be required to write about their personal histories? The question then becomes, What do we learn that is of pedagogical importance from the difficulties a Chinese student confronts in a contrived L2-English-class writing assignment? Would the Chinese student also use an indirect approach in his or her disciplinary writing in Chinese? Disciplinary writing requires rhetorics other than those used in L2 English writing classes. To make any claims about whether these students transfer first-language writing patterns into their second-language writing, it might make more sense for us to look at writing tasks they are familiar with, for example, writing in their disciplines. But most of the work on student writing in contrastive rhetoric has not looked at disciplinary writing but only at writing produced in English classrooms. It is possible that, apart from nonnative language usage (errors), the disciplinary writing of L2 engineering students is indistinguishable in its rhetorical form from that of NES engineers. But this is a domain that contrastive rhetoric has ventured into very little.

In fact, we know little about L2 students' writing across the curriculum. My research into this area indicates that although writing in, for example, a geography or speech pathology class requires NES and L2 students to adjust to new class requirements, L2 students adjust as well as NES students do. Furthermore, according to research on L2 students writing across the curriculum, they are quite successful at it and do well in their non-English courses (Johns, "Interpreting"; Leki and Carson). Though teachers of other disciplines may complain about L2 students' grammatical errors or lack of background in specific areas, such as United States history (Johns, "Faculty Assessment"), nowhere in the contrastive-rhetoric literature do we find evidence of professors complaining that L2 writing exhibits unfamiliar patterns of organization or a contrastive rhetoric. Features of L2 writing that are mentioned, such as use of poetic language or proverbs, far from disconcerting professors, are sometimes admired as different from ordinary, run-of-the-mill student writing, perhaps "quaint," but not worse for that quaintness. Thus contrastive-rhetoric research findings might be more directly useful to writing teachers if researchers broadened their scope by looking beyond texts written for English classes, by investigating possible contrasts in L2 and NES students' writing across the disciplines. It is possible that these differences would prove to be trivial.

Like contrastive-rhetoric research methodologies, contrastive-rhetoric findings cause concern. They suffer from being overgeneralized, overinterpreted, and oversimplified. In our enthusiasm for the genuine insights generated by contrastive-rhetoric studies, we must guard against being satisfied with traditional contrastive-rhetoric explanations of the differences writers exhibit. We might also be cautious about ascribing to contrastive rhetoric difficulties L2 writers have writing in English, when in fact the difficulties are caused by writing in a new language, not a new rhetoric. Eva Hoffman's poignant description of her problems with sensing the full effect of words in English and the Chinese student's account of the ease with which he or she writes in Chinese compared with English (see Connor's article in this section) are examples not of contrastive rhetoric but of the difficulty of operating in a second language, of retrieving vocabulary, of using a second language to access memories stored as reality mediated through a different first language.

A potentially fruitful approach to the study of writing in other cultures is the examination of L1 literacy training in those cultures. But here we must be cautious about overinterpretations. Contrastive-rhetoric studies have suggested, for example, that creativity in writing is not required of Chinese students and note that instead of developing creativity or critical thinking Chinese children memorize slogans, sayings, or texts such as those in the *Book of Three Hundred Tang Poems* (see Ballard and Clanchy; Unger). But this practice proves nothing about creativity. Furthermore, the Chinese National Unified Entrance Examination to Universities and Colleges includes not merely an essay but an essay competition. On what basis can a competition be judged if all the contestants are required to do is reproduce memorized material without exhibiting creativity? Assuming all competitors can memorize to more or less the same extent and have memorized the same texts, only creative use of that material could distinguish one candidate from the next.

It is also important not to allow contrastive-rhetoric or cross-cultural explanations to get in the way of critical self-analysis. It may be inaccurate to describe international students as passive in class simply because they do not speak out or ask questions. The usual cross-cultural explanation is that L2 students are not encouraged to ask questions in their home countries (see Harris's article in this section). Yet not speaking out or asking questions is not a very accurate indicator of passivity; furthermore, by implied contrast, this analysis portrays NES students as active, questioning, mentally alive, and intellectually engaged and suggests that they systematically test everything the professor says against their own well-considered ideas. Anyone who has taught NES students will recognize that such a flattering portrayal is problematic.

The danger in accepting the traditional contrastive-rhetoric explanations for writing differences or cross-cultural explanations for behavioral differences (which note, for example, that in their home countries ESL students do not criticize their teachers) is that such explanations risk turning ESL students into cardboard characters whose behavior is simply determined by these cultural norms and who have no individual differences or subtleties obscured by these behaviors. In the question of whether international students criticize their teachers, there is the implication that because they do not publicly criticize, they never criticize or perhaps cannot criticize. Yet one has only to become closer with these students to find that they most certainly can and do criticize not only teachers but also institutions and other authorities. Surely the Chinese revolution of 1949 and the 1989 uprising at Tiananmen Square say something about the ability and willingness to criticize.

Contrastive rhetoric oversimplifies not only other cultures and rhetorics but also English. Contrastive-rhetoric tradition seems to accept as doctrine that written English is straightforward and direct, moving in a straight line from one point to the next. Certainly English textbooks direct students to the formula of topic sentence plus development with examples plus conclusion. (Actually, many L2 students say that they were taught the same pattern in their native languages [Liebman], and yet contrastive rhetoric notes deviations from this pattern among L2 writers but not among writers in English.) English writing may, in fact, be taught according to this formula, and in school-sponsored writing students may follow this formula. Yet professional writers do not write this way in English (Braddock). The book *Eight Little Piggies*, by one of the most appreciated American essayists of this day, Stephen Jay Gould, provides an example. In the chapter "Ten Thousand Acts of Kindness," Gould begins by telling the story of a young person who stole a fossil from a national park and then returned the fossil with a note apologizing for the theft. (This must be one of the acts of kindness referred to in the chapter title, we might think.) The essay goes on to discuss the importance of fossils. (What is the connection to kindness? we ask.) Then Gould describes his theory of punctuated equilibrium. (Hmm, maybe the publisher accidentally put the wrong title on this chapter.) Gould finally performs a literary pirouette and links fossils, punctuated equilibrium, and the relative frequency and effects of acts of kindness versus acts of cruelty.

It is a beautiful, and typical, Gould essay. But it is far from the straight-line development form that supposedly characterizes English.

Contrastive rhetoric has perhaps been too eager to find patterns and to impose cross-cultural explanations on anything that looks like one. This is not to say that traditional contrastive-rhetoric character-izations have no basis in reality, only to caution against overgeneral-ized, overinterpreted, or oversimplified explanations of other cultures. The failure to recognize contrastive rhetoric's limitations and the un-qualified acceptance of its oversimplified findings may be to blame for a reductive contrastive-rhetoric-based pedagogy that focuses too in-sistently on patterns of organization (a criticism also leveled against contrastive-rhetoric research itself) and that emphasizes form over content.

The overemphasis on product in contrastive-rhetoric research and contrastive-rhetoric-based pedagogy is not inevitable, however. Writ-ing processes instead of written products might be examined from a cross-cultural perspective. But the differences revealed in Silva's re-view of composing-process literature are not cross-cultural differences but differences in composing processes created by writing in a first or a second language. There may be cross-cultural differences in com-posing processes as well, but we have little evidence of them to date. In fact, L1 and L2 composing-process literature argues against specifi-cally cultural differences in writing processes. Valerie Arndt's study of six Chinese students, for example, shows that writing processes differ widely among individuals of the same culture, a finding we also see in the literature on writing processes among native English speakers.

Thus contrastive-rhetoric research methodology, data interpretation, and pedagogical applications have all been criticized. Other, more po-litical, ideological, or philosophical questions about contrastive rheto-ric have not been raised. Terry Santos has described ESL as heretofore nonideological, driven by pragmatic concerns to equip L2 students as quickly as possible for academic life in an English-speaking country. The wisdom, justice, and ideological implications of requiring confor-mity to English mainstream norms have rarely been challenged in print. ESL is depicted as free of the guilt and self-doubt first-language writing professionals in this country encounter as they struggle with their conflicting goals of respecting native English-speaking students' right to their own language, particularly for speakers of nonstandard dialects, and of helping these students develop the linguistic tools to accomplish their goals within society. As Jeff Smith says about first-language composition instruction, "Suppose . . . that our students told us they had come to the university . . . to have their way into the domi-nant culture *smoothed*. Would it be our job as teachers to facilitate that aim or to thwart it? I think this is a genuinely hard question, posing as it does a choice we may face between serving our consciences and serving students" (732). The right to one's own language, in this sense, is not usually an issue for L2 students, at least not for visa students who plan to return to their home countries after completing their educations in the United States. They quite obviously have and will maintain their own languages and cultures, with or without the advocacy of their English writing teachers.

Other ideological questions have, however, been raised about ESL. James Tollefson challenges the survival English taught to refugees both for its ideological content (e.g., refugees are taught that if they work hard and apply themselves, they too will be equipped to join our consumer society) and for its linguistic content (e.g., refugees are taught "how to ask for permission, but not how to give orders; how to apologize, but not how to disagree; how to comply, but not how to complain; and how to ask about American customs, but not how to explain their own" [75]). Elsa Auerbach presents practical and ideological arguments against an English-only pedagogy in adult literacy classes and for the use of bilingual peer aides in such classes. Closer to contrastive-rhetoric concerns has been the issue of world Englishes (i.e., the varieties of English spoken and written in parts of the world such as India, Nigeria, or Hong Kong) and the complaint that the ESL establishment as embodied in TESOL has ignored the local forms of knowledge of these communities (Canagarajah). But the ideological implications of contrastive rhetoric have not yet been fully explored.

This inattention seems especially odd since contrastive rhetoric is a study of difference, and yet contrastive-rhetoric rarely invokes obvious questions raised by the study of difference: Just how different are we, and what should we do with the recognition of our differences? The study of difference can be progressive because, as I note above, it can help us regard cultural norms as relative rather than absolute. But it can also lead to regressive and limiting, even blinding, stereotypes and unwarranted categorical distinctions among groups. We see the tendency to make categorical distinctions in the failure of contrastive-rhetoric literature in general to acknowledge that English is not categorically different from other languages. Over and over we see that the stylistic or rhetorical devices said to characterize, for example, Chinese writing (the use of proverbs) or Japanese writing (indirectness) or Thai writing (introspection)—all appear to some extent, depending on the writing context, in English as well. And everything described as English (topic sentences, straight-line development) appears to some extent in other languages. These differences are more like relative degrees of reliance on some rhetorical feature to produce a particular effect than categorical differences. To be excellent, Chinese writing must include citations from the work of well-known Chinese authors. To be elegant, English writing also often includes citations of William Shakespeare, Henry James, even Will Rogers; to be erudite, English writing may pointlessly include explanations of Latin or Greek origins of English words. (Do we not read or hear lecturers make statements like "*Revising* means to 'resee'" or "I educate, from the Latin *educare* meaning 'to lead, to draw out'"?) These devices play the same role across rhetorics, to portray the utterer in a flattering light.

The categorical distinctions to which contrastive rhetoric seems to be prone blind us to these similarities. In reading Harris's discussion of writing-center culture, for example, we may be led to conclude that there are radical differences in ESL and NES students' assumptions about writing centers. Because we do not have information here on how NES students answered the questionnaire on their expectations or frustrations related to the writing center, we might assume that NES students share the expectations and assumptions of the writing-center staff whereas nonnative students do not. Yet the writing-center literature often expresses the frustration of staff members who are confronted with NES students who simply understand the writing center to be an editing service. Otherwise, why would writing-center staff members receive training to resist the impulse merely to edit their clients' work or explain rules of grammar?

The suppression of similarity has a distancing and exoticizing effect. We writers of mainstream (North American, British, Australian) English experience ourselves as the norm, as straight-line, direct writers, and we experience the exotic other as, finally, irrelevant, though perhaps also quaint and thus appealing. This is the ominous side of contrastive rhetoric: it suggests that, instead of helping us understand ourselves within a global context, the choices we make and the choices others make, contrastive rhetoric makes the other utterly dismissible. I would argue that, as Alastair Pennycook writes in another context, the danger of contrastive rhetoric is its potential encouragement of "a form of cultural essentialism whereby cultural behavior is ascribed to each supposed cultural group in deterministic fashion, . . . a form of cultural exclusivism whereby the practices of the 'other' are cultural while our own remain the norm" (279).

Beyond the issues raised by the categorical distinctions that contrastive rhetoric seems to encourage arises the other crucial question: What should we do with differences once we recognize them? One option is to celebrate and maintain them. Carol Severino discusses the possibility of such a "separatist" pedagogy that would maintain the differences between minority and majority cultures and that would require the dominant culture to accept the other ("Implications"). Each student's voice would be encouraged and glorified in its individuality or, perhaps for L2 students, in its representation of another culture. Robert Land, Jr., and Catherine Whitley even suggest that the dominant culture must permit the survival of such diversity to stay alive itself. But it appears dominant cultures will more often attempt to maintain dominance by suppressing the other, either erasing differences through denial ("We are all the same, that is, like me") or rendering the other irrelevant—exoticizing it, applauding its quaintness, or, as in contrastive rhetoric, affirming and even exaggerating differences—and then colonizing the other ("You are different from us and must learn our ways, at least while you are with us").

The possibility of celebrating or maintaining differences does not seem to arise readily in thinking about L2 writing. For example, as part of an exploration of contrastive rhetoric in a graduate class on ESL rhetoric and composition, my students and I read essays written for the Chinese National Unified Entrance Examination to Universities and Colleges (Jie and Lederman). When asked if any of the essays translated into English seemed to violate NES norms, my students agreed that a long discussion of the beauty of nature did not fit in a letter protesting the building of a factory, which was the exam task. Although they agreed that this section was probably the most interesting, most impassioned, and most revealing of the author's voice, the NES teachers and teacher trainees also agreed that, were they advising the writer, they would suggest cutting that section to make the text more typical of written English. The Chinese TESL students in the class all agreed that it was the quality of this very section that would probably most impress and positively influence the ratings of the Chinese judges of the exam competition. No one, however, felt that the author should be encouraged to retain this difference for an English-speaking audience.

Perhaps this is as it should be. ESL students consistently ask for the linguistic tools they need to succeed in their work in English, not for the right to maintain the differences they bring from their own languages. In this respect their thinking resembles the reasoning of writers like Richard Rodriguez and educators like Lisa Delpit, who voice the plea from members of United States minority communities that their children be taught "proper" English, not encouraged to use the English they speak at home, which will do them little good anywhere else.

Thus the prevailing attitude among ESL writing professionals appears based on an assumption that world rhetorics are separate but equal and that to succeed in the English rhetorical environment, L2 students need to learn and reproduce English norms. The potential colonizing effects of this practice have not specifically emerged as a topic in contrastive-rhetoric literature but are part of the larger issue of English as world language in domains such as business, airline traffic control, and scientific research publications.

While teaching English norms, however, the ESL community has simultaneously attempted to expand its non-ESL colleagues' horizons. The ESL community has been greatly concerned about the failure rates of L2 students on writing exams (Janopoulos; Ruetten; Sweedler-Brown). L2 writing professionals insist that non-ESL colleagues who evaluate L2 writing exams must first be educated about a variety of ESL issues, for example, the persistence, even among accomplished writers, of discourse accents (like spoken foreign accents); the insignificance of local errors such as improper preposition or article choice, which should not be allowed to cloud perceptions of writing quality; or the existence of contrastive rhetorics. Thus, while helping ESL students gain access to English norms, the ESL community has sought to create and maintain an atmosphere of tolerance for differences in L2 writing outside the ESL classroom.

If we ask what, then, the contribution of contrastive rhetoric to L2 writing instruction has been, we find that its essential insight, that differences exist, has not advanced much beyond its initial pronouncement almost thirty years ago. Since that time, research in contrastive rhetoric has worked to prove, or sometimes disprove, the existence of contrastive rhetoric and to fill in the details, teasing out more differences. Contrastive-rhetoric researchers have apparently not been very much interested in exploring the ideological implications of their work, and sometimes teachers have been too eager to embrace questionable conclusions of contrastive-rhetoric research. Such a final tally may seem disappointing, but linguists and cognitive scientists have long asserted that individuals remain unaware of the workings of their own background cognitive apparatus, such as language, unless their system is explicitly put into contact with and compared with other systems (Lucy). Contrastive rhetoric can most usefully be seen not as the study of internally driven, culture-specific rhetorical patterns but rather as the study of differences or preferences in the pragmatic and strategic choices that writers make in response to external demands and cultural histories. Seen this way, contrastive rhetoric can clearly make a contribution to a pedagogy that views writing instruction as the effort to make all students, not just non-English-speaking students, aware of the options and choices appropriate in a variety of text types and writing contexts.

PART IV

Sociocultural and Pedagogical Tensions

Introduction

The essays in this section address larger issues—sociopolitical conflicts in the larger society—and examine how these conflicts are played out in writing programs and classrooms. Juan Guerra discusses a pedagogy that builds on the experience that students bring to the classrooms; his essay challenges monocultural approaches to teaching writing. Mary Soliday's essay, in questioning the pedagogy of difference, focuses on the dilemma of the teacher's stance as mediator between ethnically, racially, and culturally diverse students and the institution. Henry Evans departs radically from a traditional multicultural paradigm and outlines an Afrocentrist philosophy and writing pedagogy, a point of view often suppressed in composition studies. Carol Miller describes underrepresented students' perplexed responses to and conflicts with their seemingly well-designed and well-meaning composition classes in a large state university. Like Soliday and Guerra, she urges researchers to inquire about the students' own situations, needs, and feelings. Focusing on varying degrees of culture conflict among Chicano and Chicana students, Kate Mangelsdorf describes the attitudes and writing of "students on the border." Barbara Gleason examines the conflict between the demands and results of writing assessment and those of students' other courses. In his crosstalk, Keith Gilyard challenges the authors, pointing out where they may have contradicted themselves.

The Place of Intercultural Literacy in the Writing Classroom

Juan C. Guerra

> *Because I, a* mestiza,
> *continually walk out of one culture*
> *and into another,*
> *because I am in all cultures at the same time,*
> alma entre dos mundos, tres, cuatro,
> me zumba la cabeza con lo contradictorio.
> Estoy norteada por todas las voces que me hablan
> simultáneamente
> *[soul between two worlds, three, four,*
> *my head buzzes with contradictions.*
> *I am confused by all the voices that speak to me*
> *simultaneously]*
> —Gloria Anzaldúa

When underrepresented students, especially those recruited into universities through educational opportunity programs, entered the academy in unprecedented numbers in the late 1960s and early 1970s, many of them walked into an environment for which their life experiences had not prepared them. Because state universities had increasingly shifted to open-admissions or near-open-admissions policies, a number of these students possessed limited or truncated academic experiences and very little knowledge about the culture of academia. As a consequence, many of them were dropped for academic reasons after their first semester or second quarter.

To stem the tide of dropouts among these students, universities that did not have the necessary support systems in place shifted their attention from admissions to retention in the late 1970s and instituted admissions indexes based on entering students' class ranks, grade point averages, and SAT or ACT scores. Admissions officers use these criteria to determine who among the underrepresented would be

248

given a chance to obtain a college education. Thus these universities closed their doors to students who they deemed had little hope of success and focused on recruiting contemporary representatives of W. E. B. Du Bois's "talented tenth." While these students—who make up the bulk of students of color now admitted into state universities—are better prepared academically and more likely to feel at home in an academic setting than members of the first generation of underrepresented hopefuls were, they are still asked to make difficult choices. If they hope to become members in good standing of the academic community, many of them are expected to change their "ways with words," their cultural values, and their social expectations (Heath, *Ways*).

As their writing teachers—as some of the academy's first representatives to encounter these students during their often dramatic rites of passage—we are constantly required to make choices ourselves. Will we take on the role of gatekeepers and demand these students prove to us they are willing, in David Bartholomae's words, "to speak as we do, to try on the peculiar ways of knowing, selecting, evaluating, reporting, concluding and arguing that define the discourse of our community" ("Inventing" [1985] 134)? Or will we serve as their advocates and encourage them to become agents of change willing to challenge and transform the discourse of the academy so that it more closely reflects the polyphonic discourses of their multiple and often intersecting communities?

I believe we can find an answer that transcends the limitations of this either-or conundrum. We—our students and ourselves—have more choices than we often lead ourselves to believe. Still, we cannot know how to position ourselves as teachers in this mutual dilemma until we consider the opportunities that we give our students to position themselves vis-à-vis the academic discourse community that we represent.

Is the Writing Classroom a Gateway to the Academic Discourse Community?

According to a number of specialists in composition studies, Kenneth Bruffee, David Bartholomae, and Patricia Bizzell among them, each of us participates in discourse communities that intersect to some degree and that therefore share certain conventions (Bruffee, "Collaborative Learning"; Bartholomae, "Inventing" [1985]; Bizzell, "Cognition"). Most discourse communities, however, are readily recognizable because of the peculiarity of their particular conventions. That is why some of the more extreme proponents of the academic discourse community have presented it as a "'hard-shelled' community" (Saville-Troike 20), impervious to change, into which students must be initiated. To become successful members of this community, argue these academics, these students will have to give up their native dialects or languages and learn to speak, think, and write according to the conventions and expectations of the academic community's current residents.

Many critics who take exception to how the academic discourse community is sometimes configured (Ritchie, "Beginning Writers"; Harris) or who challenge the very notion of discourse communities (Spellmeyer, *Common*), argue that the presupposition of such static configurations is dangerous because it implies that anyone who wishes to join the community not only must abide by a set of predetermined conventions but also will not be allowed to challenge and change the community's distinguishing characteristics. In other words, these critics worry that consensus is valued over conflict or dissent and thus that maintaining the status quo becomes paramount.

If we simply think of our writing classrooms as temporary gateways that our students pass through on their way to membership in this community of specially selected and highly privileged people, we will be driven to encourage a certain kind of speaking, thinking, and writing. Whatever solidarity we feel with our students, we will become gatekeepers, differentiating between those who will not forsake their identities and those who are willing to undergo the changes that will supposedly guarantee them a particular set of expected cognitive abilities. Thus we will become advocates only for those already destined to join the ranks of the "academically sound," and we will have to forgo our belief in the democratization of higher education.

What, then, is a writing teacher to do? First we must challenge the ways in which a discourse community itself is currently defined and preconstructed. We must also challenge the idea that each of us is in only one community at a time, as though discourse communities were so distinct and unchanging that moving among them literally involved crossing a border. Finally we need to encourage our students to see themselves as members of several communities at once instead of as people engaged in a one-way transition from their community to ours.

Mikhail Bakhtin and Michel Foucault posit a dialectical tension in the conflicting forces that a teacher of writing represents and between which a student often feels bound to choose. This tension offers us one of the better responses to this either-or dilemma because we can use it to critique the static view of discourse communities. On the one hand, the normative or unifying impulses, which Bakhtin calls centripetal, "seek to unify, order, and circumscribe the boundaries of discourse by pulling it toward uniformity and stasis." On the other hand, the "regenerative tendencies," which Bakhtin calls centrifugal, try "to stretch the boundaries of language, take it beyond the limits of the canon to create eclectic, idiosyncratic, hybrid forms of discourse" (Ritchie, "Beginning Writers" 161). As teachers, some of us find ourselves encouraging our students to learn the existing discourse conventions (to "recite by heart," as Bakhtin puts it) because we want them to learn how to manipulate what Bakhtin calls "authoritative discourse." Just as often, many of us find ourselves encouraging our students to challenge that discourse and to counter it by "retelling in one's own words," by enacting an "internally persuasive discourse" (*Dialogic Imagination* 341) that makes use of what Joy Ritchie calls a person's "shifting idioms and ideologies of language" ("Beginning Writers" 161).

In *The Archaeology of Knowledge and the Discourse on Language* (1982), Foucault presents a similar conceptual framework for understanding the "self-fashioning" process that student writers undergo. He too argues that writers are often confronted simultaneously by two contradictory forces (which he calls "speakers"), "Institution" and "Inclination." Like Bakhtin's centripetal force, Institution "promises the safety of roles prepared in advance of speech itself." Because it is the safe and predetermined route, it grants the writer a feeling of security and self-confidence. Inclination is also seductive in that it offers "a language without prohibitions" that grants writers an opportunity to choose "whatever roles they please" (Spellmeyer, *Common Ground* 72).

The underlying assumption of both frameworks, some would argue, is that the student writer must choose between two conflicting possibilities. If we adopt this assumption, we will have to choose between getting our students to accept and learn how to manipulate the conventions of academic discourse and encouraging them to find their individual voices and construct a discourse that represents their unique place in a conflicting system of intersecting discourses. This formulation requires students to take sides in a battle between forces that have been forever struggling to upend each other. The answer, I would argue, lies in redefining this either-or conflict as a both-and opportunity. As a consequence of the dialectical struggle between these two forces, our students can become individually empowered and "gain membership in a given community" (Ritchie, "Beginning Writers" 172).

From this perspective we can see that the writing classroom is not a mere port of entry into the academic discourse community but an initiation into a way of looking at language and the world that permits our students to engage us and one another in the process of becoming more aware of the seductiveness of language. Our students undoubtedly need to learn how authoritative discourse is constructed within a particular discourse community. To deny them the opportunity to learn how to create, manipulate, and interpret the kind of discourse that even critics of the notion of an academic discourse community have learned to use is to deny them access to the language of power (Delpit).

At the same time, we must be careful not to reify the idea of an academic discourse community by presenting it as a closed, unchanging entity that demands such strict allegiance to its conventions that all persons who enter it must be born again, must leave behind the discourse strategies and expectations they learned elsewhere. Students need to be made aware of what they already know intuitively, that there is common ground between the discourse patterns they bring and those they encounter in the university (Severino, "Where"); these patterns are not distinct and alien from each other. Students must be reminded that any discourse is dynamic and open to change and that it is their duty not only to modify their ways with words but also to challenge and transform the ways with words they are likely to encounter in the academy.

Student Resistance to Authoritative and Internally Persuasive Discourse

As teachers of writing who have lived through the radical reorientation in composition studies of the past twenty-five years, many of us believe that we have transformed our classrooms into places where students are free to engage one another actively and critically. Because we have incorporated a process approach in the teaching of writing, have developed sophisticated approaches to collaborative learning, and have begun to use multicultural readers, we believe we are on the cutting edge of pedagogy and curriculum. Unfortunately, we are sometimes so committed to what we do as individual teachers that we forget the degree to which others, especially the writing program directors who design our courses, determine how our notions of process, collaboration, and multiculturalism will manifest themselves in our classrooms. The sequencing of assignments in a first-year writing course of an educational opportunity program I taught recently is an example.

The sequence of assignments in place for several years before my arrival and for a few more after is typical of the kind of preconceived curriculum used widely in writing programs across the country. While teachers of the course had some discretion in choosing topics of interest to our students, the curriculum directed us to give the students three writing assignments in a ten-week quarter, each of which they were expected to revise twice, on schedule, over a three-week period. In Elizabeth Rankin's language, the class assignments were arranged in a modal and developmental hierarchical sequence. Modally, the sequence moved from narration and description to exposition and finally to argument. Developmentally, the sequence followed "a natural learning order, usually beginning in egocentric, subjective experience and moving outward toward integration with the 'other,' the world outside" (129). Finally, though all the assignments were related to the same topic—in my class, the role of education in our lives—the assignments were discrete and each was "regarded as an independent occasion" for engaging in writing (130).

No matter how hard I tried to give my students the sense that they were to engage as writers in the arduous act of struggling with a clash of voices, of discourses that simultaneously demanded to be heard, my agreeing to follow the sequence of assignments as they were laid out and described for us led me to privilege authoritative discourse over internally persuasive discourse and to isolate them from each other. Thus, while I implicitly encouraged them to be seduced by the voice of Inclination in their personal essays, my explicit instructions and the assignment itself demanded that they instead fulfill the expectations of the voice of Institution. As a result, my students did not have to struggle with the dialectical tension between these two forces.

For their first assignment, I instructed students as follows:

> Focus on a personal experience (yours or that of someone close to you) that you had in relation to learning and/or the educational system which (a) contradicted your (or the other person's) expectations, or (b) enlightened you (or the other person) about an important subject or person, and then, in turn, altered your (or the other person's) beliefs, values, or attitudes.

Although I implicitly challenged students to use their individual voices and engage to some degree in internally persuasive discourse, most students enacted the kind of authoritative discourse that I advocated and that was familiar to them from high school. In a class of twenty, only three students produced unconventional responses to the assignment.

Sharon (all names are fictitious), a Filipina American, was the only student in class who opted to write about another person; she wrote a piece in the third person about the social factors that prevented her mother from obtaining a formal education as a young girl in the Philippines. In a journal entry, Sharon reflected on why she decided to write about her mother instead of herself and on how she went about doing it:

> I didn't feel like writing about myself because I already know what school was like for me, but I didn't know how it was like for my mom. . . . I just started asking my mom questions about her experiences and jotted it down on paper. I continued writing without even stopping.

Jason, a young man of Eastern European Jewish descent, resisted the assignment out of frustration. At first, Jason kept suggesting he had no significant learning experience that he wanted to write about. After discussing and discarding a number of possibilities, he decided to write about his experiences with his grandparents. Instead of following the traditional chronological narrative format, he chose to tell his story as a series of vignettes separated by asterisks. In the first one, Jason sets the mood and the tone for what is to come:

> Rummaging through the closet, I found a tattered old box on the bottom shelf. Memories flooded my mind when I saw what the contents of the box were: plastic saucers, cups, a teapot, and colored baby rings. Slowly, I picked up the tea set and let the memories flow.

Several vignettes later, he returns to one of the themes he established at the outset:

> Many moves and years later, I go to visit the nursing home again. Grandpop Owen had died while I was away, and granny had aged. I no longer serve tea to granny because I am bigger than her. She doesn't recognize me, and I don't know why.

In rejecting the tight chronological strictures of authoritative discourse that every other student in class followed, Jason exploded the expected frame and revealed a series of poignant insights that a typical narrative structure would have made impossible.

The assignment affected Kim, a Korean American, more strongly and openly than anyone else in the class. After several false starts, Kim elected to write about what she had learned from attending the funeral of a close friend. Throughout our three conferences and in my comments on her three drafts, I encouraged her to use concrete language to touch her readers' emotions, and she refused. Her opposition was not only apparent in what she produced as a writer; it was also apparent socially in the curt and hard-edged replies she gave me. In my response to her second draft, I wrote:

> After reviewing your essay one more time, my feelings about it haven't changed very much. I think you have the basis for a great piece here but you need to make it come alive. This will happen only if you go past the surface events and dig deep into the meaning of what happened. Vivid details will be the icing on your cake; they will help the reader see and feel what you saw and felt and will charge the experience with the kind of energy it needs to come alive.

My response to her final draft suggests that she had moved in the direction I suggested but was still resisting:

> You seem so detached and uninterested in what's going on at the funeral; at least that's the feeling I get from your "point of view." Maybe that's something you want to explore. Do you want the reader to feel disengaged, too? Or do you want the reader to feel your sadness and the anguish of the people there? Think a bit more about the stance you've taken and decide for yourself how it is you would like your reader to interpret the experience. I guess the bottom line is this: Is your detachment and lack of interest a reflection of your attitude toward the assignment or toward the experience you're describing?

When we shifted to a more analytical and persuasive (academic) form of discourse in the second assignment (a critical analysis of a popular movie in which education was a central theme) and many students began to flounder in the transition, I decided not to provide them with a structural model to see if they could figure out the changes they would have to make. I wanted them to explore the directions in which their notions of discourse forms, both internally persuasive and authoritative, were likely to lead them. After a couple of class sessions during which most of the students tried to discover what rhetorical strategies the new approach required, Sandra, a Filipina American student, raised her hand in frustration and asked, "I'm really confused, Mr. Guerra. Can't you just tell us what *you* want us to do?"

Clearly, Sandra (and the others who joined her) wanted me to supply the scaffolding that would allow them to shift from personal narrative to more academic writing. Once I described it, the students found their footing and requested additional overt instruction and direction in writing their final essay. As Monica, a Chicana, noted in her journal after I had intervened and she had completed several drafts of the second assignment:

> Writing my second essay was harder than writing my first essay. This essay had to be a critical analysis of a movie. It was very difficult to break yourself away from the narrative and descriptive mode. . . . I found several ideas on the subject, but the problem was finding enough information to prove the statement. When I found one I could prove I began to write. I did a great deal of describing the storyline. That was a very hard mode to get out of. Eventually I ended up writing a very long essay and then pulling out as much narrative as I could or summarizing it all up.

In the first essay only Jason made use of internally persuasive notions about how to write and challenged the conventions I had explicitly set up for the students as writers. He employed personal or cultural expectations and practices and challenged or rejected the institutional restrictions often imposed in narrative writing. But Sandra, Monica, and a number of their classmates demanded that I supply them a set of conventional expectations for their final two assignments. They saw that the personal and cultural practices they brought to the classroom and their notions of how authoritative discourse functioned were inadequate to deal with the task at hand.

The conflicts that my students and I encountered are typical in classes whose assignment sequence forces the teacher and the students to try to bridge the gap between personal and academic writing. The endeavor almost always leads to a waste of energy: instead of engaging in the productive tension between internally persuasive and authoritative discourse, students spend valuable time and effort trying to identify the authoritative discourse that a teacher wants them to use. Because this problem had been prevalent in our educational opportunity writing program, Wendy Swyt, the program director from 1993 to 1995, decided to spend a year revising the curriculum as part of her dissertation work. The new curriculum avoids the personal-versus-academic split by establishing a rhetoric of inquiry approach that is both epistemic and recursive; it also allows students to link personal and academic concerns and interests in a variety of rhetorical contexts. More important, the new curriculum self-consciously encourages students to make creative use of the dialectical tension that emerges from the inevitable clash of voices and discourses in a writing classroom.

From Monocultural to Multicultural to Intercultural Literacy

In a discussion of how anthropologists have struggled to define culture, Kenneth A. Rice offers an approach that those of us concerned about how literacy can be defined should consider. A concept like culture (or literacy), Rice notes, can be defined either in essentialist or in nominalist terms. Someone who defines the concept in essentialist terms—that is, tries to answer the question What is literacy?—thinks that he or she "is talking about a phenomenon . . . when actually he [or she] is talking about a word." Thus that person tries to impose an absolutist and static definition on a dynamic phenomenon. By contrast, a nominalist definition stipulates

> how one is going to use the term by using more common terms to attach a connotation to it. There is no question of truth or falsity in nominal definitions since they simply announce an intention to use a term in a particular manner. . . . Nominal definitions are evaluated not in terms of correctness or precision, which would imply an objective phenomenal world against which to evaluate them, but in terms of usefulness for particular purposes.   (5)

The nominalist definition of literacy that I believe best suits the writing classroom is one based on Bizzell's pluralist notions of cultural literacy. "It might be said," Bizzell writes, "that a particular cultural literacy is what members of a discourse community share" ("Beyond Antifoundationalism" 662). If our job as teachers of writing were merely to initiate our students into "the academic discourse community" and help them function effectively in it, our work would be restricted to determining the discourse patterns of that community and teaching our students to manipulate these conventions competently. Our job, however, becomes complicated because many of us want our students to continue functioning in their respective discourse communities while learning to operate in an array of other discourse communities.

Some colleagues, therefore, would argue that our goal should be to assist students in developing multicultural literacy. When multicultural literacy is defined in the complex terms used by Wendy Hesford (in this volume) and other scholars interested in problematizing the notion, such a conceptualization of our goal is sufficient for our purposes. Unfortunately, most definitions of multicultural literacy tend to focus on the differences, rather than the similarities and differences, between and among the discourse practices of supposedly distinct cultural groups. Thus students are encouraged to use their cultural groups' discourse strategies while learning to manipulate academic discourse, but they are rarely encouraged to move outside this binary straightjacket.

Our goal as teachers of writing, I would argue, is to find ways to help students develop "intercultural literacy," the ability to consciously and effectively move back and forth among as well as in and out of the discourse communities they belong to or will belong to. The notion of intercultural literacy contains both common and contested grounds. Whereas the monocultural-literacy approach is hegemonic and restrictive and the multicultural-literacy approach suggests that people are literate in a number of segregated, divided, and distinct cultures, the intercultural-literacy approach not only encourages students to accept commonalities and differences but also gives students an opportunity to engage them and to integrate them into their lives.

As students move from one cultural scene that invokes a particular type of literacy to another, they do not have to adapt continually to the constraints of the existing authoritative discourse. Instead, they can bring with them a complex blend of the conflicting discourses they have encountered elsewhere. In the process, they are likely to change the existing discourse in the new cultural context as much as it changes them. Students, of course, need to be reminded that the more powerful cultural frames in any setting tend to appropriate and strip other frames of their characteristics. If they are careful, however, students will reenact the process human beings engage in whenever they move out of their closed worlds and learn to operate in the plethora of worlds that surround them.

Taking a Stance

As we stand in front of or sit in a circle with our students each semester and renew our commitment to help them attain what we consider a useful level of academic literacy, we are reminded by the daily newspapers, weekly magazines, and scholarly journals and by radio and television that the culture wars of our day are far from over (H. Gates, *Loose Canons*; Graff; Shor, *Culture Wars*). With their crisis mentalities and their flood of images of a balkanized America, the conservative elements who oppose any attempt of ours to create a multicultural curriculum struggle to keep us against the ropes of uncertainty: maybe, these adversaries say, we should stick to the basics to make sure our students get jobs in a shrinking economy and just forget about trying to engage them in a multivocal dialogue that may help them empower themselves and think critically.

In our corner between rounds, others—certain self-righteous radical elements who believe they know what's best for us and whose main reason for entering the discourse is to gain control of it—tell us the world is in constant flux, all things are relative, and the best we can do is embrace everything equally. Forget about trying to help students get jobs, they say, just do whatever you can to get them to change the world. In many ways, especially for those of us who work primarily with students of color, our perceptions of our students have been shaped by these struggles. Postmodernists, for example, encourage us to see our students as shifting social and cultural constructs without a defining center. Although there is much to be said for the newfound postmodernist notion of a multiple self that occupies a broad variety of subject positions, I would argue that we have overemphasized fragmentation of the self at a time when women and people of color are ascending and gaining power.

Our students are much more than the sum of the social and cultural forces that have shaped them. Again, though, we need not get caught up in an argument that suggests we must conceive of the self as either "the coherent, unified subject of modernity or the fragmented, dissolved subject of postmodernity" (Faigley, *Fragments* 79). Instead we must balance the intercultural with the interpersonal. Our students have not only a set of experiences that have shaped them but also what Linda Alcoff calls a "positional perspective"—that is, "a place from which values are interpreted and constructed rather than . . . a locus of an already determined set of values" (434). In Lester Faigley's words, we need to think through "the complexity of the momentarily situated subject" before we rush to judgment on this most important issue (*Fragments* 239).

And if we seek to foster a classroom environment in which we encourage critical thinking and all participants can challenge one another's beliefs, it follows that we cannot avoid letting our students know where we stand, what our positional perspective is. While advocating that our students adopt our "simple-minded dogma" is dangerous and likely to backfire, letting them know we hold a specific set of beliefs, assumptions, and values that exist in "the site of tension between authority and power on the one hand and resistance and creativity on the other" is more likely to demonstrate what it means to be actively involved in the world around us (Street 8). Such a stance also helps them realize that people don't have to live empty or cynical lives in a world without meaning. All of us can fulfill our civic duty as we try to enrich our individual lives.

While it is also important to provide readings that illustrate our concerns with issues of race, class, and gender (there is, after all, an ever-growing number of multicultural readers available) and to deal with them politically, this approach is most effective when the issues emerge from the students' experiences (as they inevitably do in a multicultural classroom) and inform their thinking. Too often we as teachers are presumptuous about who our students are and what they think about. We often assume they have had little academic experience or have done little reflecting about their circumstances in life. By having them write in journals about their place in the world and work in collaborative groups in which they can hear a multitude of voices and points of view, we can not only learn more about them and begin to see them as complex beings but also give them a chance to articulate their ideas and to place themselves in relation to the world.

Above all, each of us must "embrace the contraries" that we are going to face in the classroom, both those we must handle as teachers who want to serve our students and the academy simultaneously (Elbow, "Embracing") and those that manifest themselves in the form of conflict and with which our students must come to terms. We must not see our job as simply teaching our students the conventions of academic discourse and preparing them for some predetermined life in the real world. Instead, we must give them every opportunity to explore the clash of discourses and ideas, of different viewpoints and worldviews. As Min-Zhan Lu notes:

> Beyond the classroom and beyond the limited range of these students' immediate lives lies a much more complex and dynamic social and historical scene. To help these students become actors in such a scene, perhaps we need to call their attention to voices that may seem irrelevant to the discourse we teach rather than encourage them to shut them out.   ("Silence" 447)

Our students can become such actors most successfully if we do everything in our power to help them develop a sensitivity for and a facility with the forms of intercultural literacy that will allow them to adapt to or challenge and transform the discourses of the various scenes they encounter in their increasingly complex and dynamic lives.

The Politics of Difference:
Toward a Pedagogy of Reciprocity

Mary Soliday

In 1977 Mina Shaughnessy wrote that "from [basic writing] students we are learning to look at ourselves and at the academic culture we are helping them to assimilate with more critical eyes" *(Errors* 292). The students she wrote of represented the first generation of open-admissions students at the City College of New York (CCNY), and the differences they brought with them raised issues that would preoccupy scholars for the next two decades. Chief among these issues was the role of conflict and assimilation in teaching basic writing, traditionally one of the most multicultural classes on university campuses. Other scholarship has explored Shaughnessy's belief that basic writing programs raise critical questions about the relation between academic and minority cultures. This work questions the harmonious language used to describe multiculturalism and education (Chase; Giroux, *Schooling*; Shor, *Critical Teaching*) and calls attention to the function of social conflict and cultural struggle in basic writing and adult literacy instruction (Bartholomae, "Tidy House"; Brodkey, "On the Subjects"; Coles and Wall; Dean; Fox, "Basic Writing"; Lu, "Conflict"; Wall and Coles). It appears that in teaching writing we are teaching difference, and in teaching basic writing the difference may be intensified for both teachers and students.

Using excerpts from literacy narratives by students from diverse backgrounds, I explore below the influence of difference and assimilation on writers' representations of their learning experiences. What versions of difference do students advance when they narrate their stories of education, literacy, and language? What kinds of conflicts do they describe? What sorts of goals do they imagine for themselves? Over a four-year period I have gathered dozens of literacy narratives from students at two different schools, a midwestern university and the CCNY, where I now teach. I focus on the CCNY narratives here to examine the power and limits of a politics of difference for teaching writing in multicultural settings.

In asking what happens to basic writers when they come to college, Patricia Bizzell was one of the first composition scholars to use the idea of a discourse community to speculate about the effects of cultural and language difference on students. Because nontraditional students possess "such limited experience outside their native discourse communities that they are unaware that there is such a thing as a discourse community," they are strangers in a new language world ("Cognition" 230); "their salient characteristic is their 'outlandishness'—their appearance to many teachers and to themselves as the students who are most alien in the college community" ("What Happens" 294). Along with David Bartholomae and Mike Rose, Bizzell saw basic writers as outsiders struggling to learn a socially authoritative discourse, and she emphasized the collision between their discourse styles and those of the university (Bartholomae, "Inventing"; Rose, *Lives*).

In response to this clash of styles many teachers sought to minimize discordance by teaching students the conventions typically preferred by the academic discourse community. In a case study of a student named Dave, Lucille McCarthy tells of one student's struggles to decipher the tacit codes established by different professors at one university. If, she observes, this white, middle-class student was a "stranger" in new "academic territory" who encountered alien rhetorical styles in each of his college classes, then "students from diverse cultures may need, even more than Dave, explicit training in the ways in which one figures out and then adapts to the writing demands in academic contexts" (262). For the next few years, scholars discussed how to help strangers in a strange new land assimilate into an unfamiliar discourse community.

The idea that students from diverse communities need explicit training to adapt to new rhetorical situations became increasingly problematic, however, because of its assumption that assimilation always occurs and is a stable and desirable process. Bizzell comments that the term *initiation* is ambivalent because it reflects an ambivalent process of enculturation (*Academic Discourse* 19). By describing this process as a rite of passage experienced by millions of students, the term underscores the distinctly social function of writing, but it also implies a ritual loss of self and embrace of a way of life and worldview that mirror the linear narrative of the immigrant's assimilation into mainstream American life. This narrative of smooth integration tends, moreover, to imagine that community itself is self-contained, univocal, and free of strife (Elbow, "Reflections"; J. Harris; Severino, "Where").

These traditional ideas of initiation and community have been unsettled further by composition scholars' literacy narratives. In this autobiographical and self-reflective writing, scholars have described how learning to write academic English entails covering up certain aspects of the self, taking a detached stance that excludes certain kinds of experience, and removing traces of personal commitment and authorship (Brodkey, "Writing"; Geisler; Gilyard; Lu, "Silence"; Shen; Sommers). By describing their experiences of learning to write as enculturating journeys involving both a loss of self and a conflict with the authority of conventionality, these authors challenge the academic tendency to obscure the autobiographical in discourse and to suppress the ambivalence of adapting to various academic literacies.

Students also write narratives that foreground the difficulties of sociolinguistic assimilation. Here is the opening paragraph to an untitled literacy narrative that tells a story of cultural and linguistic dislocation (for the sake of convenience, I refer to the essay by the title "Creole"):

> I don't remember much about having any difficulties learning Creole, which is my native language or have any type of problems trying to speak it. Haiti is where I'm from and Creole is the language which is spoken among all the people living there. The thing that had bothered me to this day, while living in Haiti was the fact that, I was being taught French in school instead of Creole. This was very awkward to me when I didn't even speak the language at home or any other places except in school. I had faced one major problem while learning French. I did not want to speak French in class when I was required to do so.

Although learning French "has been a struggle for me," he continues, "I had no problems expressing my thoughts, and getting my point across, when speaking Creole. I was able to speak it fluidly without any difficulties. I wasn't concerned about making grammar mistakes." He recalls feeling a growing resistance when he entered elementary school, a "fear" and unwillingness to speak French in public. He explains how he tried "to come up with a good excuse" to avoid speaking French in front of his teachers and classmates and eventually "used [his] teachers' statements, about Creole was not a language, as [his] way out." His increasing identification with a group of boys who refused to speak the "school" languages also played a "major role in [his] inability to speak French."

The author's story took a turn, however, when his mother, who had immigrated to the United States, sent for him to live with her in New York City. He writes, "I said to myself, this dejas vous again. I thought I was going to have the same problems with English as I did with French." But that did not happen; he writes, "To my surprise I was able to understand and speak English within a year and a half." To explain his success the author contrasts the use of definite articles in both languages and then concludes, "[French] is a hard language to speak and it is also complicated. You need to know your French grammar well in order to be [able] to speak it properly." He believes that if he tries harder in the future he will learn French, and he ends the essay by saying he intends to master French someday.

"Creole" presents readers with a story of language acquisition as a complex struggle between socially subordinate and dominant languages that the author has not fully resolved. This frank account is also ambivalent and occasionally contradictory as the author attempts to come to terms with his identity, culture, and language use. While he never mastered "proper French," the author learned English in a year and a half, a contrast that he ascribes, on the one hand, to the grammatical complexity of French and, on the other, to his resentment at having to use French at the expense of the language he had always spoken at home. Similarly, although the author plainly resents "[having] grown up with this concept thinking that Creole was not a language," he is also uncertain whether he used this anger merely as an excuse not to speak French in public.

Keith Gilyard's literacy narrative, *Voices of the Self*, offers a further framework for understanding the ambivalence of "Creole." Gilyard notes that students acquire new identities along with "school English," and as evidence he narrates his story of learning to read and write in the public schools of Harlem and Corona, Queens. Describing "a kind of enforced educational schizophrenia" in the life of African American students, Gilyard explains that he learned to switch between languages to survive academically (163). Yet he wonders if this switching, which took a psychic toll on him and may not be possible for all students, should be every student's burden. "My interest is not merely in the ways Black students can learn," he writes. "I am also concerned about the psychic costs they pay. A pedagogy is successful only if it makes knowledge or skill achievable while at the same time allowing students to maintain their own sense of identity" (11). In Gilyard's story, culturally different students experience a profound sociolinguistic division—an "enforced educational schizophrenia"—because within the public school, their languages are other, private and socially devalued.

It is plausible to read "Creole" as an instance of that schizophrenia, a narrative in which a student develops a double consciousness about language. When speaking Creole the student used language "fluidly," but when he spoke French he felt so "awkward" about grammar that he couldn't address the teacher in class. His essay describes the intimate relation between learning a grammar and learning to speak or write in a different voice or identity, but in the end he does not consider this relation a major factor in his inability to learn French. While the author ends by assuring the reader that he will one day learn French, he begins by stating that he remains "bothered to this day" by the school's demand that he adapt to its preferred public language, the language of the politically dominant classes in Haiti. Sitting in a classroom in an English-speaking college, the student remembers the lingering and perhaps unresolved linguistic conflicts of the past, which provide an important framework for his writing in the present.

The author portrays a kind of resistance described elsewhere, most vividly by Paul Willis in *Learning to Labour*. Like the working-class "lads" in Willis's ethnographic narrative, the boys in "Creole" club together in their "fear and unwillingness" to speak French publicly, and they resort instead to the creative use of a private, nonstandard speech. This identification with a socially devalued and marginalized language over "school discourse" raises questions about the adequacy of traditional narratives, which seem to downplay the creative agency of individuals except for those students who make successful transitions between language worlds. The author of "Creole" forthrightly tells his readers that these transitions involve important social crossings as well.

Native-born writers whose legacy includes the biculturalism of the urban American experience also describe conflicts between languages, cultures, and sense of self. "The history of my language is quite confusing," writes one young woman:

> One would think that I should have mastered my native language before any other language. Well, the opposite happened to me, first I learned how to speak and write in Spanish, my native language. With time as I grew up in New York City, English became the language I heard, spoke and wrote the most. Many times I felt embarrassed or ashamed because I could not speak Spanish as

fluently as I did English. Presently, I feel extremely scared or intimidated when I have to speak Spanish with older Spanish professors and young Spanish speaking friends.

A native speaker of Spanish more fluent in English, this author prefers to use Spanish, a language she defines as "the offspring or child of two languages that collided with one another." Using figurative language and examples of Spanglish vocabulary to develop her narrative, she says that a language that is devalued as a "confusing" mixture actually tells a powerful story of the "collisions" between peoples and their cultures and languages. "Spanglish in itself tells the history of my people in the United States," she explains. This hybrid process of language development confused this student until she acknowledged that Spanglish, a marginalized form that hasn't gained the status of an official language, is the offspring of a history of Hispanic immigrants in the United States rather than an indication that she is unable to speak a pure version of a language.

The paper (which I refer to below as "Spanglish") is a particularly self-reflective and sophisticated discussion of the conflicts that "Creole" boldly presents but leaves unresolved. But both essays vividly depict how cultural mistrust, hybridization, and difference shape the lives of writers from diverse social backgrounds. They also call attention to the ways in which school English is defined in relation to other, outside, or impure languages or dialects. However, linguistic ambivalence is only part of the writer's story of academic strategy in these essays. Here is the opening paragraph of an essay by a basic writer from Ethiopia. He came to New York after spending two years in a Christian refugee camp in North Africa, where he struggled to learn English at night, using whatever books were available:

In 1987 I came to the USA where the national language is English. Even though I have known a little English while I was in my country, Ethiopia, in order to integrate with the American society, I was supposed to read, speak, and write in English. When I flash back to my English speaking, reading, and writing, I would say that I have started from zero degree. In the beginning of my years in the US, I had difficulties in communicating with people and explaining my ideas in writing. Since I join the City College and took ESL course, I am making a big progress. Even though still I am with difficulties on writing, compared to the previous experience I would say I make tremendous improvement.

The author tells of a long and arduous journey from "zero" to academic English. When he first arrived in New York, he found that his training in British schools made it particularly difficult to understand American accents, a problem he thought was exacerbated by his spending so much time with Ethiopian immigrants. "To familiarize [himself] with the English language," he took a job as a taxi driver and enrolled in noncredit speech ESL courses at City College to prepare for his GED. Speaking in public proved especially difficult for him, "a shy person." Reading in English was also a challenge: "In my first reading experience," he writes, "out of one book I only understood ten percent of the ideas." He describes how he taught himself to absorb new words without looking each one up in the dictionary. After passing the GED examination, the author enrolled in noncredit reading courses and prepared to take the reading test for entrance into college: after three attempts, he passed it. Then he turned to the challenge of writing; he notes, "before I came to the United States I have no experience in writing in English." He enrolled in another sequence of ESL courses that focused on writing, and in them he wrote more than he ever had ("freewriting, journals, brainstorming, and essay writing"). He concludes:

> Nothing is impossible. Practice makes perfect. As I mentioned it above, overcoming my difficulties of speaking, reading and writing in English have seemed to me like a mountain climbing. But what I have learned is facing it and doing it step by step will result to be on the top of the mountain. Now I am marching to achieve the skills of speaking, reading and writing in order to integrate with the American society.

Like the author of "Creole," the author of this essay (which I refer to here as "Mountain") portrays his learning in terms of a grave and difficult struggle to shed one language in favor of another. Both authors had to give up the languages spoken in their home communities to begin the painful task of speaking a foreign language publicly. Both authors, moreover, experienced the loss of their languages in the context of tremendous political struggles in their home countries. Like the author of "Spanglish," this author comments that his language biography reflects the historical struggles of immigrant groups in the United States.

But the terrible conflicts of the past have driven the author of "Mountain" to embrace the concept of integration and assimilation in the present. Nourished by the dream of becoming an engineer, he portrays his struggle to learn English as linear "progress," a step-by-step march toward integration with American society. Unlike "Spanglish," which describes a "confusing" history of hybridization, "Mountain" defines the struggle more clearly. If he feels conflicted about having to leave the protection of the Ethiopian community in the city and move into the dominant English-speaking world, he does not mention it; perhaps there is less conflict in his new life than in his old one as an exile and a refugee. This author finds the traditional narrative of accommodation serves his purposes as a first-generation immigrant, a mature adult working part-time to support his family and realize his dream of gaining a college degree. Like the authors of "Creole" and "Spanglish," the author of "Mountain" is a member of a marginalized language group, but unlike them, he conceives of his status in unambivalent terms. For him, college is a stepping-stone toward an integration and a move away from a past in which, among other things, he was not free to practice his religion.

Although one could argue that "Mountain" begins in postcolonial conflict in Africa, the author chooses to open his narrative in America, at the "zero degree" of his dream to "integrate with the American society." Conflict with academic language is not central to this basic writing student's narrative. Min-Zhan Lu argues, "Acculturation and accommodation were the dominant models of open admissions education for teachers who recognized teaching academic discourse as a way of empowering students"; Lu urges us not only to pay attention to "conflict and struggle in Basic Writing instruction" but also to see them "as the preconditions of all discursive acts" ("Conflict" 890). But does the model of conflict adequately replace that of acculturation? Does it provide room for the voice in "Mountain," which speaks eloquently to assimilation, another precondition for writing? Great numbers of working-class students, ethnic minorities, and new immigrants come to the academy hoping to make a better life for themselves and their children and choose to relinquish part of themselves in the process, just like most professors who write narratives of their own enculturation into academic discourse.

In essays like "Mountain," authors may mask, elude, or cover up the tensions of accommodation for many reasons. They may emphasize continuity over discontinuity because for them learning a new language does not involve the same kind of historical struggle it does for writers like the author of "Creole." For the writer of "Mountain," religion, not language per se, resonates with difference and struggle. Speaking English may not threaten his sense of cultural identity and well-being as it threatened those of the students who wrote "Creole" and "Spanglish." Equally important, the author of "Mountain" is not a postadolescent playing a role in the story most familiar to us, the middle-class rite of passage from home and high school to a four-year sojourn in the academy. In that journey the student passes from intellectual innocence to experience, so we would expect the crossing to be especially discordant and influential. But this narrative does not hold for students who do not come to college as young people ready for an initiation into the strange world of adult decisions and identities. Like the author of "Mountain," they may have established goals and well-defined, mature senses of self. For them, integration may thus be only partial.

Consider, for example, a story told by a Chinese student who lived through Mao Tse-tung's Cultural Revolution. For this author, Western books and ideas don't serve as threats of assimilation but embody a youthful dream of political resistance nearly crushed during Mao's crusades against intellectuals. The student describes how he returned home one day to find that his intellectual work had been discovered by the government: "Seeing all my diaries were in pieces and a notice on the front gate warning us never to do any anti-revolutionary action except learning Mao's thought, my heart was broken." He recalls, "I swore never to touch a pen again." Later, when he was serving a sentence at a reeducation camp on Chongming Island, the student recalls that he kept his "dream of being a novelist, a story-teller and translator" alive by studying English in secret at night with another exiled intellectual. Long before he came to the United States, the author had developed an affinity for intellectual culture, represented by Western ideas and books and nourished by his opposition to the dominant political culture in China. Like the author of "Mountain," the author of "Cultural Revolution" comes to the academy as the result of conflicts that push him toward rather than away from Western intellectual culture.

As I skim through my piles of narratives from other teachers' classes, I see that students from diverse cultural backgrounds choose to describe the connections between life at home and life at school. In contrast to Richard Rodriguez, who describes in *Hunger of Memory* how he carefully hid the signs of his intellectual life from his family, many CCNY students tell stories of how literacy is at the center of their memories of home life, stressing continuities between home and school rather than discontinuities and conflicts. These students do not always consider their cultures, in Min-Zhan Lu's phrasing, "drastically dissonant from academic culture" ("Conflict" 907). I find the narrative of an African American student from Harlem who attributes his desire for a college education to his reading of *The Autobiography of Malcolm X* at home with his father. One student born in Poland writes, "[I] vividly recall my childhood . . . [in which] my parents organized different reading and writing activities." Another raised in a New York City ghetto asserts, "My early childhood experience was with writing and reading at home before I started going to school." Basic writing students are not tabulae rasae waiting to be born anew into intellectual culture; we may see them as outlandish, but they do not.

At different points in a writer's life and in particular sociopolitical contexts, conflicted versions of difference appear in essays like "Creole" and "Spanglish." Listening carefully to these stories enriches our understanding of both the individual student's language experience and a critical part of everyone's language learning that has often been ignored in education, especially in multicultural education. But we may do our students a disservice if we assume that conflict and struggle are the necessary preconditions for all writing because this assumption restricts our ability to imagine different kinds of relations between school life and minority cultures. Although students from diverse backgrounds experience discontinuity and difference when they come to college, many also identify a strong continuity among themselves, their experiences, and the university.

While we can usefully juxtapose the ways of thinking and talking in academia with those in other cultures, it is equally useful to discover the generative points of contact between the life and language of school and that of work, family, church, and so forth. If we assume only an oppositional difference between us (the academy) and them (culturally different students), we limit the possibilities for complex relationships and various kinds of journeys for individual students. Thus the chasm between private and public languages that Rodriguez portrays in his literacy narrative becomes a dominant theme of incompatibility between cultures and their preferred languages or discourse styles.

One place to begin is to question what we as writing teachers mean when we use terms such as *basic writer* and *multicultural*. Are these terms interchangeable? Are they universal? Exactly what do we mean and to whom do we refer when we speak of diverse, culturally different, or basic writers? The cultural, political, and social complexity of black people is consistently denied in the strands of feminist and multicultural theory that emphasize difference and use it to mark social, cultural, and political differences as unbridgeable. Hazel Carby writes,

"This theoretical emphasis on the recognition of difference, of other-ness, requires us to ask, different from and for whom?" (12). Depend-ing on both the rhetorical position that a theorist takes and his or her particular teaching experience, *diversity* can have multiple meanings, which will affect the kinds of narratives we imagine for students' entry into the academy.

My use of the words *multicultural* and *basic writer* grows out of my experience as a writing teacher, scholar, and program administrator at an urban college. For me *multicultural* evokes a complex range of dif-ference that includes race, class, ethnicity, age, country of origin, and language. I see the terms *culturally diverse student, nontraditional stu-dent*, and *basic writer* as including white and black students who have delayed their college education to work or raise a family; students who have transferred from community colleges to four-year colleges or from trade schools to college; and students who are minorities, politi-cal refugees, new immigrants, second-language speakers, and first-generation college students. For me *diverse* and *basic writer* refer to new immigrants from the West Indies and Eastern Europe; working-class white, African American, and Latino and Latina students from East Harlem and Jamaica, Queens; older women finishing college edu-cations they interrupted years before; and students of all ages born in Greece, Korea, El Salvador, Colombia, Nigeria, Pakistan, Iran, Roma-nia, and the Dominican Republic.

But defining our terms isn't enough; we also need to pursue theory and ethnographic description that reveal the complexity of continuity as well as the disruption of difference. Eleanor Kutz, Suzy Groden, and Vivian Zamel have begun to do so in their ethnographic work with diverse students. From their perspective, teaching writing in multi-cultural settings is not only teaching difference: it is also teaching stu-dents to discover their cultural and rhetorical competence in telling stories, constructing arguments, and thinking critically in everyday life (at home, at work, in church or temple, in the street, or at school). Similarly, Richard Courage tells a story of communicative competence in a case study of a basic writer who built on her linguistic experiences in the ministry to succeed as an academic writer. Instead of being drastically different from academic language use, this student's rhe-torical experience in her community's church had given her skills con-gruent with those her teacher expected. She employed her social competencies in arguing points to skeptical audiences to produce per-suasive written texts in a new discourse world. Teachers do need to be aware of a politics of difference, but not one that emphasizes the discontinuities between cultures at the expense of finding the connections between students' styles and academic styles of discourse and cultural ways of knowing the world.

With support from the Fund for the Improvement of Postsecondary Education, we have developed a pilot project at CCNY that aims to enable students to describe, reflect, and build on the linguistic and rhetorical competencies they bring to the academy. Currently we are experimenting with four projects common in thirteen sections of a year-long course that mainstreams basic writers with regular freshman students. These projects allow students and teachers to investigate the relation among different cultural and language worlds, using an academic vocabulary and typical modes of discourse (e.g., description, narration, analysis, synthesis). Included are a study of the relations between oral and written narratives; the writing of autoethnography and literacy narratives; ethnographic inquiry into language use and cultural behavior; and the analysis of popular culture. Through these areas of inquiry, teachers are working with students to discover how they can bring knowledge of their cultures and competencies with their languages into the classroom for academic discussion and critique. This kind of curriculum expands the possible narratives of the "initiation" into academic discourse that have always structured much of what we do in the multicultural classroom.

We need more than one version of the relation among cultures, languages, and discourse styles so that we can remain open to voices as different as those of "Creole," "Spanglish," and "Mountain." The culture wars of the 1990s reveal that what is at stake in multicultural education is the struggle to depict human relationships in a democratic society. In the classroom, we can best approximate inclusive images of multiculturalism by promoting a dialogue that moves between students' worlds and ours to illuminate connections as well as highlight differences.

An Afrocentric Multicultural Writing Project

Henry L. Evans

I present here a theory for and conceptualizations of what I term a culturecentric project: the development of a unit of multicultural education in a particular discipline from the perspective of particular students of various cultures. In a culturecentric project varied students undertake a specific self-identified culture and identity exploration to gain a sense of their sociopolitical position. Multiple, concurrent, culturecentric projects such as whole-class and small-group presentations produce a multicultural educational environment. Key to the development of such projects are the instructor's definitions of education and culture. In this theory I define *education* as "the process of facilitating the acquisition of information, knowledge, and skills development a person receives or experiences for personal growth, intended to ensure the survival and progress of his or her cultural group." For *culture*, I employ a definition offered by Wade Nobles, a prominent Afrocentric psychologist: "A people's culture is a vast structure of language, customs, knowledge, ideas, and values which provide a people with a general design for living and patterns for interpreting reality" (54).

In United States society, cultural groups are most often distinguished as European American, African American, Latino or Latina American, Asian American, and Native American. United States elementary, secondary, and higher education is essentially fashioned so that European Americans receive an education as defined above and all other United States cultural groups do not. The frame of reference and the content of United States education are designed to promote knowledge and understanding of the European American by the European American. Other United States cultural groups are trained to support the European American cultural effort. Such an approach to education, by necessity, marginalizes other cultural groups in spite of any attempts at inclusion. Inclusion theory, I contend, marginalizes

273

students when conceptualizations and curriculum do not offer concrete means for centering the student in his or her culture or means to an enabling and emancipating situated self. For example, any paradigmatic shift by theorists of curriculum transformation that moves beyond contribution approaches or add-ons but does not provide students with access to the classical origins of their cultures and with a systematic understanding of their cultures' developments becomes truncated, privileging the students' extant access to European American classical cultures and these cultures' systematic development.

Like the authors of much of the current literature that claims to present a more equitable pedagogical approach to multicultural classroom settings, I intend this article to broaden the base of United States education and, by extension, the base of writing-instruction theory and pedagogy. Using the African American cultural group as an example, I explore the development of one culturecentric project, which has served as a model for all other cultural groups—including European Americans.

Always Already Essentialist

Unfortunately, at a time when people of color worldwide are refusing to remain on the margins of European and European American culture and history and are beginning to construct and reconstruct their histories and cultures to center themselves and form meaningful, emancipatory identities, Western academics have advanced theories of deconstruction and decentering of the self that make the advancement of emancipatory self-identity theories problematic. Thus poststructuralists perceive theories such as Afrocentricity and certain strands of feminism as essentialist, providing still another means of marginalization or dismissal and forcing proponents of these theories to acknowledge such critiques and expend time and energy justifying or refuting them. But an Afrocentric must ask, How does one decenter a self-identity that, until recently, consisted primarily of truncated and distorted received notions of African and African American history and culture, notions received from the same European and European American academic power structure that now declares African American self-identity to be so complex, shifting, and problematized by the influx of numerous histories and cultures that any culturecentric identity project (and the possible justification for claims made by African identity on United States society) is impossible?

In describing centeredness as one of the most fundamental contributions to the broadening of the Afrocentric knowledge base and of the expansion and enrichment of approaches to knowledge in general, Maulana Karenga, perhaps the foremost Afrocentric cultural analyst, admits that the current stress on deconstruction and decentering is challenging and problematic. "Most progressive scholars," he argues, "Afrocentric scholars as well as feminists and Marxists," recognize that the problem of unlimited deconstruction is that it "subverts the emancipatory possibility in ethnic, national, gender, and class theory and practice, undermines human agency by decentering the subject and denying difference—its oppositional, enriching and essential role in both education and social practice" ("Afrocentric Theory"). In short, the problem with deconstruction is that it works for the established order rather than for the oppressed.

Advancing in a similar vein an argument made by many feminists, presented in Diana Fuss's *Essentially Speaking*, I substitute *African Americans* for *women* and *European Americans* for *men*:

> [African Americans as subjects] in relation to desire, authority and textuality [are] *structurally* different from [European Americans]. [African Americans] do not necessarily have the same historical relation to identity; they have not necessarily felt "burdened by too much Self, Ego, Cogito"; and they do not necessarily start from a humanist fantasy of wholeness.   (95)

In fact, historically, the problem of constructing African American self-identity may be the opposite of European and European American self-identity construction.

While Afrocentrics respond to poststructuralist critiques, they must recognize that the core white, Western, and European self-identity (male and female), however complex it is or whatever the amount of influx and shifting occurs, remains solid, intact, the same long-established power and privilege in relation to peoples of color. No European American refuses (or decenters from) the birth-certificate right that identifies him or her as white and that secures the lifelong legal, social, and psychological privileges accompanying white identity. To the extent that poststructuralist theories deconstruct, decenter, and erase the identity formed by a four-hundred-year history of white, Western, European domination and privilege, these theories merit attention and have value for African Americans and other oppressed cultural, gender, or same-sex-preference groups in the United States.

Finally, like all forms of critical theory based in European and European American history and culture, poststructuralist theories are always already essentialist, for such theories are grounded in and make reference solely ("purely" and "essentially") to white, Western, European culture but claim to be appropriate to all cultures, as the application of such theories to African American critical theory and expressive culture indicates.

The Situated Self

Slavery, Jim Crowism, segregation, white supremacy, racism, benign neglect, and a host of other blatant and subtle means of oppression have rendered the African American sociopolitical condition unique. Unlike all other emigrant groups, who voluntarily left their countries in hope of material gains and freedom from religious and other kinds of oppression, the Africans were brought as captives to United States shores, enslaved, and later subjected to continuous oppression. The African American psychologist Hussein Bulhan states, "All situations of oppression violate one's space, energy, mobility, bonding, and identity" (124). Because a people's sociopolitical condition dictates its educational needs, multicultural education for African Americans is necessarily different from multicultural education for European Americans and other emigrant cultural groups. African American education must address these violations, particularly those that we may remedy in the classroom, violations of space (orientation, situation, and place) and identity. But like all culturecentric projects, the African American project requires a critical perspective. In *The Afrocentric Idea*, Molefi Asante, the originator of Afrocentric philosophical methodology and its most prolific theorist, writes, "The crystallization of this critical perspective I have named *Afrocentricity*, which means, literally, placing African ideals at the center of any analysis that involves African culture and behavior" (6). And in a later text, *Kemet, Afrocentricity, and Knowledge*, Asante explains, "Afrocentricity, as an aspect of centralism, is groundedness which allows the student of human culture investigating African phenomena to view the world from the standpoint of the African" (vi).

Concomitant with an Afrocentric grounding, the African American culturecentric project requires cultural and historical resurrection, reconstruction, and revitalization. Therefore teachers must make a conscious effort to seek out and learn about the scholars who have engaged and are engaging in the three Rs of the African American cultural project. Such outstanding texts as *Introduction to Black Studies*, by Maulana Karenga; the *Historical and Cultural Atlas of African Americans*, by Molefi Asante and Mark Mattson; and *Introduction to African Civilizations*, by John G. Jackson, are excellent beginnings. Not only must educators bring into the classroom the culture and history essential to African Americans' enabling and emancipatory sense of self, but they must also facilitate a systematic understanding of that history and culture. I have found I can best accomplish this effort when responding to students' final drafts of papers, when participating in whole-class responses to essay drafts, and during the class's engagement with texts. I provide information and knowledge that promote the formation of a more enabling and emancipatory sense of self-identity, and when the need arises, I help students interrogate information, concepts, and ideas that affect African American self-identity.

The above reference to a systematic understanding raises the issue of stance. Nesha Haniff, comparing Asian American and African American achievement, argues that stance is a function of the African Americans' understanding of their difference in race, color, and nationality. But, Haniff notes, African Americans are trained to view that difference as negative, while other cultural groups use their difference as a means of situating the self for achievement.

> I argue here that African Americans enter the school system with a sense of difference based on color, not on culture or nationality. The Asian American for example enters into the system with a consciousness of difference based on color, culture and nationality. It gives that student a concrete sense that this is a system very different from his life and therefore orients his stance toward learning. (250–55)

It is the systematic understanding that enables the African American student to construct a stance that orients him or her toward learning in United States society.

In *Kemet, Afrocentricity, and Knowledge* Asante writes, "All knowledge results from an occasion of encounter in place. But the place remains a rightly shaped perspective that allows the Afrocentrist to put African ideals and values at the center of inquiry" (5). I contend that an Afrocentric stance, which facilitates and validates the African American student's attempt to situate self, fosters a consciousness that provides a continuing self-motivational context and orientation for learning, an active engagement ("an occasion of encounter in place") with knowledge, and the acquisition of an authentic (enabling and emancipating) voice. These are crucial elements of invention (the initiation of the writing process) and of drafting (the self-referencing and organization of knowledge and information).

Indeed, the self-referencing of knowledge is dependent on what the African American student has been led to perceive constitutes valid knowledge. For example, one of the most problematic concepts I have encountered in the classroom and with colleagues outside the classroom is what I term "privileging white ignorance." When an African American student refers to positive contributions to civilization by Africans or African Americans of which a European American is not aware, the last is prone to refute the information, not with contrary data but with a privileged ignorance, for example, by saying "*I* never heard of that." (Individuals of other cultural groups have learned to follow suit.) Similarly, I have had African American students refuse to read drafts in the classroom or delete information from first drafts, only to find out later that they were afraid of causing conflict or of not being believed. Because my students see me as knowledgeable about African and African American history and culture, I can help them enhance their self-knowledge.

Language Style and Use

The African American psychologist James Anderson states, "Because cognition and cognitive style directly influences the style and content of language (and vice-versa), it is imperative that researchers examine cultural differences from this perspective" (6). Along with a concise summary of the African worldview and a demonstration of its manifestation in African American culture, Anderson offers tables that depict differences between Western cognition and cognitive learning styles and those of African and Eastern cultures; the titles include "Cultural Groupings of World Views," "Cognitive Style Comparison," "Comparison of Features in the Writing Styles of Holistic versus Analytic Thinkers," and "Comparison of Form and Function of Symbolic Imagery between Disparate Cognitive Processes (Speech and Writing)."

All the findings Anderson cites and explicates in his survey of cognition and cognitive-styles literature have implications for facilitating the African American student's writing process: invention, drafting, revision, proofreading, and editing—all performed recursively. Because of space limitations, however, I mention here as an example only the dichotomy of holistic versus analytic thinkers, which has implications for an important area of revision.

A holistic thinker "tends to use second person 'you,' reflects group identity, [and] tends to pull reader in as part of the writing," while the analytic thinker "can easily adopt a third person viewpoint in writing and speaking, is objective, [and] reflects a separate identity from what is going on" (7). By encouraging students to write their first drafts naturally (holistically), then explaining and validating the distinctions along the continuum between the two styles, and finally demonstrating the practical necessity of revising to an analytic writing style, I help students arrive through subsequent drafts at an approximation of the analytic style of "college writing." This approach provides students with both the motivation and a means to fulfill the requirements of their university-wide final writing exam. (During proofreading and editing sessions, I also demonstrate how grammatical agreements—subject-verb and pronoun-antecedent—used in the analytic thinking style become evident and assume an importance in writing that the indiscriminately singular-plural *you* usually used in the holistic thinking style cannot possibly assume.) This approach shows African American students that they do not have to see the components of the holistic worldview in their writing as nonacademic or in error; they come to recognize worldview differences and the sociopolitical implications of each in education and in United States society.

Furthermore, Anderson puts cognition and cognitive style in a sociopolitical context that has profound implications for African American students' writing processes:

> Never are they [white children] asked to be bicultural, bidialectic, or bicognitive. On the other hand, for children of color, biculturality is not a free choice, but a prerequisite for successful participation and eventual success. [Children of color] generally are expected to be bicultural, bidialectic, bicognitive; to measure their performance against a Euro-American yardstick; and to maintain the psychic energy to maintain this orientation. At the same time, they are being castigated whenever they attempt to express and validate their indigenous cultural and cognitive styles. Under such conditions cognitive conflict becomes the norm rather than the exception. (5)

First, Anderson's understanding demonstrates the need to expand the sociopolitical conceptualization of bilingual education to include

African Americans at different ends of the continuum of cognition and cognitive styles who speak some form of black dialect. Second, it implies that instructors must have knowledge of both the European American and the African American worldviews if they wish to mediate that sociopolitical difference, to help students maintain psychic energy for orientation, and to validate students' indigenous cultures, thus lessening cognitive conflict, which can affect the entire writing process. And third, it indicates that to mediate cognitive conflict more effectively students must be taught about the dynamics of their sociopolitical context as bicultural, bicognitive, and bidialectic people.

To construct the African American culturecentric project, an instructor must also have a clear understanding of African Americans' relation to their own language and to white standard English. Asante states Afrocentrically that a language

> exists when a community of people uses a set of agreed upon symbols to express concepts, ideas, and psychological needs. The Afrocentric scholar finds the source of a people's truth close to the language. In the United States Ebonics serves as the archetype of African American language. (*Kemet* 10)

Ebonics consists of black dialect and what Asante in *The Afrocentric Idea* and Geneva Smitherman in *Talkin and Testifyin* have demonstrated as black discourse. I add to the concept of Ebonics what I term African American Standard English (AASE). Both Black Standard English and African American Standard English have the agreed-upon set of symbols Asante discusses. But unlike black dialect, which is primarily spoken, has its own African verb structure and black vocabulary, and intentionally restricts its meanings almost exclusively to an African American community, AASE is an evolving spoken and written language that, by necessity, employs the white standard English verb structure and vocabulary, intends its meanings for all communities (including the grass roots), and operates primarily in academic arenas, mostly in African and African American scholarly texts and journals. AASE speakers and writers consciously use symbols to reflect an Afrocentric worldview, promoting the image and interest of African people.

In *Afrocentricity* Asante asserts that the African American intellectual's first order is to free Africans from racist language:

> Language is essentially the control of thought. It becomes impossible for us to direct our future until we control our language.

The sense of language is in precision of vocabulary and structure for a particular social context. . . . Black language must possess instrumentality: that is, it must be able to do something for our liberation. (31)

In an attempt to discover a truth that reflects African American reality from an Afrocentric worldview, AASE continually augments, defines, and redefines concepts and itself to provide meaningful lexical, morphological, statement, and accumulation-of-statements alternatives to the symbols of standard white English. Therefore, in Afrocentric scholarship one encounters, for example, words such as *Africoid* instead of *negroid* and *endarkening* instead of *enlightening*. Each of these terms is a more consistent, accurate, and Afrocentric reconceptualization of a Eurocentric word. *Africoid*, like *Caucasoid*, evokes a landmass origin, replacing the false *negroid*, which obscures African origins, severs continental connections, and truncates African American self-identity, relegating it to a four-hundred-year period of enslavement and oppression. There is no negroland or negroid race. *Endarkening* is a positive reversal, countering the standard English dictionary listing of negative terms involving darkness.

In *Afrocentricity*, Asante lists meaningful alternatives to Eurocentric concepts and challenges Afrocentric scholars to create others; graduate students at Temple University's Department of African American Studies have compiled an ongoing list. AASE incorporates African words to describe African American phenomena that are absent in white standard English or that have no white standard English equivalent. *Maafa*, a Yoruba term that replaces *African Holocaust* (which situates African phenomena in relation to another culture), describes the horrific events endured by Africans, from captivity to containment in west African coast dungeons to the Middle Passage to the end of the African enslavement in the Americas. Philosophical terms from throughout Africa, from classical African philosophy to the present, such as *Ntu, Muntu, Kintu, Hantu*, and *Kuntu* (which describe the essential components of Bantu philosophy) have also become standard vocabulary in AASE. The omission of words and concepts from AASE is equally important in rendering African American reality; one does not encounter, for example, the word *minority*. To perceive one's own or another's cultural group as a minority is to buy into the count-and-measure epistemological principle of European American philosophy.

Finally, words used to privilege European culture, such as the word *Continental* in *Continental philosophy*, take on a different meaning when used by African Americans. An African American who uses *Continental* refers to Continental African philosophy. Similar uses, such as *American* in reference to the United States and *classical* for European classical (as in *classical music*), demonstrate how white standard English makes claims to all of the Americas and considers European classical music *the* classical music. All cultures have classical music, and no other North or South American country regards itself as *the* America.

On the statement level, the Afrocentric scholar attempts to employ what the social science theorist David R. Burgest terms an "African humanism" to describe African phenomena. Burgest offers as an example of Euro-American antihumanism the statement "Statistics show that 50% of the infants in this community are illegitimate"; as an example of African humanism he gives the statement "Statistics show that babies are 25% of the population in this community." From an African philosophical point of view, there is no such thing as an illegitimate child. Burgest notes that to categorize babies as legitimate or illegitimate "serves as a justification and rationale for forming cohesive groups—that is for including some persons in the group and for excluding others, which is done through stigmatizing and dehumanizing the individuals or groups intended to be isolated" (44).

Afrocentric scholars also exhibit a difference on the level of meaning of accumulations of statements. For example, a non-Afrocentric scholar, commenting on a famous anthropologist's description of a rhesus monkey that, in an action unusual among animals, took control of his clan and several others and became the ruler of the entire body, states that the anthropologist "naturally" called this monkey Napoleon. Aware of European *and* African history, an Afrocentric scholar would have thought immediately of Thutmose III, an African of classical historical times whose domain spanned Africa, Europe, and Asia. The issue involves the crucial elements of reference and centeredness—not to mention historical resurrection, reconstruction, and revitalization.

Linda James Myers offers an observation similar to Asante's understanding about "a people's truth [being] close to the language":

> Words label experience, and thus give thoughts form. Language (word usage) reflects the accumulated wisdom of a people. Out of infinite sensory experience, language is created by selecting those things which are repetitive in experience and believed useful to attend. Experiences which are unlabeled at the sensory input level do not become a part of the language and typically do not intrude into consciousness. (25)

This passage, like the above references to language, describes the need for language instrumentality. By "labeling experience" important to whites, white standard English brings into consciousness its own "accumulated wisdom" and that which it perceives "useful to attend." Thus one of the most difficult problems confronting African American writers who use the lexicology and verb structure of white standard English is operating out of their own experiences, on their own ontological and axiological principles. For the African and the African American, the world is spiritual and the physical world is spirit manifest. The spiritual foundation of African American life and thus of African American language, categorized commonly as "soul" in black dialect and as the African philosophical concept of *Nommo* (word power in black discourse theory), is in white standard English, as Myers says, "unlabeled at the sensory level" and therefore does "not become part of the language."

Some have argued that African American ethnicity be understood as an interaction between and a syncretizing of the European American and the African over time. But because of the distinctions between the ontological and axiological principles grounding black dialect and United States English, I find this argument problematic and counterproductive. I view *Nommo* as a retention from traditional Africa, one of the principles of African American culture that has permitted the formation of a counterculture language (Black English) and of discourse traditions apart from and in opposition to United States English and discourse. I do not claim that African Americans are traditional Africans, but I contend that some African concepts are so vital that they have been retained intact.

Writing on the spiritual foundation of African and African American life, the Afrocentric anthropologist Donna Richards offers this description of *Nommo*:

> Nommo seeks to conceptualize the ability to activate. As there is no English equivalent for this term, it becomes difficult to explain. It is manifested in the ability of Muntu (human beings, the ancestors, the spirits, the Creator) to make use of the force within the universe in order to affect other beings. The power of Nommo is symbolized in "the word," and "the word" is the aegis of Muntu. . . . Nommo is our use of the spiritually activating principle. Nommo is will and intent. Nommo is consciousness.   (40)

I note here that Anderson includes in his survey of findings on African American cognition and cognitive style categories that reflect the concept of *Nommo*: "Thought (in speech and writing) is perceived as . . . [a] living thing, wholistic thing, doing thing," "Medium is the message," and "Medium motivates and socializes" (7). Perhaps the best conscious rendition of *Nommo* as style and consciousness is Paul Carter Harrison's *The Drama of Nommo: Black Theater in the African Continuum*, in which Harrison demonstrates through analysis and critique of African American folklore, literature, and drama the presence of the *Nommo* force-spirit in all phases of the African American experience.

African American Standard English contains the accumulated wisdom of a people. It provides not only instrumentality on lexical, morphological, and semantic levels but also an ontological base or grounding for an epistemology, axiology, and logic equal to that of (and as functional as) black dialect. Afrocentric scholars such as Asante, Myers, Richards, and Nobles engage their subjects unabashedly with the freedom and expansiveness, the instrumentality, of an evolving language derived from a material-spiritual (Afrocentric) worldview.

Finally, I have found an understanding of the evolution of African American Standard English and an appreciation of its value instrumental in educating African Americans. AASE facilitates, and lessens students' resistance to, the switch to an academically acceptable written standard English by maintaining the philosophical worldview that grounds their original language, black dialect, some form of which even most middle-class African Americans speak. Explicating and fostering the use of AASE are ways of assessing African American students' assets—starting where the students are. But one must be skilled in recognizing and reinforcing that starting place.

The Teacher-Student Relationship

In African philosophy the principle of highest value, or the axiological principle, is the establishment of positive interpersonal relationships. Therefore it is not surprising that in the past decade one of the most successful programs for African American college students, the premedical program at Xavier College, is described as follows:

> The program builds confidence and skill in its predominately black population by creating an aura of *family* in which cooperation is highly valued, *bonding* between the students and faculty is encouraged, and a maintenance of positive ethnic identity is fostered. Learning occurs in a *socially reinforcing* environment.
> (Anderson 8; emphasis mine)

All these concepts have also been demonstrated elsewhere to facilitate learning among African Americans, and all involve enhancing the student-teacher relationship.

One consequence the African American culturecentric project anticipates and fosters is a drastic change in the traditional relationship between teachers and African American student writers. This change is predicted on the following:

○ a shift in the basic (implicit or explicit) intent of writing instruction: self-knowledge (identity) becomes the grounding of writing, and teachers conceptualize writing more accurately as a tool (instrumentality) for that grounding rather than as a vessel for content—in effect, there is a true shift from the perception of the essay as final product to be corrected, to the essay as self-developmental process;

○ a transformation in the teacher's role as audience for the student's writing process, a transformation in which the instructor becomes facilitator for student self-development to promote the survival and advancement of the student's culture; and

○ a reconceptualization of the student based on the teacher's systematic understanding of African American historical and cultural knowledge.

In this dramatic restructuring of the teacher-student relationship the teacher's belief in the value and validity of the student's history and culture (and one assumes that such a belief exists, at least theoretically) is transformed into knowledge. What has existed as a generous humanistic postulation becomes grounded in historical and cultural principles that determine teacher attitude and behavior.

For new terms helpful in reconceptualizing the participants in this transformed relationship, I borrow from African-centered pedagogy. Kwame Akoto provides the terms *mwalimu* (instructor) and *mwanafunzi* (student) and has this to say about the relationship:

> The *mwalimu* must not only be involved in the study of the culture, but must be involved in a concrete and ongoing way with advancing the cultural and/or political interest of Afrikan people. The mwalimu comes before his *mwanafunzi* (students) as a representative of the whole culture. The mwalimu is entrusted with the task of inculcating the essential values of that culture and thereby guaranteeing its continuation. The mwalimu comes to the classroom representing in one sense the

limitations of tradition and the existing order. The *mwanafunzi* comes to the classroom representing the new order or unlimited potentiality.   (99)

This model of the teacher-student relationship significantly affects the teacher's role as audience in the student's writing process. It serves as a consciously structured facilitator to the student's progress in writing.

The culturecentric project for African American students is based on at least three important concepts:

- a realistic and functional sociopolitical situatedness of self, an Afrocentric worldview;
- an understanding and appreciation of one's language in itself and in relation to white standard English and of the movement to develop a language of instrumentality, African American Standard English; and
- a restructuring of the teacher-student relationship, a shift in the nature of teacher-as-audience.

In the multicultural classroom, each cultural group is entitled to an ongoing culturecentric project that takes into account its sociopolitical context in United States society. Education—and thus writing theory—must realistically reflect the needs for survival and advancement of that cultural group.

"Better Than What People Told Me I Was": What Students of Color Tell Us about the Multicultural Composition Classroom

Carol A. Miller

This essay draws on a series of interviews with students of color in first-year writing classes at the University of Minnesota, Twin Cities. What these students had to say about their writing histories, the complex interactions of their cultural and academic expectations, their experiences in composition classrooms, and the relation of all these factors to their success as writers provides important information for writing teachers. But as a member of the Cherokee Nation of Oklahoma, I have an interest in advancing a broader point: that convergences in composition and multicultural research indicate it is logical and essential to position all students, particularly students of color, as subjects rather than as objects throughout the educational enterprise. Primary data from students, especially from students of color, is invaluable in the transformation from essentially monocultural to multicultural strategies of teaching and learning.

What are these convergences? How may we, and our students, understand and benefit from them? The concentration on equity pedagogy among cultural theorists such as Paolo Freire, James Banks, Henry Giroux, and John Ogbu illustrates one such intersection and suggests a move toward common conclusions. Another is these theorists' mutual, individual, examination of the significance of specific cultural context. Ogbu, for example, distinguishing between "voluntary" and "involuntary" minorities' attitudes toward academic expectations and goals, has demonstrated that some groups and individuals perceive cultural and language differences in academic settings as barriers to overcome, while others interpret them as threats to their group identities (48). Even progressive strategies intended to help students acquire the language of academic discourse, therefore, may result in complexly ambivalent responses and outcomes. By particularizing cultural contexts of behavior and values, we understand more about the consequences of our pedagogical choices.

Over the past fifteen years, researchers in composition have paid considerable attention to the contextual factors relating writing performance and cultural transition, although only recently has there been an evolution from a largely unquestioned focus on proficiency in Standard English to the broader issues engendered within what Lisa Delpit has identified as an exclusionary academic "culture of power" (296). Moreover, the discussion of the essentially ethnocentric and unproblematized goal of teaching Standard English has almost exclusively centered on black writers. Rarely have researchers acknowledged the importance of linguistic or composing behaviors of other cultural groups or of individuals within those groups, although William Leap has since the 1970s produced studies of American Indian English demonstrating his conclusion that "just as there are many different American Indian languages and language families, there are many different varieties of American Indian English" (145). Leap's work presents one model of a specific hypothesis and methodology that reconfigures the conventional locus of American Indian writers in the classroom, liberating them from being considered solely from the perspective of deficit theory and investing them with authority as individuals who bring into the academic setting a rich and comprehensible ancestral language fluency inextricably connected to cultural identity.

In general, however, students of color have been largely ignored as resources of primary data in curricular and pedagogical reform. Russell Durst, examining almost ten years of annotated bibliographies from *Research in the Teaching of English*, noted the surprising paucity of research on writers' contexts, defined as "the nature of environments in which writers write and learn to write—the home, school, workplace, and community—and the relationships between these environments and writers' development" (400–01). Sixty percent of the contextual studies that have been produced involve elementary and preschool writers exclusively.

In the study of writing environments and their relation to development, ethnographic approaches appear to make sense (e.g., Anne DiPardo; Hull and Rose). Glynda Hull and her colleagues call for a balance of micro- and macro-level analysis of classroom activity— "shuttling in a systematic way between close linguistic cognitive study and studies of broader contexts" (323). Students' direct testimonies should significantly facilitate such balanced analysis and access to broader contexts. Further, greater reliance on students as primary informational resources may help create a cultural bridge over the chasm between oral and written language that some students must cross.

Theories about primary and secondary orality that attempt to explain interactions of technology and verbal expression have not yet fully acknowledged the ongoing importance of oral traditions in many minority cultures. In fact, Walter Ong and others (e.g., Killingsworth), in foregrounding technology as a primary agent in transformations of orality and literacy, have often unintentionally lost sight of race and ethnicity as variables affecting those transformations. If, as Ong asserts, primary and secondary orality are alike in many ways—for example, in their power to generate "a strong group sense" (136)—then why not increase the interplay of oral and written language to let one inform the other? Why not ask students about their writing abilities and use their comments as resources with important implications for the multicultural classroom? Students' testimonies constitute a sort of talking aloud and talking back that validate and take advantage of the oral traditions of the students' cultures and inform the teaching of writing in ways that have the potential to turn learners into subjects rather than objects.

What Students Had to Say

This interview study, involving twenty-one African American, Native American, and Latino and Latina students, collected students' testimonies to learn how writing classrooms might become more functional for students of color. The project involved a number of components, most notably a series of progressive interviews of two groups of first-language English-speaking students, one drawn from basic writing classes in the University of Minnesota's open-admissions General College and the other from College of Liberal Arts composition classes. ESL students were not included in the study because they commonly enroll in composition programs designed specifically for second-language speakers and writers. Ten of the students were African American, seven were American Indian, and four were Latino or Latina. The gender mix was ten women and eleven men; their ages ranged from eighteen to forty-seven. The interview instruments focused on four areas of inquiry: self-assessment of students' writing histories, processes, and overall competencies; hindsight consideration of what students believed worked and didn't work in their completed composition classes; relevance of composition course work to writing performance in other university classes; and conflicts students of color perceived between cultural identity and the specifically academic writing demanded at the university.

The interviews—thirty-one in all, since ten of our subjects participated in a follow-up interview the term after they completed the freshman writing requirement—produced considerable data. My objective here is to highlight some of the most informative insights these students of color provided about their experiences as writing students. How did they respond to progressive instructional strategies like small-group or peer revision, process emphasis, and one-on-one conferencing? Did they perceive a double bind—or any bind—between the culture and language expectations of the academic and home communities? What can educators learn from them about what is successful, or not, in writing classrooms? Generalizations based on the qualitative data of the study are necessarily indicative rather than conclusive, but examination of the responses provides a useful foundation.

One idea that emerged from the interviews is that theories of cultural or cognitive deficits do less to explain why students don't write well than does the absence of significant writing practice and preparation. In our study, fourteen students—two-thirds of our sample—reported no experience writing essays before college. Only four reported writing more than seven papers in high school, except for a few assignments they identified as creative, for example, science fiction or poetry, rather than analytic or expository. Three students reported being required to write only in a creative mode.

As might be expected, there appeared to be some correlation between students' self-perceived abilities and their preparation. Mark (all students' names are fictitious), an African American student, at first responded that in high school he "did the normal things, writing research papers, book reports, stuff like that." Responding to follow-up questions, however, he acknowledged that he "didn't write that much in high school" and had "done, like, a research paper probably once in [his] life." Not surprisingly, Mark expressed almost no confidence in his skills as a writer but ultimately considered even his minimal and uncertainly remembered experience helpful: "I'm lost at some of the things," he said, "but with the little bit of background that I have, I'm not totally lost. I have a clue."

The writing histories of these students suggest that deficits may be attributable to lack of practice and opportunity. If freshman-composition teachers overestimate their students' writing experience or fail to elicit specific information about it, an inadequately informed, blame-the-victim response to students' genuine instructional needs may result.

The importance of the most basic feature of composition class-rooms—the supervised opportunity to practice writing—was supported by students' unanimously positive responses to the question, "Do you feel your writing ability has improved as a result of the writing you've done in your university composition class(es)?" Representative student responses included the following:

> MARK: Yeah, because, like I said, I didn't write that much. This is the most writing I've done.
>
> ROBERT: Somewhat. I still have a long ways to go, but I know what is expected now, versus when I got here.
>
> KEN: I feel comfortable about my sentence structure and paragraph structure. I just feel comfortable about the whole structure of the paper.
>
> JERRY: I think it has. I can see my mistakes. I remember that I used to think after writing the first draft, that was enough and the paper was done. I believed it, and I felt like that. But now I see it and I understand it—why we write a draft more than once.
>
> MIKE: I guess in a lot of ways. My mechanics, that's improved. Configuration of my ideas has improved. And just learning how to write a paper, you know, from the draft to the final paper. That's cool.
>
> BETTY: Well, as I was telling you before, I was very insecure about my writing to begin with, and I felt very dumb. And I found that I'm not so dumb. I can do it, and it's helped me personally gain a confidence I didn't have.
>
> CATHY: I don't know if it's improved, but I feel more confident than I did before.
>
> LINDA: Yes, I think so. It's given me confidence in my knowledge, my own values of who I am.

The range of positive comments in these statements reflects increased competence and self-confidence. Embedded implicitly are outcomes that students tended to mention with some consistency at other points in the interviews. Jerry, for example, notes development of two competencies: self-critique and recursive composing process. Robert expresses relief at simply knowing what is expected; Ken speaks of attaining a level of comfort with structural components of his writing rather than merely with surface features, which students tended to talk about more frequently. Betty, Linda, and Cathy reported gaining confidence through a validation of their potential to do well within at least the portion of the academic community that composition represents. In fact, students frequently indicated that they saw the perception of increased writing ability as a component of initiation, of a perceived transition from outsider to insider status. Others considered the practice itself important, a view perhaps best expressed by Phil, an older Latino student with little previous writing experience: "I don't like writing any better, but I do it better."

The interviews identified areas of mystification that can complicate or impede students' performance but that otherwise well-planned and well-taught composition classes might never address if their teachers do not elicit information from the students. For example, students tended to confuse the meanings and thus the values of mechanics and usage. Several students, especially those who were least experienced and confident, assumed that grammar, punctuation, and effective writing were essentially the same thing. These students appeared to believe not only that surface features define good writing but that the mastery of surface features is the primary barrier to and requisite for successful performance.

These assumptions create problems for both teachers and students. They certainly complicate and imperil the teaching of effective writing. Without understanding either the vocabularies and distinctions of grammar and usage or how they relate to other components of good writing, students have apparently bought into the prioritizing of surface features. The assimilative institutional model, which mandates mechanical competence in Standard English as the primary feature of academically rewardable writing, continues to be vigorously debated, but it frequently results in confusion and naive conceptions about what good writing is and how one learns to write well. Mike, for example, when asked to describe his strengths and weaknesses as a writer, said, "I'm creative, you know. But I have problems with syntax and my vocabulary wasn't real strong. And basically just doing right, you know, punctuation and stuff like that, was weak, and syntax and form and sentence structure and paragraph structure, I think." Carol's confusion about the demands of good writing went unresolved: "You had to guess each time, is it my punctuation, is it that, or is it the words I used, or does he want me to use bigger words? It seemed like we were always guessing. And then when I got to the point where I knew how, everybody would pass their copies around and I could see everybody pretty much wrote the same way I did."

Like several other students, Mark said that creativity was a strength of his writing and that his weaknesses particularly involved "punctuation and reading." When asked to assess his strengths and weaknesses as a writer, another African American student, James, said that he didn't think he had any strengths: "I don't think I was a good writer, because I didn't like to write and I didn't like to read." At least a third of the students noted anxieties about reading skills. They consistently related reading difficulties to their weaknesses as writers and frequently expressed frustration and resignation about how this interdependence affected their academic performance. What James, for example, remembered positively about high school English was vocabulary: "I learned vocabulary words because I like to use big words. It makes me feel important or something, you know." He saw his vocabulary as a substitute for deeper-level reading skills. It gave him self-esteem by appearing to allow him to "talk the talk" of education, and he may have equated it with reading ability in the same way that many students equated mechanical competence with writing ability.

Another problem for James was confusion over the apparent arbitrariness of teacher expectations. He and several other students described responding to such expectations and other confusing aspects of writing performance by giving up on the problems—"blowing them off." In fact, the students with the least preparation and the least confidence as writers were mystified not only by performance criteria and instructor feedback but by the ways to address their confusion. As one student said when asked whether he understood and agreed with his teacher's commentary about his papers, "I really didn't. . . . I thought, forget it. She's the instructor. She's right, that's my weakest point, and she is probably right, so I'm not going to argue about it."

Students also reported general confusion about course objectives and about the purposes of specific materials and assignments, a finding especially relevant to the effects of multicultural texts and instructional strategies on performance in composition classrooms. In one required course in the freshman composition sequence that a number of the students took, the teachers chose education as the core subject for student writing because they assumed the topic would be universally meaningful. But after the course only one student was able to identify education as the core subject. Instead, after students had been asked to read and write about topics including their educational histories and goals and the educational experiences of others described in books like Jonathan Kozol's *Illiterate America* and Richard Wright's *Native Son*, students named "racism," "illiteracy," "prejudice," and "minorities" as the core topics. Although some students responded positively or neutrally to the apparent emphasis on these topics, others, like Mark, indicated a strong level of discomfort and even dysfunction.

> INTERVIEWER: Can you explain why you were uncomfortable?
> MARK: It's the topic. You're sitting in the class and you don't like sitting in class where all the rest of the students are white.

They're all from Wisconsin and Minnesota, you know, white kids. You're all talking about racism, about how dumb the niggers was, and so and so. And you're sitting there, you know. "Wow, I don't want to talk this. I don't want to listen."

INTERVIEWER: Did the instructor . . . know that you were un-comfortable? Did you ever talk?

MARK: No, I just . . . I didn't want to deal with it. I didn't want to talk about it.

INTERVIEWER: So did you have trouble writing that paper?

MARK: Yeah. I didn't really want to do it. I didn't want to have anything to do with that.

Mark's comments reflect that he felt alienated enough not to partici-pate in class, apparently because he was the only person of color in his class and was uncomfortable with race as a subject matter for writing and discussion. Other students expressed confusion or ambivalence about course substance and objectives, and these feelings, frequently coupled with and exacerbated by isolation in the classroom commu-nity, appeared to have potential to hurt their performance. Another student said, "If I wasn't comfortable with writing and telling about me, I wouldn't have done it. I wouldn't have told them about my past, or where I'd like to go, or who I am now, at all. I would have just said, 'No way.'"

The experience of Mark and his peers may teach us that, if students are to benefit fully from course objectives, texts, and writing assign-ments intended to reflect specific educational values within the com-plex dynamic of an intercultural instructional environment, they must be better prepared to understand the purposes of and connections among those course components. To accomplish this goal, instructors need to discuss the issues with students and to articulate objectives in syllabi and other course materials. It is important that teachers devise ways of monitoring and responding to students' perceptions of what they're being asked to do and why, perhaps through journal entries or conferences and through periodic course evaluations during, rather than after, the course.

Which composition class activities did the students in the study find most useful? Six named the writing practice itself, along with written and oral feedback from instructors. An impressive nineteen identi-fied individual conferences as important to improvement; five of the twenty-one said that conferencing was the most helpful class activity. One student noted that, although he had no formal conferences with his teacher, one-on-one discussion resolved his confusion about an assignment at least once: "She explained to me after class. I did understand it much better, and, you know, I wrote the paper again." Only one student responded negatively to teacher conferencing: "I don't like that. I don't like individual stuff, especially with teachers."

Seven students said that small-group or peer-response activities were most useful, but often for reasons instructors may not have anticipated. Students who expressed the lowest confidence in their abilities apparently tended to use small groups primarily not to generate ideas or to facilitate revision but to clarify what was going on in class—to have peers explain what the instructor wanted, what the assignments demanded. But small groups and peer feedback were not productive for all students. Students across all three ethnic groups, especially those who expressed the greatest writing confidence, found these activities a waste of time and complained about uninformed or indiscriminately positive peer reactions. Two of the American Indian students in the sample were particularly resistant to critiquing the writing of peers in small groups.

> LINDA: I just don't get anything out of small groups personally. I don't know if it's because I'm not aggressive in making my own opinions or whatever. I just don't. We had evaluation, and I never got anything out of my evaluations at all. Everything was, you're a great writer. Well, I know I'm not a great writer.
>
> INTERVIEWER: Did you do critiques of other people's writing in the small groups?
>
> LINDA: Yeah, and I found that extremely difficult because I'm, I don't like it because I'm Native American and the way I believe is that we do not criticize other people's . . . Maybe it's my concept of thinking, of not understanding what they want, but to me to criticize is to criticize. So I have difficulty saying that something is wrong.
>
> INTERVIEWER: Would it have been useful, would it have been possible for the instructor to talk about that as help rather than criticism?
>
> LINDA: I think if it would've been presented to me in the fashion that, instead of saying, just interfering with this other person's journey, if they would say, well, what would you do if this was your writing? That would have been more useful to me, just, what would you have done, not what's wrong with it.

Linda's response, in the context of an almost universal Native American ideal of communal and personal harmony, suggests that small-group peer critique, widely used in writing classrooms, does not automatically help all learners. Her response provides a particularly useful cue about how peer feedback could be more constructive—and could engender less resistance—if it were elicited as constructive advice rather than criticism: "What would you do?" rather than "What's wrong?"

In general, the students considered it important that they feel invested not only in their writing but in a classroom writing community that acknowledged their cultural and individual experiences as relevant. Many students spoke eloquently about differences they perceived between their "home" and academic voices and about the consequences of those differences. "Those people that say they can feel like they're in two different worlds, I guess I can understand," said one American Indian student. "It's just that I've gotten used to being around this white culture kind of thing and blowing it off. But I'm going to be like I am, and you can't say anything to me because I'm not doing anything wrong." An African American student spoke about how, through his experience in composition, he was losing the slang he brought with him: "I don't want to lose it, though, because slang is very important just in case I go back home. I had to make an adjustment. So what I'm doing now is that I'm able to keep some of my old way, but also, you know, being able to communicate with other people too. I'm using both."

Students were clearly empowered by their senses of improved writing ability and by classroom opportunities to learn and practice. "When I first started, all of a sudden I felt a lot smarter," said one. Another said, "[the class] has helped me out a lot, to prove to myself that I can go on and that I'm better than what people told me I was." Unfortunately, only three students reported being required to write in subsequent university classes, and one of them complained that he had been penalized for using the process approach he had been encouraged to develop in his composition class: when he requested early feedback from his instructor on what he considered a preliminary draft, the instructor graded the paper as a final version.

The information that the sample of students of color provides about the students' histories and experiences convincingly demonstrates the importance of students themselves as resources for creating more inclusive and functional learning environments. Several conclusions about the teaching of writing emerged from the study. One is the need for an expanded theoretical grounding—supported by detailed evaluation—in how diverse populations learn. Alternatives to universal, undifferentiated models of cognitive development require the support of quantitative studies that do not proceed from ethnocentric assumptions and that recognize numerous cultural and individual contexts. There is also a need for more qualitative research—interviews, case studies, and so on—to bring into the discussion in much greater numbers many students who have so far been more frequently talked about than talked with. Students of color have principally been objects of, rather than partners in, the construction of what are sometimes prefabricated and monolithic academic edifices.

We must perform an ongoing reexamination of our pedagogical objectives and instructional strategies, especially their consequences for students who may logically resist being socially reconstructed when that process involves behaviors of assimilation and acculturation. We need answers to questions more explicit than those we have posed so far. How do progressive strategies, or any instructional strategies for that matter, really affect students' academic performance? What students are we talking about and under what circumstances? How do we know what we think we know about these students, and whom have we asked?

Most broadly, teachers and students must find ways to reconcile the contending demands of educational systems and community forces, since to adopt unequivocally the language and values of the dominant culture means for many students to risk identity and the sense of belonging. In genuinely effective multicultural classrooms the teacher will devise strategies that allow students to use their cultural and personal traits to examine closely the components of learning and performance. Such a classroom will require not only new paradigms of cultural transaction but also the will and tenacity to carry them through. What students tell us should be fundamental to how, and whether, cultural transactions occur. As Carlos Yorio asserted, "Our students . . . *can* talk; they have opinions about what we do and what we make them do. . . . Our students will not always agree with each other and may not always be right or even sensible. But I will argue, they cannot be ignored" (33).

NOTE

I would like to thank the Center for Interdisciplinary Studies of Writing at the University of Minnesota, Twin Cities, which provided funding for the original interview study. I also wish to acknowledge the assistance of my research assistant, Caroline Evans.

Students on the Border

Kate Mangelsdorf

> *Borders are set up to form a third country—a border culture.*
> *Borders are set up to define the places that are safe and unsafe,*
> *to distinguish us from them. A borderland is a vague and un-*
> *determined place created by the emotional residue of an un-*
> *natural boundary. It is in a constant state of transition.*
> —Gloria Anzaldúa, *Borderlands / La Frontera*

This essay is about students who live and go to college on the Rio
Grande border between the United States and Mexico. Their ethnicity,
class, and language, like those of many other students in the United
States, position them on another border as well—the border that di-
vides the dominant culture from marginalized cultures. Like some
other students from marginalized cultures, many of these students
end up on the borders of our writing classrooms, where their voices
are often drowned by those of more privileged students. In this essay I
argue that we need to create classrooms in which students can cross
the lines that divide *them* from *us*, a crossing that requires students to
rethink their identities and the role of language in creating them. Such
a crossing can also allow students to understand the borders that they
live on and the effect these borders have on them and on others. In the
words of Henry Giroux, we need

> to challenge and redefine the substance and effects of cultural
> borders, . . . to create opportunities for students to be bor-
> der crossers in order to understand otherness on its own terms,
> and . . . to create borderlands in which diverse cultural resources
> allow for the fashioning of new identities within existing configu-
> rations of power.   (Introduction x)

Perceiving our classrooms as borderlands and our students as border
crossers can help us create pedagogies in which dominant and mar-

298

ginalized discourses are mutually re-formed as students and teachers work together to generate and communicate knowledge.

The students I discuss here are Chicana and Chicano, and though many Chicana and Chicano students in the United States do not live as close to the Rio Grande border as these students, they often—especially if they are recent immigrants—experience a similar clash of cultures. I derive my analysis and pedagogical suggestions from case studies, interviews, and textual studies I have conducted at a university in the Southwest. Because many of these border students live in two cultures at once, their experiences in writing classrooms can help us understand how to enable all our students, no matter what their position in our culture, to cross borders so that they can interact with, rather than simply adjust to, the dominant discourse of the academy. Below I describe some of the cultural conflicts that border students experience and suggest how teachers can use these conflicts to create borderlands in which their students can use language(s) to create new and empowered identities.

The terms *Chicana* and *Chicano* refer to Americans of Mexican ancestry. *Latina* and *Latino*, terms I also use in this essay, refer more broadly to Americans of Latin American ancestry. *Hispanic*, the term used by the United States Census Bureau, denotes Americans of Latin American and Iberian ancestry. Though I do not engage the arguments here, the use of these terms has created a heated ideological conflict among some Latinas and Latinos (for one view, see Hayes-Bautista and Chapa).

Cultural Conflicts on the Border

A border culture is unique in that the interactions of cultures in a single geographic area can create a language and belief system that is the product of neither culture alone, but rather both at once: "Two groups coming into culture with one another are mutually influential although not necessarily to the same degree" (Negy and Woods 226). At the United States–Mexico border, the Anglo-American culture is clearly more powerful, economically and politically, than the Mexican—after all, the United States seized this territory from Mexico. Nonetheless, some Chicana and Chicano border students choose to ignore the power issues associated with the mingling of these cultures, preferring to believe they can select what they like from each culture—a cultural smorgasbord, so to speak. For instance, one student wrote in an essay that being Mexican American had enabled her to enjoy both Mexican and American food and customs: "I can cook enchiladas one day, yet the next day I can prepare a burger and fries without problems." This student's strong affiliation with the dominant Anglo culture, her few personal experiences of discrimination, and her comfortable middle-class lifestyle left her with little sense of cultural conflict or awareness of difference. She was positioned in the center of the dominant culture, her Mexican background apparent to her only in her knowledge of food and holidays.

Other border students are more ambivalent, confused, and even hostile toward one or both of their cultures. In particular, female students—caught between the limitations of traditional gender roles in one culture and the promise of freer gender roles in another culture—struggle to resolve such cultural tensions. One student, Rebecca (all names are fictitious), began an essay describing the advantages of living in the Mexican culture, in particular having a united family whose members help one another out. She added, however, that women's opportunities can be limited because "in the Mexican culture men like to protect women a lot. Women sometimes feel trapped and unhappy." In another piece she wrote, "My Spanish / Mexican culture has affected me in some ways, but I always overcome it." Sandy, also Chicana, wrote of having to turn down a scholarship to an out-of-town college because her mother believed that a daughter should not move out of the house until she is married. Similarly, another Chicana student, Alicia, wrote that in the Mexican culture "men are the ones who wear the pants in the household and who go out into the wilderness of the work force. On the other hand, women are seen as fragile creatures who must never leave their parents' side until their wedding day." Alicia's parents also made her decline a scholarship, this one to a prestigious out-of-town university. Alicia wrote about this event in an essay entitled "Imprisoned by Culture." She described her response to her parents' refusal to allow her to accept the scholarship:

> Outraged by all that was happening, tears ran down my cheeks. I realized that I had spent a long part of my life working for something that would never be mine, something that would always be a vision, a mirage. This was the day that I became fully aware of how my Mexican heritage would hinder me as a female trying to survive in the world of today. . . . [This] wound will never heal.

Alicia's anger and bitterness is directed toward her Mexican culture. Other Latina and Latino students may have similar feelings toward the dominant Anglo culture because of ethnic and linguistic discrimination. In *Bootstraps* Victor Villanueva writes:

> Biculturalism does not mean to me an equal ease with two cultures. That is an ideal. Rather, biculturalism means the tensions within, which are caused by being unable to deny the old or the new. (39)

If we pretend these tensions don't exist, we encourage students to disengage themselves from their writing, even to the point of using writing to erase their identities.

Language, Resistance, and Belief

Given such powerful tensions, what can writing teachers do to help students succeed in writing classes? How can we teach critical literacy—an understanding of and appreciation for different ways of making meaning—to students of all backgrounds? How can we make our students, and ourselves, border crossers?

My pedagogical strategies are based on three assumptions. First, voices of difference need to be able to challenge the dominant discourse in the writing classroom. We need to release ourselves from the idea that teaching writing is a politically neutral process. Language, including the language we use and teach in the classroom, is never neutral; as Patricia Bizzell has noted, by privileging academic language we can invalidate other languages:

> The problem then is whether the acquisition of academic literacy, because it carries with it the political power of its origins in the privileged social classes, will crowd out whatever other cultural literacies students bring to school, unfairly devaluing and perhaps eventually extirpating them. ("Literacy" 134)

The literacies that Latina and Latino students bring to the classroom are diverse: some speak and write only English; some read and write only English but speak Spanish as well, including different Chicana and Chicano dialects; others, particularly recent immigrants, have Spanish as their primary language. Rather than devote all our attention to standard written and oral English, we need to make our classrooms places where different languages and texts intersect, so that students grapple with the significance of the different literacies in their lives.

My second assumption is derived from my experiences in the classroom, where students have sometimes resisted my attempts to include languages and cultures other than those valorized by the dominant society. I have come to believe that student resistance can be used to increase engagement and insight—although it can make teachers uncomfortable in the process. In traditional classrooms, student resistance is often manifested by apathy, silence, and absence—signs that the pedagogy fails to make connections to issues in students' lives. Ira Shor has commented, "Habits of resistance are learned early and well by many students in traditional schools. Unfortunately, these habits are carried into democratic and critical classrooms" (*Empowering* 139). Many students resist crossing borders because it's safer and easier to stay on the margins or because they're cynical about the ability of education to empower them. Furthermore, marginalized students may themselves believe that only academic literacy is valid. As Paulo Freire has put it in *Pedagogy of the Oppressed*, they may have internalized the belief system of the dominant culture to the point that they have become the dominant culture (32). In my experience, students who insist most strongly that classes should focus only on standard academic structures are often those who come from homes where English is not spoken. In response to this type of resistance, we can make our pedagogy a subject of discussion and dissension, engaging students in reflections on the goals of a writing class. The purpose of such discussion should be not consensus (which often just means that students are going along with everyone else) but challenge—the students should challenge us and their peers as we challenge them.

My last assumption is that this resistance and these challenges should reposition us in our classrooms, especially if we are members of the dominant culture teaching students on the borders of that culture. "White educators who are working with bicultural students," Antonia Darder has noted, "must first come to acknowledge their own limitations, prejudices, and biases, and must be willing to enter into dialogue with their students in a spirit of humility and with respect for the knowledge that students bring to the classroom" (70). Thus teachers as well as students can become border crossers in a mutual process of teaching and learning.

Crossing Textual Borders

To validate students' literacies as well as teach academic literacy, I try to expose students to a variety of languages and texts that connect with some, but by no means all, students in the class. Those who are in the dark about a particular phrase or idea (and this often includes me) are taught by the students who understand it. When teaching classes with Spanish-speaking Chicana or Chicano students, I often rely on texts written in English by Chicana or Chicano writers that contain some Spanish phrases. Inevitably, these writers deal with cross-cultural issues that many of the students are experiencing in their own lives. Writers I have successfully used with first-year writing students include Rudolfo Anaya (*Bless Me, Ultima*), Sandra Cisneros (*The House on Mango Street* and *Woman Hollering Creek*), Pat Mora (*Chants* and *Borders*), Arturo Islas (*The Rain God*), Antonia Wilbur-Cruce (*A Beautiful, Cruel Country*) and Gloria Anzaldúa (selections from *Borderlands / La Frontera* and the collection *Making Face, Making Soul / Haciendo Cara*). These writers deal with cultural issues such as gender pressures, feelings of otherness, and attempts to maintain cultural identity in an Anglocentric world.

As an example of how I might use one of the texts in a first-year writing classroom, let me discuss a lesson focused on the story "Little Miracles, Kept Promises," from Cisneros's *Woman Hollering Creek*. This story consists of prayers and letters written to saints by people following the tradition of pinning charms called *milagritos*, or little miracles, onto statues of saints in shrines or churches. The letters vary widely in purpose, tone, and language, from the respectful note of an elderly man praying for his wife's health to the ruminations of a young woman who has just cut her long hair. Some are written entirely in English, many in a combination of English and Spanish, and one entirely in Spanish. I ask students to explain the tradition of the *milagritos* to those who don't understand it and to translate Spanish words for the rest of the class. This process empowers students whose language, traditions, and ideas are seldom the focus of the classroom. Then, as a class, we discuss some of the rhetorical aspects of the letters—their order in the story, the effect they might have on different readers, the diversity of experiences they communicate, and the cultural and spiritual messages they convey. The writing assignments this story has produced include writing a text, such as a letter or poem, that incorporates non-English words for a specific rhetorical purpose; writing a report on the origin of the *milagrito* tradition or similar traditions in other cultures; and collaborating with other students to write an epistolary story (perhaps depicting recent immigrants writing to their families in their native lands). In collaborative writing assignments such as the last one, students from different backgrounds can be paired to encourage the sharing of diverse perspectives.

Another writing assignment that helps students cross borders is gathering data about other students' literacy practices to write ethnographies of classmates. Students can also write comparative ethnographies, examining differences in the literacy practices of people they know at school, home, or work. Thematic assignments also work well; for instance, one class did a series of writings on ritual, including a personal narrative describing a ritual in the student's life, a report on the origin of that ritual, a comparison of similar rituals in other cultures, and an interview with another person (in or outside the classroom) who has experienced an alternative form of that ritual. Other assignments include asking students to observe an important cultural symbol from a part of town they don't live in (such as a church or shrine) and asking them to assume different personae, for example, having male students write about an event from the perspective of a woman.

Students often make language an issue in these assignments. One female student wrote a personal narrative about the ritual of making tamales with her female relatives. At the beginning of the story, reluctant to participate in the ritual because she wants to be with her friends, she speaks only English to her Spanish-speaking relatives. But by the end of the story she has decided to stay with her relatives to take part in the ritual and is using some Spanish words with them. Another student wrote a report on witnessing the border patrol abusing and harassing undocumented immigrants. He quoted members of the border patrol, who were speaking only English (though many understood Spanish), and some of the immigrants, who spoke primarily Spanish. While he was drafting this report, he asked his classmates if they thought he should provide a translation of the Spanish dialogue; they thought he shouldn't, so that the readers would better experience the deep division between the two groups. Assignments that draw on students' positions in their cultures can, with the instructor's guidance, lead to discussions such as this one, in which students make connections among language, difference, and culture.

Transgressing Pedagogical Borders

Pedagogical borders are the cultural and institutional divisions that separate student from teacher and student from student. My goal in the writing classroom is not so much to eradicate these divisions as to highlight the tensions, the power relations that these borders represent. Certainly, divisions between teacher and student should not lead to the hierarchical "banking" model of education in which, as Freire has put it, "the students are the depositories and the teacher is the depositor" (*Pedagogy* 58). But as teachers, we are constantly torn between our need to act as coaches and the institution's need to have us act as gatekeepers, to borrow Peter Elbow's terminology ("Embracing"). Although I know of no technique to get around this dilemma, strong collaborative learning activities (such as small-group discussions, collaborative writing assignments, and peer revision groups) can help move the center of gravity away from the teacher and toward the students. As Carol Stanger notes, in a collaborative class "power flows from the teacher to everyone in the room, and then from student to student" (43).

But such a sharing of power does not happen spontaneously in a collaborative class, for students tend to replicate power relations they have learned from the dominant culture in their collaborative student groups. In a study of students working on a report for an engineering class, Elizabeth Flynn and her colleagues found that male students sometimes dominated female students, relegating them to secretarial roles. Among my Chicana and Chicano students, I have noticed linguistic inequities in addition to gender inequities; students with limited English fluency tend, out of embarrassment, to participate less than others do in oral and written work. Rotating the position of group leader or manager can help ensure that easily dominated students have a chance to assert their views or demonstrate their skills. And when students discuss a controversial topic, I ask them to present a majority and a minority report to the class, so that quieter students will not feel they must always agree with their classmates. (The emphasis in traditional Latina and Latino culture on community consensus creates pressures to agree.) In general, teachers must intervene a great deal in collaborative learning activities to allow all students' voices to be heard.

Thus when I argue for the need to transgress pedagogical borders, I am suggesting that teachers take a very active, interventionist role in the classroom. This active role is well illustrated in Ira Shor's description of a problem-posing curriculum (*Empowering*). Problem posing, as conceived by Freire and adopted by Shor, uses material from students' lives as a starting point to engage students actively in knowledge making. In Shor's model, the teacher begins the learning process by posing a problem to the students (one the students might have suggested), such as What is good writing? or What factors in society can limit or help personal growth? (237). Students reflect on the problem, write about it, share their writing, and present their ideas to the class—and the teacher then synthesizes the responses and represents the problem to the students. After further reflection, drafting, peer editing, and evaluation, Shor then presents to the class what he calls a "dialogic lecture," in which he offers his views, which may differ from the students'. Shor writes:

> Serious educators have a right and a responsibility to share their academic knowledge and perspectives. They must not impose their values or interpretations on students, but when their turn comes in a participatory process they can set an example of the love of knowledge, of a well-informed mind, and of a critically thinking intellectual and citizen.   (247)

A key idea here is that the students, as well as the teacher, participate in the forum, so that they know they can add to or disagree with the teacher's and one another's views. It is the teacher's responsibility to ensure that all students contribute to the forum.

Forging a New Identity

Eventually, students who straddle the border between two cultures will be able to embrace the ambiguities and multiplicities in their lives, to create "the new consciousness" in which, as Gloria Anzaldúa describes, the "intercultural split will heal" (*Borderlands* 86). Another Latina writer, Aurora Levins Morales, has described the wholeness that can emerge from the mingling of cultures; in "Child of the Americas," she writes:

> I am a child of the Americas,
> a light-skinned mestiza of the Caribbean,
> a child of many diaspora, born into this continent at a
>   crossroads.
> . . . .
> I am new. History made me. My first language was spanglish.
> I was born at the crossroads
> and I am whole.   (50)

This wholeness is not a result of homogenization, of becoming a member of one culture or the other. Instead, it represents a new way of experiencing the world, in which differences, contradictions, and tensions are examined and appreciated. As writing teachers, we have a tremendous opportunity to help our students, and learn from them, as they cross the borders in their lives.

When the Writing Test Fails: Assessing Assessment at an Urban College

Barbara Gleason

> *Why some people be mad at me sometimes*
> *They ask me to remember*
> *but they want me to remember*
> *their memories*
> *and I keep on remembering mine.*
> —Lucille Clifton

More than any other public institution, schools have tested the potential for progress in social justice, equal opportunity, and individual liberty. As social institutions, schools have also come to reflect existing inequalities in our culture, conserving and transmitting the traditions, values, and customs of the politically empowered. American schools have thus both provided sites for social change and conserved the status quo. This polarity has frequently yielded theoretical diatribe and miscommunication rather than productive dialogue and collective action. Unfortunately, this has often been true in the public debates about open-admissions policies in urban colleges and their corollary in literacy instruction, basic writing.

To understand the basic writing movement and the accompanying issue of assessment apart from issues of access to higher education is to miss the essence of basic writing. While it is patently obvious that questions about pedagogy are at stake, these issues are inevitably embedded in a sociopolitical context that shades in perspective on nearly every pedagogical question or theory posed. Discussions about teaching and evaluating basic writers are inextricably bound to questions about who merits access to institutions of higher learning, how such decisions should be made, and who should make them. Moreover, the very language used frames these issues from the start: *basic skills, assessment, academic standards, standard English, minimal competency,* and now *multiculturalism* are all value-laden terms that codify educational positions and signal political alignments.

What follows is a descriptive study of the experiences of three City College of New York students with the City University of New York's Writing Assessment Test (WAT). This study grows out of a profound need to understand the system of assessment that envelops and shapes curriculum at CUNY's seventeen junior and senior colleges. As a writing program administrator, I have observed the special circumstances of students taking the WAT and participated in programs designed to help students pass the test. Although my study focuses narrowly on the CUNY assessment practices, the issues raised here bear on the general practice of evaluating student writers solely on the basis of a timed writing test.

I intend this study to address one aspect of the complexities involved in admitting to colleges and universities students of diverse cultural, ethnic, class, and linguistic origins. Although it entails analysis of grammar, discourse, and idiomatic usage, my intent is not to reveal patterns or peculiarities of student language, nor even to evaluate students' writing competencies, but to disclose the ironies and indeed the virtual impossibilities of using a timed test of writing to screen fairly and accurately a multicultural student population for placement into or out of remediation or to assess minimal competency in writing, literacy, or academic preparedness.

The CUNY Writing Assessment Test

The CUNY Writing Assessment Test originated as part of the faculty response to a 1976 mandate from the Board of Higher Education, now called the Board of Trustees of CUNY. Concerned about public accountability in the midst of a catastrophic fiscal crisis, the board was itself responding to public charges of grade inflation and declining academic standards vis-à-vis CUNY's 1970 open-admissions policy. The mandate was written into the BHE's minutes for the meeting of 5 April 1976:

> RESOLVED, That students moving to the upper divisions of a four-year college either from the lower division of the college or from a community college within the University system or outside of it must provide evidence, in accordance with a standard to be determined by the Chancellor, that they have attained a level of

proficiency in basic learning skills necessary to cope successfully with advanced work in the academic disciplines.

Explanation: With the inception of the Open Admissions Program, the University and its faculty have liberalized the grading process so as to maximize opportunities for students. In the process, the grading system has been abused to the extent that very little incentive has been provided the student where he or she is doing less than average work. The intent of these resolutions is to have students' transcripts accurately reflect their performance and to maximize the available instructional resources.   (42)

Just how significant and widespread grade inflation was at CUNY between 1970 and 1976 is difficult to ascertain, but internal documents indicate it was of some concern. At City College, for instance, Mina Shaughnessy addressed grade inflation in her 1973 report on the Basic Writing Program, arguing that the high rate of student failure, not grade inflation, was of real concern for the basic writing classes.

When it became clear that faculty members would have to respond to the board's mandate, a task force of CUNY professors responded by forming three committees, one each for reading, writing, and math, which remain operational today as advisory committees for the CUNY assessment tests. These three committees provided recommendations for the three skills tests that now constitute the CUNY Freshman Skills Assessment Program, which operates out of the central administrative office and, more than any other structural agent, serves to bind together a rather loosely federated system of seventeen community and senior colleges.

Since its inception in 1978, the CUNY Writing Assessment Test has commanded national attention and served as a model for testing at many other colleges and universities (Lyons; Brick; Judith Fishman; Troyka; Bruffee, "Beginning"). Along with the California State University English Placement Test in the 1970s, the CUNY WAT represented a progressive approach to writing assessment because it substituted students' writing samples for a multiple-choice format. Although not all early reports were favorable (see Judith Fishman), the test was embraced wholeheartedly by all CUNY colleges as part of a broad-based initiative on behalf of open-admissions students. To ensure the creation and maintenance of needed support services at the campuses, CUNY required that students take the tests after being admitted and that they retake the tests repeatedly until all three tests were passed.

The issue of access to the test and to appropriate instruction has legal implications. Minimal competency testing in the high schools has been challenged in the courts with partial success. One issue addressed in lawsuits is whether students have opportunities to prepare for the test in advance and to take the test several times. However, the basic charge that such tests discriminate against certain groups of students may not be addressed adequately even by these measures. According to Merle Steven McClung, "Programs that require a student to pass as a prerequisite to a high school diploma in particular have potential for discrimination against students. Some of these programs may not only be unfair to students, they may be illegal as well" (652). Stephen T. Schroth argues that standardized competency tests like the CUNY WAT discriminate against students from poorly funded school districts:

> Standardized tests are a remnant of an age when Blacks and other minorities were believed genetically inferior. The use of national testing firms assures uniformity among all tests administered across the country. Nevertheless, such competency tests fail to consider the disparity in quality and funding between the various schools in any one state. This disparity in funding disproportionately affects minority students because their test scores have been shown to be more dependent upon funding than white students' test scores.   (267)

The CUNY WAT soon came to serve a dual purpose—as a placement test for remediation and a test of minimal competency for admittance to upper-division courses (beyond sixty credits). Unlike the land-grant colleges, where open-admissions policies dating back to the first Morrill Act of 1862 tend to have a revolving-door effect, CUNY aimed to admit and retain its students, shifting the blame for failure from the student to the institution itself. Thus the Freshman Skills Assessment Program embodied CUNY's unified commitment to open admissions in the 1970s, and it continues to do so.

The CUNY WAT consists of a choice of two issue-statement prompts that require students to take a position and write an argument. The sample test below is excerpted from the second edition (1983) of a pamphlet prepared by the CUNY Task Force on Writing:

> Directions: You will have fifty minutes to plan and write the essay assigned below. You may wish to use your fifty minutes in the following way: 10 minutes planning what you are going to write; 30 minutes writing; 10 minutes rereading and correcting what

you have written. You should express your thoughts clearly and organize your ideas so they will make sense to a reader. Correct grammar and sentence structure are important. Write your essay on the lined pages of your booklet. You may use the inside of the front cover of the booklet for preliminary notes. You must write your essay on *one* of the following assignments. Read each one carefully and then choose either A or B.

A. It always strikes me as a terrible shame to see young people spending so much of their time staring at television. If we could unplug all the TV sets in America, our children would grow up to be healthier, better educated, and more independent human beings. Do you agree or disagree? Explain and illustrate your answer from your own experience, your observations of others, or your readings.

B. Older people bring to their work a lifetime of knowledge and experience. They should not be forced to retire, even if keeping them on the job cuts down on the opportunities for young people to find work. Do you agree or disagree? Explain and illustrate your answer from your own experience, your observations of others, or your reading.

There are several criticisms of this test: the questions require cultural knowledge that students may not possess; the time limit restricts revision, a primary focus of writing classes; and the test discriminates unfairly against second-language speakers. Most problematic, the WAT screens for a number of variables, not all predictive of successful college writing: speed in producing a first draft, cultural knowledge, mastery of standardized forms of written English, test-taking ability, handwriting, spelling, and ultimately culture, class, and ethnicity. And many students who repeatedly fail the WAT fare well in their college courses, as is illustrated by the case of David Patel below (all names are fictitious).

Students take the WAT and the other two assessment tests on the day they are officially admitted to CUNY. No entering CUNY freshman or matriculated transfer student may register without having taken the three assessment tests. Currently, all seventeen CUNY colleges use the WAT as the primary means of placement in remedial writing courses (although they are not required to do so). Most of the colleges use it as a requirement for exit from these courses, as students enrolled in remedial courses are not permitted to register in the "college-level" curriculum. Thus this test (as well as the other two assessment tests) both keeps students in the college by attempting to prepare them in remedial courses and excludes students from the regular curriculum ostensibly for their own good. Only a few colleges have addressed this problem, including Herbert H. Lehman College, where innovative programs allow students to enroll in the credit-bearing curriculum while coenrolled in remedial reading, writing, math, and ESL. However, most CUNY colleges, including City College, simply exclude students from the regular curriculum when they fail one assessment test or more. As of spring 1991, City College no longer uses the WAT as an exit exam for basic writing, so students are allowed into the core curriculum after successful completion of the basic writing courses—should they fail the WAT in the first place.

The central administrative office has only two mandates with regard to scoring the CUNY WAT: that two readers of each essay use the official 6-point scale and that each college submit periodically to an audit in which a group of official CUNY readers rescores a sample of a college's tests to check the statistical reliability of scores. Otherwise, each college is free to determine its own system of reading the tests. The question of who reads the exam is important, as are issues such as the readers' preparation for scoring the exam, their motivation, and their compensation. While at least one CUNY college requires adjunct faculty members to score the exam without compensation, many colleges hire adjunct faculty members at an hourly rate to score the exams. Until spring 1994, the WAT at City College was scored for free by full-time English department faculty members (most of whom did not regularly teach composition); selected adjunct faculty members are now paid to read and score it. Each college must also decide whether to include ESL instructors in the scoring process, whether to provide special instructions for the scoring of ESL students' tests, and how to conduct the norming sessions. Each college institutes its own system for students to challenge the test scores.

Special state-funded programs are available to help students who fail the assessment tests. The tests are used somewhat ironically as measures of the success of such programs although the failure rates on the tests necessitate the programs in the first place. Thus without the tests (or some alternative) state funds for special programs would not be forthcoming, and without the failure rates on the tests state funds for special programs would not be needed. Among these special state-funded programs are the Intersession Basic Skills Immersion Program, the Freshman Year Program, and the Prefreshman Summer Immersion Program.

In January 1992, I taught an intersession workshop for students who had failed the WAT. After an intensive three-week course divided into three sections, fifty-nine students took the WAT again, with only fourteen passing. As I came to know the students and their writing, I became deeply interested in the reasons why they could function satisfactorily in City College courses but still fail to pass the WAT. I have since followed the paths of some of those students to discover how they would fare in their courses and when, if ever, they would pass the WAT. The three students described below were enrolled in that intersession workshop.

Hua Zhang

In 1988, Hua Zhang immigrated with his wife and daughter from China to the United States, settling in New Jersey. He was thirty-seven years old. Hoping for a "better life," Zhang arrived with a college degree in English from Jinan University in Canton and three years of experience as an English teacher—two years at a middle school before his college education and one year teaching evening classes after completing his degree. Within a year of his arrival, Zhang separated from his wife, moved to New York City, and enrolled at City College, where he failed the CUNY WAT and placed into Basic Writing II. In an unusual turn of events, Zhang enrolled in Basic Writing I and II during the same semester and received a Pass and an A respectively. In the meantime, he failed the WAT two more times and enrolled in my intersession workshop.

In the workshop, Zhang showed a quiet determination to develop his English proficiency and his writing ability, while appearing to lack confidence in his already considerable language expertise. Speaking in halting, unsteady phrases, Zhang explained that, although he had no English-speaking friends, he watched television and read regularly to develop his competency in English. Not surprisingly, his writing exhibited greater fluency and control of form than one might expect of an immigrant of three years. At age forty-one, Zhang approached his writing with an ability to consider alternative views and with an awareness of audience, qualities sometimes lacking in other students' writing. But these strengths manifested themselves more distinctly in Zhang's in-class writing than in his Writing Assessment Test performance. Below is the complete essay Zhang wrote upon his entrance to City College.

Topic

The Supreme Court has ruled that schools may search students for weapons without a warrant. Although most students don't bring weapons to school, these searches are needed to protect the majority of students from the violence of a few.

Essay

I agree that schools may search students for weapons without a warrant for protection of the majority of students.

In America, the people can get a gun easily comparing with the situation of my motherland. Influenced by the violence in T.V. or the film, some students like to play with a gun, especially the boys. They don't know the result of firing a gun very much without the professional training. In a fighting or a quarrel with other people, maybe they cannot control themselves, but there is a limitation of firing. Can you shoot a student to death just for a blow or quarrel? Of course not. You should call the police or security guard if you are in the danger.

Many students would feel uneasy if they know a few students have guns with them. If there is a gun fighting, they would be hurted easily, besides, their stuty and life in the school would be disturbed, they cannot concentrate themselves on the classes.

During the cultural revolution in China in 1960's, some students in the school got the guns, they fought among themselves, they wanted to be heros, just like the one in the film. Many student died in the battle.

To pass the CUNY WAT, writers must receive a score of 4 or higher on the 6-point scale. Scores of 4 and 3 are described as follows:

4 The essay shows a basic understanding of the demands of essay organization, although there might be occasional digressions. The development of ideas is sometimes incomplete or rudimentary, but a basic logical structure can be discerned. Vocabulary generally is appropriate for the essay topic but at times is oversimplified. Sentences reflect a sufficient command of standard written English to ensure reasonable clarity of expression. Common forms of agreement and grammatical inflection are usually, although not always, correct. The writer generally demonstrates through punctuation an understanding of the boundaries of the sentence. The writer spells common words, except perhaps so-called "demons," with a reasonable degree of accuracy.

3 The essay provides a response to the topic but generally has no overall pattern of organization. Ideas are often repeated or undeveloped, although occasionally a paragraph within the essay does have some structure. The writer uses informal language occasionally and records conversational speech when appropriate written prose is needed. Vocabulary often is limited. The writer generally does not signal relationships within and between paragraphs. Syntax is often rudimentary and lacking in variety. The essay has recurrent grammatical problems, or because of an extremely narrow range of syntactical choices, only occasional grammatical problems appear. The writer does not demonstrate a firm understanding of the boundaries of the sentence. The writer occasionally misspells common words of the language.

The differentiation between a 3 and a 4 is a fundamental determinant of a student's future at City College and all other CUNY colleges. The problems with this system of evaluation become apparent when one applies it to the reading of an essay.

We can identify the following rhetorical features in Zhang's essay: an early, direct communication of a thesis, a set of reasons in support of the thesis, the use of the academically preferred third person in all but two sentences and the thesis statement, the use of a rhetorical question, an emergent (albeit undeveloped) comparison of United States culture with Chinese culture, a consideration of students with guns as well as students without guns, and a sense of paragraph definition by topic. Considering that Zhang had been in the United States for just one year and eight months when he took the test, we might judge his performance a dramatic success. In fact, the readers of his essay were divided in their opinions: one scored the essay a 4 and the other scored it a 3. A third reader resolved the discrepancy with a score of 3, officially placing Zhang into Basic Writing II.

What caused the last two readers to fail the essay and thus judge Zhang unprepared for college-level courses (even though he had a college degree in his own country and had actually majored in English)? If we examine sentence-level forms, we find that although he spelled nearly all words correctly, his essay has shortcomings in idiomatic usage, verb forms, articles, and punctuation. Evidence of his second-language learning appears in such phrasing as "comparing with," "a gun fighting," and "they cannot concentrate themselves on the classes." Since there are no articles in Chinese and since English articles are highly idiosyncratic, it is not surprising that Zhang would have trouble with this language feature. And although he uses commas rather than periods occasionally, his use of them indicates an awareness of syntactic units that will facilitate his learning of punctuation. So should Zhang have been placed into remedial writing and excluded for a semester from the regular curriculum? Even though he completed Basic Writing I, Basic Writing II, and the intersession workshop, Zhang still failed the WAT on his fourth attempt. He finally passed on his fifth attempt in the summer of 1992 (six months after the intersession workshop) and is now planning a career as a bilingual teacher in the New York City public schools. In 1995 he won an English department award for an essay he wrote for a world humanities course.

James Pearson

James Pearson, an African American student, entered City College at the age of twenty in spring 1992. Having scored a 6 out of 12 on the WAT (two readers gave him a score of 3), James placed into Basic Writing II and passed his reading and math assessment tests on the first attempt. Unlike Zhang, James was confident in his ability to begin college-level courses immediately, so his goal in taking the workshop was to test out of Basic Writing II and qualify for enrollment in college-level courses. When I saw James's written work and heard him speak in class, I was surprised he had failed the WAT, and I asked him about his previous writing and his experience taking this test. James described a long history of reading and writing that included daily reading of books, newspapers, and magazines and writing for his high school newspaper. In class, his eloquence and soft-spoken manner established him as both authoritative and accessible to other students. Always considerate of his classmates, James regularly helped others as a tutor and mentor. Although he was one of the younger students and certainly the newest to City College, James's strengths as a speaker and a writer were quickly apparent to all, and so it was no surprise when he passed the WAT at the end of the workshop. (He was the only one of fifteen students in this section who did pass.)

When I asked James why he thought he had failed the WAT, he said that he had not known he would have to write an essay and so was not mentally prepared and that he spent the first half-hour thinking about the question and what he wanted to say. Here are the prompt and James's essay:

Topic

Young people often look up to entertainers and athletes as role models. Many people criticize the celebrities because of the poor example they set in conducting their lives. But like others, celebrities should be free to make their own choices about the way they live.

Essay

Today's society has many problems; Racism, drugs, sexism, and a host of other isms which destroy even the slightest chance of this being a model society. How we pick our role models or should I say, how our role models are picked causes problems for the followers of these so called role models. Before we get into entertainers and athletes as our role models, we must first deal with what a role model should be. Role models should be people who at one polarity perform great acts, feats, and are the best at what they do. It is this the other polarity which society has neglected. At the other polarity we have character role models should have Integrity, values, morals, and be the best when not performing greatness. I'm starting over.

Before I get into entertainers and athlete's as role models, we must first deal with what a role model should be. At one polarity role models should be people who perform great acts, feats and are the opitimy as what they do. At the other polarity we have character role models should have integrity, morals, values and maintain the same level dignity while performing as when not performing.

Today's society has many problems; drugs, racism, sexism and a host of other isms that destroy even the slightest chance of this being a model society. So what makes us think society can pick our role models? Society says if you have money, or can play a sport well, or can entertain within the boundaries accepted by society you automatically become a role model, regardless of character when not in the spotlight.

Magic Johnson exemplifies my statement in that on one hand, here we have a man who is a basketball legend can play the . . . [James ended the essay in mid-sentence.]

The scoring of James's essay illustrates how divergent readers' impressions can be: one reader scored the essay a 6 and the other, a 3. The discrepancy was resolved by a third reader, who scored the essay a 3, placing James in Basic Writing II. What might have led to such a wide variance?

In addition to recognizing that James was working out his ideas in revision on this essay, the first reader might have appreciated the use of such terms as *polarity, epitome* (misspelled as "opitimy"), and *exemplified*. This reader may also have valued James's distinction between two kinds of role models. We can discern in James's prose a fluency of language revealed by such syntactically varied constructions as the following: "How we pick our role models or should I say, how our role models are picked causes problems for the followers of these so called role models." Here James demonstrates that he can use syntactic options to convey meaning, to wit, that we do not always intentionally choose our role models.

This essay reveals some of the problems with the six-point scale: there is no guarantee that all the elements in an essay will fall into the same scoring category. For example, language use may suggest a 5 or 6 while organization and development point to a 3 or 4. In James's essay, his language use appears to be relatively strong, but his essay development and organization could understandably be given a three. An essay awarded a 3, the scoring guidelines say, "provides a response to the topic but generally has no overall pattern of organization. Ideas are often repeated or undeveloped. . . ." But some readers might decide the essay "shows a basic understanding of the demands of essay organization" and so deserves a four, since it displays a structuring of ideas even at this early drafting stage. Ultimately, the reader might ask whether James's essay indicates that its author merits placement in basic writing and exclusion from the core curriculum.

Since James passed the retest and went directly into the regular curriculum, we can chart his progress in his first two semesters. In his first semester, he received a B in freshman writing, an A in Math, an A in sociology, a pass in freshman orientation, a C in psychology, and a B in black studies. In his second semester, James earned a C in philosophy, a B in United States society, a B in economics, and an A in world civilization. Since he made Bs on tests and quizzes, James believed his C in philosophy to be an error and he planned to challenge the grade. On the recommendation of his freshman writing instructor, James was hired as a writing-center tutor in fall 1992, and he quickly achieved a reputation as an accomplished tutor. During that semester, he attended an out-of-town writing-center conference, attended and spoke at a Composition Committee meeting (as the only student present), and wrote a news report for the Composition Program newsletter. In short, for someone who failed his writing skills test and placed in a remedial course, James achieved rather remarkable success in his first year of college. James is majoring in political science and plans to become an entertainment lawyer or a politician.

David Patel

David Patel arrived in the United States from Sri Lanka in 1987 at the age of eighteen. Between 1986 and 1988 David, whose first language is Tamil, was learning English and preparing to attend college in the United States. In 1988 he enrolled in a college in Long Island where he completed two remedial writing courses. Because they are labeled remedial, these writing courses did not transfer to City College when he was admitted in fall 1989. Although David failed the CUNY reading-assessment test by just a few points, he passed the math test with a perfect score of 12. David passed the reading test on his second attempt. His experience with the WAT, however, contrasted dramatically with his experience on the other two tests: David failed the writing test eleven times.

How could David be able to pass his reading and math tests and attain a 3.13 GPA (out of 4.0) over 109 credits but unable to pass the WAT? On examining all eleven of David's writing tests, I learned that he had nearly passed the WAT twice, each time receiving a 3 and a 4 from the first two readers. On one of his tests, David's scores were a 1 and a 2, which would place him in Basic Writing I as an entering freshman. Oddly, he obtained this score on his seventh attempt, after he had already received five total scores of six (two readers scored the essays a 3) and one total score of 5 (a 2 and a 3).

A look at the topic and the first two paragraphs of David's third essay reveal some of the difficulties that he and his readers experienced with his writing test:

Topic

New York, like many other states, has a lottery to help raise money for special purposes. Some people, however, feel that the lottery takes advantage of human weaknesses. They would like to see the lottery abolished. Do you agree or disagree?

Essay

Lottery is a well known word. Many people think that lottery helps a lot of people, but some public think that (it) pulls people toward the bad habits. However, I feel that lottery should not be abolished because it helps to improving New York City in many ways. The money, NYC gets from lottery, is helping to the homeless and maintaining the city. Lottery would be an easy way to become a millioner, and this would protect the New Yorkers from increasing tax.

Main part of the money that the New York City makes from lottery is spent on homeless and maintaining the subways and buses. The city's one of the biggest problems is homeless. New York City needs millions of dollars to help homeless, and the rate of homeless is also increasing everyday. Where does the New York City get the big amount of the money to help these people? Lottery plays a big roll in this game. Everybody knows that New York City is the busiest city in the world where millions of people are traveling everyday. Eventhough there are many subways and buses runing, many people are complaining about the service because they are very crowded in the morning and eveing. The money, N.Y.C. collects from lottery, takes a big roll to improve this system.

The first two readers scored the essay a 4 and a 3; the third reader resolved the discrepancy with a score of 3. The strengths of the essay lie primarily at the discourse level (David presents his thesis and reasons for favoring the lottery), and the weaknesses result largely from second-language transfer errors at the sentence level (e.g., misuse of articles and problems with idiomatic usage). When I spoke to David about this test four years later, he told me that he thought his lack of knowledge about the subject had weakened his writing; he had since learned that the money from the lottery goes to education, not to the care of the homeless or to the public transportation system. I doubt that David's misinformation affected his score, because the readers seem to look primarily at form; but David's writing may well have been hampered by lack of confidence.

David took this test as the final exam for an ESL remedial writing course; because he failed it, he was supposed to repeat the course. But instead, taking a not-uncommon approach, he simply decided not to repeat the course and to continue with his major courses, which he somehow managed to do without taking any other writing course until fall 1992, when he enrolled in the full-credit freshman writing course. David's manipulation of the bureaucracy illustrates an ingenuity not atypical of City College students. David just kept progressing through the system, doing well in his engineering courses and getting his advisers to waive the sixty-credit WAT requirement. But by the end of the fall 1992 semester, when he had accumulated 109 credits, David was told by a dean in the School of Engineering that he could not continue to enroll in courses unless he passed the WAT (even though he had a

GPA of 3.13). After David registered in the CUNY WAT intersession workshop for the second time, his instructor advised him to appeal the score on one of his writing tests, which he did successfully. In the appeals process at City College two members of the English faculty read, reread, and score the exam. Here are David's topic and essay:

Topic

Because of continuous increases in college tuition costs, many students are not able to attend the college of their choice. Education should be a right, not a privilege, and if students are academically qualified for the college that they choose, the federal government should pay their college tuition.

Essay

A country's future depends on the students. Nowadays college dropouts are increasing tremendously. One of the reasons is that the tuition fee is very expensive. Many people believe college education must be free, so many poor students who can not afford to pay for the tuition can go to college. Of course, colleges must be free. Many students will be encouraged to study, and the country can have a good future.

Drugs is everywhere in New York City. Most of the drug addicts and dealers are teenagers who are college dropouts. Most of the these people believe that the society is not paying any attention to them such as helping for their education. It is very hard to get a job. Especially if you do not have any kind of degree, the chances are very slim. I am not saying the society should offer them a job. By changing no money for their studies. Many students feel college is very tough: if the city does not take any proper action, it is like adding fuel to fire. The number of college dropouts will increase.

The future of a country is the students. Our country is going down the hill as far as education is concerned. Our educational system is criticized by many countries especially mathematics. Many college science professors are froginers. Two years ago in the state of OHIO only one man had qualified to teach mathematics in a university. It is embarrasing for the whole nation. We are the best in the world, but as far as the education is concerned, we are almost at the bottom. Many poor students are not be able to pay their college fees, and the students must be encouraged to study by charging them no money for their college education.

> Would you like to see a radical improvement in our educational system? Would you like to see our studuent competting other countries in education? Let the universities be free of charge for education.

This test, which the original readers gave a 2 and a 3, received two fours on reevaluation. What criteria might the second pair of readers have used to pass this essay? To begin with, the essay clearly meets "the basic demands of essay organization," as stipulated by the lead sentence in the description of an essay meriting a four; there is a clear thesis in the introduction and each subsequent paragraph presents a reason in support of the thesis. In his conclusion, David makes effective use of a rhetorical question and an imperative statement, which suggests some degree of rhetorical competence. Granted, the essay structure is mechanical, clearly in the mode of a five-paragraph essay, but this is exactly what gets rewarded on the WAT. Readers generally want to ascertain as quickly as possible whether the student can use paragraphs to organize an essay. As for language use, we find in this essay a stronger control of articles and fewer trespasses in idiomatic usage than in the earlier writing sample, but writers often work out these issues in editing their work, which students cannot practically do in a timed test. There are five spelling mistakes and one nonstandard use of punctuation (before the sentence beginning "Especially"). There is one subject-verb agreement error ("Drugs is everywhere") and one clearly nonstandard verb form ("Many poor students are not be able to pay their college fees"). The question is whether these nonstandard language forms should cause David to fail this fifty-minute timed test. Clearly the first two readers thought they should, but the second two readers disagreed.

The CUNY WAT and City College Students

What common ground, if any, can we find among these three students? More than anything else, we find that the WAT's numerical score itself fails to capture the complex potential of the students. The timed writing test and its interpretive scoring mechanism cannot begin to assess a student's history, motivation, ingenuity, creativity, work habits, sense of self, interpersonal intelligence, or sheer courage in the face of seemingly insurmountable obstacles. Most students pass the WAT by the end of their first semester, but failure rates for the 1986 through the

1990 cohorts indicate that whites consistently pass the test more frequently than do Asians, blacks, and Latinos and Latinas. Moreover, second-language speakers are not differentiated from first-language speakers in this database and each group is tested exactly the same (Silverman).

Take Zhang, whose writing tests repeatedly indicate inadequate preparation for college-level work. Here is a man who survived the hardships of Mao's Cultural Revolution (and intends to write about this experience), attained a college degree and taught English for three years in China, immigrated to the United States, and determined to make a new life for himself as a bilingual educator. How likely is a fifty-minute timed writing test to predict the success of a man with this history and this goal? And, alternatively, how accurate is the test as an indicator that he needs remediation as a "prefreshman" in a radically multicultural academic environment?

Or consider James, a young man whose personal presence inspires the confidence of his peers and his elders. A student who has read newspapers, magazines, and books regularly for years and who wrote for his high school newspaper. A college freshman already planning to attend law school. Can we really be certain that a timed writing test can gauge his literacy and thus predict the likelihood of his succeeding if he is admitted directly to the academic mainstream? James's first two semesters substantiate that the test is fallible at least sometimes, and for every James there are many other students who did not know about the intersession workshop, did not recognize its significance, or had to work during the daytime, when the class was scheduled.

Let us also take into account David, the immigrant from Sri Lanka whose principal aim at City College was to study engineering. By talking to friends and advisers, David learned that he did not really have to repeat his remedial writing course or pass the WAT to continue progressing through the system. All he had to do was succeed in his courses and persevere, retaking the WAT regularly to indicate his serious intent. A close reading of David's writing test allows us to recognize the role that second-language influence plays in the readers' scoring. We might describe David's writing as "accented," as is his speech and the speech of most students and not a few teachers at City College. Should we conclude that David's accent makes him unfit to attend or graduate from City College? More fundamentally, will his graduation from City College devalue the real or imagined worth of the degree itself? After all, even when he graduates, David's writing will still be accented, and his mathematical competence will continue to overshadow his writing ability.

In 1973, the City College professor of English Edward Quinn wrote that "numbers—reading levels, SAT's, math achievement, dropout rates—are to the educational enterprise what the score is to the game. They measure and judge and discriminate, but they are not the game itself." Quinn reflected further that "the failure shows up in the statistics, the success in the life of the student" (30). These words ring as true today as they did then, in the earliest years of open admissions at CUNY. Yet the temptation of the numerical score remains as seductive as ever in this age of economic recession, budgetary slashing, and public demands for accountability. After Bill Clinton included national testing in his 1992 campaign platform, state initiatives for minimal competency testing in literacy and numeracy began to rise. Of course, the cost of other measures of evaluation at first seem prohibitive, but they are arguably less so when weighed against the cost of failing large numbers of students at institutions like City College and placing those students into remedial courses. Each year approximately half of City College students fail the WAT and are placed into remediation (sixty-one percent in fall 1991). This practice raises serious questions about using one timed test of writing for placing students into remedial writing courses and thus barring them from the regular, credit-bearing college curriculum.

A special report issued by CUNY Chancellor Ann Reynolds after the students in this study had taken their assessment tests advises (but does not require) all CUNY colleges to use multiple criteria for placing students into remediation and for passing students out of these courses. As for the WAT's use as a "rising junior exam," a CUNY task force is currently searching for another means of assessing the writing competency of students who are continuing beyond sixty credits.

Cross-Talk: Toward Transcultural Writing Classrooms

Keith Gilyard

Should our work as writing instructors serve to maintain the status quo? Or should our classrooms become forums for social criticism? These are the horns of a rather fractious rhetorical dilemma in our profession. But the six writers in this section do not construe the politics of writing instruction so simply. Nor should they. Moving beyond notions of binary opposition, they provide a necessary and welcome complication of discussion about pedagogy. But we need clarity, even about complexity, and I hope to contribute a bit more as I join the conversation and respond to their essays, some of which complement and yet challenge others, some of which tell on themselves.

Juan Guerra advances the first and perhaps most forceful argument against the either-or fallacy. He believes that students continue to develop a matrix of communicative capabilities in writing classrooms. He favors, therefore, lending institutional legitimacy to several forms of discourse and making academic decisions reflecting the fact that all of us, including first-year writing students, belong simultaneously to several discourse communities. Guerra thus reformulates talk about conformity versus rebellion into a both-and credo, aiming to help students improve their total language packages, not to eradicate and replace items or to encourage resistance only. Such a proposal implies an understanding of code, a principle of linguistic choice. Code, as Michael Gregory and Susanne Carroll explain, "controls the verbal repertoire of the individual, his capacity to encode meaning lexically and grammatically. Code therefore determines which options will be selected as appropriate to the given situation" (80).

The essential factor in language learning is not exposure to verbal forms but rather engagement in situations in which the learner perceives the use of those forms to be meaningful. Ironically, Guerra subscribes to the notion of teaching academic discourse, an idea that ignores the learning histories of academics, who were probably not

325

taught in first-year composition courses to write the way they do. They learned through immersion in their majors, disciplines, and careers. It puzzles me, in fact, that anyone wants to claim to be teaching academic discourse, for I certainly would not attempt to teach first-year writing students any of the jargon-laden prose, some of which I myself generate, used to theorize literacy. Where do people learn to express "the problematizing of discourse communities that privilege hegemonic nondialogic language practices"? Not in writing courses. Standard Written English is a better description of what we are trying to solicit, more or less, than academic discourse is. Students will write as we do, to paraphrase David Bartholomae, only to the extent that they become us ("Inventing").

To his credit, though, Guerra keeps focusing on inquiry as opposed to relatively passive acquisition. Certain questions raised by students seem indispensable. How does this particular language variety work? How can I add it to what I do? Do I need to? Should I? Why? One calls discourse into question to learn it fully. This line of reasoning is so persistent in Guerra's essay that a little theoretical vagueness in other areas is a minor distraction. More troubling is that the classroom activities he describes do not coincide with his best conceptions. At times, for example, his report of classroom exchanges reflects insufficient student input. I would love a more detailed account of how Guerra urged his student Kim to show more and tell less. I have the same objection to his recounting of his advice to Sandra on moving from narrative to abstract writing. I understand why rhetorical stance became a crucial issue but not why it wasn't the first issue, given Guerra's theoretical persuasion. It seems the general problem of persona would have been posed ahead of specific writing tasks so students would have felt vested in assignments from the outset.

Mary Soliday shares Guerra's rejection of dichotomous thinking about the politics of writing courses. Soliday cautions us to avoid essentializing students by relsying on monolithic frameworks such as difference theory. Her warning is worth stressing, though one would hope that after witnessing the contentious discourses of African Americans on Clarence Thomas, of Native Americans on casino gambling, and of women on feminism, to name just a few, all teachers would realize the mixed bag that is our nation contains many smaller mixed bags. Differentiation is natural, as is commonality. But conditions of inequity outside school put commonality under strain. Differentiation in school becomes a major problem, therefore, when school systems refuse to acknowledge and allow for differences that matter—only students can fully know what they are, which is why we have to listen carefully.

One difference I care a lot about, one not fully acknowledged by Soliday, is the one between myself and Richard Rodriguez. He regards the suppression of the language some students bring to school as a necessary evil. I see it as merely evil. A certain rupture accompanies any learning, but we must remember that systematizing harsh consequences for linguistic variation has hurt far too many. In a similar vein, I wonder if the distinction between home language values and school language values is of any use beyond the early primary grades. As I indicate in *Voices of the Self*, the aspirations I learned at home were congruent with those taught in school. The big rift, underplayed by Soliday, was between a segment of the larger African American community and the school, specifically between a prized black-militant posture and a cherished academic pursuit of the American dream. John Edgar Wideman's *Brothers and Keepers* helps illuminate this divide by illustrating how two brothers from the same household adopted radically different roles in school, the immediate community, and the larger society. *Home* does not necessarily equal *community*, though Soliday at times uses the terms interchangeably, which causes some confusion. And although Soliday excerpts immigrant students' autobiographies to show how their authors affirm an assimilationist mission of schools, she may not be fully aware that immigrants' adaptive strategies are unappealing to many so-called minorities. John Ogbu, for example, has long cited motivational divergence between immigrants and minorities. Or as Victor Villanueva, drawing on Ogbu's and Mario Barrera's research, has recently addressed the matter:

> The immigrant seeks to take on the culture of the majority. And the majority, given certain preconditions, not the least of which is displaying the language and dialect of the majority, accepts the immigrant. The minority, even when accepting the culture of the majority, is never wholly accepted. There is always a distance.
>
> (*Bootstraps* 23)

The immigrant-minority division does not always hold true, as Kate Mangelsdorf points out, but it often does. As strong as Soliday's presentation of a pedagogy of commonality is, it would be stronger if it included the work of students concerned with permanent rejection or with selling out. We could use, say, some B-boy and B-girl autobiographies that explore how their authors, who form a significant population at open-admissions universities like Soliday's, grapple with the clash between street culture and academic culture, how they attempt study toward a degree while their oversized, beltless pants sag (crazily in our view, stylishly in theirs) below their waistlines.

Carol Miller would agree with this point, as she is specifically concerned with representing a multitude of student viewpoints in our writings about students. Like Soliday, she investigates students' literary histories, but she seems more aware of the potential for variety. She knows Ogbu's work, for example, and she knows that conflict between community and school may be a more powerful determinant of behavior than dissonance, or allegiance for that matter, between home and school. Perhaps Miller's most important point, as she ponders the cultural transactions that need to take place in class, is that we have to pay attention to how students perceive our courses and understand or fail to understand our intentions. As she notes, we are often quick to assess what went wrong in class and to theorize anew while taking for granted that students comprehended what we asked of them.

Henry Evans injects much more color, pun intended, into the intertextual dialogue. I do not have space for a lengthy evaluation of the Afrocentric paradigm, but Evans surely makes admirable use of it as he fuses Afrocentricity with elements of composition theory. One may easily disagree with his proposals. His critique, however, is hard to refute as he explains the damage caused by academic structures that preserve white privilege and ridicules, much as Henry Giroux does, the occasional, weakly conceived attempts at inclusion (*Schooling*). Evans argues that if educators are ignorant of the power and validity of a given culture's logic, then formal educational experience will not enable students of that culture, because it will fail to promote the centered self, the Afrocentric self, in the specific case of African Americans, that these students need. Evans, like Guerra, blames academia for popularizing notions of decentering when African Americans, in their view, most require centering.

But this rumination about centering and decentering is not Evans's strong suit. We African Americans have known about psychic multiplicity or cultural hybridity long before contemporary critics came on the scene. As a whole, we never have escaped a sort of Du Boisian duality. Studying all the African cosmology in the world, as much as students may appreciate it, will not guarantee that they behave in an Afrocentric manner. It will place rich Afrocentric ideas at their disposal. That is all we can ensure. The self Evans envisions is really fluid: it has to be if Evans is to transform it Afrocentrically. But an African American self will not necessarily accord the greatest weight to Afrocentricity. Evans's argument against views of decentering implies an understanding that a socially constructed "I" is an "I" nonetheless. To be consistent, then, he would have to concede that when African Americans assert an "I-ness," they are centered in the sense he means, whether or not they are Afrocentric. A person could be centered in Islam, for example, a religion toward which some Afrocentric scholars have been antagonistic.

All that said, I still see tremendous worth in the course he proposes, and I endorse it, partly because I know it will not always produce the results he expects. Instructors may place African ideals and values at the center of inquiry, but students will use all the modes of inquiry they know, some possibly overlapping Afrocentricity but not identical to it. It is a worthwhile mingling, perhaps the most enlightened or, more to the point, endarkened manifestation of inclusion theory. And if folks actually wanted to adopt Afrocentricity wholeheartedly, it would not bother me at all. It occurs to me that Mark, the alienated African American student in Miller's essay, might have benefited considerably from Evans's program. Miller stands against proceeding from ethnocentric assumptions, and I generally agree, but everyone carries at least a little cultural baggage anyway, and the specific cultural assumptions Evans advocates might suit particular African Americans like Mark.

In fact we need Evans to expand his work. Although he is theoretically explicit, we could use a clearer picture of how he applies his curriculum in the classroom. Learning African American Standard English suggests more than lexical enrichment. How does one learn the "Standard English" part?

No doubt I would disagree vigorously with parts of the book-length work I hope Evans produces, but I am enamored with the prospect that, in a decade of shallow multicultural rhetoric, it could offer an in-depth view of African Americans and composition. The more I hear about multiculturalism, the more I recall how, during my tenure as a substance-abuse counselor, someone impressed on me that America's cure for a headache is to create a bigger headache. He was referring to the clinical use of opium to treat alcoholism, morphine to treat opium addiction, heroin to treat morphine addiction, and methadone to treat heroin addiction. Posed as method, rather than more accurately as physical description or indicator of concern, multiculturalism is the larger headache created because we have not dealt sufficiently, under rubrics like *integration, open admissions, special programs*, and *preparation for the mainstream*, with the cultures certain groups have brought to campus. So in an era of increasing diversity we pursue a new ideal fraught with problems of even greater magnitude, which we can only solve, as Evans challenges, by inspecting cultures, one by one, more deeply than we have.

Mangelsdorf's article adds border cultures to the list of cultures in the classroom and perhaps even declares their primacy. The best practical example of dealing with various cultures in classrooms in this section, her essay demonstrates the creative and positive responses to cultural tension that supportive educational environments can yield. No slip-shod talk about multiculturalism dominates her classroom; what transpires is something I would call *transculturalism*, in which students who are respected and taken seriously are willing to entertain and possibly embrace new cultural constructs. It is not assimilation, but a synthesis conducted from a position of cultural strength. Unlike Evans, Mangelsdorf rejects the idea of a static self. She presents no Chicanocentric or Chicanacentric curriculum or any culturecentric project such as Evans suggests. Her students Rebecca, Sandy, and Alicia don't appear to be good candidates anyway. They have a firm grip on their culture of nurture but want to relinquish its limitations on women. Theirs is a thoughtful, gender-based criticism of ethnic sentiment. Ethnicity is specific enough for Evans; Mangelsdorf prefers to concentrate on the individual in transition.

Conspicuously absent from the discussion to this point is the movement of students in and out of the writing courses being described. Barbara Gleason addresses this matter as she demonstrates that the CUNY Writing Assessment Test does not accurately evaluate writing ability or predict academic success. I read WATs for twelve years and supervised their scoring for four of those years, so I have firsthand knowledge of the testing system Gleason so ably assesses. Many of my students understandably mulled over the exam questions just as her student James Pearson did. When I deliberate about issues, I proceed in much the same way. After just fifty minutes, the length of the WAT, this essay looked a lot more like James's exam paper than like any you would see in a book on educational theory. I found it impossible to express any of the major ideas in this paper to my satisfaction in less than an hour. I've worked on this paper in New York, Illinois, and Texas, on a word processor, over the course of weeks. And I'm not satisfied yet. I finished it because it was due. Ironically, I had to convince my students that no one, least of all the test makers, cared about their opinions on the exam questions. I had to make an effort to get them not to take the exam seriously in an intellectual sense, advice that puzzled many of them, who found it hard to fathom that anyone would bother to make up meaningless test questions.

While Gleason's critique is generally persuasive, one of the things I miss in her work is consideration of how the test frequently drives curriculum. Before our department discarded the WAT as an exit instrument, many courses emphasized test-taking rather than writing; in an extreme case, one instructor taught students to memorize openings, transitional phrases, and conclusions, so that they could prewrite some forty to fifty percent of the WAT, doing minimal slot-fitting in response to particular prompts. The instructor, an adjunct, was fired when it was discovered that all his students wrote pretty much the same paper, but although his approach was viewed as wacky, it made sense in a test-driven curriculum that hadn't been examined critically enough within the department. I hope it is safe to say that most of us would not spend a semester on rote exercises, but this instructor would not have done so either, I later found out, had he not felt that his employment was contingent on his students' WAT performance.

The final exam is now two hours long. It allows for more drafting, reflecting, and revising, but there is still a gulf between it and an assessment instrument consistent with a process pedagogy that might involve portfolio assessment. But neither Gleason nor the others describe an alternative placement and exit structure.

I must mention too that Gleason sidesteps a crucial discussion of general academic standards. In arguing that the WAT is a poor predictor of academic success, she asks how students who fail the WAT, sometimes repeatedly, can otherwise be so successful in college. How indeed? Although the question is resolved in her mind, and to a large extent in mine, I nonetheless realize the legitimacy of asking whether standards have been compromised to accommodate certain students, resulting in grade inflation. Gleason indicates that the question was raised in the seventies, but she fails to report results. At any rate, the case against the WAT should not hinge on the simple assertion that students are failing it but making it through school anyway, especially when we don't get to see the writing done in other courses. The more convincing argument is that despite failing the WAT students are successful in a rigorous curriculum in which they must fulfill writing assignments to attain good grades. We need to see the kind of writing students like James Pearson, Hua Zhang, and David Patel do in other courses, not simply report on their grades. We need prolonged case studies of writing across the curriculum. Gleason can perhaps lead us in this venture.

I resist making a formal conclusion at this point because I am still hearing these texts talk to one another and to me. The texts articulate basics of a transcultural model, but new wrinkles seem to be emerging. In short, we ain't done. I will say that this has been the most rewarding professional discussion I have been involved with in a long time and that the other writers in this section had a much harder task than I did. They spoke first.

Notes on Contributors

Susan Blalock, associate professor at the University of Alaska, Fairbanks, is interested in writing pedagogy and writing centers and in nineteenth- and twentieth-century British literature. She is working on systems to deliver tutoring through computers, fax machine, and interactive television to ethnically diverse remote populations. Her book *A Reference Guide to the Secular Poetry of T. S. Eliot* is forthcoming from G. K. Hall.

Johnnella E. Butler, professor of American ethnic studies and adjunct professor of women's studies and English at the University of Washington, is interested in African American literature, comparative American ethnic literature and theory, and pedagogy and faculty development. Her publications include *Black Studies: Pedagogy and Revolution* and *Transforming the Curriculum: Ethnic Studies and Women's Studies* (coedited with John C. Walters). Forthcoming are three edited collections: *Ancestry, Discourse, and African American Literature; Marrowbone: Ancestry and American Ethnic Literature*; and *Generative Practice: Teaching and Diversity*.

Kermit E. Campbell, assistant professor of English at the University of Texas, Austin, is tracing rhetorical traditions that extend from early African cultures to African diaspora cultures, particularly African American culture. He has published in the *Journal of Advanced Composition* and in the proceedings of the conference of the Association of University English Teachers of South Africa. His book project, tentatively titled *Rapping: An African American Vernacular Rhetoric*, will intersect several strands of African American vernacular culture, including language, literacy, and music.

Virginia A. Chappell is associate professor of English at Marquette University; previously, she taught at the Educational Opportunity Program Writing Center at the University of Washington. She studies and publishes articles about composition pedagogy and about the rhetorics of civic discourse, common sense, and expert testimony. Her current project is on the rhetoric of Vaclav Havel's political writing and its relevance to the challenge of the concept *E pluribus unum* in the contemporary United States.

Ulla Connor, professor of English and adjunct professor of women's studies at Indiana University–Purdue University, Indianapolis, is a native of Finland and has taught ESL and linguistics in the United States for twenty years. She has published articles on second language reading and writing in *Language*

Learning, Research in the Teaching of English, TESOL Quarterly, and *Applied Linguistics*. Her publications also include the book *Contrastive Rhetoric: Cross-Cultural Aspects of Second Language Writing*.

Esha Niyogi De, lecturer in the writing programs at the University of California, Los Angeles, is interested in interdisciplinary approaches to the teaching of writing, gender and feminist studies, and Asian American studies. She is exploring the politics of gender, race, and class in the English language learned and written by South and Southeast Asian (Asian diasporic) women. She has published in Renaissance and medieval English literature and is completing a book on translation theory and imperialism.

Henry L. Evans, professor of educational foundations at Hunter College of the City University of New York, teaches basic writing and is developing a program for teacher educators. He is working on a collection of essays about teaching writing from an Afrocentric perspective. His fiction and essays have appeared in the periodicals *Essence, Persia*, and *Balaam's Ass / Fiction* and the collections *Amistad III, Illuminating Tales of the Urban Black Experience*, and *A Writer's Worlds*. "Race, Culture, and Composition" will appear in *Race, Rhetoric, and Composition*, edited by Keith Gilyard.

Keith Gilyard, professor of writing and English and director of the writing program at Syracuse University, is interested in student literacy narratives and in African American rhetoric and literature. He taught writing for fourteen years at the City University of New York and has served on the executive committees of the Conference on English Education and the Conference on College Composition and Communication. He has published the books *Voices of the Self: A Study of Language Competence*, which received an American Book Award, and *Let's Flip the Script: An African American Discourse on Language, Literature, and Learning*. He is currently editing the collection *Race, Rhetoric, and Composition*.

Barbara Gleason, assistant professor of English at City College, City University of New York, teaches first-year writing and graduate courses in the MA program in language and literacy. She coordinates a FIPSE-funded pilot project in writing program development with Mary Soliday. Her publications include *Composition in Four Keys: Inquiring into the Field through Nature, Art, Science, and Politics* (with Mark Wiley and Louise Wetherbee Phelps) and *Cultural Tapestry: Readings for a Pluralistic Society* (with Faun Bernbach Evans and Mark Wiley).

Donna Uthus Gregory is a communications consultant with McKinsey and Company, Inc., where she designs courses in cross-cultural communication and helps enrich corporate conceptions about the way writing works. She taught in the University of California, Los Angeles, writing programs for eleven years. She published a chapter in *Making Connections*, edited by Malcom Kiniry and Patricia Chittendon, and edited *The Nuclear Predicament: A Sourcebook*. Through the MacArthur Foundation Program on International Peace and Security, she researched and published on the rhetoric of the national security debate. She is interested in the analysis of professional and corporate discourse.

Michelle Grijalva, assistant professor of American Indian studies and English at the University of Arizona, teaches American Indian literature and the oral tradition. She is completing a book, *Between Silence and Sanction*, about the oral traditions and histories of Indians of the Southwest, specifically the Pasqua Yaqui, the Tohono O'odham, and the Hohokam. An essay by the same title appears in *American Identities: Contemporary Multicultural Voices*, edited by Robert Pack and Jay Parini.

Juan C. Guerra, assistant professor of English at the University of Washington, teaches courses on literacy, ethnography, the teaching of writing, and Chicana and Chicano autobiography. He has published essays in *Discourse Process* and *Education and Urban Society*. He is studying the language practices of Mexican immigrants in Chicago and is working on a book tentatively titled *By Right and Ritual: The Communicative Practices of Mexicanos in a Chicago Comunidad*.

Liz Hamp-Lyons, chair professor of English at Hong Kong Polytechnic University, is interested in ESL writing, writing assessment and pedagogy, and discourse analysis. She edited *Assessing Second Language Writing in Academic Contexts*, cowrote *Portfolios and College Writing* (with W. Condon), and has written numerous articles.

Muriel Harris, professor of English and director of the writing lab at Purdue University, is interested in writing center theory and practice, individualized instruction in writing, and writing in online environments and online writing labs. Her work includes *The Prentice-Hall Reference Guide to Grammar and Usage*, *Teaching One-to-One: The Writing Conference*, and numerous chapters and articles on writing center theory and practice. She is the editor of the *Writing Lab Newsletter*.

Wendy S. Hesford, assistant professor of English at Indiana University, teaches courses in cultural studies, composition, and literary studies. She is completing her first book, titled *Autobiographical Frames: Pedagogy and the Politics of Identity*. She has published in *Feminist Teacher* and *Transformations* and has essays forthcoming in *Genres: Mapping the Territories of Discourse*, edited by Wendy Bishop and Hans Ostrom, and *In Other Words: Feminism and Composition Studies*, edited by Susan C. Jarratt and Lynn Worsham.

Sandra Jamieson, director of composition and assistant professor of English at Drew University, is a British citizen who has been teaching writing in the United States since 1984. She is interested in composition studies, literary theory, and noncanonical American writers, as well as how writing instruction creates identities for students in composition classes and writing centers. Her text *Writing across the Curriculum/Writing in the Disciplines* is forthcoming.

She has written *The Bedford Guide to Teaching Writing in the Disciplines: An Instructor's Desk Reference* with Rebecca Moore Howard; "Texts, Contexts, and Teaching Literature by African American Women," in *Understanding Others: Cultural and Cross-Cultural Criticism and the Teaching of Literature*, edited by Joseph Trimmer and Tilly Warnock; and "The United Colors of Multicultural-ism," in *Cultural Studies in the 1990s*, edited by Michael Morgan and Susan Leggett.

Ilona Leki, professor of English at the University of Tennessee, Knoxville, is interested in applied linguistics, academic literacy, and second-language writing. She is doing a longitudinal study of the acquisition of academic literacy by a group of ESL students. She has published *Understanding ESL Writers: A Guide for Teachers, Academic Writing: Exploring Processes and Strategies*, and *Reading in the Composition Classroom* with Joan Carson. Her publications include "Coping Strategies of ESL Students in Writing Tasks across the Curriculum," in *TESOL Quarterly*, and "Good Writing: I Know It When I See It: Matching Student and Teacher Expectations," in *Academic Writing in a Second Language: Essays on Research and Pedagogy*, edited by Diane Belcher and George Braine.

Bonnie Lisle, coordinator of placement and director of the first-year intensive program in writing at the University of California, Los Angeles, is interested in transforming curriculum and pedagogy for multiethnic classrooms. She also studies the politics of literacy and learning, contrastive rhetoric, and narrative theory. Her publications include *Rereading America: Cultural Contexts for Critical Thinking* (with Gary Colombo and Robert Cullen) and *Frame Work: Culture, Storytelling, and College Writing* (with Sandra Mano and Gary Columbo).

Kate Mangelsdorf, associate professor of English at the University of Texas, El Paso, is interested in multicultural issues in the teaching of writing and in ESL writing, basic writing, and teacher education. She has been published in *Teaching English in the Two Year Colleges, Two-Year College English: Essays for a New Century* and the *Journal of Second Language Writing*. With Evelyn Posey, she has written a developmental-writing textbook, *Your Choice: A Basic Writing Guide with Readings*. Her essay "Literature in the ESL Classroom: Reading, Reflection, and Change" will be published in *Adult ESL: Issues, Politics, and Perspectives*, edited by Trudy Smoke.

Sandra Mano, lecturer in the writing program at the University of California, Los Angeles, is developing curricula for helping underprepared students. With Bonnie Lisle and Gary Colombo, she has written *Frame Work* (see the entry for Lisle). She has published *American Mosaic: Multicultural Readings in Context* with Barbara Rico and "New Themes for English B: Negotiating Boundaries within the Multicultural Canon," in *The Canon in the Classroom*, edited by John Alberti.

Carol A. Miller, associate professor of American Indian studies and American studies at the University of Minnesota, Twin Cities, is a member of the Cherokee Nation of Oklahoma. She teaches and writes about American Indian literature and is working on a study of converging narrative strategies in the fiction of contemporary American Indian women writers. Her interview project on students of color in composition classrooms was supported in part by a grant from the Center for the Study of Interdisciplinary Writing at the University of Minnesota.

Gail Y. Okawa, assistant professor of English at Youngstown State University, is interested in literacy, cultural rhetorics, and sociolinguistics, especially the representation and use of autobiographical narrative in such studies. She is writing chapters for *Race, Rhetoric, and Composition*, edited by Keith Gilyard, and for *Ethnicity and the American Short Story*, edited by Julie Brown. She has a chapter in *Writing Centers in Context*, edited by Joyce Kinkead and Jeannette Harris, and coauthored an article with Thomas Fox on multicultural voices in the writing center for *Writing Center Journal*. Her book project on lives of English teachers of color is tentatively titled *Carving Our Own Faces: The Making of Language and Literacy Teachers of Color*.

Cecilia Rodríguez Milanés, assistant professor of English at Indiana University of Pennsylvania and cochair of the NCTE Latino(a) Caucus, is interested in emergent American literature, especially writing by women of color; womanist theory; cross-genre writing; and multicultural education. She is coediting a collection of essays entitled *Nation-Building in the Academy: Scholars of Color Speak Out*. Her publications include "Risks, Resistance, and Rewards," in *Composition and Resistance*, edited by C. Mark Hurlbert and Michael Blitz, and "Racism and the Marvelous Real," in *Social Issues in the English Classroom*, edited by C. Mark Hurlbert and Samuel Totten. Her fiction and poetry have appeared in several collections, including *Iguana Dreams, Paper Dance, Little Havana Blues*, and *Under the Pomegranate Tree*.

Carol Severino, associate professor of rhetoric and director of the writing lab at the University of Iowa, is interested in how culture and social context affect writing and the teaching of writing. She has published in the *Journal of Basic Writing*, the *Journal of Second Language Writing, Writing Center Journal, Writing Lab Newsletter, Metropolitan Universities*, the *Iowa Journal of Communication*, and *Urban Education* (forthcoming). She is completing a book about the history of academic opportunity programs tentatively titled *The 'Urban Mission' and the Academic Opportunity Program: Los Angeles, Chicago, and New York Stories*.

Tony Silva, assistant professor of English at Purdue University, is interested in second-language writing and writing instruction. With Ilona Leki, he cofounded and edits the *Journal of Second Language Writing* and is chair of the CCCC Special Interest Group on Second Language Writing. He has published in *College Composition and Communication, TESOL Quarterly, Writing Program Administrator*, and the *ELT Journal*. He is exploring ethical issues in the treatment of second-language writers.

Mary Soliday, assistant professor of English at City College, City University of New York, is interested in basic writing, language and literacy issues, writing centers and peer tutoring, and cultural studies. She has published essays in *College English, College Composition and Communication*, and *Writing Center Journal*. With Barbara Gleason, she codirects a FIPSE-funded project in writing program development that is also the subject of a book she is writing that concerns reconceiving remediation in four-year colleges.

Denise Troutman, associate professor of American thought and language and linguistics at Michigan State University, is interested in African American women's language, Black English, sociolinguistics, and discourse analysis. She has an essay "The Tongue or the Sword: Which Is Master?" in Geneva Smitherman's collection *African American Women Speak Out on Anita Hill / Clarence Thomas*. "We Be Strong Women: An Assertion and Defense of the Language Patterns of African American Women" will appear in *Black Women in the Academy: Defending Our Name 1894–1994 / Papers from the Conference*, edited by R. Kilson.

Works Cited

Abrahams, Roger. *Deep Down in the Jungle: Negro Narrative Folklore from the Streets of Philadelphia*. Hatboro: Folklore Associates, 1964.

Adams, Ansel. *Born Free and Equal: Photographs of the Loyal Japanese-Americans at Manzanar Relocation Center, Inyo County, California*. New York: US Camera, 1944.

Akoto, Kwame. *Nationbuilding: Theory and Practice in African Centered Education*. Washington: Pan Afrikan World Inst., 1992.

Alarcon, Norma. "The Theoretical Subject(s) of *This Bridge Called My Back* and Anglo-American Feminism." Anzaldúa, *Making* 356–69.

Alcoff, Linda. "Cultural Feminism versus Poststructuralism: The Identity Crisis in Feminist Theory." *Signs* 13.3 (1988): 418–19.

Allaei, Sara K., and Ulla M. Connor. "Exploring the Dynamics of Cross-Cultural Collaboration in Writing Class Rooms." *Writing Instructor* 10 (1990): 19–28.

Althusser, Louis. "Ideology and Ideological State Apparatuses (Notes towards an Investigation)." *"Lenin and Philosophy" and Other Essays*. Trans. Ben Brewster. New York: Monthly Review, 1971. 127–86.

Anaya, Rudolfo. *Bless Me, Ultima*. Berkeley: Quinto Sol, 1972.

Anderson, James. "Cognitive Styles and Multicultural Populations." *Journal of Teacher Education* Jan.-Feb. 1988: 2–9.

Anderson, Janice Walker. "A Comparison of Arab and American Conceptions of 'Effective' Persuasion." *Intercultural Communication*. Ed. Larry A. Samovar and Richard E. Porter. 6th ed. Belmont: Wadsworth, 1991. 96–106.

Angelou, Maya. *I Know Why the Caged Bird Sings*. 1969. New York: Bantam, 1971.

Anzaldúa, Gloria. *Borderlands / La Frontera: The New Mestiza*. San Francisco: Spinsters–Aunt Lute, 1987.

———, ed. *Making Face, Making Soul / Haciendo Cara: Creative and Critical Perspectives by Women of Color*. San Francisco: Aunt Lute, 1990.

———. "Speaking in Tongues: A Letter to Third World Women Writers." *This Bridge Called My Back: Writings by Radical Women of Color*. Ed. Cherríe Moraga and Gloria Anzaldúa. 2nd ed. New York: Kitchen Table: Women of Color, 1983. 165–74.

Applebee, Arthur N., Judith A. Langer, and Ina V. S. Mullis. "Learning to Be Literate: Reading, Writing, Reasoning." *Education Digest* Dec. 1987: 6–8.

Armor, John, and Peter Wright. *Manzanar*. New York: Times, 1988.

Arndt, Valerie. "Six Writers in Search of Texts: A Protocol Based Study of L1 and L2 Writing." *English Language Teaching Journal* 41 (1987): 257–67.

Asad, Talal. "The Concept of Cultural Translation in British Social Anthropology." *Writing Culture: The Poetics and Politics of Ethnography*. Ed. James Clifford and George E. Marcus. Berkeley: U of California P, 1984. 146–62.

Asante, Molefi Kete. *The Afrocentric Idea*. Philadelphia: Temple UP, 1987.

———. *Afrocentricity*. Trenton: Africa World, 1988.

———. *Kemet, Afrocentricity, and Knowledge*. Trenton: Africa World, 1990.

Asante, Molefi Kete, and Mark Mattson. *Historical and Cultural Atlas of African Americans*. New York: Macmillan, 1991.

Atari, Omar Fayez. *A Contrastive Analysis of Arab and American University Students' Strategies in Accomplishing Written English Discourse Functions*. Diss. Georgetown U, 1983. Ann Arbor: UMI, 1984. 8401491.

Auerbach, Elsa. "Reexamining English Only in the ESL Classroom." *The TESOL Quarterly* 27 (1993): 9–32.

Baker, Houston A., Jr. *Blues, Ideology, and Afro-American Literature: A Vernacular Theory*. Chicago: U of Chicago P, 1984.

Bakhtin, Mikhail. *The Dialogic Imagination: Four Essays by M. M. Bakhtin*. Trans. Michael Holquist and Caryl Emerson. Ed. Michael Holquist. Austin: U of Texas P, 1981.

———. *Marxism and the Philosophy of Language*. Trans. Ladislav Matejka and I. R. Titunik. Cambridge: Harvard UP, 1986.

Baldwin, James. "A Talk to Teachers." Simonson and Walker. 3–12.

Ball, Arnetha F. "Cultural Preference and the Expository Writing of African-American Adolescents." *Written Communications* 9.4 (1992): 501–32.

Ballard, Brigid, and John Clanchy. "Assessment by Misconception: Cultural Influences and Intellectual Traditions." *Assessing Second Language Writing in Academic Contexts*. Ed. Liz Hamp-Lyons. Norwood: Ablex, 1991. 19–35.

Banks, James A. *Multiethnic Education: Theory and Practice*. Boston: Allyn, 1994.

Barna, Laray M. "Stumbling Blocks in Intercultural Communication." *Intercultural Communication*. Ed. Larry A. Samovar and Richard E. Porter. Belmont: Wadsworth, 1991. 345–53.

Barratt, Michelle. "Some Different Meanings of the Concept of 'Difference': Feminist Theory and the Concept of Ideology." *The Difference Within*. Ed. Elizabeth Meese and Alice Parker. Philadelphia: Benjamins, 1989. 37–47.

Barrera, Mario. *Race and Class in the Southwest: A Theory of Racial Inequality*. South Bend: U of Notre Dame P, 1979.

Bartholomae, David. "Inventing the University." *When a Writer Can't Write: Studies in Writer's Block and Other Composing Process Problems*. Ed. Mike Rose. New York: Guilford, 1985. 134–65.

——. "Inventing the University." *Journal of Basic Writing* 5 (1986): 4–23.

——. "The Tidy House: Basic Writing in the American Curriculum." *Journal of Basic Writing* 12 (1993): 4–21.

Bartholomae, David, and Anthony Petrosky. *Facts, Artifacts, and Counterfacts: Theory and Method for a Reading and Writing Course*. Portsmouth: Boynton, 1986.

Belsey, Catherine. "Constructing the Subject: Deconstructing the Text." *Feminist Criticism and Social Change*. Ed. J. Newton and D. Rosenfelt. London: Methuen, 1985. 45–64.

Benson, Beverly Ann. *A Qualitative Analysis of Language Structures in Compositions Written by First and Second Language Learners*. Diss. U of Kansas, 1980. Ann Arbor: UMI, 1980. 8026712.

Benveniste, Emile. *Problems in General Linguistics*. Miami: U of Miami P, 1971.

Berlin, James A. "Composition and Cultural Studies." Hurlbert and Blitz, 47–55.

——. "Contemporary Composition: The ·Major Pedagogical Theories." *The Writing Teacher's Sourcebook*. Ed. Gary Tate, Edward P. J. Corbett, and Nancy Myers. 3rd ed. New York: Oxford UP, 1994. 9–21.

——. "Rhetoric and Ideology in the Writing Class." *College English* 50 (1988): 477–94.

Bernstein, Susan David. "Confessing Feminist Theory: What's 'I' Got to Do with It?" *Hypatia*. 7 (1992): 120–47.

Berthoff, Ann E. *The Making of Meaning: Metaphors, Models, and Maxims for Writing Teachers*. Montclair: Boynton, 1981.

Berthoff, Ann E., with James Stephens. *Forming Thinking Writing*. 2nd ed. Portsmouth: Boynton, 1988.

Biber, Douglas. *Variation across Speech and Writing*. New York: Cambridge UP, 1988.

Bingham, Sam, and Janet Bingham, eds. *Between Sacred Mountains: Navajo Stories and Lessons from the Land*. Tucson: U of Arizona, 1986.

Bissex, Glenda L. "Small Is Beautiful: Case Study as Appropriate Methodology for Teacher Research." *The Writing Teacher as Researcher: Essays in the Theory and Practice of Class-Based Research*. Ed. Donald A. Daiker and Max Morenberg. Portsmouth: Boynton, 1990. 70–75.

Bizzell, Patricia. *Academic Discourse and Critical Consciousness*. Pittsburgh: U of Pittsburgh P, 1992.

——. "Beyond Anti-foundationalism to Rhetorical Authority: Problems Defining 'Cultural Literacy.'" *College English* 52 (1990): 661–75.

——. "Cognition, Convention, and Certainty: What We Need to Know about Writing." *Pre/Text* 3.3 (1982): 213–43.

——. "Literacy in Culture and Cognition." Enos 125–37.

——. "What Happens When Basic Writers Come to College?" *College Composition and Communication* 37 (1986): 294–301.

Blanchard, Fletcher A. "Combatting Intentional Bigotry and Inadvertently Racist Acts." *Chronicle of Higher Education* 13 May 1992: B1–2.

Bloom, Alfred. *The Linguistic Shaping of Thought: A Study of the Impact of Language on Thinking in China and the West*. Hillsdale: Erlbaum, 1981.

Bloomfield, Morton, and Einar Haugen, eds. *Language as a Human Problem*. New York: Norton, 1974.

Board of Higher Education of the City University of New York. Minutes. 5 Apr. 1976.

Braddock, Richard. "The Frequency and Placement of Topic Sentences in Expository Prose." *Research in the Teaching of English* 8 (1974): 287–302.

Brent, Doug. *Reading as Rhetorical Invention: Knowledge, Persuasion, and the Teaching of Research-Based Writing*. Urbana: NCTE, 1992.

Brick, Allan. "The CUNY Writing Assessment Test and the Teaching of Writing." *Writing Program Administration* 4.1 (1980): 28–34.

Britton, James. "A Quiet Form of Research." *Reclaiming the Classroom: Teacher Research as an Agency for Change*. Ed. Dixie Goswami and Peter R. Stillman. Portsmouth: Boynton, 1987. 13–19.

Britton, James, et al. *The Development of Writing Abilities*. London: Macmillan, 1975.

Brodkey, Linda. "On the Subjects of Class and Gender in 'The Literacy Letters.'" *College English* 51 (1989): 125–41.

———. "Writing on the Bias." *College English* 56 (1994): 527–47.

Brooks, Phyllis. "Peer Tutoring and the ESL Student." *New Directions for College Learning Assistants* 3 (1981): 45–52.

Brown, Cecil. *The Life and Loves of Mr. Jiveass Nigger*. New York: Ecco, 1969.

Brown, Claude. *Manchild in the Promised Land*. New York: Signet, 1965.

Brown, Gillian, and George Yule. *Discourse Analysis*. London: Cambridge UP, 1983.

Brown, Hubert Rap. *Die Nigger Die!* New York: Dial, 1969.

Brown, Roscoe C., Jr. "Testing Black Student Writers." Greenberg, Wiener, and Donovan 98–108.

Bruffee, Kenneth A. "Beginning a Testing Program: Making Lemonade." Greenberg, Wiener, and Donovan. 93–97.

———. "Collaborative Learning and the 'Conversation of Mankind.'" *College English* 46 (1984): 635–52.

———. "Peer Tutoring and the 'Conversation of Mankind.'" *Writing Centers: Theory and Administration*. Ed. Gary A. Olson. Urbana: NCTE, 1984. 3–15.

Bulhan, Hussein. *Frantz Fanon and the Psychology of Oppression*. New York: Plenum, 1985.

Bullock, Richard, John Trimbur, and Charles Schuster, eds. *The Politics of Writing Instruction: Postsecondary*. Portsmouth: Boynton, 1991.

Burgest, David. "The Racist Use of the English Language." *Black Scholar* Sept. 1973: 37–45.

Burtoff, Michelle J. *The Logical Organization of Written Expository Discourse in English: A Comparative Study of Japanese, Arabic, and Native-Speaker Strategies*. Diss. Georgetown U, 1983. Ann Arbor: UMI, 1985. 8428443.

Butler, Judith. *Gender Trouble: Feminism and the Subversion of Identity*. New York: Routledge, 1990.

Cahalan, James M., and David B. Downing, eds. *Practicing Theory in Introductory College Literature Courses*. Urbana: NCTE, 1991.

Cai, Xiaomin. "Behavioral Characteristics of Oriental ESL Students in the Writing Center." *Writing Lab Newsletter* 18.8 (1994): 5–6.

Campbell, Cherry. *Writing with Others' Words: The Use of Information from a Background Reading Text in the Writing of Native and Non-native University Composition Students*. Diss. U of California, Los Angeles, 1987. Ann Arbor: UMI, 1988. 8721021.

———. "Writing with Others' Words: Using Background Reading Text in Academic Compositions." *Second Language Writing: Research Insights for the Classroom*. Ed. Barbara Kroll. New York: Cambridge UP, 1990. 211–30.

Campbell, Kermit E. "*The Signifying Monkey* Revisited: Vernacular Discourse and African American Personal Narratives." *Journal of Advanced Composition* 14.2 (1994): 463–73.

Canagarajah, A. Suresh. "Comments on Ann Raimes's 'Out of the Woods: Emerging Traditions in the Teaching of Writing': Up the Garden Path: Second Language Writing Approaches, Local Knowledge, and Pluralism." *TESOL Quarterly* 27 (1993): 301–06.

Carby, Hazel V. "The Multicultural Wars." *Radical History Review* 54 (1992): 7–18.

Carino, Peter. "What Do We Talk about When We Talk about Our Metaphors: A Cultural Critique of Clinic, Lab, and Center." *Writing Center Journal* 13 (1992): 31–42.

Carlson, Sybil B. "Cultural Differences in Writing and Reasoning Skills." Purves, *Writing* 227–60.

Carson, Joan G. "Becoming Biliterate: First Language Influences." *Journal of Second Language Writing* 1 (1992): 37–60.

Catano, James V. "The Rhetoric of Masculinity: Origins, Institutions, and the Myths of the Self-Made Man." *College English* 52 (1991): 421–36.

Caywood, Cynthia L., and Gillian R. Overing. *Teaching Writing: Pedagogy, Gender, and Equity*. New York: State U of New York P, 1987.

"CCCC Secretary's Report, 1988–89." *College Composition and Communication* 40 (1989): 362–65.

"Certiorari Denied." *NCJAR Newsletter* (National Council for Japanese American Redress). 10.9 (1988): 1.

Chaplin, Miriam T. *A Comparative Analysis of Writing Features Used by Selected Black and White Students in the National Assessment of Educational Progress and the New Jersey High School Proficiency Test*. Research Report 88–42. Princeton: Educ. Testing Service, 1988.

Chappell, Virginia A., Randall Hensley, and Elizabeth Simmons-O'Neill. "Beyond Information Retrieval: Transforming Research Assignments into Genuine Inquiry." *Journal of Teaching Writing* 13.1-2 (1994): 209–24.

Chase, Geoffrey. "Accommodation, Resistance and the Politics of Student Writing." *College Composition and Communication* 39 (1988): 13–22.

Choi, Yeon Hee. "Text Structure of Korean Speakers' Argumentative Essays in English." *World Englishes* 7 (1988): 129–42.

———. *Textual Coherence in English and Korean: An Analysis of Argumentative Writing by American and Korean Students*. Diss. U of Illinois, Urbana, 1988. Ann Arbor: UMI, 1989. 8908652.

Churchill, Ward. *Fantasies of the Master Race: Literature, Cinema, and the Colonization of American Indians*. Monroe: Common Courage, 1992.

Cisneros, Sandra. *The House on Mango Street*. Houston: Arte Publico, 1984.

———. *Woman Hollering Creek and Other Stories*. New York: Vintage, 1991.

The City University of New York Writing Skills Assessment Test. New York: Office of Academic Affairs, City U of New York, 1983.

The City University of New York Writing Skills Assessment Test Evaluation Scale (Refined 1981–82). New York: Office of Academic Affairs, City U of New York, 1982.

Clark, Beverly Lyon, and Sonja Wiedenhaupt. "On Blocking and Unblocking Sonja: A Case Study in Two Voices." *College Composition and Communication* 43 (1992): 55–74.

Clark, Gregory. *Dialogue, Dialectic, and Conversation: A Social Perspective on the Function of Writing*. Carbondale: Southern Illinois UP, 1990.

Clark, Herbert H., and Eve V. Clark. *Psychology and Language: An Introduction to Psycholinguistics*. San Diego: Harcourt, 1977.

Clifford, James. *The Predicament of Culture: Twentieth-Century Ethnography, Culture, and Art*. Cambridge: Harvard UP, 1988.

Clifford, John. "Composing in Stages: The Effects of a Collaborative Strategy." *Research in the Teaching of English* 14 (1981): 37–53.

———. "The Subject in Discourse." Harkin and Schilb 38–51.

Clyne, Michael. "Cultural Differences in the Organization of Academic Texts: English and German." *Journal of Pragmatics* 5 (1981): 61–66.

Code of Fair Testing Practices in Education. Washington: Joint Committee on Testing Practices, 1988.

Coles, Nicholas, and Susan V. Wall. "Conflict and Power in the Reader-Responses of Adult Basic Writers." *College English* 49 (1987): 298–314.

Columbo, Gary, Robert Cullen, and Bonnie Lisle, eds. *Rereading America: Cultural Contexts for Critical Thinking and Writing*. 2nd ed. Boston: Bedford, 1992.

Committee on Conference on College Composition and Communication Language Statement. "Students' Right to Their Own Language." *College Composition and Communication* 25 (1974): 1–18.

Conference on College Composition and Communication. *The National Language Policy*. Urbana: NCTE, 1992.

Connelly, F. Michael, and D. Jean Clandinin. "Stories of Experience and Narrative Inquiry." *Educational Researcher* 19 (1990): 2–14.

Connor, Ulla. "A Contrastive Study of Persuasive Business Correspondence: American and Japanese." *Global Implications of Business Communications*. Ed. J. Bruno. Houston: U of Houston P–Clear Lake, 1988. 57–72.

———. "Linguistic/Rhetorical Measures for International Persuasive Student Writing." *Research in Teaching of English* 24.1 (1990): 67–87.

———. "Research Frontiers in Writing Analysis." *TESOL Quarterly* 21 (1987): 677–96.

———. "A Study of Cohesion and Coherence in English as a Second Language Students' Writing." *Papers in Linguistics* 17 (1984): 301–16.

Connor, Ulla, and Robert Kaplan. *Writing across Languages: Analysis of L2 Text*. Reading: Addison-Wesley, 1987.

Connor, Ulla, and Melinda Kramer. "Writing from Sources: Case Studies of ESL Graduate Students in Business Management." *Academic Writing in a Second Language: Essays on Research and Pedagogy*. Ed. Diane Belcher and George Braine. Norwood: Ablex, 1995. 155–82.

Cook, William. "Writing in the Spaces Left." *College Composition and Communication* 44 (1993): 9–25.

Courage, Richard. "The Interaction of Public and Private Literacies." *College Composition and Communication* 44 (1993): 484–96.

Daniels, Harvey A., ed. *Not Only English: Affirming America's Multicultural Heritage*. Urbana: NCTE, 1990.

Daniels, Roger, Sandra C. Taylor, and Harry H. L. Kitano, eds. *Japanese Americans: From Relocation to Redress*. Salt Lake City: U of Utah, 1986.

Darder, Antonia. *Culture and Power in the Classroom*. New York: Bergin, 1991.

Dasenbrock, Reed Way. "Teaching Multicultural Literature." Trimmer and Warnock 35–46.

Davidson, Donald. *Inquiries into Truth and Interpretation*. Oxford: Clarendon, 1984.

Dean, Terry. "Multicultural Classrooms, Monocultural Teachers." *College Composition and Communication* 40 (1989): 23–37.

Decker, Randall E., and Robert A. Schwegler, eds. *Patterns of Exposition*. 13th ed. New York: Harper, 1991.

Delpit, Lisa D. "The Silenced Dialogue: Power and Pedagogy in Educating Other People's Children." *Harvard Educational Review* 58.3 (1988): 280–98.

Dennett, Joann Temple. *Writing Technical English: A Comparison of the Process of Native English and Native Japanese Speakers*. Diss. U of Colorado, Boulder, 1985. Ann Arbor: UMI, 1986. 8528478.

Dingwaney, Anuradha, and Lawrence Needham. "Feminist Theory and Practice in the Writing Classroom: A Critique and a Prospectus." *Constructing*

Rhetorical Education: From the Classroom to the Community. Ed. Marie J. Secor and Davida Charney. Southern Illinois UP, 1992. 6–25.

DiPardo, Anne. *A Kind of Passport: A Basic Writing Adjunct Program and the Challenge of Student Diversity.* Urbana: NCTE, 1993.

Du Bois, W. E. B. "The Talented Tenth." *A W. E. B. Du Bois Reader.* Ed. Andrew G. Paschal. New York: Macmillan, 1971. 31–51.

Dunsmore, Roger. "A Navajo High School and the Truth of Trees." *Studies in American Indian Literatures* 3 (1991): 36–40.

Durst, Russell. "The Mongoose and the Rat in Composition Research: Insights from the *RTE* Bibliography." *College Composition and Communication* 41.4 (1990): 393–408.

Eastman, Arthur M., et al., eds. *The Norton Reader.* Shorter 8th ed. New York: Norton, 1992.

Ede, Lisa, and Andrea Lunsford. *Singular Texts / Plural Authors: Perspectives on Collaborative Writing.* Urbana: Southern Illinois UP, 1990.

Eggington, William G. "Written Academic Discourse in Korean: Implications for Effective Communication." Connor and Kaplan 153–68.

Elbow, Peter. "Embracing Contraries in the Teaching Process." *College English* 45 (1983): 327–39. Rpt. in *The Writing Teacher's Sourcebook.* Ed. Gary Tate and Edward P. J. Corbett. 2nd ed. New York: Oxford UP, 1988. 219–31.

——. "Reflections on Academic Discourse: How It Relates to Freshmen and Colleagues." *College English* 53 (1991): 135–56.

——. *Writing with Power.* New York: Oxford UP, 1981.

Elbow, Peter, and Pat Belanoff. *A Community of Writers: A Workshop Course in Writing.* New York: Random, 1989.

Ellsworth, Elizabeth. "Why Doesn't This Feel Empowering? Working Through the Repressive Myths of Critical Pedagogy." *Harvard Educational Review* 59.3 (1989): 297–324.

Enkvist, Niles E. "Text Linguistics for the Applier: An Introduction." Connor and Kaplan 1–43.

Enos, Theresa, ed. *A Sourcebook for Basic Writing Teachers.* New York: Random, 1987.

Erickson, Frederick. "School Literacy, Reasoning, and Civility." Ed. Eugene R. Kintgen, Barry M. Kroll, and Mike Rose. *Perspectives on Literacy.* Carbondale: Southern Illinois UP, 1988. 205–26.

Evers, Larry, prod. *Iisaw: Hopi Coyote Stories, with Helen Sekaquaptewa.* Words and Place: Native Literature from the American Southwest. Videocassette. Clearwater, 1978.

——, prod. *In This Song I Walk.* Words and Place: Native American Literature from the Southwest. Videocassette. Clearwater, 1978.

——, prod. *Natwaniwa: A Hopi Philosophical Statement.* Words and Place: Native Literature from the American Southwest. Videocassette. Clearwater, 1978.

—, prod. *Running on the Edge of the Rainbow: Laguna Stories and Poems, with Leslie Silko*. Words and Place: Native Literature from the American Southwest. Videocassette. Clearwater, 1979.

Faigley, Lester. "Competing Theories of Process: A Critique and a Proposal." *College English* 48 (1986): 527–42.

—. *Fragments of Rationality: Postmodernity and the Subject of Composition*. Pittsburgh: U of Pittsburgh P, 1992.

Fanon, Frantz. *Black Face, White Masks*. New York: Grove, 1967.

—. "Racism and Culture." *Toward the African Revolution: Political Essays*. Trans. Haakon Chevalier. New York: Grove, 1964. 29–44.

Farr, Marcia. "Essayist Literacy and Other Verbal Performances." *Written Communication*. 10.3 (1993): 4–38.

Farr, Marcia, and Harvey Daniels. *Language Diversity and Writing Instruction*. New York: ERIC, 1986.

Farrell, Thomas. "Literacy, the Basics, and All That Jazz." Enos 27–44.

Fishman, Joshua A. "Planned Reinforcement of Language Maintenance in the United States: Suggestions for the Conservation of a Neglected National Resource." *Language in Sociocultural Change: Essays by Joshua A. Fishman*. Ed. Anwar S. Dil. Stanford: Stanford UP, 1972. 16–47.

—. "The Sociology of Language: Yesterday, Today and Tomorrow." *Current Issues in Linguistic Theory*. Ed. R. W. Cole. Bloomington: Indiana UP, 1977. 51–75.

Fishman, Judith. "Do You Agree or Disagree: The Epistemology of the CUNY Writing Assessment Test." *Writing Program Administration* 8.1–2 (1984): 17–25.

Flannery, Kathryn T. "Composing and the Question of Agency." *College English* 53 (1991): 701–13.

Flower, Linda, and John F. Hayes. "A Cognitive Process Theory of Writing." *College Composition and Communication* 32 (1981): 365–87.

Flynn, Elizabeth. "Composing as a Woman." *College Composition and Communication* 39 (1988): 423–35.

Flynn, Elizabeth, et al. "Gender and Modes of Collaboration in a Chemical Engineering Design Course." *Journal of Business and Technical Communication* 5 (1991): 444–62.

Foucault, Michel. *The Archaeology of Knowledge and the Discourse on Language*. Trans. A. M. Sheridan Smith. New York: Pantheon, 1972.

—. *The Archaeology of Knowledge and the Discourse on Language*. Trans. Rupert Swyer. New York: Pantheon, 1982.

—. *Discipline and Punish: The Birth of the Prison*. Trans. Alan Sheridan. New York: Pantheon, 1977.

—. "What Is an Author?" *Language, Counter-memory, Practice*. Ithaca: Cornell UP, 1977.

Fox, Thomas. "Repositioning the Profession: Teaching Writing to African American Students." *Journal of Advanced Composition* 12 (1992): 291–303.

——. *The Social Uses of Writing: Politics and Pedagogy*. Norwood: Ablex, 1990.

Fox, Tom. "Basic Writing as Cultural Conflict." *Journal of Education* 17.1 (1990): 65–83.

Freedman, Diane P. *An Alchemy of Genres: Cross-Genre Writing by American Feminist Poet-Critics*. Charlottesville: U of Virginia P, 1992.

Freire, Paulo. *Pedagogy of the Oppressed*. Trans. Myra B. Ramos. New York: Continuum, 1970.

——. *The Politics of Education: Culture, Power, and Liberation*. Trans. Donaldo Macedo. South Hadley: Bergin, 1987.

Freire, Paulo, and Donaldo Macedo. *Literacy: Reading the Word and the World*. South Hadley: Bergin, 1987.

Fuss, Diana. *Essentially Speaking: Feminism, Nature, and Difference*. New York: Routledge, 1989.

Gates, Henry Louis Gates, Jr. *Bearing Witness: Selections from African-American Autobiography in the Twentieth Century*. New York: Pantheon, 1991.

——. *Loose Canons: Notes on the Culture Wars*. New York: Oxford UP, 1992.

——, ed. *Reading Black, Reading Feminist: A Critical Anthology*. New York: Meridian, 1990.

——. *The Signifying Monkey: A Theory of African-American Literary Criticism*. New York: Oxford UP, 1988.

——. "The Weaning of America." *New Yorker* 19 Apr. 1993: 113–17.

Gates, Roberta Dixon. *An Analysis of Grammatical Structures in Compositions Written by Four Groups of Students at Southern Technical Institute: Indo-Iranian, Latin-Romance, Sino-Tibetan, and American*. Diss. Georgia State U, 1978. Ann Arbor: UMI, 1979. 7817575.

Gebhardt, Richard C. "Diversity in a Mainline Journal." *College Composition and Communication* 43 (1992): 7–10.

Geisler, Cheryl. "Exploring Academic Literacy: An Experiment in Composing." *College Composition and Communication* 43 (1992): 39–54.

Gere, Anne Ruggles. "Practicing Theory / Theorizing Practice." *Balancing Acts: Essays on the Teaching of Writing in Honor of William F. Irmscher*. Ed. Virginia A. Chappell, Mary Louise Buley-Meissner, and Chris Anderson. Carbondale: Southern Illinois UP, 1991. 111–21.

Gergen, Kenneth J., and Mary M. Gergen. "Narrative Form and the Construction of Psychological Science." *Narrative Psychology: The Storied Nature of Human Conduct*. Ed. Theodore R. Sarbin. New York: Praeger, 1986.

Gilyard, Keith. *Voices of the Self: A Study of Language Competence*. Detroit: Wayne State UP, 1991.

Giroux, Henry A. *Border Crossings: Cultural Workers and the Politics of Education*. New York: Routledge, 1992.

———. *Ideology, Culture, and the Process of Schooling*. Philadelphia: Temple UP, 1981.

———. Introduction. *Rewriting Literacy*. Ed. Candace Mitchell and Kathleen Weiler. New York: Bergin, 1991. ix–xvi.

———. "Postmodernism as Border Pedagogy: Redefining the Boundaries of Race and Ethnicity." Giroux, *Postmodernism* 217–56.

———, ed. *Postmodernism, Feminism, and Cultural Politics: Redrawing Educational Boundaries*. Albany: State U of New York P, 1991.

———. *Schooling and the Struggle for Public Life: Critical Pedagogy in the Modern Age*. Minneapolis: U of Minnesota P, 1988.

———. *Theory and Resistance in Education: A Pedagogy for the Opposition*. South Hadley: Bergin, 1983.

Giroux, Henry A., and Peter McClaren, eds. *Between Borders: Pedagogy and the Politics of Cultural Studies*. New York: Routledge, 1994.

Goldstein, Lynn M., and Susan M. Conrad. "Student Input and Negotiation of Meaning in ESL Writing Conferences." *TESOL Quarterly* 24 (1990): 443–60.

Gonzalez, Roseann Duenas. "When Minority Becomes Majority: The Changing Face of English Classrooms." *English Journal* 79 (1990): 15–23.

Goodlad, John. *A Place Called School*. New York: McGraw-Hill, 1984.

Gould, Stephen Jay. *Eight Little Piggies: Reflections in Natural History*. New York: Norton, 1993.

Graff, Gerald. *Beyond the Culture Wars*. New York: Norton, 1993.

Greenberg, Karen L., Harvey S. Wiener, and Richard A. Donovan, eds. *Writing Assessment: Issues and Strategies*. New York: Longman, 1986.

Greene, Maxine. Foreword. *Stories Lives Tell: Narrative and Dialogue in Education*. Ed. Carol Witherell and Nell Noddings. New York: Teachers Coll., 1991. ix–xi.

Gregory, Dick. *Nigger: An Autobiography*. New York: Washington Square, 1964.

Gregory, Michael, and Susanne Carroll. *Language and Situation: Language Varieties and Their Social Contexts*. London: Routledge, 1978.

Haas, Christina, and Linda Flower. "Rhetorical Reading Strategies and the Construction of Meaning." *College Composition and Communication* 39 (1988): 167–83.

Hairston, Maxine. "Diversity, Ideology, and Teaching Writing." *College Composition and Communication* 43 (1992): 179–93.

Hamp-Lyons, Liz. "Raters Respond to Rhetoric in Writing." *Interlingual Processes*. Ed. Hans Deckert and Gunther Raupach. Tübingen: Gunther Narr, 1989. 229–44.

———. "Second Language Writing: Assessment Issues." *Second Language Writing: Insights for the Classroom*. Ed. Barbara Kroll. New York: Cambridge UP, 1990. 69–87.

Haniff, Nesha Z. "Epilogue." *College in Black and White: African American Students in Predominantly White and in Historically Black Public Universities*.

Ed. Walter Allen, Edgar G. Epps, and Nesha Z. Haniff. Albany: State U of New York P, 1991. 247–56.

Hansen, Kristine. "WAC Readers: What Are They?" Conf. on Coll. Composition and Communication Convention. Chicago. 22 Mar. 1990.

Harkin, Patricia, and John Schilb, eds. *Contending with Words: Composition and Rhetoric in a Postmodern Age*. New York: MLA, 1991.

Harris, David P. *The Organizational Patterns of Adult ESL Student Narratives: Report of a Pilot Study*. ERIC, 1983. ED 275 150.

Harris, Joseph. "The Idea of Community in the Study of Writing." *College Composition and Communication* 40 (1989): 11–22.

Harris, Muriel. "Individualized Instruction in Writing Centers: Attending to Writers' Cross-Cultural Differences." *Intersections: Theory and Practice in the Writing Center*. Ed. Joan Mullin and Ray Wallace. Urbana: NCTE, 1994. 96–110.

———. *Teaching One-to-One: The Writing Conference*. Urbana: NCTE, 1986.

Harrison, Paul Carter. *The Drama of Nommo: Black Theater in the African Continuum*. New York: Grove, 1972.

Hashimoto, I. "Voice as Juice: Some Reservations about Evangelic Composition." *College Composition and Communication* 38.1 (1987): 70–80.

Hayden, Julian. "Talking with the Animals." *Journal of the Southwest* 29.2 (1987): 224–27.

Hayes-Bautista, David E., and Jorge Chapa. "Latino Terminology: Conceptual Bases for Standardized Terminology." *American Journal of Public Health* 77 (1987): 61–68.

Heath, Shirley Brice. *Ways with Words: Language, Life, and Work in Communities and Classrooms*. New York: Cambridge UP, 1984.

———. "Where Is the Crisis in American Literacy?" *Education Digest* Feb. 1987: 19.

Henderson, Mae Gwendolyn. "Speaking in Tongues: Dialogics, Dialectics, and the Black Woman Writer's Literary Tradition." Gates, *Reading* 116–42.

Henning, Barbara. "The World Was Stone Cold: Basic Writing in an Urban University." *College English* 53 (1991): 674–85.

Hersey, John. "A Mistake of Terrifically Horrible Proportions." Armor and Wright 3–66.

Herskovits, Melville J. *The New World Negro: Selected Papers Written by Melville J. Herskovits*. Ed. Frances Herskovits. Bloomington: Indiana UP, 1966.

Higginbotham, Evelyn Brooks. "African-American Women's History and the Metalanguage of Race." *Signs* 17.2 (1992): 251–74.

Hill, Carolyn Erickson. *Writing from the Margins: Power and Pedagogy for Teachers of Composition*. New York: Oxford UP, 1990.

Hillerman, Tony. "Sacred Ground." *National Geographic* May-June 1989: 44–61.

Hinds, John. "Contrastive Rhetoric: Japanese and English." *Text* 3 (1983): 183–96.

———. "Inductive, Deductive, Quasi-inductive: Expository Writing in Japanese, Korean, Chinese, and Thai." *Coherence: Research and Pedagogical Perspectives*. Ed. Ulla Connor and Ann M. Johns. Alexandria: TESOL, 1990. 87–110.

———. "Reader versus Writer Responsibility: A New Typology." Connor and Kaplan 141–52.

Hirokawa, Keiko. "An Investigation of Native/Non-native Speaker Examination Essays." *Papers in Applied Linguistics—Michigan* 1 (1986): 105–31.

Hirsch, E. D., Jr. *Cultural Literacy: What Every American Needs to Know*. Boston: Houghton, 1987.

Hoffman, Eva. *Lost in Translation: A Life in a New Language*. New York: Penguin, 1989.

Holt, Grace. "Metaphor, Black Discourse Style, and Cultural Reality." *Ebonics: The True Language of Black Folks*. Ed. Robert L. Williams. Saint Louis: Inst. of Black Studies, 1975. 86–95.

hooks, bell. "Essentialism and Experience." *American Literary History* 3 (1991): 172–83.

———. *Talking Back: Thinking Feminist, Thinking Black*. Boston: South End, 1989.

Houston, Jeanne Wakatsuki, and James D. Houston. *Farewell to Manzanar*. New York: Bantam, 1974.

Hu, Zhuang Lin, Dorothy F. Brown, and L. B. Brown. "Some Linguistic Differences in the Written English of Chinese and Australian Students." *Language Learning and Communication* 1 (1982): 39–49.

Hull, Glynda, and Mike Rose. "'This Wooden Shack Place': The Logic of an Unconventional Reading." *College Composition and Communication* 41.3 (1990): 287–98.

Hull, Glynda, et al. "Remediation as Social Construct: Perspectives from an Analysis of Classroom Discourse." *College Composition and Communication* 42.3 (1991): 299–329.

Hunt, Earl, and Franca Agnoli. "The Whorfian Hypothesis: A Cognitive Psychology Perspective." *Psychological Review* 98 (1991): 377–89.

Hurlbert, C. Mark, and Michael Blitz, eds. *Composition and Resistance*. Portsmouth: Boynton, 1991. 47–55.

Hurston, Zora Neale. *Dust Tracks on a Road*. 1942. New York: Perennial-Harper, 1991.

———. *Mules and Men*. 1935. New York: Quality, 1990.

Indrasuta, Chantanee. *A Comparison of the Written Compositions of American and Thai Students*. Diss. U of Illinois, Urbana, 1987. Ann Arbor: UMI, 1988. 8721663.

————. "Narrative Styles in the Writing of Thai and American Students." Purves, *Writing* 206–26.

In the White Man's Image. Narr. by David McCullough. The American Experience. PBS. 17 Feb. 1992.

Islas, Arturo. *The Rain God: A Desert Tale.* Palo Alto: Alexandrian, 1984.

Jackson, John G. *Introduction to African Civilizations.* New York: Citadel, 1990.

Jacoby, Jay, and Stan Patten. "Changing the Way We Teach: The Role of the Writing Center in Professional Development; or, The Virtue of Selfishness." *The Writing Center: New Directions.* Ed. Ray Wallace and Jean Simpson. New York: Garland, 1991. 157–67.

Jamieson, Sandra. "Rereading Readers: The Use of Textbook Readers in College-Level Composition Classes." Diss. State U of New York, Binghamton, 1991.

————. Rev. of *Norton Reader: Shorter Eighth Edition. Focuses* 6 (1993): 15–16.

————. "The United Colors of Multiculturalism: Rereading Composition Textbooks." *Mainstream(s) and Margins: Cultural Studies in the 90's.* Ed. Michael Morgan and Susan Leggett. Westport: Greenwood, 1996. 62–84.

JanMohamed, Abdul R., and David Lloyd. "Introduction: Minority Discourse— What Is to Be Done?" *Cultural Critique* 6 (1987): 5–17.

Janopoulos, Michael. "University Faculty Tolerance of NS and NNS Writing Errors: A Comparison." *Journal of Second Language Writing* 1 (1992): 109–21.

Jarratt, Susan. "Feminism and Composition: The Case for Conflict." Harkin and Schilb 105–23.

Jie, Gao, and Marie Jean Lederman. "Instruction and Assessment of Writing in China: The National Unified Entrance Examination for Institutions of Higher Education." *Journal of Basic Writing* 7 (1988): 47–60.

Johns, Ann M. "Faculty Assessment of ESL Student Literacy Skills: Implications for Writing Assessment." *Assessing Second Language Writing in Academic Contexts.* Ed. Liz Hamp-Lyons. Norwood: Ablex, 1991. 167–79.

————. "Interpreting an English Competency Examination: The Frustrations of an ESL Science Student." *Written Communication* 8 (1991): 379–401.

Jordan, June. "Nobody Mean More to Me Than You and the Future Life of Willie Jordan." *On Call: Political Essays.* Boston: South End, 1985. 123–39.

Journal of Second Language Writing. Norwood: Ablex.

Journet, Debra. "Ecological Theories as Cultural Narratives." *Written Communication* 8 (Oct. 1991): 446–72.

Kachru, Yamuna. "Linguistics and Written Discourse in Particular Languages: Contrastive Studies: English and Hindi." Purves, *Writing* 50–69.

————. "Writers in Hindi and English." Purves, *Writing* 109–37.

Kail, Harvey, and John Trimbur. "The Politics of Peer Tutoring." *WPA: Writing Program Administration* 11.1–2 (1987): 5–12.

Kaplan, Robert B. "Contrastive Rhetoric and Second Language Learning: Notes toward a Theory of Contrastive Rhetoric." Purves, *Writing* 275–304.

———, ed. *Contrastive Rhetoric: Annual Review of Applied Linguistics*. New York: Cambridge UP, 1983.

———. "Cultural Thought Patterns in Intercultural Education." *Language Learning* 16 (1966): 1–20.

Karenga, Maulana. "Afrocentric Theory at the Edge of the Twenty-First Century." Dept. of African American Studies, Temple Univ., Philadelphia. 19 Mar. 1993.

———. *Introduction to Black Studies*. 2nd ed. Los Angeles: U of Sankore P, 1993.

Kilborn, Judith. "Tutoring ESL Students: Addressing Differences in Cultural Schemata and Rhetorical Patterns in Reading and Writing." MinneTESOL Conference. Saint Paul. 2 May 1992.

Killens, John Oliver. *The Cotillion*. New York: Trident, 1971.

Killingsworth, M. Jimmie. "Product and Process, Literacy and Orality: An Essay on Composition and Culture." *College Composition and Communication* 44 (1993): 26–39.

Knoblauch, C. H. "Rhetorical Constructions: Dialogue and Commitment." *College English* 50 (1988): 125–40.

Kobayashi, Hiroe. "Rhetorical Patterns in English and Japanese." *TESOL Quarterly* 18 (1984): 737–38.

———. *Rhetorical Patterns in English and Japanese*. Diss. Columbia U, 1984. Ann Arbor: UMI, 1985. 8424236.

Kochman, Thomas. *Black and White Styles in Conflict*. Chicago: U of Chicago P, 1981.

Korzenny, Felipe. "Relevance and Application of Intercultural Communication Theory and Research." *Intercultural Communication*. Ed. Larry A. Samovar and Richard E. Porter. Belmont: Wadsworth, 1991. 56–61.

Kozol, Jonathan. *Illiterate America*. Garden City: Anchor, 1985.

Kutz, Eleanor, Suzy Q. Groden, and Vivian Zamel. *The Discovery of Competence: Teaching and Learning with Diverse Student Writers*. Portsmouth: Boynton, 1993.

Kwatchka, Patricia. *Oral and Written English of the Koyukon Athabaskan Area*. APEL Research Reports, vol. 4. Nenana: Yukon Koyukuk School District, 1988.

Kwatchka, Patricia, and Charlotte Basham. "Literacy Acts and Cultural Artifacts: On Extensions of English Modals." *Journal of Pragmatics* 14 (1990): 413–29.

Lacan, Jacques. Ecrit: *A Selection*. Trans. Alan Sheridan. New York: Tavistock, 1977.

Land, Robert, Jr., and Catherine Whitley. "Evaluating Second Language Essays in Regular Composition Classes: Toward a Pluralistic US Rhetoric."

Richness in Writing: Empowering ESL Students. Ed. Donna Johnson and Duane Roen. New York: Longman, 1989. 284–93.

Lanham, Richard. *A Handlist of Rhetorical Terms*. 2nd ed. Berkeley: U of California P, 1991.

Layton, Marilyn Smith, ed. *Intercultural Journeys through Reading and Writing*. New York: Harper, 1991.

Leap, William. "American Indian English." *Teaching American Indian Students*. Ed. Jon Reyhner. Norman: U of Oklahoma P, 1992. 143–53.

LeFevre, Karen Burke. *Invention as a Social Act*. Carbondale: Southern Illinois UP, 1987.

Leki, Ilona. "Twenty-Five Years of Contrastive Rhetoric: Text Analysis and Writing Pedagogies." *TESOL Quarterly* 25 (1991): 123–43.

———. *Understanding ESL Writers: A Guide for Teachers*. Portsmouth: Boynton, 1992.

Leki, Ilona, and Joan G. Carson. "Students' Perceptions of ESL Writing Instruction and Writing Needs across the Disciplines." *TESOL Quarterly* 28 (1994): 81–101.

Lester, James D., ed. *Interactions: The Aims and Patterns of Writing*. Belmont: Wadsworth, 1988.

Liebman, JoAnne D. "Toward a New Contrastive Rhetoric: Differences between Arabic and Japanese Rhetorical Instruction." *Journal of Second Language Writing* 1 (1992): 141–65.

Ling, Amy. "I'm Here: An Asian American Woman's Response." *New Literary History* 19 (1987): 151–60.

Linn, Michael. "Black Rhetorical Patterns and the Teaching of Composition." *College Composition and Communication* 26 (1975): 149–53.

Linnarud, Moira. *Lexis in Composition: A Performance Analysis of Swedish*. Lund, Swed.: Liber Forlag Malmo, 1986.

Lorde, Audre. "The Master's Tools Will Never Dismantle the Master's House." *Sister Outsider: Essays and Speeches by Audre Lorde*. Freedom: Crossing, 1984. 110–13.

Lu, Min-Zhan. "Conflict and Struggle: The Enemies or Preconditions of Basic Writing?" *College English* 54 (1992): 887–913.

———. "From Silence to Words: Writing as Struggle." *College English* 49 (1987): 433–48.

Lucy, John. *Reflexive Language: Reported Speech and Metapragmatics*. New York: Cambridge UP, 1993.

Lyons, Robert. "The City University of New York Writing Assessment Test: A Faculty-Generated Model," *Writing Program Administration* 4.1 (1980): 23–27.

Macrorie, Ken. "To Be Read." *Rhetoric and Composition: A Sourcebook for Teachers and Writers*. Ed. Richard L. Graves. 3rd ed. Upper Montclair: Boynton, 1994. 81–88.

Madden-Simpson, Janet, and Sara M. Blake, eds. *Emerging Voices: A Cross-Cultural Reader*. Fort Worth: Holt, 1990.

Mahmoud, Amal Abdul-Ghany. *A Functional Analysis of Written Compositions of Egyptian Students of English and the Implications of the Notional Functional Syllabus for the Teaching of Writing*. Diss. Georgetown U, 1982. Ann Arbor: UMI, 1983. 8321349.

Malcolm X. *The Autobiography of Malcolm X*. New York: Ballantine, 1965.

Malotki, Ekkehart, with Michael Lomatuway'ma. *Earth Fire: A Hopi Legend of the Sunset Crater Eruption*. Flagstaff: Northland, 1987.

Mann, Richard Phillip. *A Statistical Survey of Transitional Device Usage among Writers of English as a Second Language and Native Writers of English*. Diss. Ohio State U, 1986. Ann Arbor: UMI, 1986. 8618816.

Martin, J. E. *Contrastive Rhetoric: Implications of a Revised Approach to Text*. ERIC, 1991. ED 329 118.

Masayesva, Victor, prod. *Itam Hakim, Hopiit: We the Hopi*. Videocassette. Is, 1984.

Matalene, Carolyn. "Contrastive Rhetoric: An American Writing Teacher in China." *College English* 47 (1985): 789–808.

Matalene, H. W. "Walter Mitty in China: Teaching American Fiction in an Alien Culture." Trimmer and Warnock 124–36.

Mauranen, Anna. "Contrastive ESP Rhetoric: Metatext in Finnish-English Economics Texts." *English for Specific Purposes* 12 (1993): 3–22.

McCarthy, Lucille. "A Stranger in Strange Lands: A College Student Writing across the Curriculum." *Research in the Teaching of English* 21 (1987): 233–65.

McClung, Merle Steven. *Fordham Law Review* 7 (1979): 651–712.

McCuen, Jo Ray, and Anthony C. Winkler, eds. *Readings for Writers*. 6th ed. San Diego: Harcourt, 1989.

McIntosh, Peggy. "White Privilege and Male Privilege." Working Paper 189. Wellesley, Wellesley Coll. Research on Women, 1988.

———. "White Privilege: Unpacking the Invisible Knapsack." *Peace and Freedom* July-Aug., 1989: 10–12.

McLaren, Peter. "Schooling the Postmodern Body: Critical Pedagogy and the Politics of Enfleshment." Giroux, *Postmodernism* 144–73.

Messer-Davidow, Ellen. "The Philosophical Bases of Feminist Literary Criticisms." *New Literary History* 19 (1987): 65–103.

Meyer, Emily, and Louise Z. Smith. *The Practical Tutor*. New York: Oxford UP, 1987.

Miller, George, ed. *The Prentice-Hall Reader*. Englewood Cliffs: Prentice, 1986.

Miller, Keith D. *Voice of Deliverance: The Language of Martin Luther King, Jr., and Its Sources*. New York: Free, 1992.

Miller, Suzanne M., and Barbara McCaskill, eds. *Multicultural Literature and Literacies: Making Space for Difference*. Albany: State U of New York P, 1993.

Mishima, Yukio. *The Sound of Waves*. New York: Knopf, 1956.

Mohan, Bernard A., and Winnie Au-Yeung Lo. "Academic Writing and Chinese Students: Transfer and Developmental Factors." *TESOL Quarterly* 19 (1985): 515–34.

Mohanty, S. P. "Us and Them: On the Philosophical Bases of Political Criticism." *Yale Journal of Criticism* 2.2 (1989): 1–31.

Momaday, N. Scott. "Man Made of Words." *The Remembered Earth: An Anthology of Contemporary Native American Literature*. Ed. Geary Hobson. Albuquerque: Red Earth, 1979. 162–73.

———. *The Way to Rainy Mountain*. 1969. Albuquerque: U of New Mexico, 1976.

Mora, Pat. *Borders*. Houston: Arte Publico, 1986.

———. *Chants*. Houston: Arte Publico, 1984.

Morales, Aurora Levins, and Rosario Morales. *Getting Home Alive*. Ithaca: Firebrand, 1986.

Morrison, Toni. "A Slow Walk of Trees." *The Bedford Guide for College Writers*. Ed. X. J. Kennedy, Dorothy M. Kennedy, and Sylvia A. Holladay. 3rd ed. Boston: St. Martin's, 1993. 496–99.

Mura, David. "Strangers in the Village." Simonson and Walker. 135–54.

Myers, Greg. "Reality, Consensus, and Reform in the Rhetoric of Composition Teaching." *College English* 48 (1986): 154–74.

Myers, Linda James. *Understanding an Afrocentric World View: Introduction to an Optimal Psychology*. Dubuque: Kendall, 1988.

Neel, Jasper. *Plato, Derrida, and Writing*. Carbondale: Southern Illinois UP, 1988.

Negy, Charles, and Donald J. Woods. "The Importance of Acculturation in Understanding Research with Hispanic-Americans." *Hispanic Journal of Behavioral Sciences* 14 (1992): 224–47.

Niggaz With Attitude. "Real Niggaz Don't Die." *Niggas4life*. Audiocassette. Priority, 1991.

Nobles, Wade. *Africanity and the Black Family: The Development of a Theoretical Model*. Oakland: Inst. for the Advanced Study of Black Family Life and Culture, 1985.

Norment, Nathaniel. *Contrastive Analysis of Organizational Structures and Cohesive Elements in Native and ESL Chinese, English, and Spanish Writing*. Diss. Fordham U, 1984. Ann Arbor: UMI, 1984. 8409265.

North, Stephen M. "The Idea of a Writing Center." *College English* 46 (1984): 433–46.

Nystrand, Martin. *The Structure of Written Communications: Studies in Reciprocity between Writers and Readers*. New York: Academic, 1986.

Oberman, Cerise. "Question Analysis and the Learning Cycle." *Research Strategies* 1 (1983): 22–30.

Ogbu, John U. "Minority Education in Comparative Perspective." *Journal of Negro Education* 59 (1990): 45–57.

Ohmann, Richard. *English in America: A Radical View of the Profession.* New York: Oxford UP, 1976.

Oi, Kyoko Mizuno. *Cross-Cultural Differences in Rhetorical Patterning: A Study of Japanese and English.* Diss. State U of New York, Stony Brook, 1984. Ann Arbor: UMI, 1985. 8422565.

Okawa, Gail Y. "Redefining Authority: Multicultural Students and Tutors at the Educational Opportunity Program Writing Center at the University of Washington." *Writing Centers in Context.* Ed. Joyce A. Kinkead and Jeanette G. Harris. Urbana: NCTE, 1993. 166–91.

Okawa, Gail Y., Thomas Fox, Lucy J. Y. Chang, Shana R. Windsor, Frank Bella Chavez, Jr., and LaGuan Hayes. "Multi-cultural Voices: Peer Tutoring and Critical Reflection in the Writing Center." *Writing Center Journal* 12 (1991): 11–32.

Olsen, Tillie. "Here I Stand Ironing." *Anthology of American Literature.* Ed. George McMichael et al. 4th ed. New York: Macmillan, 1989. 1067–71.

Ong, Walter. *Orality and Literacy: The Technologizing of the Word.* New York: Methuen, 1982.

Ostler, Shirley E. "English in Parallels: A Comparison of English and Arabic Prose." Connor and Kaplan 169–85.

Ouaouicha, Driss. *Contrastive Rhetoric and the Structure of Learner-Produced Argumentative Texts in Arabic and English.* Diss. U of Texas, Austin, 1986. Ann Arbor: UMI, 1987. 8700260.

Papke, David Ray. *Narrative and the Legal Discourse: A Reader in Storytelling and the Law.* Liverpool: Devorah Charles, 1991.

Parbst, John R. "Off-Topic Conversation and the Tutoring Session." *Writing Lab Newsletter* 19.1 (1994): 1+.

Park, Young Mok. "Academic and Ethnic Background as Factors Affecting Writing Performance." Purves, *Writing* 261–72.

Pennycook, Alastair. "The Complex Contexts of Plagiarism: A Reply to Deckert." *Journal of Second Language Writing* 3 (1994): 27–85.

Perkins, David N. "Reasoning as Imagination." *Interchange* 16 (1985): 14–26.

Perrin, Robert. "Textbook Writers and Textbook Publishers: One Writer's View of the Teaching Canon." *Journal of Teaching Writing* 7 (1988): 67–74.

Perry, Ruth. "A Short History of the Term *Politically Correct.*" *Beyond PC: Toward a Politics of Understanding.* Ed. Patricia Aufderheide. Saint Paul: Graywolf, 1992. 71–79.

Personal Justice Denied: Report of the Commission on Wartime Relocation and Internment of Civilians. 2 vols. Washington: Commission on Wartime Relocation and Internment of Civilians, 1983.

Phillips, Susan. *The Invisible Culture: Communication in Classroom and Community on the Warm Springs Indian Reservation.* New York: Longman, 1983.

Ponsot, Marie, and Rosemary Deen. *Beat Not the Poor Desk*. Montclair: Boynton, 1982.

Purves, Alan C. "Rhetorical Communities, the International Student, and Basic Writing." *Journal of Basic Writing* 5 (1986): 38–51.

———, ed. *Writing across Languages and Cultures: Issues in Contrastive Rhetoric*. Newbury Park: Sage, 1988.

Quandahl, Ellen. "The Anthropological Sleep of Composition." *Journal of Advanced Composition* 14.2 (1994): 413–30.

Quinn, Edward. "The Case for Open Admissions: 'We're Holding Our Own,'" *Change* Summer 1973: 30–34.

Ragan, Peter H. "Applying Functional Grammar to Teaching the Writing of ESL." *Word* 40 (1989): 117–27.

Raimes, Ann. "What Unskilled ESL Students Do As They Write: A Classroom Study of Composing." *TESOL Quarterly* 19 (1985): 229–58.

Rankin, Elizabeth. "From Simple to Complex: Ideas of Order in Assignment Sequences." *Journal of Advanced Composition* 10.1 (1990): 126–35.

Reid, Joy Maurine. *Quantitative Differences in English Prose Written by Arabic, Chinese, Spanish, and English Students*. Diss. Colorado State U, 1988. Ann Arbor: UMI, 1989. 8911827.

Reigstad, Thomas, and Donald McAndrew. *Training Tutors for Writing Conferences*. Urbana: NCTE, 1984.

Reither, James A. "Writing and Knowing: Toward Redefining the Writing Process." *College English* 47 (1985): 620–28.

Reither, James A., and Douglas Vipond. "Writing as Collaboration." *College English* 51 (1989): 855–67.

Rice, Kenneth A. *Geertz and Culture*. Ann Arbor: U of Michigan P, 1980.

Richards, Donna. *Let the Circle Be Unbroken: The Implications of African Spirituality in the Diaspora*. Trenton: Red Sea, 1989.

Ritchie, Joy S. "Beginning Writers: Diverse Voices and Individual Identity." *College Composition and Communication* 40 (1989): 152–74.

———. "Confronting the 'Essential' Problem: Reconnecting Feminist Theory and Pedagogy." *Journal of Advanced Composition* 10.2 (1990): 249–73.

Rodriguez, Richard. *Hunger of Memory*. New York: Bantam, 1982.

Rodríguez Milanés, Cecilia. "Racism and the Marvelous Real." *Social Issues in the English Classroom*. Ed. C. Mark Hurlbert and Samuel Totten. Urbana: NCTE, 1992. 246–57.

———. "Risks, Resistance, Rewards." Hurlbert and Blitz 115–24.

Rosa, Alfred, and Paul Eschholz, eds. *Models for Writers*. 3rd ed. New York: St. Martin's, 1989.

Rose, Mike. "The Language of Exclusion: Writing Instruction at the University." *College English* 47 (1985): 341–59.

———. *Lives on the Boundary: A Moving Account of the Struggles and Achievements of America's Underclass*. New York: Penguin, 1989.

Rosenblatt, Louise M. *Literature as Exploration*. New York: Appleton, 1938.

Ruetten, Mary. "Evaluating ESL Students' Performance on Proficiency Exams." *Journal of Second Language Writing* 3 (1994): 85–96.

Russ, Joanna. *How to Suppress Women's Writing*. Austin: U of Texas P, 1983.

Said, Edward. *Orientalism*. New York: Vintage, 1979.

Saldívar, Ramón. *Chicano Narrative: The Dialectics of Difference*. Madison: U of Wisconsin, 1990.

Santos, Terry. "Ideology in Composition: L1 and ESL." *Journal of Second Language Writing* 1 (1992): 1–15.

Sarris, Greg. "Storytelling in the Classroom: Crossing Vexed Chasms." *College English* 52 (1990): 169–85.

Saville-Troike, Muriel. *The Ethnography of Communication*. New York: Blackwell, 1982.

Scarcella, Robin Cameron. *Cohesion in the Writing Development of Native and Non-Native English Speakers*. Diss. U of Southern California, 1984. Ann Arbor: UMI, 1984.

———. "How Writers Orient Their Readers in Expository Essays: A Comparative Study of Native and Non-native English Writers." *TESOL Quarterly* 18 (1984): 671–88.

Schön, Donald A. *The Reflective Practitioner: How Professionals Think in Action*. New York: Basic, 1983.

Schroth, Stephen T. "Competency Testing: The Hidden Risk of School Reform." *Law and Inequality* 7 (1989): 265–98.

Scollon, Ron, and Suzanne B. K. Scollon. *Interethnic Communication*. Fairbanks: Alaska Native Lang. Center, 1980.

———. *Narrative, Literacy, and Face in Interethnic Communication*. Norwood: Ablex, 1981.

Scribner, Sylvia, and Michael Cole. *The Psychology of Literacy*. Cambridge: Harvard UP, 1981.

Severino, Carol. "The Sociopolitical Implications of Response to Second Language and Second Dialect Writing." *Journal of Second Language Writing* 2 (1993): 181–201.

———. "Where the Cultures of Basic Writers and Academia Intersect: Cultivating the Common Ground." *Journal of Basic Writing* 2 (1992): 4–15.

Shapiro, Nancy. "Rereading Multicultural Readers: What Definition of 'Multicultural' Are We Buying?" Cincinnati. Conf. on Coll. Composition and Communication Convention. 21 Mar. 1992. ERIC ED 346 472.

———. Review essay. *College Composition and Communication* 42 (1991): 524–30.

Shaughnessy, Mina. *Basic Writing Program Report, 1973–74*. New York: City Coll. of New York, 1973.

———. *Errors and Expectations*. New York: Oxford UP, 1977.

Shen, Fan. "The Classroom and the Wider Culture: Identity as a Key to Learning English Composition." *College Composition and Communication* 40 (1989): 459–66.

Shor, Ira. *Critical Teaching and Everyday Life*. Chicago: U of Chicago P, 1987.

———. *Culture Wars: School and Society in the Conservative Restoration, 1969–1984*. London: Routledge–Kegan Paul, 1986.

———. *Empowering Education*. Chicago: U of Chicago P, 1992.

Showalter, Elaine. "Women and the Literary Curriculum." *College English* 32 (1971): 855–62.

Silko, Leslie Marmon. "Language and Literature from a Pueblo Indian Perspective." *English Literature: Opening Up the Canon*. Ed. Leslie A. Fiedler and Houston A. Baker, Jr. Baltimore: Johns Hopkins UP, 1979. 54–72. Rpt. in *Critical Fictions: The Politics of Imaginative Writing*. Ed. Philimina Mariani. Seattle: Bay, 1991. 83–93.

Silva, Tony. *A Comparative Study of the Composing of Selected ESL and Native English Speaking Freshman Writers*. Diss. Purdue U, 1990. Ann Arbor: UMI, 1991. 9031389.

Silverman, Ed. *SKAT Writing Test Results for the 1986 to 1990 Cohorts*. New York: City Coll., City U of New York, Office of Institutional Research, 1992.

Simonson, Rick, and Scott Walker, eds. *Multi-cultural Literacy: Opening the American Mind: The Graywolf Annual, Five*. Saint Paul: Graywolf, 1988.

Sledd, James. "Bi-dialectalism: The Linguistics of White Supremacy." *English Journal* 58.9 (1969): 1307–29.

Smith, Jeff. "Allan Bloom, Mike Rose, and Paul Goodman: In Search of a Lost Pedagogical Synthesis." *College English* 55 (1993): 721–44.

Smith, Sidonie. *A Poetics of Women's Autobiography: Marginality and the Fictions of Self-Representation*. Bloomington: Indiana UP, 1987.

Smitherman, Geneva. "'The Blacker the Berry, the Sweeter the Juice': African American Student Writers and the National Assessment of Educational Progress." *The Need for Story*. Ed. Anne H. Dyson and Celia Genishi. Urbana: NCTE, 1994. 80–101.

———. "NAEP Writing Research." NCTE Convention. Detroit. Nov. 1984.

———. *Talkin and Testifyin: The Language of Black America*. Detroit: Wayne State UP, 1986.

Smitherman-Donaldson, Geneva. "Opinion: Toward a National Public Policy on Language." *College English* 49 (1987): 29–36.

Sommers, Nancy. "Between the Drafts." *College Composition and Communication* 43 (1992): 23–31.

Soter, Anna O. "The Second Language Learner and Cultural Transfer in Narration." Purves, *Writing* 177–205.

Spellmeyer, Kurt. *Common Ground: Dialogue, Understanding, and the Teaching of Composition*. Englewood Cliffs: Prentice, 1993.

————. "A Common Ground: The Essay in the Academy." *College English* 51. (1989): 262–76.

————. "Foucault and the Freshman Writer: Considering the Self in Discourse." *College English* 51 (1989): 715–29.

Spivak, Gayatri, and Ellen Rooney. "In a Word: Interview." *Differences* 1.2 (1989): 124–56.

Stalker, Jacqueline W., and James C. Stalker. "A Comparison of Pragmatic Accommodation of Non-native and Native Speakers in Written English." *World Englishes* 7 (1988): 119–28.

Stanger, Carol. "Sexual Politics of the One-to-One Tutorial Approach." *Teaching Writing: Pedagogy, Gender, and Equity*. Ed. Cynthia Caywood and Gillian Overing. Albany: State U of New York P, 1987. 31–44.

Steele, Shelby. *The Content of Our Character: A New Vision of Race in America*. New York: St. Martin's, 1990.

Steinbeck, John. *The Grapes of Wrath*. New York: Viking, 1958.

Street, Brian V. "Introduction: The New Literacy." *Cross-Cultural Approaches to Literacy*. Ed. Brian V. Street. New York: Cambridge UP, 1993. 1–21.

Sundquist, Eric J. "The Japanese-American Internment: A Reappraisal." *American Scholar* 57 (1988): 529–47.

Swales, John. *Genre Analysis*. New York: Cambridge UP, 1991.

Sweedler-Brown, Carol. "ESL Essay Evaluation: The Influence of Sentence-Level and Rhetorical Features." *Journal of Second Language Writing* 2 (1993): 3–17.

Swyt, Wendy. *Discursive Pedagogies: A Post-process Analysis of the College Writing Course*. Diss. U of Washington, 1995.

Tapahonso, Luci. *A Breeze Swept Through*. Albuquerque: East End, 1987.

Tateya, Kanae. "Culture Shock: Schools in the US and Japan." *Kaleidoscope: St. Cloud State University's Multicultural Arts Magazine* Spring 1992: 10–11.

Tedesco, Janis. "Women's Ways of Knowing / Women's Ways of Composing." *Rhetoric Review* 9.2 (1991): 245–56.

Tollefson, James W. *Alien Winds: The Reeducation of America's Indochinese Refugees*. New York: Praeger, 1989.

Trimbur, John. "Consensus and Difference in Collaborative Learning." *College English* 51 (1989): 602–16.

————. "Peer Tutoring: A Contradiction in Terms?" *Writing Center Journal* 7.2 (1987): 21–28.

————. "Taking the Social Turn: Teaching Writing Post-process." *College Composition and Communication* 45 (1994): 108–18.

Trimmer, Joseph, and Tilly Warnock, eds. *Understanding Others: Cultural and Cross-Cultural Studies and the Teaching of Literature*. Urbana: NCTE, 1992.

Troutman, Denise. "Oral and Written Discourse: A Study of Feature Transfer." Diss. Michigan State U, 1987.

Troyka, Lyn Quitman. "The Phenomenon of Impact: The CUNY Writing Assessment Test." *Writing Program Administration* 8.1-2 (1984): 27–36.

Truth, Sojourner. "Ain't I a Woman." *Issues in Feminism: A First Course in Women's Studies*. Ed. Sheila Ruth. Boston: Houghton, 1980. 463–64.

Unger, Jonathan. "Post–Cultural Revolution Primary-School Education: Selected Texts." *Chinese Education* 10 (1977): 4–34.

United States. Army. Western Defense Command and Fourth Army. *Final Report, Japanese Evacuation from the West Coast, 1942*. Washington: GPO, 1943.

United States. Bureau of the Census. *Current Population Reports*. Washington: GPO, 1990.

Uribe, Virginia, and Karen M. Harbeck. "Addressing the Needs of Lesbian, Gay, and Bisexual Youth: The Origins of PROJECT 10 and School-Based Intervention." *Coming out of the Classroom Closet: Gay and Lesbian Students, Teachers, and Curricula*. Ed. Karen M. Harbeck. New York: Haworth, 1992. 9–28.

Valdés, Guadalupe. "Bilingual Minorities and Language Issues in Writing." *Written Communication* 9 (1992): 85–136.

Villanueva, Victor, Jr. *Bootstraps: From an American Academic of Color*. Urbana: NCTE, 1993.

———. "Considerations for American Freireistas." Bullock, Trimbur, and Schuster. 247–62.

Walker, Alice. "Everyday Use." *The Norton Anthology of Short Fiction*. Ed. R. V. Cassill. 2nd ed. New York: Norton, 1981. 1421–28.

Walker, Scott, ed. *The Graywolf Annual, Seven: Stories from the American Mosaic*. Saint Paul: Graywolf, 1990.

Wall, Susan, and Nicholas Coles. "Reading Basic Writing: Alternatives to a Pedagogy of Accommodation." *The Politics of Writing Instruction: Postsecondary*. Ed. Richard Bullock, John Trimbur, and Charles Schuster. Portsmouth: Boynton, 1991. 27–46.

Wallace, Michelle. "Variations on Negation and the Heresy of Black Feminist Creativity." Gates, *Reading* 52–67.

Webb, Sarah Jones. *Using Figurative Language in Epistemic Writing: The Purposes and Processes of First and Second Language Writers*. Diss. U of Texas, 1988. Ann Arbor: UMI, 1989. 8901414.

Weglyn, Michi. *Years of Infamy: The Untold Story of America's Concentration Camps*. New York: Morrow, 1976.

West, Cornel. "Diverse New World." *Debating PC: The Controversy over Political Correctness on College Campuses*. Ed. Paul Berman. New York: Bantam, 1992. 326–32.

White, Edward M., and Leon Thomas. "Racial Minorities and Writing Skills Assessment in the California State University and Colleges." *College English* 42 (1981): 276–83.

Whiteman, Marcia Farr, ed. *Writing: The Nature, Development, and Teaching of Written Communication*. Hillsdale: Erlbaum, 1981.

Whorf, Benjamin L. *Language, Thought, and Reality*. Cambridge: MIT, 1956.

Wideman, John Edgar. *Brothers and Keepers*. New York: Holt, 1984.

Wilbur-Cruce, Eva Antonia. *A Beautiful, Cruel Country*. Tucson: U of Arizona P, 1987.

Willis, Paul E. *Learning to Labour: Why Working-Class Kids Get Working-Class Jobs*. Westmead, Eng.: Saxon, 1977.

Wong, Jennifer. "Conservative Scholars See 'Multiculturalism' as a Plague." *Chronicle of Higher Education* 19 Sept. 1990: A41.

Wright, Richard. *Native Son*. 1940. New York: Perennial, 1987.

Xu, George Qiaoqi. *An Ex Post Facto Study of Differences in the Structure of the Standard Expository Paragraphs between Written Compositions by Native and Nonnative Speakers of English at the College Level*. Diss. Indiana U of Pennsylvania, 1990. Ann Arbor: UMI, 1990. 9022655.

Yamada, Mitsuye. "Masks of Woman." Anzaldua, *Making* 114–16.

Yau, Margaret S. S. "A Quantitative Comparison of L1 and L2 Writing Processes." TESOL Convention. San Antonio, 8 Mar. 1988.

Yorio, Carlos. "The Other Side of the Looking Glass." *Journal of Basic Writing* 8.1 (1989): 32–45.

Young, Art. "College Culture and the Challenge of Collaboration." *Writing Center Journal* 13.1 (1992): 3–15.

Young, Linda Wai Ling. "Inscrutability Revisited." *Language and Social Identity*. Ed. John J. Gumperz. Cambridge: Cambridge UP, 1982. 72–84.

Young, Richard. "Paradigms and Problems: Needed Research in Rhetorical Invention." *Research in Composing*. Ed. Charles R. Cooper and Lee Odell. Urbana: NCTE, 1978. 29–47.

Zawacki, Terry Myers. "Recomposing as a Woman—An Essay in Different Voices." *College Composition and Communication* 43 (1992): 32–38.

Zikopoulos, Michael, ed. *Open Doors: 1991–1992*. New York: Inst. for Intl. Educ. 1992.

Index